2000

University of St. Francis Library
3 0301 00214567 6

P9-ASN-773

The Developmentally Appropriate Inclusive Classroom in Early Education

The Developmentally Appropriate Inclusive Classroom in Early Education

Regina Miller
University of Hartford

Delmar Publishers
I(T)P® An International Thomson Publishing Company

Albany • Bonn • Boston • Cincinnati • Detroit • London • Madrid
Melbourne • Mexico City • New York • Pacific Grove • Paris • San Francisco
Singapore • Tokyo • Toronto • Washington

Delmar staff:
Publisher: Diane L. McOscar
Sponsoring Editor: Erin O'Connor
Production Coordinator: James Zayicek
Art and Design Coordinator: Timothy J. Conners
Editorial Assistant: Glenna Stanfield

Printed in the United States of America

For more information, contact:

Delmar Publishers
3 Columbia Circle, Box 15015
Albany, New York 12212-5015

International Thomson Publishing
Berkshire House
168-173 High Holborn
London, WC1V7AA
England

Thomas Nelson Australia
102 Dodds Street
South Melbourne 3205
Victoria, Australia

Nelson Canada
1120 Birchmont Road
Scarborough, Ontario
M1K5G4, Canada

International Thomson Publishing GmbH
Konigswinterer Str. 418
53227 Bonn
Germany

International Thomson Publishing Asia
221 Henderson Bldg. #05-10
Singapore 0315

International Thomson Publishing Japan
Kyowa Building 3F
2-2-1 Hirakawa-cho
Chiyoda-ku, Tokyo 102
Japan

1 2 3 4 5 6 7 8 9 10 XXX 01 00 99 98 97 96 95

Library of Congress Cataloging-in-Publication Data

Miller, Regina, 1946-
The developmentally appropriate inclusive classroom in early education / Regina Miller.
p. cm.
Includes bibiographical references and index.
ISBN 0-8273-6704-X
1. Early childhood education—United States—Curricula.
2. Mainstreaming in education—United States. I. Title.
LB1139.4.M55 1995
372.21—dc20 95-1337
CIP

Contents

Reviewers

David Finn, EdD
University of Hawaii at Manoa
Honolulu, HI

Mary Frances Hanline
The Florida State University
Tallahassee, FL

Barbara Lowenthal, EdD
Northeastern Illinois University
Chicago, IL

James McCrory, PhD
Mary Baldwin College
Staunton, WA

AmySue Reilly, PhD
Auburn University
Auburn University, AL

Jo Robertson
Emporia State University
Emporia, KS

Kristine Slentz, PhD
Western Washington University
Billingham, WA

Preface

This book is the result of many years of applied work and teaching in the field of early childhood education. My many years of working with all kinds of children and parents, as well as undergraduate and graduate students, have helped refine my ideas and applications of what is appropriate and meaningful for young children. All the people with whom I have worked and the research and reading I have done over time have cemented for me the concepts of what constitutes appropriate, healthy practice for all children. What seems to be important is that we remember that children are children first. How they think, talk, walk, sing, draw, or dance are characteristics of their abilities and should not be the only way to look at children.

The emphasis of this book is on the exploration of the role of developmentally appropriate curriculum and practice through the implementation of integrated thematic curriculum in the early childhood years. Sound developmentally appropriate practice makes good sense for all children. A key component of developmental appropriateness is meeting the needs of each child at his or her own level. The concept of appropriateness for each child translates into a very wide range of children and an equally wide range of behaviors, skills, abilities, and personalities. If the focus of the program is on meeting the needs of all children through activities and experiences of interest to them, all children should be able to grow and develop to their maximum potential.

An important feature of this book is the application of theory to practice. Examples of practical situations are drawn from classroom experiences to teach through story-telling. These examples are meant to enhance the learning of the early childhood student while demonstrating theory into practice.

The book contains current information reflecting the latest research and practice in the field of early childhood education and the integration of children with disabilities in inclusive early childhood settings.

This book is organized into three parts. The first part, Chapters 1 through 3, introduces the concepts of developmentally appropriate curriculum and practice, integrated thematic play based curriculum, and the elements to consider when developing the integrated curriculum.

Part two of the book, Chapters 4 through 12, concerns the planning and implementation of the integrated curriculum. Emphasis is placed on this approach to curriculum planning and implementation as being appropriate for all children in inclusive early childhood classrooms. At the end of Chapter 4 several case studies are introduced to the reader. Each of these cases contains information about the disability or multiple disabilities of the child described. The subsequent Chapters, 5 through 11 cover activity areas one would commonly find in an early childhood program: art, sensory, manipulatives and small blocks, dramatic play in the large blocks and housekeeping corners, large motor development, music and movement, and language and literacy. Each of these chapters discusses the importance of the activities for young children, the objectives for the area, developmentally appropriate activities and materials, and reintroduces each of the cases first introduced in chapter 4. This information relates to the modifications required in order to include the child in activities in the area discussed in the chapter so the child might participate to his or her maximum ability. Chapter 12 includes sample planning to offer the reader clear examples of the planning process and to offer a developed theme to implement. The theme is developed with overall objectives for the theme, objectives for each activity, and modifications indicated to enable the inclusion of all types of children. It is important to remember child as a unique being that each may need greater or fewer modifications than are indicated. There are no recipes to working with children with or without disabilities. As we get to know children in our classrooms, we are better able to provide more meaningful experiences for them, collectively and individually.

Part three provides the reader with information about working with parents and families, working with specialists, and observation and assessment. The emphasis in this part is on cooperation and collaboration. Teachers in inclusive classrooms need the assistance of parents and specialists to help them carry out their objectives for children with disabilities so that these children may grow and develop to their maximum ability.

Each of the chapters, except for chapter 12 have discussion questions intended to stimulate thought and discussion for both individual students and for small groups of students.

The appendix provides early childhood video resources that can be used as supplementary learning for the material covered in this book. Some of these video resources are also appropriate to be shared with parents in group meetings or with specialists who are new to the provision of service in inclusive early childhood settings.

There are many people who deserve considerable thanks. To the parents of children with and without disabilities who were enrolled at the University of Hartford Early Childhood Center over the years, I thank you for your trust and for sharing my vision of a school for all children. Without you, the knowledge acquired and stories collected which are included in this book would not have been possible. You have all added to the richness of the field as well as to the richness of my life.

Thanks also are due to the undergraduate and graduate students at the University of Hartford who over the years shared in the implementation of the vision of a school for all children. These students added to the richness of experience provided for children while enriching their own experiences. Many of these students are now practitioners in the field and are providing integrated experiences for children in other communities. Without all of you, my life and the lives of many children and parents would not have been the same.

To the women who have served as head teachers at the center I give my heartfelt thanks for the devotion to the job and to the vision of the school. To Joanne Klein, Patty Miller, Lesley Keener, Barbara Koff, and Nancy McVey—I could never have done it without you. You supported, cooperated, collaborated, and nurtured ideas, children, and adults. You put into practice the ideals of an integrated setting where all children could maximize their potentials.

To my colleagues at the University of Hartford and in the community and to my friends who were encouraging and understanding during the writing of this manuscript, I thank you. When I sometimes thought I would not have the time or fortitude to finish this work, you assured me that I could do it.

The photographs in this book are the product of a very talented young woman, Rebecca Kandel. She was willing to work quickly when my schedule necessitated it and her schedule necessitated that she be working on other things. My heartfelt thanks go to her with the hope that we may collaborate on other projects in the future.

To the people at Delmar who believed enough in the concept of this book to encourage the development of the idea from the start, I thank you. I am sure that I would have never done this without your approval of the concept so early on.

Last but not least, this book would have never been possible without the inspiration and support of my family. My parents and sisters have always been involved in teaching, appreciating, and enjoying children. All during his childhood, my son Perchik allowed me to be the kind of working mom I wanted and needed to be. He was always interested in and took pride in my work and I was always interested and invested in his activities. I thank you Perchik for the opportunities you gave me to learn more about children on a continuing and developmental basis. My husband Don, my best friend and supporter, has always been there for me and allowed me the space and time I needed to create, teach, and learn. Late nights at the computer and more pizza than we have ever eaten in our married life allowed this project to come to fruition. I dedicate this work to you both.

CHAPTER 1

Introduction

KEY TERMS

developmentally appropriate curriculum and practice
age appropriateness
individual appropriateness
whole child
developmental evaluation process
constructivist theory
inclusion
specialists
collaboration
consultation

DEVELOPMENTALLY APPROPRIATE CURRICULUM AND PRACTICE

Developmentally appropriate curriculum and practice has become the focal point of early childhood educators across this country and other countries as well. The National Association for the Education of Young Children (NAEYC, 1987) in a position statement on developmentally appropriate practice in early childhood programs serving children from birth through age eight defined the concept of developmental appropriateness as having two dimensions: **age appropriateness** and **individual appropriateness**.

Age Appropriateness

Knowing whether materials, equipment, or curriculum content is right for children requires a strong knowledge of child development. When an individual teacher knows about the typical physical, social, emotional, language, and cognitive development of children, then that teacher will understand what needs to go into the framework of an age-appropriate classroom and age-appropriate activities. A teacher who does not have command of this information will have difficulty with planning and implementing activities that are comfortable for children while still encouraging them to grow and develop. Once learned, this content needs to be reviewed and refreshed because teachers often begin to confuse age appropriateness based on the developmental levels of children they have recently had in their classes. If a teacher has an extremely precocious group of children one year, the next group of children may be compared with that precocious group rather than looked at relative to their true ages. We know that for some children, chronological age and developmental level are very different. A child may be highly verbal but not at the same level of functioning in any other area of development. This may be true for any area or combination of areas of development. This brings us to the next component of developmental appropriateness:

Individual Appropriateness

Child development knowledge affords teachers the opportunity to see the uniqueness in each and every child. Although we know that children develop along predictable patterns and timetables, there is considerable variation within each individual child. Teachers cannot decide to interact with children in just one way just as they cannot have one curriculum set in stone or one way of presenting curriculum to all children. There is no one magic prescription that makes all things right for all teachers and all children. If that were the case, life in the classroom would be static, dull, and boring.

What makes the early childhood period exciting and vibrant is the fact that each day is a challenge due to the very differences presented by individual children who come to our classrooms. Although we must recognize that children are unique, it is not enough to recognize that at a global level. Teachers must observe children in their classrooms under a variety of conditions in order to learn about the children and their special ways of doing and learning. We know that some children approach new people and materials with caution and others jump right in. Children have different personality styles and different learning styles. One learns about these styles or ways in which children approach their worlds from observation of children while they are engaged in what is the most normal activity for all children—play. Play is the natural medium for young children to learn, grow, and develop. Play affords children opportunities to explore, discover, attempt varying roles, relate to others, and exercise creativity (Smilansky, 1990). Play is transforming and can reveal the poetry of a child's inner life and the history of childhood itself (Bakken, 1990). Play needs to be child initiated, child directed, and teacher supported. Play is not something children do until they are ready to learn, play is what children do that readies them to learn. Play is developmental and is an integral component of the provision and implementation of developmentally appropriate curriculum and practice.

GUIDELINES FOR DEVELOPMENTALLY APPROPRIATE PRACTICE

The NAEYC guidelines for developmentally appropriate practice focus on curriculum, adult-child interaction, relations between home and program and developmental evaluation of children. Each of the topics discussed under the guidelines can be analyzed independently but when considered collectively form the basis for a comprehensive framework that attends to the critical components of early childhood curriculum and practice.

These guidelines for ensuring developmentally appropriate practice are also appropriate for the early education of children with disabilities. Wolery, Strain, and Bailey (1992) noted that the guidelines for developmentally appropriate practice alone are not likely to be sufficient for many children with disabilities. A match must also be made on the basis of the unique learning needs presented by the children with disabilities within the framework of an environment and learning activities that are chronologically age appropriate. This translates into children with disabilities learning in classrooms with their age-appropriate peers with the supports necessary to enable this practice to be effective.

Between 1991 and 1993 several articles appeared that cautioned the field of early childhood special education against abandoning early childhood special education practices in favor of developmentally appropriate practices (Carta, Schwartz, Atwater & McConnell, 1991; Carta, Schwartz, Atwater & McConnell, 1993; Johnson & Johnson, 1992). The article by Carta, Schwartz, Atwater, and McConnell (1993) discussed the many areas of overlap between what is considered quality practice in early childhood special education and in the developmentally appropriate practice guidelines. The article was written in response to criticism by other authors over what was perceived to be a devaluing of principles of developmentally appropriate practice. The authors list the current indicators of quality practice in early childhood special education that overlap with developmentally appropriate practice as:

- the importance of individualization (to enable children with disabilities to be active participants in educational settings with nondisabled peers)
- the deemphasis of standardized assessment (a view shared by both early childhood special education and developmentally appropriate practice)
- the integration of curriculum and assessment (another shared perspective)
- the importance of child-initiated activities (another shared perspective)
- the importance of active engagement (another shared perspective)
- the emphasis on social interaction (a shared perspective with early childhood special education acknowledging that specific training for children with disabilities may be required in this area)
- the importance of cultural diversity (another shared perspective)

Johnson and Johnson (1993) in a rejoinder to Carta et al. point out that early childhood special education is a field of education and developmentally appropriate practice is a set of guidelines for practice within a field of education. They point out that NAEYC is revising developmentally appropriate practice taking into account cultural factors and special education concerns so as to have a more comprehensive and sensitive set of guidelines. As the fields of early childhood special education and early childhood education become more integrated, the practices of the two fields may come closer together. Research on practice and the outcomes of practices will continue to inform practitioners of "best practices" for young children with and without disabilities.

Developmentally Appropriate Curriculum

When one speaks about developmentally appropriate curriculum, one speaks about curriculum planned to be appropriate for the age span of children within the program. One also needs to be aware that once a teacher begins to work with a group of children and begins to learn more about individual children within the group, the curriculum might change drastically. Curriculum should be driven by the different needs, levels of functioning, and interests of the children in the group. Curriculum planned in the summer before a teacher even knows the children in the class is curriculum that will not be sensitive to individual learners. Curriculum developed under those conditions is also curriculum bound to fail because it was not designed specifically for the group.

When planning developmentally appropriate curriculum, all aspects of development need to be taken into consideration. A curriculum that focuses in on cognitive development at the expense of planning for and nurturing the development of the physical child does not take into consideration the **whole child**.

Planning for the development and education of the whole child means that children will not become "specialists" in the areas of language or social development. It means that children will be encouraged to develop evenly across all areas of development. It is not uncommon for adults to pay considerable attention to the strengths of individual children because it is rewarding for adults to engage children in activities in which the child is particularly interested or at which the children are successful. It is far more appealing for most adults to work with children under pleasant conditions than to work with children under stressful, less success-oriented conditions when they are attempting to address weaker areas of development.

Developmentally appropriate curriculum focuses on integrating learning rather than departmentalizing learning. Children learn through interaction with children, materials, and adults. In developmentally appropriate curriculum, children learn through direct experiences not by learning about persons, places, and things from someone always telling them about them. In a developmentally appropriate environment, children learn science, social studies, language arts, and math through reading books and listening to stories, engaging in sensory experiences, participating in cooking experiences, being involved with art activities, taking part in dramatic play, using manipulatives, taking field trips, building, creating, and sharing all of these experiences with their peers and the adults in their classrooms.

Children learn through concrete activities with real materials. If you would like a child to learn about flowers and retain this learning, you must provide flowers for the child to see, feel, smell, and touch. Seeing a picture of a flower does not replace the actual experience of having flowers in front of the child. Seeing and handling one flower does not replace the opportunity of seeing and handling several different types of flowers. Seeing the variety of flowers allows the child to make comparisons about the shapes, colors, textures, smell, and complexity of the different flowers. Having these different experiences allows children to broaden their horizons about the definition of the word flower. All of this information contributes to the child's evolving data base. It allows children to pair this information with information gathered from other experiences they will collect along the educational path they will follow for many years to come. Obviously, all learning cannot take place under these conditions because the entire world cannot be brought to each individual classroom but developmentally appropriate curriculum must provide as much of these types of experiences as possible.

Not every child is interested in the same thing at the same time. Therefore, children should be able to choose from an array of activities and materials, those activities that are of specific interest to the child. Teachers themselves may have particular interests and want to develop curriculum around those interests. Some teachers delight in developing units around bears or dinosaurs. Some teachers have a particularly strong interest in art or music. Other teachers love to cook with children while other teachers are afraid to cook with children because they do not even cook for themselves and the very thought of having to follow a recipe scares them. Commandeering the selection of curriculum topics is appropriate only if the children are interested in these topics. Force feeding curriculum does not accomplish anything. As adult learners, looking back on our childhood experiences, teachers can recall having the unfortunate experience of being made to endure a learning situation that was not of interest. Teachers all remember how little was learned under those conditions. All former students remember hoping it would be over as soon as possible.

Any early childhood classroom will find children who are operating at different developmental levels; no two children develop at exactly the same rate. Thus, teachers need to provide varying levels of complexity as well as a variety of activities for children within the framework of the same curriculum topic. Since children learn by observation as well as by doing, many children learn from watching other children work with materials and concepts that are a little beyond their own current personal reach. It does not have to frustrate children when they cannot yet engage in something that other children can. Within the correct nurturing, responsive environment with adults supporting any growth and develop-

FIG 1.1 Time to play and explore enhances development.

ment, children come to admire their peers' abilities while they themselves continue to grow and develop. Responsive adults create an accepting, sharing environment.

Time as a factor in curriculum

Children need time to work with activities and materials. Many children come from home environments where time is a luxury. Children are often rushed, crowded, or overwhelmed by stimuli. This means that in the school environment, rigid time schedules with short intervals for activity are not sensitive to the needs of the children in that class. Teachers also need time within the day to connect with children facilitating their play and activity without intruding. This type of teacher behavior allows for encouragement, questioning, stimulation, and reinforcement of thinking and learning.

Diversity as an Element of Curriculum

Children also need exposure to peoples and practices different from those within the culture of their own families. This means that curriculum needs to focus on multicultural, gender fair, and anti-bias experiences in a natural, non-contrived manner (Derman-Sparks, 1989). Teachers need to support the diverse populations of children and families that are becoming part of the culture of the schools in which they teach. Teachers need to model for children the acceptance and knowledge of diversity in order to facilitate the children absorbing the importance of being accepting of and responsive to those different from themselves.

Balance of Activity in Planning Curriculum

Developmentally appropriate curriculum should provide for a balance of quiet and active engagement during the course of the day. Teachers should strive to achieve a balance of activity throughout the day. Some children come from home environments that are noisy all the time or are painfully quiet and controlled all the time.

The following is an example of a child coming from a home with a very specific atmosphere.

CASE STUDY

A family lived in a small apartment building above an older couple who could not handle any noise. When the mother was home with the preschool age child during the day, the child was not allowed to wear her shoes, run, jump, or play with wheel toys because if she did, the people downstairs would bang on the ceiling to register their complaints. As a result of this controlled environment, the little girl was very timid and controlled. Due to the fact that the mother always looked for quiet activities to do with her daughter, the child was very skilled in fine motor activities. Mother and daughter spent a lot of time dusting, washing, working with dough, doing art projects, and learning how to do crafts. When this child came to preschool, she presented a picture of very uneven development. She excelled in fine motor activities, was very quiet, evidenced few peer social skills, and demonstrated language skills that were very adult oriented. Her preschool teachers worked very hard to help her develop a more balanced developmental profile by encouraging gross motor activity as well as peer and adult appropriate language and social activity. When a teacher knows the conditions under which a child lives, the teacher can plan for activities to balance those experienced at home to help provide an overall balance of activity.

Outdoor experiences in early childhood curriculum

Developmentally appropriate curriculum should provide for outdoor experiences. Outdoor time as part of the curriculum is not simply a time to let off steam but should be, as much as possible, integrated into the current curriculum. Children generally do not spend as much time outdoors as they did in years past. Some children live in neighborhoods that are not safe or conducive to outdoor play. Some children do not get home until it is quite dark and they leave the house when it is still dark. These children really need to spend some time outdoors. Early childhood educators aware of these factors can provide enriching outdoor activity so that children will not miss out on the benefits of vigorous, imaginative outdoor play.

Adult-Child Interaction

In a developmentally appropriate program, adults respond to children in a direct and timely fashion. They respond to children based on their needs, messages, and abilities. Sometimes as teachers are getting to know the children in their classrooms, it is very important to be in contact with the family in order to learn the "cues" to watch for. What may seem like a silly behavior on the part of one child may in fact be a sincere social attempt that is misperceived by adults and peers.

The following episode is an example of the importance of family contact early on and throughout the time we work with a child.

CASE STUDY

During a summer session, a three-year-old Asian boy joined a preschool class. His mother told the teachers that he was very quiet but he loved to play with cars. The teachers made sure to incorporate small cars into their plans the very first day he attended school. This boy evidenced himself to be a very involved active observer of children playing with cars but would not join in. This puzzled the teachers somewhat and at the end of the day, the head teacher talked to the mother again about what her son liked to do. She assured the teacher that his favorite activity was indeed playing with cars. It was decided to put out more cars the next day and to make sure that this child had access to them. The next day the same thing happened. He observed, laughed, and smiled but did not move in the direction of the cars. Once again, the teacher consulted with the mother. She told the teacher she would speak to the child during the course of the evening to try to figure out why he was not interested in playing with the cars. The following day mother and child came to school with the mother reporting the conversation she had had with her son the night before. It seemed as though she had done such a good job of teaching her young son to make sure that he did not play with toys belonging to others that he exercised the utmost control in staying away from the cars at school. Each day by the time this mother and child arrived at school, other children were already engaged in active play. The child assumed that the toys these children were using belonged to them so he did not touch them. His mother explained the situation to him and vowed to get to school earlier so that he would see the beginning of the day. From then on, with the facilitation of his teacher, this little boy was a very active participant in the play in the classroom and did not need to be invited or cajoled into activity for very long. The communication established between the teacher and the mother helped to identify key variables having impact on the child. When the situation was understood, the teacher knew what role to play in encouraging the child to become an active participant in the classroom.

Adults as facilitators and models

Younger children may need an adult to facilitate for them or model appropriate behavior for them. There are many adults who think that telling a child to "go play" is all that needs to be said or "get to work" is the only instruction needed. Children would most usually be engaged in more appropriate behavior if they only knew how to engage in that behavior or knew what comprised the targeted behavior. These are the children who need an adult to model that behavior.

An example of adult assumptions concerning what children know and do not know concerns a daily instruction delivered to a child as his mother left him at school each day.

CASE STUDY

The mother would tell him to remember to behave and he would respond by saying that he would. This was not a child for whom appropriate behavior came easily. He was very bright, highly verbal, drank from a bottle at home and still wore diapers. He was three years old. At home, his head was filled with so much information that he was almost like a machine that was capable of dispensing facts about animals, birds, trees, flowers, and various other topics. He was easily frustrated by children who were not interested in him or his facts. His spontaneity often got him into trouble. One day as the teacher preempted a block from flying across the room toward a peer, the child was asked what he was doing. To the surprise of the teacher, he responded that he was behaving! Teacher and child sat down immediately for a very quick but serious discussion about the word "behave." When asked to define what the word meant, he responded with great seriousness that it meant to be bad! That misconception was cleared up very quickly by explaining to the child what the word actually meant. The mother was informed about the content of the discussion that had taken place that day. She was surprised to learn that the child did not know the meaning of the word. What was learned from this incident was that this child needed to have words defined for him. It was also learned that he needed to observe models of appropriate behavior because it could not be assumed that he knew what the appropriate behavior would be in any given situation.

Adults provide guidance and support

Children may need physical support, reassurance, or redirection. Some children need to be physically redirected and supported until they are involved with an activity or with a new group of children. As children get older, they may need more support in terms of words rather than physical support. Some children really need adults to reassure or confirm with a wink or a nod. Other children need adults to reflect on their behavior and give them words to explain or describe what they have experienced or what they are feeling. Again, the only way to know the appropriate way to support children and help them through each episode in which they would benefit from adult facilitation rather than adult intervention, is through circulating through the classroom, spending time with children on the various tasks and activities in which they engage, listening to their language, watching their play and peer interactions, and observing them first hand. Children respond well to adults with whom they have spent time and have built a trust relationship. Children know when adults are sincerely interested in them and respond positively to their supportive attempts. When an adult is not sincere in his or her feelings towards a child, the adult becomes more like a machine operating in the environment saying and doing the right things with little or no substance behind it. Children do not respond positively to this type of attention from adults. Respect and trust develop over a period of time and from a point of familiarity.

Children look to adults for support in their interactions, in their play and in their task-related behavior. Some children are accustomed to having adults solve their problems for them and may need time to learn how to respond to an adult whose style is to help the child solve the problem unassisted. Under these conditions, children learn that there is usually more than one way to handle a situation and more than one way to answer a question or solve a problem.

Through their own behavior, adults model and facilitate the development of self-esteem in children by respecting, accepting, listening to, and comforting children. Children learn to separate themselves as people from the behaviors in which they engage. They learn that while a particular behavior may not be appropriate, there is more to them as individuals than that specific behavior. Developmentally appropriate practice prescribes that adults may never engage in the neglect of children; scream at children in anger; inflict physical or emotional pain; criticize a child's person or family by ridiculing, blaming, teasing, insulting, namecalling, threatening, or using frightening or humiliating punishment. Adults should not laugh at children's behavior, nor discuss it among themselves in the presence of children or non-teaching adults. Adults should nurture, care, praise, support, guide, redirect, and discuss things with children. Adults should find a time to discuss children's behavior away from the children and adults not involved in teaching the children (i.e., parents, visitors).

Adults deal with stress

Children today are often under a lot of stress. Stress can be broadly defined as an environmental change that interferes with normal functioning by triggering some kind of emotional tension in the person (Garmezy, 1984). The various situations in which children live and the situations in which they spend time during the day may contribute to this stress. A family member being ill, losing a job, or leaving home for another job may result in considerable stress. Divorce is very disruptive to families and particularly so to young children in those families (Mediros, Porter &

Welch, 1983). The resulting changes in life style, economic level and living arrangements continue to be sources of stress. Some children experience remarriage and the blending of families as another source of stress. Divorce may create a change in child care arrangements with some children entering or spending more hours in child care.

Routine events in the life of a family such as relocation to a different dwelling, the birth of a new sibling, or having a sibling with disabilities may cause considerable stress in some young children (Honig, 1986a). Other routine events such as the death of a pet, a friend moving away, moving to a new house, relatives visiting for long periods of time, or a parent away on business for an extended period may also produce stress. The following is an example of a stress producing situation.

CASE STUDY

The mother of a young boy shared a concern with a guest speaker after a parent night in a community preschool. The father of the child was in the military and was away for long periods of time. The child developed an interest in and seemed to want to own a doll. The father was set against it and told the mother she was never to get him a doll. The mother went along with the directive for a period of time but finally gave in because the child seemed to miss his father so much when he was away. The mother related that she told the child he could not play with the doll or even show the doll to the father when he was at home. When the father was home, the doll stayed in the closet. The mother wondered if she had created a new problem while attempting to deal with an existing one.

Homelessness is another reason children experience stress. While homelessness is not as prevalent a source of stress, it is becoming an increasing problem. Homelessness is disruptive, unsettling, and unhealthy. Children living in shelters often do not sleep or eat well, have health problems, attend school irregularly, and lose many or all of their personal possessions. There is limited privacy in some shelters and the routine familiar to the child is disrupted.

Some young children live in neighborhoods filled with violence. They spend their time indoors because parents are fearful of allowing them outdoors to play. Many children have seen family members or other people get shot or die from gunshots. These events are increasing in the cities and in other areas as well. Some children have been victims of physical abuse or neglect, sexual abuse or emotional abuse, or neglect. Some children present obvious signs of abuse (i.e., cuts, welts, bruises, burns) or neglect (i.e., medical or educational neglect, signs of inadequate food, clothing, bathing, shelter, or supervision). It is more difficult to identify children who suffer from emotional abuse or neglect. There are many reasons why children act out or withdraw. One of the reasons may be emotional abuse or neglect. The classroom teacher with knowledge of child development is in a good position to observe changes in behavior patterns which over time may be strong indicators of abuse (Meddin & Rosen, 1986).

Some children react strongly to what they hear through the media. Adults listening to the news may be unaware that children are also listening. What is heard may be frightening but the child may be unable to find the words to inform the adult of the experience. The fear produces stress for the child.

Some children appear to be stressed without an apparent external cause. Some children are very hard on themselves and create stress in their own lives. They have a very intense need to be first, best, prettiest, smartest, most clever, or most popular. When a teacher encounters a child presenting this kind of profile, it might be easy to assume that this competitiveness comes from the home environment. After meeting the parents, it might become obvious that the stress could not possibly come from home. The stress is definitely self-induced.

Some children are stressed because they feel a strong need to be the biggest when there is no hope that they will ever attain that stature in life. A child in a class several years ago was always asking his peers what size their clothes were. He spent considerable time each day anguishing about the fact that he was almost five and wore size seven and another child was just four and wore size eight. How could that be? Attempts at logic, and examples to demonstrate size and age relationships did not work to appease this child. He knew he was the oldest in the class and in his mind that meant that he had to be the biggest. The teachers in this classroom helped this size conscious child to see past numbers and to experience people for what they were and what they had to offer.

Adults must be sensitive to the signs of stress and help children find appropriate stress-reducing activities and techniques. Honig (1986b) lists twenty ways teachers can help children cope with stress:

1. Notice when a child is stressed.
2. Demonstrate self-control and coping skills yourself.
3. Enhance children's self-esteem.
4. Encourage each child to develop a special interest or skill that can serve as an inner source of pride and self-esteem.
5. Use proactive intervention to avoid unnecessary stress.
6. Help children understand the consequences and implications of negative acting out behaviors on others and on themselves.

7. Acknowledge children's feelings and encourage verbal mediation.
8. Help children distinguish reality from fantasy.
9. Use gentle humor.
10. If the stressor on a child is peer aggression, focus directly on the stressor.
11. Help children view their situation more positively.
12. Structure classroom activity to enhance cooperation.
13. Modify classroom situations and rules.
14. Find individual talk time with troubled children.
15. Mobilize other children to help.
16. Use bibliotherapy.
17. Have regular classroom talks in a safe, calm atmosphere.
18. Use art.
19. Encourage children to act out coping skills with dolls, puppets or other dramatic play.
20. Involve parents.

Adults model self-control and conflict resolution

Another area in which children learn from the adults in their presence is in the area of self-control. Self-control rather than control by others is important because people who have self-control are trustworthy and responsible, they can be counted on to do the right thing, and they can make choices on their own behalf (Hendrick, 1992). Children learn self-control when they are treated with dignity and respect as well as through the use of discipline techniques that guide children by setting clear expectations and fair limits. As children get older, they can participate in setting their own limits with adults guiding them as to the reasonableness of the limits. Children need adults to help them learn that making a mistake is not terrible. They need to learn that there is something to be learned from each mistake made. Children learn to accept this if they see adults make mistakes, correct them, and go on with their lives. Children need adults to help them find more meaningful behavior in which to engage rather than to be told "No" without an alternate behavior. Children often engage in certain behaviors because they do not know or have any other behaviors in their repertoire. Children need to be taken seriously when they talk about their frustrations, fears, and feelings. Sometimes what a child takes so seriously may seem comical to an adult who knows that life has many more frustrating moments ahead. However, to the young child, the situation is very serious. One needs to listen to these feelings and validate them while not attending to them so seriously that the child will become even more frustrated and self-absorbed.

Some children come from homes in which there are few positive role models who engage in conflict resolution. This is either because nobody at home engages in conflicts or the role models at home are negative rather than positive. When children can see adults model conflict resolution skills, they learn from the observation and internalize the behaviors. Rules that are worth having are rules worth patiently reinforcing. Children also need to understand the rationale for rules that have been established. Long lectures delivered when they challenge rules may detract from understanding. Rules might be more effective when children know that adults develop them to keep children safe.

Children who have yet to develop self-control may need guidance. Guidance is an ongoing process and is related to discipline, which some associate with a reaction to misbehavior by a child who does not follow the rules (Morrison, 1988) and management. When children are involved in meaningful activity there is much less opportunity or need to misbehave. Developing meaningful activities for all children helps to promote inclusion. Having a well thought out plan for guidance provides for attention paid to appropriate behaviors while children are helped to learn appropriate behaviors when they are not aware of or are not skilled in the behaviors expected of them in given situations. In this way, all children with and without disabilities will be able to enjoy the activities of an inclusive classroom.

Adults are supervisors

The last critical component of adult-child interaction is that of responsibility for supervision of all children at all times. Supervision means recognizing that children need opportunities for increasing independence as they acquire skills during the course of the year. This realization comes from time spent with the children.

Relations Between Home and Program

The most positive outcomes are effected during the early childhood period when parents and teachers work together within a framework of shared decision making (Berger, 1987). Parents should be encouraged to observe and participate in the child's program as much as possible. In some early childhood programs, it is the responsibility of the teacher to establish and maintain frequent contacts with families. In other programs, the family is given ample opportunity through a variety of avenues to establish a relationship with the teacher; the choice is theirs. Establishing relationships with parents may be difficult. Some parents have difficulty letting anyone get close to them. They prefer that teachers not call, even if the call is intended to share a wonderful incident that happened at school that day. One must respect the privacy of parents while attempting to build trust and rapport with the family. Understand that the reason some parents have problems coming to visit the school is because those people had less than positive experiences during their own schooling and as a result they carry a lot of baggage. The physical act of coming to school brings to surface some negative memories for them. Try to help to turn that negative experience around by creating a warm, responsive environment for parents as well as for children. A teacher needs to recognize that one person may not be able to accomplish this task alone.

Teachers are the logical source of information concerning child development, appropriate resources for materials, activities, and referrals for children. Teachers need to be available for conferences and other forms of communication with families. Sometimes this means having conferences at unusual times of the day in order to accommodate parent work or school schedules. Teachers need to be ready for conferences and avoid interruptions to prevent resentment on the part of the parents (Hendrick, 1992). When parents feel welcome and a vital part of a child's program, it is easier to establish a pattern of parent as partner in education which is crucial to the future success of the child. Once this partnership is well established, parents feel comfortable raising their concerns about their children, asking for advice from teachers, or just sharing.

A relationship based on respect and trust affords those who have the educational responsibility for children the opportunity to share developmental information about the child. Shared information helps parents, teachers, and other involved professionals to make appropriate decisions about children and their educational programs and allows for planning ahead for transitions.

Developmental Evaluation of Children

Decisions about placement and curriculum for children must be based on a **developmental evaluation process**. A critical component of the process of developmental evaluation is observation by teachers and information gathered from parents (Hills, 1992). Developmental assessments should not be used to deny access to children of legal entry age for specific programs. The process of developmental evaluation should be used to develop and provide appropriate programs for children. Developmental evaluation of children should assist in the process and practice of inclusion. Observation as assessment, the linking of curriculum and assessment and other issues in assessment are presented in detail in Chapter 15.

HOW CHILDREN LEARN

Young children in the early childhood years who are in the preoperational period according to Piaget's stages of development, learn through authentic experiences presented to them in a manner that is safe and appropriate to their level of development. Although children have very vivid imaginations, experience is what fuels the imagination. A child who enjoys a richness of experience is a child who has conversation to share with adults and children. This type of child is curious for more experience and information and through the experience, constructs his or her own frame of knowledge. An activity experienced personally is an activity remembered. These are the experiences that are the basis for the "remember when we . . ." statements children often make. A point of information that is only verbally presented to a young child is most usually a point of information not remembered by the child (Williams & Kamii, 1986).

Observation as a tool for learning how children learn

Watching the natural play and activity of young children provides us with the vehicle for understanding the ways in which children learn. A young child at play or work invests great energy in the activity. The child is really striving to perfect skills, attempt new behaviors and make sense of the world. There is no other way to duplicate these experiences.

Children can learn through observation but this kind of learning does not afford the child the same opportunities as actually being involved in the discovery oriented, hands-on process. What a child does, a child learns. The more often a child engages in an experience, the more the learning that is based on the experience is cemented. This is one reason that children love to repeat the same activity. Knowledge is not something that is poured into the child by an external source, but something the child has to construct for herself or himself. This is why Piaget's theory is also called **constructivist theory** (Forman & Hill, 1980). When making an observation of a young child at play at home or in school, seeing a child working hard to complete a puzzle might be a common sight. What would also be a common sight would be to see the child dump the puzzle over and begin to redo it immediately upon completion of the puzzle. An adult with a strong knowledge of child development understands that repetition is comforting as well as challenging to a young child. Children invent their own challenges when repeating tasks. A child might want to see if he or she could repeat the task with one hand, in less time, or without any assistance from an adult or peer. The child may also enjoy completing the same puzzle because the sense of accomplishment it brings is worth repeating.

Children learn through interactive materials

Children learn through experiences with interactive materials. These interactive materials consist of:

- dramatic play materials, doll house and accessories, hollow blocks
- small unit blocks and accessories, Legos, woodworking, manipulatives (items that fit together)
- materials for tactile play such as water, sand, clay, mud, goop

- a variety of art media
- equipment for gross motor play
- materials for games such as musical games, board games, outdoor games and thinking games.

In our modern technological world, it is very common to find many toys that do many things. These toys basically perform for children and while some children may find these toys entertaining for a while, they are not the most appropriate for young children. Young children need toys that allow them to interact with the materials. They need toys that require the child to be active and not just an observer. Toys that "perform" prevent the child from being involved in the action because the action of the toy is automated. The child is then left to just watch the action or listen to some sounds. After a very little time, you will see the child leave the toy and probably begin to play with the box and wrappings that previously surrounded the toy.

Learning is enhanced through feedback

Children need to have feedback to motivate them to continue to be involved in activity. The feedback may consist of success with the materials being worked with or feedback from peers or adults who comment positively about what the child has accomplished with the materials.

Children learn through interactions

Children also learn through interactions with their peers and adults. Children who spend considerable time alone miss out on valuable opportunities for learning. Children do grow and develop from the experiences they have during the time spent exploring by themselves but there is a great difference between being given the opportunity to explore with supervision and support versus being left alone with no stimulation or support.

Children need time to learn

Another key factor in the learning process for young children is time. If children are rushed through activities their learning tends not to be enhanced. Children know how much time they need to spend with materials and on specific tasks. Adults really should not prejudge the amount of time needed for children to accomplish certain learning. Some children react to being rushed by digging their heels in and resisting the attempts to move the child along. Urging a child to hurry up and move faster may result in actually encouraging the child to take twice as long as necessary. Each child, as a unique individual developing along a fairly predictable course, needs as much time as required to realize his or her developmental potential. Rushing children through development does not help a child get to the next level of development with assurance and stability. Children who are rushed often require time later on to readdress certain aspects of development. While they could have become very self-assured and competent learners, rushed children may indeed become very dependent learners and dependent personalities (Elkind, 1987). These were children who needed more time to develop evenly across all areas of development instead of being pushed in one or two areas at the expense of the others. Some parents and teachers confuse the early interests of young children as indicators of life-long interests or talents. A child who demonstrates an early interest in cars or planes may be saturated with those items. For each birthday, holiday, or "I love you" present from parents or other relatives, the child may receive one of these treasures. This may result in serious overkill and eventually turn the child off to any interest in these items.

Children learn through integrated experiences

Children need exposure to all kinds of experiences and materials in order to allow them to determine what they like to do and discover what they do well. Since children learn best through real experiences, these experiences should cover a broad range of themes. Repetition is a key element of learning, and continual exposure to activities and information presented in an integrated manner is critical to stimulate and support the learning of the young child. Presenting children with bits of information introduced in a scattered fashion may prevent rather than enhance learning. Often, schools have special weeks that highlight one particular theme such as ethnic diversity. This is an excellent example of the type of theme and activity that should permeate the entire curriculum (Derman-Sparks, 1992). How much can one expect a child to learn and assimilate learning into life when the subject matter is touched on for such a short time? How much value can be attributed to this learning? Those who are responsible for planning learning experiences for young children need to do their planning based on what we know about how children learn rather than how learning opportunities might have been presented previously.

Successful learning depends on the provision and implementation of meaningful curriculum. This enables children to make sense of what they are learning and to connect their experiences in ways that lead to rich conceptual development (Bredekamp & Rosegrant, 1992). The urgency to have children perform at certain levels according to state or local assessments may trigger thought concerning the implementation of programs claiming quick and sure results. Teachers also need to be empowered to stand strong in their beliefs concerning what is right for young children. This may be difficult for new teachers or teachers who are new to a particular school. Teachers may be easily intimidated by their peers, by parents of children in their classes, and by administrators.

Trends in education have come and gone (i.e., programmed instruction, individualized skill-based reading programs, purely academic programs). Most have gone because they often focused on teaching children in a manner that did not support a child's natural predisposition to learn. What they did focus on was skills and pushing a child ahead. Children who "produce" are not to be gathered as trophies to be placed on shelves. Children have the right to develop without pressure. They have the right to quality appropriate education. This education should reflect life and the normal process of development. This education should reflect the respect due to children and those who take the responsibility of early childhood educator so seriously. Working with young children is one of the most important kinds of work a person can choose as a lifelong career. It should be undertaken by individuals who get into the field because they want to help children develop expertlike, deep understandings of a discipline by making schools more like hands-on museums and schooling more like serving apprenticeships (Gardner, 1991).

INCLUSION

Inclusion refers to the commitment to educate each child, to the maximum extent appropriate, in the school and classroom he or she would otherwise attend. Inclusion has an underlying philosophy that all children belong together (Salisbury, 1991). It involves bringing the support services to the child (rather than moving the child to the services) and requires only that the child will benefit from being in the class (rather than having to keep up with the other children). The concept of inclusion moves well beyond the concept of mainstreaming in that inclusion is broad based and mainstreaming usually means having a child with special needs as part of one or more periods of a school day. When the concept of mainstreaming was first introduced, children were mainstreamed for lunch, art, or music. The child with special needs was not part of the regular class on a full-time basis.

Inclusion means that children with special needs are totally integrated into the activity of the classroom. A majority of early childhood programs for children without disabilities report that they enroll at least one child with disabilities (Wolery, Holcombe, Brookfield, Huffman, Schroeder, Martin, Venn, Werts & Flemming, 1993). Effective inclusion is characterized by its virtual invisibility. Children with disabilities are not clustered into groups of persons with similar disabilities. They are no longer in separate classrooms labeled "LD Resource," "ED," or "EMR." These children with disabilities are able to be included in the classroom because appropriate supports are provided directly to the child in the classroom. These supports may include a special educator, a personal aide (paraprofessional) for the child who serves as a facilitator for the child, supportive personnel such as a physical therapist, occupational therapist, speech and language therapist, vision specialist, or technology specialist. The child may use a computer to facilitate learning and communication. The child may have adaptive equipment or furniture. The most important conceptual component of inclusion is that the child with special needs has every right to be in the same classroom with age-appropriate peers who are in turn able to provide the child with special needs with normal models of language, social interaction, and cognitive functioning.

CASE STUDY

The parents of a preschool child with disabilities wished the child to be enrolled in a community preschool program. When the mother called the school to discuss coming for a visit, she indicated to the director that her child was disabled. The director informed the mother that there had been many children with disabilties in that school over the years and the school identified the practice of inclusion as an important part of the mission of the school. The mother was so eager for her child to be a child first and a child with disabilities second. The child was eventually enrolled in the school and with the child came an aide, a speech and language therapist, a physical therapist, an occupational therapist, a vision consultant, an adaptive physical education teacher, a special education teacher and a technology consultant. All of these people, in cooperation and collaboration with the classroom teachers and the parents, worked to establish communication and the integration of the child into the classroom environment through the use of adaptive equipment (switches, communication devices, etc.) added to the child's participation in as many regular classroom activities as could be adapted.

Benefits of inclusion for children with disabilities

Wolery and Wilbers (1994) review the current research on the practice of inclusion in preschool programs. They state that the benefits of preschool are well known and are supported by early childhood educators who practice inclusion as well as by the professionals who prepare those teachers. They also indicate that the research shows that families of children with and without disabilities appear to have positive feelings about preschool inclusion. The authors reinforce the fact that many of the proposed benefits of inclusion do not happen without purposeful and careful supports to promote them.

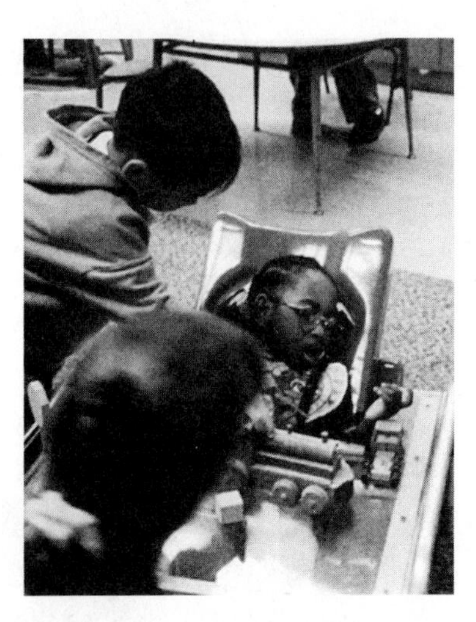

FIG 1.2 Children with and without disabilities at play.

Benefits of inclusion for children without disabilities

Children in an inclusive classroom who do not have disabilities benefit from the experience of interacting with a child with disabilities. When inclusion is practiced on a regular basis from the early childhood years on, major benefits to the children without disabilities can be seen in several areas. Children learn to be comfortable around individuals with disabilities from not only being around them, but by interacting with them, learning with them, and learning from them. Parents of children with disabilities see the potential peers have for influencing appropriate behavior in their children. Parents of children without disabilities see their children respecting other children and learning acceptance and the value and dignity of life in a very different way. Inclusion is a practice that supports an anti-bias curriculum approach. The early childhood years are prime for redirecting energy to the provision of what is every child's right and due—the right to an appropriate program that is designed to meet the needs of every child at the level of the child at that point in time.

THE CHILDREN IN AN INCLUSIVE CLASSROOM

Children in an inclusive classroom are children with and without disabilities. They are all the children who will benefit from exposure to a developmentally appropriate curriculum as well as to opportunities to interact with their age-appropriate peers. They are children who may need assistance and support in order to maximize their potential no matter what classroom they are in. Children in an inclusive classroom in a public school are children from the neighborhood. In a non-public school setting, they are children whose parents have chosen a particular school for them based either on the curriculum the school offers, the diversity of the school population, the proximity to the parents' work location, or any other reason parents choose particular schools for their children. The point is that an inclusive setting accepts children at whatever level they are without attempting to determine in September whether a child will be on "grade level" at the end of the year. Even the most seasoned educator avoids predicting exactly where any child will wind up at the end of the year. What educators do know is whether a setting has the potential to enable a child to learn, grow, and develop to the best of his or her potential. If one can say that an educational environment has the potential for accomplishing that, then the setting is indeed appropriate for inclusion of children with special needs.

THE TEACHERS IN AN INCLUSIVE CLASSROOM

The teachers in inclusive classrooms are most typically regular early childhood educators. They are teachers who through their training, have been prepared to understand child development, ages and stages of development, and the creation and implementation of developmentally appropriate curriculum and practice as a means of providing mindful curriculum. This means that they have experience accommodating varying levels of development in one classroom. It also means that they are skilled in meeting the needs of children across all areas of development. What this means is that the typically well-prepared, early childhood educator is experienced in planning a variety of activities to meet the needs and interests of the often multi-age population that constitutes an early childhood classroom. These teachers are used to having children engage in different activities at the same time. They are used to having art, books, blocks, dramatic play, manipulatives, science discovery, and possibly other activities taking place at the same time. They are used to taking a particular activity and modifying it to enable a younger or less skilled child to participate in the activity. They are used to accepting each child at the developmental level he or she presents and working with each individual child to maximize the experience the child has in the classroom.

There is currently much being published concerning the role of the regular early childhood program/classroom as the site of educational programs for children with special needs (Fowell & Lawton, 1992; McLean &

Hanline, 1990; Wolery, Strain & Bailey, 1992). The field of special education has been the focal point for the education of young children with special needs for many years. In recent years (Cavallaro, Haney & Cabello, 1993; Guralnick, 1990; Odom & McEvoy, 1990) there has been considerable research and writing to support the concept of inclusion with the regular early childhood educator as the facilitator in the provision of an appropriate program. With all children with special needs, it is understood that the regular educator cannot provide everything the children need in terms of education and therapeutic needs. Whether the children in an inclusive classroom are children with severe disabilities or children with mild disabilities, regular educators, early childhood special educators, and specialists in the area of identified disability need to join forces to provide an integrated, developmentally appropriate program for each child, according to specific, identified special needs. Joining forces means working together in the true sense of working as a team. Without this team effort, the child will not reach maximum potential.

Including children with special needs in the regular early childhood environment does not minimize the special needs a child actually has but it does provide a more active environment with more potential for the child with disabilities to observe normalized behaviors and for the adults in the setting to facilitate the development of such behaviors. The regular education environment emphasizes positive, normal behaviors while helping children to work through their deficit areas. The early childhood educator sees emerging behaviors and skills and rearranges the environment to stimulate the occurrence of new behaviors.

There is another "teacher" in the inclusive environment. This "teacher" has not had any formal preparation but is often more effective in stimulating the development of a greater behavioral repertoire than any other teacher in the classroom. This "teacher" is the peer without disabilities in the inclusive classroom. As discussed previously, no adult model can replace the modeling done by a peer. The rapport that develops between children in classrooms is often the most beneficial component of the classroom program.

Teachers in early childhood classrooms are often accustomed to working as part of teaching team. Prior to a first grade classroom, it would be very rare to find an early childhood professional working alone in a classroom. The team in an early childhood classroom may consist of teachers with the same credentials and experience. The team may also consist of a teacher, a paraprofessional, a parent assistant, and a student intern. Once an early childhood classroom becomes an inclusive environment, the team working in the early childhood classroom may add **specialists** to the group. Such specialists might include a speech and language professional, a physical therapist, an occupational therapist, a vision specialist, a special education liaison teacher, or an adaptive physical education teacher. The specialists who come into the classroom to become part of the team working with the child(ren) with special needs works within the program offered in the classroom. This is a critical component of the delivery of service to the child with special needs. **Collaboration** and **consultation** are very important parts of the service delivery model in inclusive education. This topic will receive much more attention in Chapter 14.

SUMMARY

The concept of developmental appropriateness has two dimensions: age appropriateness and individual appropriateness. Teachers must observe children in their classrooms under a variety of conditions in order to learn about the children and their special ways of learning. Children have different personality styles and different learning styles.

Play is the natural medium for young children to learn, grow and develop (Bredekamp, 1987; Moyer, Egerston & Isenberg, 1987; Piaget, 1962). Play affords children opportunities to explore, discover, attempt varying roles, relate to others, and exercise creativity. Play needs to be child initiated, child directed, and teacher supported.

The NAEYC guidelines for developmentally appropriate practice focus on curriculum, adult-child interaction, relations between home and program, and developmental evaluation of children. These guidelines for ensuring developmentally appropriate practice are also appropriate for the early education of children with disabilities. As the fields of early childhood special education and early childhood education become more integrated, the practices of the two fields may come closer together.

Developmentally appropriate curriculum provides for integrated learning driven by the different needs, levels of functioning, and interests of the children in the group. All aspects of development need to be taken into consideration when planning for the development and education of the whole child. Children learn through direct interaction with children, concrete activities and real materials, and adults. In a developmentally appropriate classroom, children can make choices.

All children need time to work with activities and materials and teachers need time to connect with children. Children need exposure to peoples and practices different from those within the culture of their own families. Teachers need to model for children the acceptance and knowledge of diversity. Developmentally appropriate curriculum should provide for a balance of quiet and active engagement during the course of the day as well as for outdoor experiences.

In a developmentally appropriate program, adults respond to children in a direct and timely fashion, facilitate for, or model appropriate behavior for them. Children may need physical support, reassurance, or redirection. Children look to adults for support in their interactions, in their play, and in their task-related behavior. Adults model and facilitate the development of self-esteem in children by respecting, accepting, listening to, and comforting children.

Adults must be sensitive to the signs of stress in young children and help children find appropriate stress-reducing activities and techniques. Children learn self-control when they are treated with dignity and respect as well as through the use of discipline techniques that guide children by setting clear expectations and fair limits. Adults are supervisors of children at all times children are with them.

Parents and teachers who work together within a framework of shared decision making add to the growth and development of young children. Decisions about placement and curriculum for children must be based on a developmental evaluation process. A critical component of the process of developmental evaluation is observation by teachers and information gathered from parents. Young children in the early childhood years learn through authentic experiences. Watching the natural play and activity of young children provides the vehicle for understanding the ways in which children learn. Children learn through experiences with interactive materials. They need feedback to motivate them. They learn through interactions with peers and adults. Activities and information presented in an integrated manner are critical to stimulate and support the learning of the young child.

Inclusion refers to the commitment to educate each child, to the maximum extent appropriate, in the school and classroom he or she would otherwise attend with the provision of support services brought to the child. There are benefits of inclusion for children with disabilities as well as benefits of inclusion for children without disabilities.

The teachers in inclusive classrooms most typically are early childhood educators. Including children with special needs in the regular early childhood environment does not minimize the special needs a child has. The regular education environment emphasizes positive behaviors while helping children to work through their deficit areas. Peers without disabilities in an inclusive environment have the potential to contribute much to the richness of the experiences of peers with disabilties. The team involved in teaching in an inclusive early childhood classroom may consist of a teacher, a paraprofessional, a parent assistant, a student intern, and specialists. Collaboration and consultation are very important parts of the service delivery model in inclusive education.

DISCUSSION QUESTIONS

1) The mother of a young boy shared a concern with a guest speaker after a parent night in a community preschool. The father of the child was in the military and was away for long periods of time. The child developed an interest in and seemed to want to own a doll. The father was set against it and told the mother she was never to get him a doll. The mother went along with the directive for a period of time but finally gave in because the child seemed to miss his father so much when he was away. The mother related that she told the child he could not play with the doll or even show the doll to the father when he was at home. When the father was home, the doll stayed in the closet. The mother wondered if she had created a new problem while attempting to deal with an existing one. What would you say to this mother? What could you suggest to her that she do to make the situation less confusing for the child?
2) You are a new teacher in an old established early childhood program. You have very strong ideas about the infusion of an anti-bias approach into the curriculum. Once you begin to settle into the job, you realize that the program director and the teachers have an established curriculum that identifies weekly themes that are offered in a set sequence. They have followed this curriculum for many years. How will you handle this situation?
3) You respond to a telephone inquiry concerning the early childhood program in which you work. The family making the inquiry wants to know the philosophy of the program. You discuss developmentally appropriate curriculum and practice and indicate that the program includes children with disabilities. The parent seems uncomfortable with this information. What will you say in response to this parent?
4) Describe two situations you have observed in which activities could have been presented in a manner making them more accessible and developmentally appropriate for all children in the class.
5) Think about a situation in which you worked with a child or observed a child who was experiencing stress. What did you do or could you have done to alleviate the stress?
6) Friends of yours ask for your advice about the selection of toys for their children for birthday gifts. Their children are four, six, and eight years old. What suggestions will you give them and what can you tell them about the developmental importance and appropriateness of the items you suggest?

REFERENCES

Bakken, M. (1990). In the foreward to E. Klugman & S. Smilansky (Eds.). *Children's play and learning: Perspectives and policy implications* (p. xi). New York: Teachers College Press.

Berger, E. (1987). *Parents as partners in education: The school and home working together*. Columbus, OH: Merrill Publishing Company.

Bredekamp, S. (Ed.). (1987). *Developmentally appropriate practice in early childhood programs serving children from birth through age 8*. Washington, DC: NAEYC.

Bredekamp, S., & Rosegrant, T. (1992). Reaching potentials through appropriate curriculum: Conceptual frameworks for applying the guidelines. In S. Bredekamp & T. Rosegrant (Eds.), *Reaching potentials: Appropriate curriculum and assessment for young children, Volume 1*. Washington, DC: National Association for the Education of Young Children.

Carta, J., Schwartz, I., Atwater, J., & McConnell, S. (1991). Developmentally appropriate practice: Appraising its usefulness for young children with disabilities. *Topics in Early Childhood Special Education, 11*(1), 1–20.

Carta, J., Schwartz, I., Atwater, J., & McConnell, S. (1993). Developmentally appropriate practices and early childhood special education: A reaction to Johnson and McChesney Johnson. *Topics in Early Childhood Special Education, 13*(3), 243–254.

Cavallaro, C., Haney, M., & Cabello, B. (1993). Developmentally appropriate strategies for promoting full participation in early childhood setting. *Topics in Early Childhood Special Education*, 13(3), 293–307.

Derman-Sparks, L. & the A. B. C. Task Force. (1989). *Anti-bias curriculum: Tools for empowering young children*. Washington, DC: National Association for the Education of Young Children.

Derman-Sparks, L. (1992). In S. Bredekamp, & T. Rosegrant (Eds.), *Reaching potentials: Appropriate curriculum and assessment for young children, Volume 1*. Washington, DC: National Association for the Education of Young Children.

Elkind, D. (1987). *Miseducation: Preschoolers at risk*. New York: Alfred A Knopf.

Forman, G., & Hill, F. (1980). *Constructivist play: Applying Piaget in the preschool*. Monterey, CA: Brooks/Cole.

Fowell, N., & Lawton, J. (1992). An alternative view of appropriate practice in early childhood education. *Early Childhood Research Quarterly*, 7, 53–73.

Gardner, H. (1991). *The unschooled mind*. New York: Basic Books.

Garmezy, N. (1984). Stressors of childhood. In N. Garmezy & M. Rutter (Eds.), *Stress, coping and development in childhood* (pp. 43–84). New York: McGraw-Hill Book Co.

Guralnick, M. (1990). Major accomplishments and future directions in early childhood mainstreaming. *Topics in Early Childhood Special Education, 10*(2), 1–17.

Hendrick, J. (1992). *The Whole Child: Developmental education for the early years.* New York: Merrill Publishing Company.

Hills, T. (1992). Reaching potentials through appropriate assessment. In S. Bredekamp & T. Rosegrant (Eds.), *Reaching potentials: Appropriate curriculum and assessment for young children, Volume 1.* Washington, DC: National Association for the Education of Young Children.

Honig, A. (1986a). Stress and coping in children (Part 1). *Young Children, 41*(4), 50–63.

Honig, A. (1986b). Stress and coping in children (Part 2). *Young Children, 41*(5), 47–59.

Johnson, J., & Johnson, K. (1992). Clarifying the developmental perspective in response to Carta, Schwartz, Atwater, and McConnell. *Topics in Early Childhood Special Education, 12*(4), 439–457.

Johnson, J. & Johnson, K. (1993). Rejoinder to Carta, Schwartz, Atwater, and McConnell. *Topics in Early Childhood Special Education, 13*(3), 255–257.

McLean, M., & Hanline, M. (1990). Providing early intervention services in integrated environments: Challenges and opportunities for the future. *Topics in Early Childhood Special Education,* 10(2), 62–77.

Meddin, B., & Rosen, A. (1986). Child abuse and neglect: Prevention and reporting. *Young Children, 41*(4), 26–39.

Morrison, G. (1988). *Education and development of infants, toddlers, and preschoolers.* Glenview, IL: Scott, Foresman/Little, Brown College Division.

Moyer, J., Egerston, H., & Isenberg, J. (1987). The child-centered kindergarten. *Childhood Education, 63*(4), 235–242.

Odom, S., & McEvoy, M. (1990). Mainstreaming at the preschool level: Potential barriers and tasks to the field. *Topics in Early Childhood Special Education,* 10(2), 48–61.

Piaget, J. (1962). *Play, dreams and imitation in childhood.* New York: Norton.

Salisbury, C. (1991). Mainstreaming during the early childhood years. *Exceptional Children, 58*: 146–155.

Smilansky, S. (1990). Sociodramatic play: Its relevance to behavior and achievement in school. In E. Klugman & S. Smilansky (Eds.), *Children's play and learning: Perspectives and policy implications* (pp. 18–42). New York: Teachers College Press.

Williams, C., & Kamii, C. (1986). How do children learn by handling objects? *Young Children, 42*(1), 23–26.

Wolery, M., Strain, P., & Bailey, D. (1992). Reaching potentials of children with special needs. In S. Bredekamp & T. Rosegrant (Eds.), *Reaching potentials: Appropriate curriculum and assessment for young children* (pp. 92–111). Washington, DC: National Association for the Education of Young Children.

ADDITIONAL READINGS

Allen, K. (1992). *Mainstreaming in early childhood education.* Albany, NY: Delmar.

Bricker, D., & Cripe, J. (1992). *An activity-based approach to early intervention.* Baltimore: Paul H. Brookes.

Elkind, D. (1993). *Images of the young child: Collected essays on development and education.* Washington, DC: National Association for the Education of Young Children.

McCracken, J. (Ed.). (1986). *Reducing stress in young children's lives.* Washington, DC: National Association for the Education of Young Children.

Neugebauer, B. (Ed.). (1992). *Alike and different: Exploring our humanity with young children* (rev. ed.). Washington, DC: National Association for the Education of Young Children.

Peck, C., Odom, S., & Bricker, D. (Eds.). (1993). *Integrating young children with disabilities into community programs.* Baltimore: Paul H. Brookes.

Quint, S. (1994) *Schooling homeless children: A working model for America's public schools.* New York: Teachers College Press.

Roopnarine, J., & Honig, A. (1985). The unpopular child. *Young Children, 40*(6), 59–64.

Safford, P., Spodek, B., & Saracho, O. (Eds.). (1994). *Early childhood special education: Yearbook in early childhood education, volume 5.* New York: Teachers College Press.

Scales, B., Almy, M., Nicolopoulou, A., & Ervin-Tripp, S. (1991). *Play and the social context of development in early care and education.* New York: Teachers College Press.

Wallerstein, J., Corbin, S., & Lewis, J. (1988). Children of divorce: A ten-year study. In E. Hetherington & J. Arasteh (Eds.), *Impact of divorce, single-parenting and stepparenting on children* (pp. 198–214). Hillsdale, NY: Paul Erlbaum, Associates.

Werner, E. (1984). Resilient children. *Young Children, 40*(1), 68–72.

Wolf, S. (1969). *Children under stress.* London: The Penguin Press.

CHAPTER 2

Integrated Thematic Play and Curriculum

KEY TERMS

thematic curriculum
emergent curriculum
integrated curriculum
discipline
punishment and guidance
self-discipline
emotional climate
ongoing assessment
respect

OVERVIEW OF THEMATIC APPROACH

The term "thematic approach" is currently used widely in the field of early childhood education (Seefeldt, 1989). **Thematic curriculum** is curriculum that focuses on one topic or theme at a time. Thematic curriculum is a vehicle for managing curriculum while achieving developmental appropriateness. Each theme developed allows the activities and concepts planned to integrate all learning opportunities for the children for whom the curriculum is planned. Children at differing stages of development approach concepts from different levels. They bring different experiences to the activities provided for them. A developmentally appropriate curriculum is neither child directed nor teacher directed but a result of interaction between teachers and children, with both contributing ideas and reacting to them to build on meaningful themes (Cassidy & Lancaster, 1993).

Determining Appropriate Themes for Young Children

Although children can benefit and gain something from almost any theme, there are many themes that are more appropriate for children at different ages and stages than others. How does one determine what themes are appropriate for a particular group of children? How do you know where to start? One way to start is to make observations of the children in your classroom within free play situations. When you make these observations, you will see some children gravitate to equipment with wheels while other children will gravitate to materials that relate to daily living situations or role playing. Some children will be slow to get started, while other will jump right in. If a teacher-initiated topic is not appropriate for the group, the waning interest of the children will serve as a strong indicator (Cassidy & Lancaster, 1993). In addition to observing children while they play or engage in social interactions with their peers, listening to questions that the children ask will provide a lot of information about their interests. When presented with an array of materials, observe which materials the children use when they make their own choices rather than when the choices are made for them. Observe which books children select to "read" when given free choice. Listen carefully to the comments that children make when they are asked what they might like to talk about at a time designated for discussion. All of these opportunities allow teachers to determine clues to themes that would be intrinsically interesting to the children in that particular classroom at that particular time.

Making Connections for Young Children

Children learn best through learning that is related and learning that is discovery oriented. Children begin to make connections relative to their learning when one activity supports the next. Books, writing, art activities, music, and dramatic play opportunities that relate to one theme afford children the opportunity to learn, practice, explore, and internalize information about one theme at a time. Themes that emerge from brainstorming, a happening, or introduction of materials are interconnected and flow from one to the other as children ask questions and develop new interests

(Cassidy & Lancaster, 1993). Learning that takes place under these conditions is learning that is remembered. It is not learning that has to be memorized because the children have been actively involved with their learning rather than passive recipients of information handed to them in written or oral form.

Consider this example the next time you attempt to "teach" something to a young child without having the child be actively involved in the learning process. A visit to a preschool identified as being science based once produced an observation of a teacher attempting to fill the children full of science facts. These children were asked to sit down at the end of the morning and listen to the teacher present 10–15 facts about the animal of the day. They were each given a ditto sheet with these facts to bring home to show their parents what they had "learned" about the animal of the day. On the reverse side of the ditto sheet was an outline of the animal of the day. The children were supposed to color in the animal. This was the science curriculum for that school. During the presentation of the animal facts, the children were inattentive, they sat too close together, and appeared to learn nothing. The teacher did not seem to take note of the behavior of the children in front of her. If she did notice the inappropriate behavior, it was clear that she had no idea that the manner and content of this type of lesson was inappropriate for this age group. Even when teaching adults, this type of learning is not even appropriate for all content. Imagine trying to learn to drive a car by being told all the steps one has to engage in order to make the car start to move. That certainly would not be an effective or safe way of learning to drive.

Thematic Learning—A Process for the Entire Year

Thematic curriculum is not a very new concept. Teachers have been introducing themes such as community helpers, Thanksgiving, or other holidays for many years. These themes are usually introduced at specific times during the year and are offered as something "special" for children around a holiday season or special school-wide event. Children usually respond to these kinds of activities with excitement because it allows them to be actively involved, work with a friend, select a place in the classroom to work on their special activities, and experience a sense of "freedom" they do not experience on a regular basis. Teachers seem to enjoy this approach to learning and treat is as a nice "break" from the normal routine. Some teachers feel threatened by this approach because the behavior of the children is so different than the behavior normally seen when the daily routine consists of structured learning, skill, and drill. The different behavior the children exhibit is not negative behavior but the teachers may not know what really stimulates that behavior and may have the sense that they are losing control. They mistake exuberance and excitement for lack of control.

What is being advocated here is that the thematic approach be offered as the vehicle for learning all year long. It is an approach that should be offered to children on a regular basis instead of a "special occasion" basis. It is an approach that goes beyond simply isolating the holiday of the month and using that as the focus of the curriculum for the month. John Dewey introduced thematic curriculum during the Progressive Era. It was introduced as part of the project approach he felt was meaningful for children. Dewey felt that through the project approach to curriculum, children would come to see themselves as part of the community in which they lived. Dewey saw the necessity for curriculum to be meaningful to the lives of children so that they would be learning for a purpose and not learning because some adult in the school environment told them that it was important for them to learn something specific (Dewey, 1938). Other examples of thematic curriculum were found in the Open Education movement of the 1960s.

Supporters of developmentally appropriate thematic curriculum do not advocate a return to these two approaches as they were previously implemented. What they do advocate is the application of the philosophical essence of these two approaches, in combination with curriculum and child development research conducted over the last 20–30 years, and using what has been learned about assessment of young children. All of this is formulated into a common sense approach to thematically presented and integrated curriculum. What this means is that the excitement of hands-on learning is combined with the acknowledgement of the importance of skill acquisition. It is recognized that these are not two distinctly different agendas for learning. Integrated learning affords the teacher the opportunity to embed skill development in activities that are meaningful to the children. It may often mean that the learner may not recognize that he or she is engaged in skill development or practice because the practice takes place within the framework of an activity that is exciting and useful. What is also recognized is that there is a developmental sequence to skill acquisition which translates into "earlier is not always better". This means that if a child evidences an interest in something as discovered within a thematic curriculum unit, the child may then pursue further interest in that area. Each child, with the support and facilitation of the teacher, is able to choose meaningful learning episodes. What it does not mean is that if a child evidences serious interest in something, that that activity should be the only academic area the child is encouraged to be involved in. If a child shows early interest and ability in the area of math, for example, that interest will not be diminished by activity in music, art, language arts, or any other area of study. In fact, math learning will be supported by explorations in other activity areas. Encouraging the development of a well-rounded child who delights in learning of all kinds should be the goal of an early childhood educator.

Jones and Nimmo (1994) use the term **emergent curriculum** to document the process of developing curriculum. They point out that emergent curriculum is sensible but not predictable and requires that teachers trust in the power of play. Jones and Nimmo support the notion that no teacher invents curriculum from scratch. Teachers read about or observe what other teachers have developed, reflect on it as it fits their own personal needs and the needs of the population they teach, and make it their own. The authors use an interesting metaphor for explaining the concept of emergent curriculum. The curriculum does not emerge just from the children. The children are a source of curriculum but only one of the possible sources. Teachers are the stage directors while the children are the models and coplayers. The teacher as the responsible adult is the organizer who sets the stage, times the acts and holds it all together.

DEFINITION OF INTEGRATED CURRICULUM

Integrated curriculum is a term that is often interchanged with or associated with the term thematic curriculum. Integrated curriculum is used as a framework for organizing all the organized learning that will take place in the classroom. Integrated curriculum is thematic by nature because the theme that is chosen as the focus of study is what integrates the learning opportunities in the classroom. Integrated curriculum allows the teacher to relate the major content areas of language arts, math, science, and social studies as well as the arts to the theme being studied. The integration of all these curriculum areas allows the child who is weak in one content area to have successful experiences with the content of the theme within the other content areas being integrated into the theme. Integrated curriculum also allows the child who might not choose to engage in activities in a particular area such as science, to become involved in this area of study because the science content for that particular integrated theme is couched within a food activity, an arts activity, or a dramatic play activity. For example, a child who shies away from scientific equipment might be very motivated to use a magnifying glass when asked to help the teacher discover clues by being a detective within the classroom. That same child might also be encouraged to make "discoveries" related to food, plants, shells, or rocks, when given the magnifying glass to use and maybe also a detective's hat and coat to wear while role-playing the part. Integrated curriculum affords all children access to the concepts and content of the curriculum specified within the unit of study. It allows the teacher to apply the information gathered about the children in the classroom to their learning advantage rather than acquiring information about the children only to fill out forms.

Bredekamp and Rosegrant (1992) propose that the primary purpose of curriculum should be to help children develop personal integrity and fulfillment while also enabling them to think, to reason, and to make decisions necessary to participate fully as citizens in a democracy. To accomplish this goal, the authors advocate the need for children to experience "mindful" curriculum that enables them to make sense of what they are learning and to connect their experiences in ways that lead to rich conceptual development.

CURRICULUM TO ACCOMMODATE ALL CHILDREN

Standard curriculum approaches focusing on the use of a text book and work book or work sheets often precludes many children from participation in the class and certainly precludes many children already in the class from meeting with success. If a child has difficulty with the physical mechanics of writing due to poorly developed muscles, delayed development, or a permanent deficit, traditional standard curriculum would mean that this child would not be able to demonstrate his or her command of the material covered in the classroom.

FIG 2.1 Children functioning on different developmental levels can engage in shared experiences.

Accommodating Classroom Participants

Within an integrated curriculum, the child described above would have several other options for demonstrating command of the information learned. The child might be able to play the role of a reporter and "report" the information via a tape recorder or through an oral presentation to the class. If the equipment is available, this "report" may be video-taped. The child making this video tape might really benefit from watching the tape at a later time. Watching the tape might provide a means of building self-esteem for the child and prove to be a genuine motivator for other children in the class. Sharing the tape with the parents during a parent-teacher conference or sending it home for the parents to view may allow them to see a demonstration of skills and ability that they did not know their child possessed. The child might be able to use the class computer to record the information that previously had to be hand written. The computer could be used as another tool for playing the role of "reporter" for the class. For a child with language delay or permanent deficit, technology might assist the child in communicating information previously kept within the child. The way in which technology affords some children the opportunity to be "heard" is found in the following example of a preschool age child.

CASE STUDY

Several years ago, a child came to an early childhood program with no productive language and no mobility. His diagnosis was cerebral palsy. When the child was born, his mother was told that he would never amount to anything but she was not ready to give up on him. She proposed that she serve as his classroom aide so that she could see what interested him in order to know what she could be doing with him at home. That sounded like a wonderful idea to the director. This child was afforded the opportunity on a daily basis to engage in every activity possible within the program. This often meant that the teachers all had to be quite ingenious and persistent. After a few weeks, it was quite apparent to teachers, his peers, and certainly to his mother that his receptive vocabulary was quite sophisticated. This child listened to everything and laughed, with his whole body, when something funny occurred. From this information, the teachers went on to see this child utilize computer technology to communicate his ideas. This child, when given the right tools, appeared to be a gifted child. He began using the computer by writing sentences with all words spelled perfectly. Nobody taught him how to do this. One of the first things he wrote about was how he felt when people looked at him like he was stupid because he could not talk. He said he understood why people thought that but he did not like it. He also wrote about how he felt when doctors talked about him in front of him, as though he was not even there. All the adults the child came in contact with certainly learned a lot from this one little boy. Without a doubt that he continues to teach all of his teachers and peers as he continues his education in regular classrooms with peers without disabilities. If the computer had not been made available to this child, it may not have been possible to learn how intelligent he was and how much he had already absorbed from the environment.

Program Accommodations

No matter what the developmental and/or skill level of the child, the integrated curriculum approach can provide the child with a fair and very exciting opportunity to learn and to demonstrate mastery of the learning that has taken place. The teacher who works within the format of an integrated curriculum, through the provision of a variety of activities and learning opportunities, has many chances to observe children mastering the targeted information and behaviors. This observation-based data informs the teacher about the appropriateness or inappropriateness of the curriculum being offered (Hills, 1992). If the curriculum appears to be of interest to only a few children, the teacher will see that very clearly. The curriculum topic may be appropriately offered later in the year or after another topic or two are first provided for the children. What the teacher may observe is that one or two children are having trouble with some of the activities offered within the integrated curriculum. The teacher may then see specific things that could be done to modify certain activities to make them accessible to those children who are having difficulty. Possibly, the curriculum objectives did not take into account the prerequisite skills necessary to ensure that all children would be successful. With this observational information as well as authentic assessment information gathered from activities in which the children engage within the framework of the integrated curriculum, the teacher is then in a position to decide whether to continue with modifications of the curriculum or activities, or whether to move on to another theme entirely to allow for the possibility of returning to this theme at a later point.

Curriculum Fits the Children

The most important point to remember is that an integrated curriculum approach allows the teacher to ensure that all children will be accommodated within the framework of the curriculum. No longer should there be a case of a teacher saying that a particular child does not fit in the class due to the fact that the child cannot do the assigned work. The integrated curriculum approach affords each child the opportunity to participate in the curriculum at an appropriate level. Different levels of ability, different styles of learning, different rates of learning are all part of this curriculum approach and are the bases for the actual process of curriculum development. Curriculum cannot be developed "once and for all" within this approach because the very differences among individual children and groups of children drive the curriculum. This is not always an easy lesson for some teachers to learn. Some teachers who previously found comfort in having a curriculum script to follow often seek to find another way to develop a script for integrated curriculum. Although one can develop a core for each thematic integrated curriculum unit, it will never be offered the same way to different groups of children because it is the very nature of the individual differences that children bring to each group that make curriculum exciting, dynamic, and ever-changing.

CHILD POPULATIONS AND CHILD AGE CONSIDERATIONS

One question about the integrated curriculum approach asks whether there is a type of child for whom this approach is not appropriate? All children who are able to benefit from being part of an inclusive classroom can benefit from and participate in integrated curriculum units. In the same classroom, children who are able bodied, of average intelligence, or gifted are learning alongside children with mild to severe physical disabilities, learning disabilities, health problems, mental retardation, autism, or language deficits. Because of the open-ended integrated curriculum unit, children are able to participate at different levels and get as much out of the experience as they are ready to take in at the time.

Integrated Curriculum: Flexible Not Static

Integrated curriculum is the most natural manner of learning. It is not a contrived learning environment in which an activity is predetermined by the structure of a static "package" handed down as the universal way in which to teach young children. Usually these "packages" have been developed by professionals who do not live within the community and do not know the needs of the children you are teaching. They may know textbook development very well. They cannot know about the children in your class. Only you can design the right "prescription" for learning in your room at that particular time.

Integrated Curriculum: Age Considerations

When one refers to the early childhood education period, one refers to children from birth to eight years of age. Although it would be highly unusual to find this wide an age span in one particular classroom, it is not unusual to find an age differential of two years (i.e., 3–5 year-olds, 5–7 year-olds, or 6–8 year-olds). With this in mind, the principle of practice is that the younger the children and the more diverse their backgrounds, the wider the variety of teaching methods and materials required (Bredekamp, 1987). Since in this integrated approach, the learning in all traditional content areas occurs primarily through hands-on learning centers and projects accomplished individually, in pairs, or in cooperative groupings, children have many different opportunities to learn. They may learn from the adults who work with them in the classroom, they may learn from the materials and activities provided for them, may learn from peers. In this way, all learners of all ages in the early childhood period may be accommodated.

BENEFITS OF THE INTEGRATED CURRICULUM APPROACH

Benefits to Children

There are many benefits to the implementation of developmentally appropriate, thematically based integrated curriculum. The children who have the opportunity to learn within the framework of an environment that supports the implementation of this approach are the greatest beneficiaries. These are children who do not need to be bored or frustrated by traditional, static curriculum. These are the children who are able to develop a love for learning that is life long, and stems from learning what and when they are interested in learning. These are children who will learn in environments that accept their interests and abilities and appreciate them rather than chastise them for not knowing the "right" answer or not being able to color inside the lines. These are children who will benefit from learning from others who have different skills, interests, and abilities. These children will develop positive self-esteem based on an orientation of success and acceptance. Another benefit to children in a developmentally appropriate classroom is that they can take over more of their own learning (Barclay & Breheny, 1994). They advocate accomplishing this through cooperative learning, parent involvement, using upper-grade children as buddies, and permitting children to perform independent or collaborative research and writing.

Benefits to Teachers

Teachers benefit from the integrated curriculum approach because it empowers them to create, develop, and implement curriculum that is meaningful to them as teachers and allows them to meet the interests and needs of the children in their classes. Teachers are encouraged to be creative and not to remain static. Teachers implement integrated curriculum network with other teachers who also implement integrated curriculum in their classrooms. Teachers benefit because they are more in control over what happens in their own classrooms due to the fact that they are setting their own goals and objectives and undertaking their own assessments based on what has taken place in their own classrooms. Teachers also benefit from their own professional development that takes place within the activities of researching, developing, and implementing new integrated curriculum units.

Much thought goes into the development of an integrated curriculum. Much of the thought begins with a web that allows teachers to explore the possibilities of a topic relative to materials and ideas to determine if they are worth doing. The process of brainstorming usually generates ideas for developmentally appropriate activities. At that time, thought should be given to the way in which the ideas can be implemented to meet the needs of all children in the class, children with and without disabilities. This process of brainstorming develops into an initial plan with the true test of appropriateness being when the children have a chance to explore (Jones & Nimmo, 1994).

Benefits to Parents

Most parents are not in the classroom on a regular or consistent basis, yet parents do benefit from the integrated curriculum approach because it allows them to be closer to what their children are learning. Children come home with more information about what they did in school because the learning was active and involved their entire beings. Researchers and early childhood authorities (Morrison, 1988; Read, Gardner & Mahler, 1987) have found that parents are interested not only in what happens to their children while at school, but also want to know what they can do to help their children both at home and school. Integrated curriculum allows parents to engage in home activities that bridge the relationship between home and school. It empowers parents in the role of home teacher because it suggests related activities, field trips, and books to read. It allows parents to share their own expertise in the content of each unit of integrated curriculum. Parents benefit from involvement with the education their children receive. In turn, children benefit from their parents' involvement in their school programs. Children feel more positive about activities and experiences that are validated by the attention their parents pay to these activities and experiences (Berger, 1987).

CLASSROOM DISCIPLINE AND MANAGEMENT

One of the most difficult areas of expertise to develop is within the area of classroom discipline and management. Much has been written on the topics of classroom **discipline** and management, yet many teachers continue to have problems with both. The goal of discipline is to help children learn socially acceptable behavior and to learn to develop internal controls related to these socially acceptable behaviors.

Defining Discipline

One problem within the area of discipline is with terminology. Many people use the terms discipline, guidance, or punishment as though they meant the same thing (Deiner, 1993). The manner in which an individual uses a term will affect children differently. Gartrell (1987) defines discipline as behavior which is designed to encourage self-control. Discipline is a form of teaching. If one accepts this definition, then it is assumed that a child misbehaves out of lack of knowledge and that discipline should supply the knowledge a child needs to behave appropriately.

Punishment and guidance can be considered two forms of discipline. Punishment involves the presentation of a negative consequence for a behavior deemed to be inappropriate (Gartrell, 1987). Punishment may cause the inappropriate behavior to diminish or disappear but it may also cause positive behaviors to disappear. The child may associate the environment and the adults in the environment with the punishment. This does not achieve the desired outcome. There is another element to consider in the implementation of punishment. Some adults become too reliant on punishment as a discipline technique. The control and power experienced through the use of punishment may become gratifying to the person delivering the punishment. This is not a healthy situation for adults or children.

Guidance (or positive discipline techniques) encourage the development of good self-concepts, prosocial behavior and an ability to engage in self-control (Gartrell, 1987). Guidance is an ongoing process that creates a positive climate in the classroom thus avoiding the isolated incidents of punishment. In this atmosphere of positive guidance, children learn and are rewarded for appropriate behavior as well as learning that there are consequences for inappropriate behavior. In this environment, children learn to act responsibly and control their own behavior.

Role of the Teacher

The most well developed, most creative curriculum plans in the world will not be implemented to their maximum potential if a teacher is not skilled in management and discipline. Skills in these areas are critical to the success of integrated curriculum implementation. When a classroom environment is calm and orderly and a teacher is aware of where children are at all times, both in a physical sense as well as a conceptual sense, children can be freer to choose activities and enjoy mobility in the classroom. An example of a well-organized, well-managed classroom environment can be found in the following story.

CASE STUDY

A visitor came to a mixed-age group preschool class several years ago. This visitor arrived during the free choice of planned activities and sat down to observe. After observing for a while, she asked the head teacher what was wrong with the children in the class. The question seemed quite surprising. Included the class at that time were two children with special needs. The teacher explained the situation to the visitor. The visitor informed the teacher that she was not referring to the children with special needs, but to the entire class. She was concerned because the room was so quiet and there were no children running around. It was explained that the children were all engaged in meaningful activity within a carefully planned environment. The visitor replied that was exactly what she did in her classroom but her room was always so noisy and chaotic! After the head teacher paid a reciprocal visit to the classroom of the visitor, the difference between the two environments became very clear. In the classroom of the visitor, all materials she owned were out on the shelves all of the time. There was no thematic planning, there was no facilitation of play. There was, however, serious traffic control, a very high level of noise and a lot of "putting out fires." In other words, it was a daily free-for-all! This is a very good example of a classroom that has no management or discipline plan. In this environment, children had to "be disciplined" on a regular basis because there were no guidelines for behavior and no appropriate models for behavior. Children engaged in behavior and teachers reacted to those behaviors. This is not an ideal learning situation for children. This is also not an ideal working environment for teachers.

Facilitating Self-Discipline

Some teachers are uncomfortable with the notion of external controls in a classroom. What they would rather see is children exercising self-discipline. **Self-discipline** in children has to do with developing self-reliance, an inner structure, self-monitoring skills, and a self-awareness. All of these are behaviors that will stay with a child throughout a lifetime.

Discipline imposed from an adult is something that often does not stay with a child when the adult is not in the environment. Think back to your early school years. When the teacher stepped out of the room for a moment (if she dared to do so or was allowed to do so), were there several children who acted out in some way? If the answer is yes, then the classroom teacher in that classroom had a false sense of discipline. The atmosphere of discipline prevailed only when the teacher was present. This means that some of the children never internalized a sense of discipline from the authoritarian discipline atmosphere imposed in the classroom. The children in that classroom who were "good" in the absence of the teacher were children who were self-disciplined. This is what we should strive for in every classroom. However, we should probably not strive to achieve this atmosphere of discipline with the same methods used by authoritarian teachers.

What we need to do is engage children in learning; maintain the excitement and sense of accomplishment that accompanies this excitement and not worry about the fact that this exhilarating environment produces a higher level of "healthy" noise and a greater level of "healthy" movement within the classroom. Hendrick (1992) suggests ten practical ways to stop discipline situations before they start. These could be renamed ten ways to promote self-discipline in young children. The list is as follows:

1. Reward behavior you want to see continued; don't reward behavior you wish to discourage
2. Be persistent
3. Consistently position yourself so that you are able to see a large area of the room or play yard at the same time
4. When trouble repeats itself, analyze the situation and try changing it rather than nagging the child
5. Emphasize the positive rather than the negative; always tell the child the correct thing to do
6. Warn ahead of time to make transitions easier
7. Arrange the environment to promote positive interactions
8. Have as few rules as possible, but make the ones you do have stick
9. When supervising children, plan ahead
10. Keep the day interesting

Attending to the Emotional Climate of the Classroom

A healthy **emotional climate** in the classroom is one that promotes pro-social behavior and an excitement for learning. You will notice that the term "good behavior" is not used here; pro-social behavior is used. This is specifically because "good" is not as easy to define as it may seem. To a teacher who has personal self-esteem problems and needs children to be so "good" as to be submissive at all times, "good" means that a child does nothing without asking permission, never leaves his or her seat, follows every rule (and there are probably many of them), never speaks above a whisper, and certainly does not ask many questions. The emotional climate of the room is subdued to a point that is unhealthy and may even be perceived to be a very depressed atmosphere. A teacher clearly influences what happens in the classroom but a teacher is also influenced by what happens in the classroom. This is what is meant by the emotional climate in the classroom.

Poor self-esteem taints the perceptions of others and how they feel about teachers. Children respect teachers who respect themselves and the children in their classrooms. Teachers who respect children dignify them by understanding the natural development of children. Children deserve to learn in an environment that is supportive of their development and appreciative of their uniqueness and individuality. Teachers who employ positive guidance approaches facilitate children's development. Positive approaches are nurturing and educational in nature. Children are not told to behave, they are invited to engage in another activity, or their behavior is redirected. This other behavior is explained to them or demonstrated to them.

When implementing positive approaches, teachers use a variety of techniques to enable children to engage in more positive behavior. Teachers use a variety of techniques because they recognize that the uniqueness of children requires individualized management approaches as well as instructional approaches. These teachers also recognize that inappropriate behavior interferes with child social development. Children acquire reputations quite easily. A child who is frightened by another child due to the misbehavior of that other child will find it difficult to quickly forget that behavior. A teacher who is sensitive to the developmental nature of classroom management will know that there is a different way to handle each incident that occurs in the classroom. Teachers in a team teaching situation support one another in managing the behavior of the children in the classroom. Children do not benefit from exercising control over one or two teachers while complying with the requests and instructions of other teachers. It is not always initially obvious to any team of teachers that particular children only listen to one or two teachers in the classroom. Some children are offensive in their non-compliance, causing the teachers who have been offended by them to tend to stand clear of those particular children or give them instructions in a tentative way, then leave the area and pray that the child will comply. When the child does not comply, these teachers may make an obvious decision to ignore the non-compliance because they know the behavior the child is capable of and they do not want to deal with it. By avoiding the screams or physical behaviors the child might exhibit when confronted about inappropriate behavior, the teachers are actually giving license to the behavior. It is very true that some behaviors are best ignored. These are behaviors that do not interfere with the rhythm of the day and pose no threat of harm to other children or adults. However, when a behavior is of the nature that may be harmful to others or is disrupting the entire class, then the behavior must be confronted and an age-appropriate behavior intervention must be implemented.

Matching the Approach to the Child

There are many fine examples of age-appropriate interventions to be found in the literature (Essa, 1990). The important variable to keep in mind is that what constitutes an appropriate intervention for one child may not be an appropriate intervention for another child. One cannot read one journal article or one text on behavior management and declare oneself an expert behavior manager. It is always best to consult with colleagues or a behavior consultant when developing a behavior management plan for an individual child or for an entire class.

One of the problems in the implementation of behavior management plans is that frequentl, the plan is developed without thinking about the consequences of implementation. Often, developed behavior management plans are so complex and have many components with so many procedures to follow that the adults in the room have difficulty remembering all of the components. Can you imagine how confused the children would be? When children cannot easily understand what is expected of them, the confusion invites misbehavior. When children are dealt with inconsistently, when one teacher implements one procedure and another teacher does something entirely different, children often wind up pitting one teacher against the other. Some children are quite expert at this since they have much practice successfully engaging in this behavior at home. When a classroom is run on the basis of known rather than unknown expectations, the emotional climate of the room will be conducive to the promotion of prosocial behavior. When this is the climate, the teacher is then able to focus his or her energies towards the development and implementation of stimulating units of integrated curriculum while conducting ongoing assessments of children.

The Importance of Ongoing Assessment

Ongoing assessment is a critical component of a well managed classroom. When teachers consistently engage in the collection of a variety of kinds of information on the children in the classroom, they will always be able to see potential problems before they become problems. Anticipating problems before they flare up helps to maintain a well-managed classroom. Ongoing assessment will also inform teachers about the developmental level of the children in the class and will allow the teachers to plan curriculum accordingly (Hills, 1992). Assessment and planning are partners in the process of curriculum development. One cannot know what to introduce next if one does not know how the material already presented has been received. Planning and assessment are key components to a well-managed classroom.

Respect Promotes a Healthy Emotional Climate

The goal of a well disciplined early childhood classroom should be to see a classroom full of young children who listen to each other because they are interested in each other, and who admire and value each other and what each one is able to accomplish. These classrooms are filled with young children who respect each other and treat each other with dignity. Classrooms should be filled with young children who recognize differences in each other but approach these differences with a sense of appreciation rather than prejudice. Respect fills classrooms with young children who are developing with a sense of purpose and direction and who need less and less external management as the year goes on.

A well-managed classroom contributes to all of these characteristics. Teachers can establish this kind of classroom using well-developed, positive guidance strategies and by modeling all the behaviors children will learn. Teachers need to listen to children and genuinely care for the children they teach. They need to listen to and care for the people they work with. They need to show children that one can recognize differences without acting negatively toward those differences. They need to model **respect** toward their co-workers, colleagues and the children's parents. Children who are enveloped and embraced by genuinely courteous, polite behavior have a greater likelihood of developing these behaviors naturally and cherishing these values, unlike children who grow up within a climate of rude, crude, and impolite behavior. Since the world has become ruder and more impolite in recent years, it is up to us as early childhood educators to set the tone for a different pattern of behavior, a different way of living. Children deserve to be educated in well managed, disciplined environments. They deserve to have order in their young lives.

SUMMARY

Thematic curriculum focuses on one topic or theme at a time and is a vehicle for managing curriculum while achieving developmental appropriateness. Each theme developed allows the activities and concepts planned to integrate all learning opportunities for the children. Children at differing stages of development bring different experiences to activities provided for them. A developmentally appropriate curriculum is a result of interaction between teachers and children contributing ideas and reacting to them to build on meaningful themes.

Many themes are more appropriate for children at different ages and stages than others. One way to know which themes are appropriate is to make observations of the children at play. If a theme is inappropriate, the lack of interest of the children will serve as a strong indicator. When children make their own choices rather than when the choices are made for them, it becomes easier to learn of their interests.

Children learn best through learning that is related and learning that is discovery oriented because it allows them to make connections relative to their learning. The thematic approach promotes the excitement of hands-on learning combined with the reality of skill acquisition.

Integrated curriculum is thematic by nature because the theme chosen as the focus of study integrates the learning opportunities in the classroom. Integrated curriculum allows the teacher to relate the major content areas of language arts, math, science, social studies, and the arts to the theme being studied. This affords the child who is weak in one content area to have successful experiences with the content of the theme within the other content areas.

Within an integrated curriculum, regardless of the developmental or skill level, the child can be presented with a fair and very exciting opportunity to learn and demonstrate mastery of the learning that has taken place. The approach allows the teacher to fit the curriculum to the child at the appropriate level. All children can benefit from and participate in integrated curriculum units in an inclusive classroom where able-bodied, of average intelligence, or gifted children learn alongside children with mild to severe physical disabilities, learning disabilities, health problems, mental retardation, autism, or language deficits.

In the integrated approach, learning in the content areas occurs primarily through hands-on learning and projects accomplished individually, in pairs, or in cooperative groupings. Children learn from adults, materials and activities, and from peers. Children, teachers, and parents are the many who benefit from developmentally appropriate, thematically based integrated curriculum.

The goal of class discipline is to help children learn socially acceptable behavior and to learn to develop internal controls related to these socially acceptable behaviors. Discipline is behavior designed to encourage self-control. Guidance (or positive discipline techniques) encourages the development of good self-concepts, prosocial behavior, and an ability to engage in self-control. The role of the teacher is to create an environment conducive to the development of self-discipline. What constitutes an appropriate intervention for one child may not be an appropriate intervention for another child. Anticipating problems before they become problems through the use of ongoing assessment will also inform teachers about the developmental level of the children in the class and will allow the teachers to plan curriculum accordingly.

Classrooms filled with young children who respect each other, treat each other with dignity, who recognize differences in each other, but approach these differences with a sense of appreciation rather than prejudice is an important goal of an integrated curriculum. Teachers can establish this kind of classroom through well-developed, positive guidance strategies and through modeling all the behaviors a teacher wants to see in children.

DISCUSSION QUESTIONS

1) A grandparent brings a grandchild to school and with the child holding on to her hand, informs you that the only way the grandchild in her care is going to behave for you is if you hit the child. The grandparent gives you permission to do it. What can you say to this person and to the child to set a different tone?
2) You are required to visit a classroom to make an observation. You call the number of a teacher that someone in your neighborhood has given you. Since you do not know anything about the school the teacher works in, you ask for some information about the class. The teacher tells you that it is a kindergarten class that has 24 children who are all on different levels. Three of the children have language problems and two of them are children with mild physical disabilities. The teacher also informs you that in this classroom, all children are treated the same way. There is no special treatment. Everyone is expected to accomplish the same work in the same manner, and behave according to the rules of the classroom. You decide to reflect on the information given to you over the phone before you make an appointment to visit. What are your thoughts about what you heard? Will you schedule a visit?
3) The parents of a child in the first grade are concerned because the child does not have any workbooks or worksheets to do. The parents asks you what you think about this since they know that you are studying early childhood education. What will you tell them? What will you tell them to look for instead of looking for workbooks and worksheets?
4) Think back to your early years in school. What are your memories of classroom activities? Why do you remember them? Who are the people you most remember? Why do you remember them?
5) You have been given an assignment that requires you to brainstorm ideas for two themes appropriate for young children with another person in your class. You set a date to get together and the other person in-

dicates that she thinks it would be easier to choose at least one holiday, such as Thanksgiving, as a theme. You are not comfortable with the idea. Discuss what you would say to your classmate when you get together. What other themes could you suggest as alternatives and why?

6) Discuss the ways in which you could find out what interested the children in your class. Once you had that information, what would it allow you to do?

REFERENCES

Abraham, M., Morris, L., & Wald, P. (1993). *Inclusive early childhood education—A model classroom*. Phoenix, AZ: Communication Skill Builders.

Berger, E. (1987). *Parents as partners in education: The school and home working together*. Columbus, OH: Merrill Publishing Company.

Bredekamp, S. (1987). *Developmentally appropriate practice in early childhood programs serving children from birth through age 8*. Washington, DC: National Association for the Education of Young Children.

Bredekamp, S., & Rosegrant, T. (1992). Reaching potentials through appropriate curriculum: Conceptual frameworks for applying the guidelines. In S. Bredekamp & T. Rosegrant (Eds.), *Reaching potentials: Appropriate curriculum and assessment for young children, Volume 1*. Washington, DC: National Association for the Education of Young Children.

Cassidy, D., & Lancaster, C. (1993). The grassroots curriculum: A dialogue between children and teachers. *Young Children, 48*(6), 47–51.

Deiner, P. (1993). *Resources for teaching children with diverse abilities—birth through eight*. Fort Worth, TX: Harcourt Brace Jovanovich College Publishers.

Dewey, J. (1938). *Experience and education*. New York: Macmillan.

Dodge, D. (1989). *The creative curriculum for early childhood*. Washington, DC: Teaching Strategies, Inc.

Eliason, C. & Jenkins, L. (1994). *A practical guide to early childhood curriculum*. New York: Merrill.

Essa, E. (1990). *Practical guide to solving preschool behavior problems* (2nd ed.). Albany, NY: Delmar Publishers Inc.

Gartrell, D. (1987). Punishment or guidance? *Young Children, 42*(3), 55–61.

Hendrick, J. (1992). *The whole child*. New York: Merrill.

Hendrick, J. (1994). *Total learning—Developmental curriculum for the young child* (5th ed.). New York: Merrill.

Hills, T. (1992). Reaching potentials through appropriate assessment. In S. Bredekamp & T. Rosegrant (Eds.), *Reaching potentials: Appropriate curriculum and assessment for young children, Volume 1*. Washington, DC: National Association for the Education of Young Children.

Jones, E., & Nimmo, J. (1994). *Emergent curriculum*. Washington, DC: National Association for the Education of Young Children.

Krogh, S. (1990). *The integrated early childhood curriculum*. New York: McGraw-Hill Publishing Company.

Morrison, G. (1988). *Education and development of infants, toddlers and preschoolers*. Boston: Scott, Foresman & Co.

Peters, J., Bunse, C., Carlson, L., Doede, L., Glasenapp, G., Haydon., Lehman, C., Templeman, T., & Udell, T. (1992). *Supporting children with disabilities in early childhood programs*. Monmouth, OR: Teaching Research Publications.

Read, Gardner, & Mahler, (1987). *Early childhood programs: Human relationships and learning*. New York: Holt, Rinehart & Winston.

Seefeldt, C. (1989). *Social studies for the preschool-primary child*. Columbus, OH: Merrill.

Watkins, K. & Durant, L., Jr. (1992). *Complete early childhood behavior management guide*. West Nyack, NY: The Center for Applied Research in Education.

Wortham, S. (1994). *Early childhood curriculum—Developmental bases for learning and teaching*. New York: Merrill.

ADDITIONAL READINGS:

Berry, C. & Mindes, G. (1993). *Planning a theme-based curriculum: Goals, themes, activities, and planning guides for 4's and 5's*. Glenview, IL: GoodYear Books.

Canter, L. (1976). *Assertive discipline: A take-charge approach for today's educator*. Seal Beach, CA: Canter & Associates.

Charles, C. (1989). *Building classroom discipline: From models to practice* (3rd ed.). New York: Longman.

Cuffaro, H. (1994). *Experimenting with the world: John Dewey and the early childhood classroom*. New York: Teachers College Press.

Day, B. (1994). *Early childhood education—Developmental/experiential teaching and learning* (Fourth edition). New York: Merrill.

Dolinar, K., Boser, C., & Holm, E. (1994). *Learning through play: Curriculum and activities for the inclusive classroom*. New York: Delmar Publishers Inc.

Eliason, C., & Jenkins, L. (1994). *A practical guide to early childhood curriculum*. New York: Merrill.

Greenberg, P. (1989). Learning self-esteem and self-discipline through play. *Young Children, 44*(2), 28–31.

Kostelnik, M. J., Soderman, A. K., & Whiren, A. P. (1993). *Developmentally appropriate programs in early childhood education*. New York: Merrill.

Kostelnik, M., Ed. (1991). *Teaching young children using themes*. Glenview, IL: GoodYear Books.

Kostelnik, M., Stein, L., & Whiren, A. (1988). Children's self-esteem: The verbal environment. *Childhood Education, 65*(1), 29–32.

Krogh, S. (1990). *The integrated early childhood curriculum.* New York: McGraw-Hill Publishing Company.

Marion, M. (1991). *Guidance of young children* (3rd ed.). Columbus, OH: Merrill.

Miller, D. (1990). *Positive child guidance.* Albany, NY: Delmar Publishers Inc.

Shipley, D. (1993). *Empowering children: Play-based curriculum for lifelong learning.* Scarborough, Ontario: Nelson Canada.

Trostle, S. L., & Yawkey, T. D. (1990). *Integrated learning activities for young children.* Boston: Allyn & Bacon.

Van Hoorn, J., Nourot, P. M., Scales, B., & Alward, K. R. (1993). *Play at the center of the curriculum.* New York: Merrill.

CHAPTER 3

Developing the Integrated Curriculum

KEY TERMS

space
furniture
equipment
materials
schedule
facilitator
communication

There are many factors to consider when developing an integrated curriculum. One is to know that the children who will be the consumers of this curriculum need to be the primary consideration. There are certain concrete factors that go into the thinking involved in developing an integrated curriculum. One needs to look at the space in which one teaches, the equipment available, the equipment to be designated as first priority to obtain, the materials and books available, and the materials and books to be designated as first priority to obtain. Another important factor to consider is the schedule or routine outlined as a guide to follow. Finally, it is important to consider how all the activities planned for the classroom will actually be facilitated. In other words, how is it all going to happen?

SPACE

Teachers are usually not fortunate enough to be able to design our own classrooms in terms of the overall physical structure. If given the opportunity to do so, it would be an overwhelming task and one that should usually be approached with caution. Although in your dream classroom you may think you know exactly what you want, in reality, once a decision is made that one might have to live with, one is almost afraid to make that final commitment. Although complaints are raised about existing space and the constraints it imposes, teachers can play around with the rearrangement of the space as much as humanly possible without the guilt of knowing that a **space** was designed that is less than perfect!

Space Supports Development

The early childhood environment should support the development of children (Essa, 1992). An age-appropriate environment takes into consideration adequate space per child, accessibility of materials and equipment, and the provision of personal space dedicated to the personal belongings of each child in the class. Activity space clearly identified for specific activities enhances the activities in the classroom and promotes child involvement.

Space Supports Integrated Curriculum and Inclusion

A room that does not have any built-ins that cannot be moved is the kind of space that works best within an integrated curriculum format for a program that includes children with disabilities. The ideal space is flexible and fluid. It allows for configuration and reconfiguration of interest centers, quiet corners, space for medium-size groups, and whole group activities. It also allows for widening pathways between activity areas so that children with physical disabilities who may or may not require the use of adaptive equipment can have easier access to the areas. The ideal space has access to water, toilet facilities, as well as access to outdoors. The space should have a carpeted area as well as an area that is tiled. The carpeted area must be securely fastened to the floor to prevent all children from tripping. Tile floors should be clean but not highly waxed to prevent children unsteady on their feet from slipping and falling.

FIG 3.1 Floor space is often ideal for supporting inclusion.

Space Impacts on Behavior

The physical environment has impact on the behavior of a child (Thomson & Ashton-Lilo, 1983). Children with disabilities are sometimes inhibited by space that is overcrowded with people or furniture. Some children with visual disabilities have difficulty crossing what they perceive to be barriers. These children with visual deficits may need assistance passing through an open doorway the first few times. Some blind children will not cross a threshold that is perceived or existing. This may translate into the child staying in one part of a room. It would be up to the teacher in the environment to encourage exploration of space for that child. Inclusion of this child in the classroom would be enhanced by the child moving more freely from one area of the room to another.

If a room has two levels, a ramp may need to be installed to accommodate the child with physical disabilities. If the room has a loft area, that area may be totally inaccessible to the child with physical disabilities. Whatever is planned for the loft area needs to be made accessible to children in another area of the room.

Crosser (1992) points out the need for considering the importance of the effect of space on behavior prior to the start of the school year. The space should not be so cluttered that children and adults do not have any breathing or thinking space, but the space should not have any consistently wide open spaces. Cluttered space stifles some children and adults. Uncluttered space enhances concentration and stimulates a sense of order, which might be missing in the lives of some of the children. Wide open spaces may be exciting and inviting to some children, but this excitement may work to the detriment of the emotional climate in the classroom. A wide open space might invite a spontaneous game of football. Some children might avoid a large open area while others might just pile on top of each other in the center of it.

Space for Storage

No matter how much storage space one has in any classroom, there is never enough. Storage space should receive serious consideration because a lack of storage space may encourage very cluttered areas that become uninviting to children. Lack of storage space also may deter a teacher from creating additional theme boxes or from acquiring additional materials and books. Safety issues need to be a factor when thinking about storage.

CASE STUDY

In a traditionally arranged second grade classroom with twenty four children sitting at individual desks, the teacher had developed many activities and activity areas for the children to use. Each scrap of construction paper that was left over after the children completed a project was stored in a series of cardboard storage boxes kept under a table in the back of the room. The boxes were overstuffed and stacked on top of each other. The teacher wanted the children to use that paper when they needed less than a whole sheet of paper for a project. However, the children were so overwhelmed by the quantity and disorganization of the paper, they did not use it and instead used the whole sheets of paper for their needs. In the stored paper area, there was too much paper out at once and the overstuffed boxes were too heavy for the children to move. This prevented the children from using these resources. They used the resources that were more inviting and more safely stored. In that environment, a child with special needs would probably have considerable difficulty accessing the paper resources or other resources because the room was so crowded and overwhelming. Storage and usage need to be considered simultaneously to maximize the use of available resources and to make them accessible. Children like the security of organization—similar things belong together in an accessible manner (Crosser, 1992).

Space to Meet the Needs of Activity

The space as it exists in a classroom needs to be looked at very carefully to determine whether particular areas of the room are more conducive to certain kinds of activities. For example, setting up the art area closest to the sink area and on the tiled floor makes a lot of sense in terms of setting up and maintaining activities without considerable teacher intervention. If the sink is accessible to the children, they will hopefully be able to use it independently or with minimal adult assistance. In a multi-age classroom the younger children might be able to use the sink with some peer assistance. If a child with physical disabilities is unable to reach the faucets, a pan with water or a wet cloth can be made available to the child in order for the child to be able to engage in self-help activity. A block area with little space for building might also inhibit a child with adaptive equipment from frequenting the area because of the closeness of the space.

The space in the classroom must allow for and promote a flow of activity. Interest areas set up in railroad car fashion (see Figure 3.2) so that each activity must be walked through to get to the next activity probably

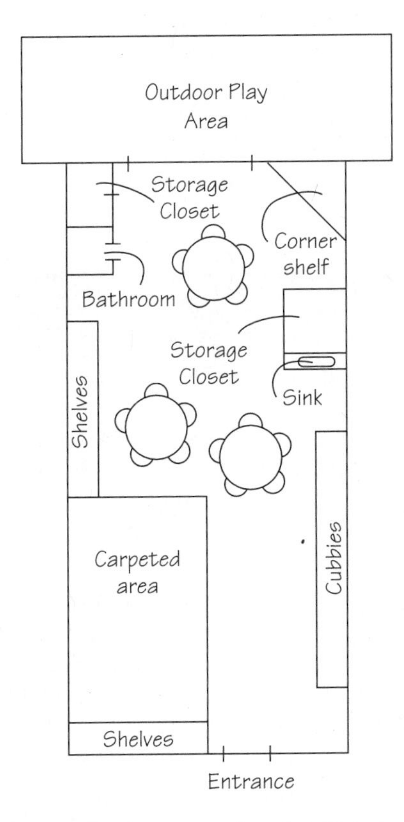

FIG 3.2 An example of railroad car room design.

inhibits the flow of activity. This kind of set-up would create a very distracting atmosphere for the children and adults as well. This kind of arrangement could also promote behavior problems because children would be getting in each other's way. All children might have difficulty surveying the activities available because the line of vision may be obstructed by the first few activities set up in the classroom. Many children might develop the positive technique of moving from area to area before selecting an area in which to begin the day. For children with disabilities, who are either not able to easily move from one area to another, whose vision precludes being able to see from one end of the room to another, or whose attention span encourages flitting behavior rather than positive exploration, this type of room arrangement might inhibit rather than support learning and appropriate behavior.

The space in the classroom should take into account the need children have for working on long-term projects. An area of the room that could be designated for ongoing project work that could be remain in that location over time, would make for an ideal situation. Children could add to their individual or cooperative projects thus enriching the experience gained from the implementation of the project approach. In addition, the children would be able to use the projects developed by their peers to enhance their own learning. If space allowed, the children could connect their projects to create a total environment or an in-depth study of a larger topic.

CASE STUDY

In a kindergarten classroom of modest size, the teacher was interested in having the children work on extended projects about the greater geographic area in which the school was located. In order to accomplish this, she removed most of the tables and chairs from her room for a period of several weeks. The children began to create structures representing urban, suburban, and rural areas. They each worked on their own structures to begin with, and then they began to work with each other. When the structures were almost completed, the children decided that they needed to put down roads to connect the parts of their community. After they made the roads, they determined that they needed vehicles, traffic lights, public buildings, and parks. The children learned through their own creations as well as through the creations of their peers. When the unit of study came to a natural conclusion, the children looked forward to the next big project they could work on. They did not miss all those tables and chairs.

The layout of the inclusive classroom in which integrated curriculum takes place should also receive careful attention. Materials and equipment must be presented on safe, durable shelves that allow children to safely access the materials by themselves. This independent access allows for children to determine choices of materials and activities without the teacher having to worry about the safety of the child's independence.

The layout of the classroom should also include interest or activity centers with discernible boundaries. This enhances classroom management because when there is a clear delineation between activity areas, teachers do not need to spend time repeating rules to children about what materials belong where or that what they choose to work with must be used at the table across the room. The layout of the classroom should also take into consideration the alternating of quiet and noisy activities. Activities that require considerable concentration should not be placed next to a woodworking activity or a very active dramatic play area. A book corner is better placed away from a lively large or small block area.

Children will use activity areas that are in spaces having clear paths leading to them. When an area does not appear to be receiving much attention from the children, the flow of activity should be analyzed to try to determine how the room may be rearranged. The following chart (see Figure 3.3) is an example of an analysis of activity flow resulting in moving the book area to another area of the room.

The layout of the classroom should also make sure that there are some places that provide for the privacy of children. The following is an example of the need for private spaces within the classroom.

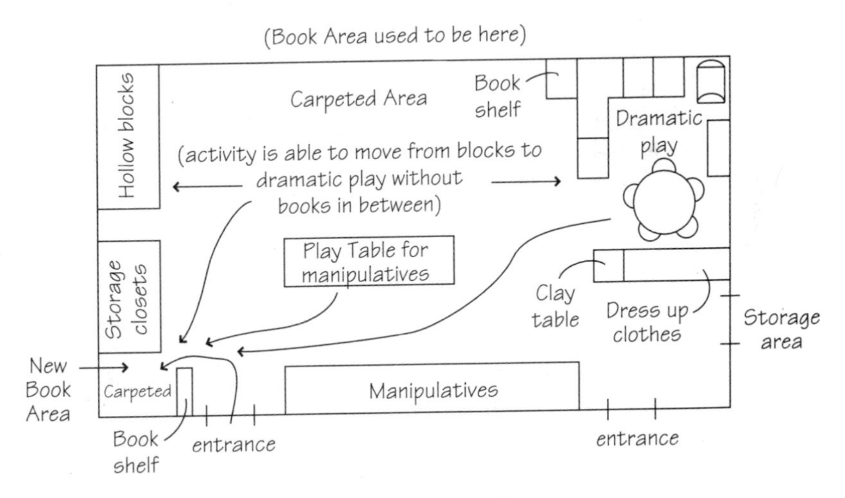

FIG 3.3 Analysis of activity flow created by rearranging areas of the room.

CASE STUDY

In a mixed-age group classroom, two children identified the need to have a quiet hide-away each day. These two children, one boy and one girl, used their quiet places to engage in some very serious discussions about their feelings and experiences. They were very supportive of each other. From being able to listen unobtrusively to their conversations, it was clear to the teacher that this young boy of four years of age had found a soul mate in this four-year-old girl. When they did not find a "ready made" space in the classroom, they would create their own space by sitting together under a table. This observation reinforced the importance for children to create or allow the creation of those occasional quiet spaces, both indoors and outdoors.

Finding Additional Space

Teachers tend to think of their allocated space as the floor, wall, and sometimes ceiling space within the boundaries of the four walls in their classrooms. They may often think longingly about space in the school that is not used on a regular basis and think about how wonderful it would be to be able to use those spaces for activities or for storage of the wonderful materials that might not be needed on a daily basis. Collective thinking and planning between teachers may yield a plan for how to gain access to those spaces and use them to the advantage of children in the early childhood classes. In addition, collaborating together with other teachers may yield a wonderful plan for sharing space and equipment with each other. When the class next door is out of the room for 20 minutes or more, a small group from your class might be able to use that next door space for a special activity or for some quiet times just reading books. This, of course, all depends on adequate staffing and the relationships that exist between teachers. Think of the message conveyed to children when teachers support each other and their programs in this way. Think of the message to the administration from the implementation of this practice. All too often, teachers are discouraged from working collaboratively instead of being encouraged to work collaboratively. Collaboration often reduces the resources necessary to create exemplary programs and builds a very effective sense of camaraderie and collegiality. Teachers benefit from the cooperation and collaboration and, of course, the children benefit as well from the extras that are often the result of collaborative efforts.

Designs for Appropriate Space

There is considerable variation found among the physical spaces used for early childhood programs. Some programs are housed in public school

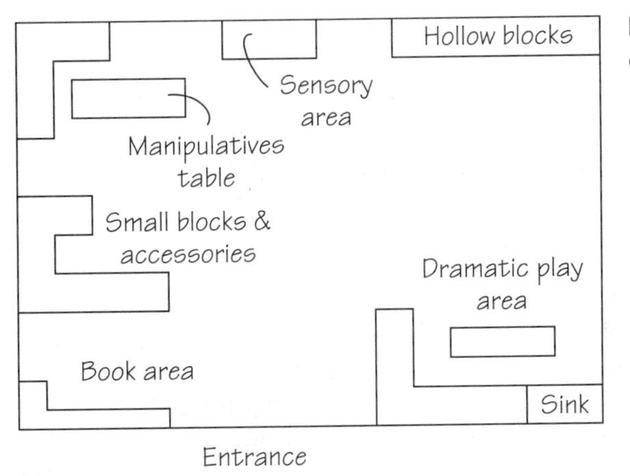

FIG 3.4 Preschool classroom design.

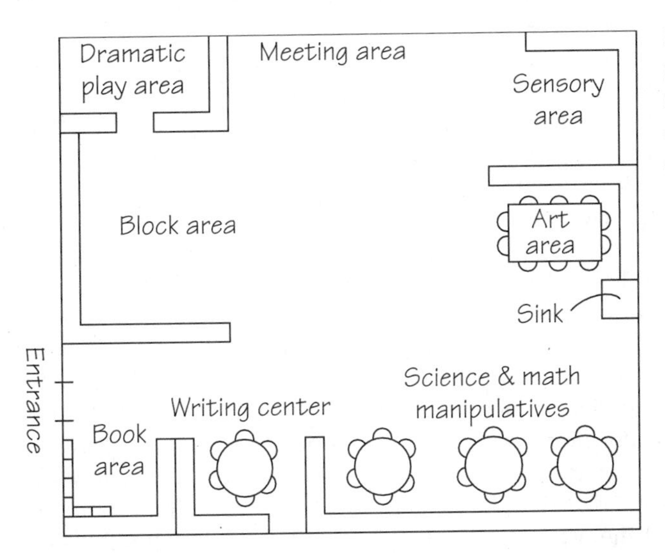

FIG 3.5 Kindergarten, first, and second grade classroom design.

buildings, some in portable buildings, some in church buildings. Early childhood programs in the community can be found in store fronts, converted barns, museum buildings, old carriage houses, and former railroad stations. As a result, it would be difficult to design one perfect space but it is possible to look at some possibilities for developmentally appropriate spaces for young children. The factors one would take into consideration beyond issues of size and shape of the space would include: location of doors and windows, the lead levels of wall and ceiling coverings indoors, and the soil and any painted surfaces outdoors, asbestos, accessibility, and whether the space is used by other groups of children or adults. What follows (see Figures 3.4 and 3.5) are some flexible sample room designs that could be modified as needed.

FURNITURE AND EQUIPMENT

Sometimes, teachers are reluctant to begin to plan for and implement curriculum in a format other than what they had been doing for many years. Some of these feelings of reluctance may be due to lack of information as to what the expectations of this different approach may actually entail; some may be due to lack of self-esteem. Still others may be hesitant to change because they think that they do not have all the "right" **furniture** or **equipment** to implement this different approach correctly.

Implementation of the thematic integrated curriculum approach does not require special furniture or equipment. Some early childhood curriculum approaches do require specific equipment within their programs (i.e., Montessori), but in order to implement integrated curriculum, you need space, children, ideas, creativity, materials, resources, and resourcefulness. There are teachers who would rather have as little equipment and furniture in their rooms as possible because they like to have children work on the floor or on rugs rather than on tables which may be too confining for them. One does not have to have an audio-visual cart to be able to use records, tapes, and filmstrips with children. It may be nice to have one in order to more easily organize and move these materials but it is certainly not necessary. Teachers sometimes say that they would certainly include water or other sensory play into their classrooms if only they had the right table for it. While the right table does make it easier to put things out for children, deep dishpans and other containers make for very adequate and portable sensory containers. A few years ago two teachers were receiving consultation concerning their implementation of a more "hands-on" integrated approach. The consultant was delighted to find a lovely brand new water table in each of their rooms. When the consultant remarked about how fortunate they were to have sensory tables in their rooms and questioned as to how these tables were used in their rooms, one teacher looked at the other and said, "Oh, that's what this thing is supposed to be used for!" When asked what they had been using them for, one of the teachers removed the table top in her room and shared that it had been used for storing new boxes of crayons and paper. So you can see that inheriting all the right equipment and materials does not make a developmentally appropriate, thematic integrated curriculum. One needs to understand the reason behind the need for certain equipment in order to use it successfully and to the advantage of the children in the class.

Some of the problems encountered concerning equipment and furniture stem from a tendency of some teachers who work with young children to be more concerned about the cleanliness and "perfect shape" the items are in rather than how much use the equipment gets and how much these items are adding to their programs and to the development of the children in the room. Remember that equipment and furniture will last many years with proper care, even if the children use them with vigor.

In an inclusive classroom, there are certain pieces of furniture and equipment that are necessary in order to accommodate the special positioning and support requirements of children with physical disabilities. The children who require the use of these floor sitters (see Figure 3.6), special chairs (see Figure 3.7), standers (see Figure 3.8), or other adaptive equipment (see Figure 3.9) will either arrive with the child or soon after the child arrives, the appropriate pieces will be procured by the school system. If the child is of preschool age, the school system or another agency that provides support funds and activities for the child will procure what the child needs. The therapist associated with the child will

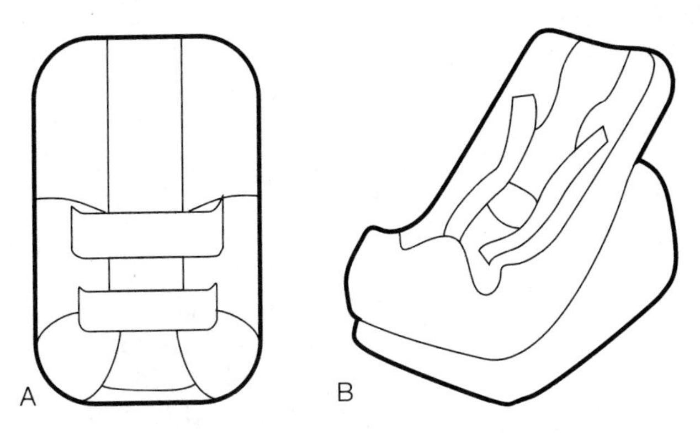

FIG 3.6 An example of a corner floor sitter (A). An example of a floor sitter wedge (B) .

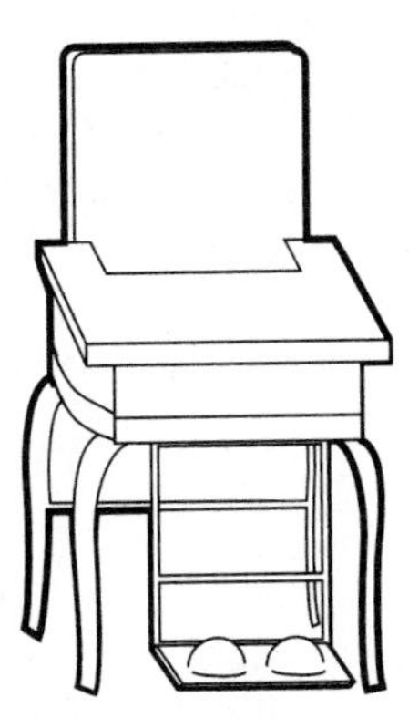

FIG 3.7 A sample youth activity chair.

FIG 3.8 A sample adaptive stander

FIG 3.9 Stabilizing play frame that holds a book or puzzle

need to demonstrate proper positioning of the child in the equipment. Improper placement in a chair or stander is more detrimental to a child than not having a stander to use. Demonstration and practice with the therapist guiding the teacher will help the teacher to develop skill in positioning and the confidence necessary to support the inclusion of the child. In addition to appropriate chairs and standers, large therapeutic balls, side lying boards, therapy bolsters, scooter boards, or therapy wedges might add to the collection of equipment that joins a child in school. Each company produces pieces of specific equipment and furniture that have different features that might best support the specific needs of certain children. For some children, there is no manufactured furniture or equipment that meets all their needs. If this is the case, the appropriate therapist will work on modifying what does exist to best meet the needs of the child. The most critical reason for the concern about proper positioning for children is that proper positioning creates the optimal physical structure for learning. If a child is sitting or standing in the best position possible, the child will be able to gain maximum mobility of extremities and the head. This allows the child to have a better visual orientation so as to gain more from the stimulus materials placed before him or her.

MATERIALS AND BOOKS

The essence of the developmentally appropriate thematic integrated curriculum is the provision of a variety of activities being offered to children in a related manner. The idea is to have many different activities that relate to a theme so that children will have the opportunity to choose activities that interest them and are at their developmental level. Some of these activities require no materials at all but other activities require the children to use materials to solve problems or create their own "props" to be included in the activity in which they will engage.

The most appropriate **materials** to be included in a classroom based on integrated curriculum are open-ended materials that may be used for multiple purposes. Manipulative materials that may be put together in many different ways and incorporated into other activities are a good example of an open-ended, multiple-use material. Children do not tire of using these materials because each time they use them, the experience they had with the materials the previous time increases the potential they have for creating new and different things with each subsequent use. Manipulative materials may be used individually or with peers and this makes them not only manipulative, fine motor materials but adds a social dimension to their use as well. These materials may be used to create something realistic or something from the imagination. When children offer to share information about what they have made, a conceptual, verbal component is added to their experience. Some of these materials may be modified for use with children with disabilities or larger versions of the materials make the experience accessible to children whose motor dexterity interferes with the successful use of regular manipulative materials. The importance, use, and modification of these materials will be discussed in more detail in Chapter 7.

Another type of material for open-ended use would be anything children can use to engage in dramatic play. Containers, baskets, bags of different sizes, shapes and purposes, clothing, hats, and family related props are all wonderful to have around so that children may incorporate them into their play, depending on what roles they are playing and what theme they are carrying out. Children may use a backpack one day to pack a picnic and use it another day to carry all that is needed while exploring new lands. Some teachers think that children need every prop, doll, and piece of kitchenware sold in the largest early childhood catalogues in order to have the best experience possible. Although it is nice to have a variety of materials in this area, it is also important to keep in mind that the more realistic things children have to use, the less imagination and creativity they bring to the situation. Dramatic play materials may require slight modifications for use by children with disabilities so as to make it possible for these children to use the materials more independently.

Materials that help children explore and find out about things are very important materials to have. Magnifying glasses, scales, magnets, and magnetic things are examples of things that help children make discoveries. These materials stimulate the use of a child's senses and provide for long-lasting learning. Books are certainly materials that help children find out about things. We are fortunate today to have so many wonderful books at many different levels which deal with different topics specifically written for the age ranges that exist within the early childhood period. Books should be available to be "read" by children individually, in pairs, and in small groups. Books should be available for teachers to read to children. These books may be regular size books or big books. There should also be books that may be used as resources for information for those times that children ask questions that require a "Let's find out together!" response. Books are often incorporated into ongoing play when children are carrying out themes such as community resources (library, book store, school), or packing to go on a trip (family packs activities for the car or train or bus). In addition to regular books, stories on tape, filmstrips, and movies provide alternative modes for children who do not attend to regular books. These materials should be used to support the development of interest in books and reading but not as a permanent substitute for the regular use of books as a component in the implementation of integrated curriculum.

Materials for the sensory area, for art exploration, to support music and movement activities, and large motor play should also be as open ended and exploratory as possible. When these materials as well as those mentioned previously are used in this manner, they serve the needs of children at their own level of development. A child working with materials in an open-ended fashion will be afforded the opportunity to continue to grow and develop at a rate comfortable for the child. This translates into the child being provided with age appropriate as well as individually appropriate experiences. This is healthy for all children regardless of the level of functioning. The child will be provided with an environment of encouragement and acceptance. This approach uses materials to the best advantage of the children and the teacher.

Well-stocked cabinets in an early childhood classroom filled with the latest and best materials should not be misconstrued as the one sign of developmentally appropriate, integrated curriculum. The manner in which the materials are presented to the children, their accessibility, and the open-ended way in which the children are encouraged to explore and play with the materials are the indicators of appropriate maximum use of materials.

CASE STUDY

A parent once shared a story with the director of a preschool program. The parent had a four-year-old child she was eager to have enrolled in the school run by the director. The parent shared that the child had attended another school the previous year that contained so many wonderful materials. While the mother was impressed with the materials and the precise manner in which they were displayed on the shelves, she was concerned that the materials seemed to remain on the shelves. When the mother asked a teacher why the materials were never out when she came to pick up the child, the teacher told her that they were not used at that time of the day. When the mother had occasion to come to the school to pick the child up at different times of the day, the materials were always on the shelves and the answers were always the same. The mother began to think that the children rarely used the materials and that there was more concern about the cleanliness and orderliness of the materials rather than how to use the materials to the best advantage. More detailed information about materials may be found in Chapters 5 through 11.

SCHEDULE AND ROUTINE

In addition to the components of the integrated curriculum discussed already, it is very important to consider what type of **schedule** lends itself well to the purposes of the integrated learning experience. What this entails is thinking about the types of activities that are best provided within the same time block. In addition, it is important to think about what length of time would be appropriate for the provision of those activities without rushing children through them and without leaving so much time that children become bored with the activities and begin to engage in nonpurposeful activities of their own creation.

Schedules that Support Choices

When children are free to choose their own activities within a large enough block of time, they will be able to select and engage in meaningful activity. When children make choices, they are on the long road to developing responsibility (Kelman, 1990). If adults in the environment were to arbitrarily decide that children should rotate activities in 15-minute time blocks, this could prove to be extremely counterproductive to the goals of an integrated curriculum. Children need appropriate amounts of time for play to develop. Christie and Wardle (1992) contend that insufficient play time is responsible for low-quality play in many classrooms. Too little time appears to inhibit two important areas of play: group-dramatic play and constructive play.

Another less than ideal notion would be to assign children to specific activity or interest areas based on the choice of the teacher. The teacher might think that this would be the best way to ensure that all children sampled all of the interest centers and activities. This is not, however, how it would really work because you would probably wind up assigning children to activities they were not ready to engage in, and that in turn would disrupt or destroy the experience of the other children in the group. It would make it very difficult for the teacher facilitating that activity to motivate the child who does not want to be there. Many years ago, a kindergarten teacher was observed to assign children to activity areas for an entire week. For the entire week the children would find themselves with the same small group of children (not of their choosing) engaging in the same activity. This might mean that the group was assigned to puzzles or pegboards. It might also mean that they were assigned to the playhouse. Although a playhouse is a much more open-ended "assignment," being there with children one would not necessarily choose to play with made it a less-than-ideal learning situation for the children in the class. One can imagine that this teacher implemented this procedure of assigning children to areas because it was easier than monitoring children in their self-selected activities. It was also probably a foolproof way to maintain a very quiet kindergarten classroom. It also was an extremely foolproof way to make sure that the first schooling experience for many children in the class was less than desirable.

Schedules that Support Time to Think

One of the problems some children have in their home environments is that they are not given enough time to explore and experiment. When they begin to engage in some meaningful activity they are often told to stop what they were doing so they can be rushed off to their next structured, organized activity. Although organized, purposeful activity is beneficial, too many children experience this kind of activity to excess while not having enough time to experience "time" to "be" and to engage in activities of their choosing. One of these activities might be to just lie on the floor thinking or imagining. Another might be to initiate a long term activity that will occupy the free time the child has over the next several weeks. The daily schedule at school should include some time for meaningful thought and imagining wonderful things.

Schedules that Account for Active and Quiet Periods

A schedule that is sensitive to the developmental needs of the early childhood period takes into account that a young child needs active periods and quieter periods. The children also need time to be part of a small group and time to be part of a larger group. They need time to be outdoors or have similar types of experiences if the weather prohibits them from being outdoors. They also need time to eat. These time periods need to alternate so that all active and all quieter times are not clustered.

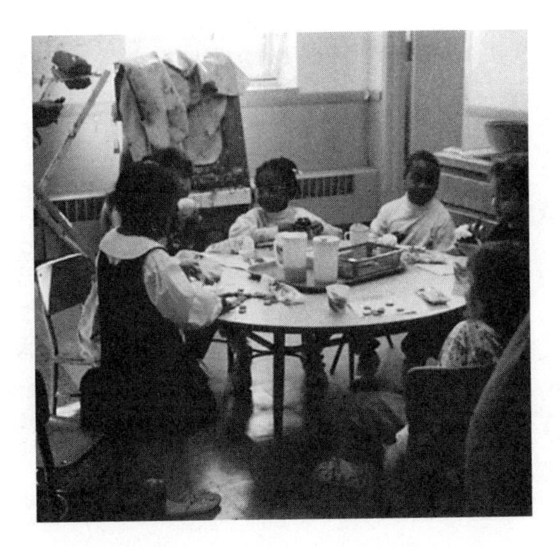

FIG 3.10 Snack eaten in small groups provides for a quiet time during the day.

Schedules that Supports Flow of Activity

Schedules and routines are guidelines for the flow of activity during any given school day. What determines exactly how long each period lasts is the quality of activity and the interests of the children. Some days you will find that children have shorter attention spans. This may be due to some special activity that is scheduled to take place at school, or an upcoming birthday or holiday. Sometimes children have short attention spans due to lack of sleep due to family circumstances, positive or negative. Some children exhibit short attention spans due to lack of food. A quick change of plans that will enable children to eat earlier or be engaged in a less active activity will salvage the day before children get into a negative behavior pattern for the entire day. Rigidly adhering to a schedule does nothing to promote positive experiences for children or adults. Sticking to a schedule to make sure that "everything gets done" indicates that the teacher in the room really does not understand child development or classroom management. A developed schedule is a framework to guide the flow of activity. Different parts of the day might require a change in space or at the very least, transitioning from one activity to another. Transitions may be made easier by alerting children to the change that will soon take place, supporting the children through the change, and capturing their attention through the use of appropriate signals (Crosser, 1992).

FIG 3.11 Children enjoy using the computer as a quiet activity.

Schedules Should Reflect Diversity of Activity

Each day, the schedule and routine should include joy. That means that each child should have a pleasant sense of anticipation. Each child will probably not equally enjoy each part of the school day. Some children like to start the day with a quiet activity (see Figure 3.11). Some children may have had limited experience playing outdoors and may not immediately enjoy the activity as much as other children. Some children seem to be extremely sensitive to wind, cold, or humidity. Some children love "circle time" while others merely tolerate it. Some do not appreciate circle time because they are not able to see small visual displays or hear everything that goes on. To make the activity more appealing to these children with disabilities, care needs to be taken in planning for the materials used during the activity so as to accommodate the children.

Some children love snacks and lunch while others have such finicky appetites or special needs concerning swallowing and eating that eating is really not yet a pleasurable time of the day. For a child for whom food is not appealing, engaging the child in the preparation or choice of food may increase the interest. Occupational therapy for the child with a feeding disorder will help to diminish the problem over time. Some children will find that eating at home is not as much fun as eating with peers and will develop better eating habits and routines through pleasurable food experiences at school.

The following example demonstrates the value of children anticipating pleasant activity.

CASE STUDY

In a second grade classroom, the children could handle just about anything else as long as they knew that their teacher would read to them at the end of the day from a "chapter book." This end of the day "treat" was both joyful and served as an excellent motivation and management technique. The children learned that if they took too long at transitions during the day, the reading time at the end of the day would be shorter. Interestingly, at one point, this teacher thought she needed to implement a formal management plan involving a "reward" given to the children at the end of the day. The teacher decided that if the children were "good" during the day, she would give them a piece of candy at the end of school. What she quickly learned was that the candy was not at all rewarding compared to the story reading she usually provided for them. The teacher quickly abandoned the candy routine and went back to her usual rewarding reading with great success. The following are some samples of appropriate schedules that support activity by allowing adequate blocks of time for all children to be able to engage in activity without rushing and for teachers to move about the room facilitating activity and learning. What follows are some sample schedules that provide a balance of activities:

Preschool Age Program	*Full Day with half-day options*
8:00– 9:00	Early drop, meet with parents, children play
9:00–10:15	Free choice of planned activity
10:15–10:30	Clean-up, toileting, story
10:30–10:45	Snack time
10:45–11:15	Outdoor play
11:15–11:40	Circle time
11:40–12:00	Individual activity time
11:15–12:00	Circle time
12:00–12:45	Lunch (some children leave before or after lunch)
12:45– 1:30	Play and prepare for nap
1:30– 2:30 or 3:00	Nap
3:00	Snack
3:00– 5:00	Planned activities including indoor and outdoor weather permitting, staggered departure

FIG 3.12 Sample schedule for flexible enrollment pattern. Children spend minimum of half-day at school but can stay for lunch and extended day.

Kindergarten to Third Grade	*Full-Day Program*
8:45– 9:15	Arrival, group time, activity selection
9:15–10:30	Rotating activity areas
10:30–11:00	Snack and whole language group activity
11:00–12:15	Rotating activity areas
12:15–12:30	Transition for lunch
12:30– 1:00	Lunch
1:00– 1:30	Outdoor activity
1:30– 2:50	Afternoon activity areas
2:50– 3:00	Preparation for dismissal

(Special periods such as library, physical education, art, and music scheduled as activities outside the classroom will necessitate schedule adjustments on specific days of the week.)

FIG 3.13 Sample schedule for full-day kindergarten program.

Kindergarten	*Half-Day Program*
8:45– 9:15	Arrival, group time, activity selection
9:15–10:30	Rotating activity areas
10:30–11:00	Snack and whole language group activity
11:00–11:55	Rotating activity areas
11:55–12:00	Preparation for dismissal

FIG 3.14 Sample schedule for half-day kindergarten program.

FACILITATION OF ACTIVITY

One of the most difficult components of implementing integrated curriculum for many teachers to master is the idea of teacher as facilitator, not teacher as director. Teachers often say that they chose early childhood education as a career because they wanted to teach. In their minds this means that the teacher is the one to be in control of all learning that takes place in the classroom. In a way, some teachers are rewarded by peers, parents, and administrators relative to the amount of authority the teacher exerts over the students in her classroom. In the minds of some, good teachers are those whose classrooms are quiet and whose students are in their seats at all times. In those kinds of classrooms, teachers plan for every move children make and everything that they, the teachers, will say and do. This means that there is no spontaneity and that children are expected to have specific responses to teacher questions. While this style of organizing a classroom may be gratifying to the adult who needs a strong sense of control in order to feel successful, this rigidity can serve to stifle the children in the class. The children in the class will be discouraged from being spontaneous or creative. Under these conditions, some children may even stop responding altogether.

Teacher as Facilitator

Teacher as **facilitator** is also teacher as role model. Sometimes people forget that teachers are people first. By virtue of the fact that they are people, their people skills should be obvious to all who come into the classroom. Teachers should speak softly to children in order to encourage the use of soft tones of voice in children. Teachers who yell when trying to communicate with children teach them that yelling is perfectly fine as long as you have something you want others to know. Teachers need to model courteous behavior and to extend common classroom courtesies. If children are not allowed to sit on tables, then teachers should not sit on tables. If children are discouraged from leaving the table with food in their mouths or hands, then teachers should not walk around with food in their hands or food in their mouths. If children may not chew gum in school, then teachers should not chew gum in school. Creating a climate of positive talk about each other means that teachers should also engage in positive talk about children, colleagues, and parents. Children do learn from the adult models in their environments. With so many children suffering from the lack of positive models in their homes and communities, not to mention the media, it is of the utmost importance that the models they encounter in school are powerfully positive. Listen carefully to the children when they play teacher and you will hear exactly what kind of influence you are exerting on the children. Hopefully, it will be something you are proud to see and hear.

Teachers Engage in Activity with Children

Another way that teachers provide models within the integrated curriculum is to engage in activity with children. Rather than presenting a model of exactly how something should or must be done, children should be shown that the activity is an enjoyable one. In this way, the teacher serves as an assistant to the child to enhance, sustain, or extend the play experience (Hendrick, 1992). Sometimes children with limited or no previous experience with art materials have the idea that using markers or paints or glue causes permanent change to the body. They may also be afraid that if any color were to get on their clothing, there would be punishment at home. While teachers certainly are unable to control parental responses to child behaviors, parent education at the start of the school year will help parents to understand the importance of using free-flowing art materials and thus make it easier for the teacher to facilitate the engagement of the child in those activities. If a child is still hesitant to engage in activity, if you assure the child that you will speak to their parents about how to remove the paint from clothing, the child may feel comfortable enough to try something new.

Teacher as Parent Communicator

This brings up a very critical component of facilitation of activity within the integrated curriculum—**communication** with parents. Communication with parents allows the parents to become partners in your endeavors. Since most parents of the children in your class will not have experienced education in the same way their children are experiencing it in your class, they may not be 100 percent supportive of what you are doing unless you help them to understand the value of what you are doing. Making parents your allies is critical to the success of developmentally appropriate practice and to the role of teacher as facilitator (Stipek, Rosenblatt & DiRocco, 1994). The manner in which this education of parents takes place needs to be sensitive to the individual differences in parents—their life styles, their level of education, their work and school schedules. Some parents are very involved in the education of their children while others are minimally involved. No matter what the level of involvement, all parents need to be informed so they can support their children as well as lend support to your program. If they are educated to understand the basic philosophy of learning by doing and understand that the implication of this approach means that there are activities and projects rather than worksheets, then they will not chastise their children for forgetting to bring their papers home. Parents also need to learn how to ask their children the right kinds of questions so that their children will want to share information with them. Sometimes a teacher will encounter a "difficult" parent (Boutte, Keepler, Tyler & Terry, 1992). If the teacher reaches out to establish an authentic relationship, the effort will go a long way to ease difficulties. Once the difficulties have been worked out, the children, teachers, and parents will together be able to facilitate what happens in the classroom. Sometimes a parent will decide to remove a child from a school because it may appear that there are difficulties or differences that cannot be worked out (Jacobs, 1992). When this happens, it is important to make the situation as positive as possible for the child. Jacobs (1992) makes important suggestions to accomplish this difficult task, including slowing the transition process to give time for appropriate preparation, encouraging and guiding the parent to make a plan with the child to leave the school, supporting the parents' plan as much as possible, being sensitive to what a child leaving a class can mean to those children remaining in the classroom, assisting the classmates to say farewell to the child in their own way, being sensitive and supporting the parents of classmates, being prepared for delayed reactions, and being open to criticism and helping staff learn from this experience.

Teachers Encourage Engagement of all Children

Facilitation of activity in the integrated curriculum classroom means that teachers encourage children to engage in activity and encourage children to feel good about their explorations. Teachers need to encourage but not "do" for children. Sometimes the temptation is very great for some to actually make something for a child so the child will have something to take home or so that child is not the only one in the class who does not have a project completed. This temptation may be very strong as it relates to children with disabilities. A teacher may be very sensitive to the expectations of parents of children with disabilities. The teacher may feel that the parent will gain more confidence if the child brings things home from school. Often, the child with special needs is not able to relate the events of the day to the parents so having actual "productions" made by the child will serve to inform the parents of the activity of the day. If one really understands and supports the child's role in learning, it will be perfectly fine for a child to choose not to engage in a particular project or activity or not be ready to participate. The role of the teacher relative to children with disabilities is to attempt to find a way to adapt the activity or adapt the environment to facilitate a child to engage in the activity. If the child is not able to do so, an alternate activity should be provided that is as similar to the activity as possible, thus encouraging involvement.

With a child without disabilities, what one must be careful to note is whether this happens once or twice or whether this is a consistent pattern that needs a different tactic. Understanding child development allows the teacher to know that some children take to one kind of activity before another and that individual differences are sometimes so strong that a particular child will not ever want to participate in a specific activity. While teachers must respect children and their choices, they must also try to provide each child with the fullest experience possible. Sometimes a child may be encouraged to participate in something if allowed to participate with a favorite peer. Other times this specific activity may become very interesting to a child if a parent comes to school for a "sharing day" and shares that activity with the child. Still other children may be most interested in an activity when an older child, an admired child, has a strong interest in the same activity. While forcing a child to engage in a particular activity is not in the best interests of the child, it is in the best interests of the child to do everything possible to ensure that the child has had every opportunity possible to sample the experience.

Many teachers working with young children do so because they love the age group. In addition to that, they love working with the materials that the children work with. It is very appropriate to be involved with the children and to participate in activities, but it is a not appropriate to plant yourself in an activity and stay there from start to finish (Hendrick, 1992). The teacher in an integrated curriculum classroom should be involved but should also be mobile. That does not mean flying from one activity to another but it does mean getting around to make sure that everything is going well and that all children are involved. It is critical to make assessments of children while they choose and participate in activities.

Each classroom needs a plan for supervising activity that makes sure that all areas that need coverage have enough coverage. This means that in order to provide a safe, stimulating environment, teachers need to think through all of the activities they have planned for the day so that there will not be several activities provided that need constant supervision (i.e., cooking, woodworking, and the final piece of a make-your-own-book activity).

Teachers should be careful to make children their first priority while they are in the classroom. This means that phone calls, visitors, paperwork, team meetings, and consultations need to take a back seat during the day. Periods of time when children are in special activities or eating lunch might be better times for distractions and activities that take up teacher time.

SUMMARY

The many factors to consider when developing an integrated curriculum include the children, space, equipment, materials and books, schedule, or routine and how all the activities will be facilitated.

The early childhood environment should support the development of children taking into consideration adequate space per child, accessibility of materials and equipment, and the provision of personal space dedicated to the personal belongings of each child in the class. Activity space identified for specific activities enhances the activities in the classroom and promotes child involvement. The kind of space that works best within an integrated curriculum format for a program that includes children with disabilities is flexible and fluid. It allows formation of interest centers, quiet corners, space for medium-size groups and whole-group activities, and widening pathways between activity areas so children with physical disabilities can have easier access to the areas. The ideal space has access to water and toilet facilities as well as access to outdoors. The space should be carpeted and tiled where necessary.

The physical environment has impact on the behavior of a child. Children with disabilities are sometimes inhibited by space overcrowded with people and furniture. The space should not be cluttered nor should it have any consistently wide-open spaces.

Storage space should receive serious consideration. Lack of storage may deter a teacher from creating additional theme boxes or from acquiring additional materials and books. Safety issues need to be a factor when creating storage.

Space should meet the needs of activity. The space in the classroom must allow for and promote a flow of activity. The space in the classroom should take into account the need children have for working on long-term projects. The layout of the inclusive classroom in which integrated curriculum takes place should also receive careful attention. Materials and equipment presented on safe, durable shelves that allow children to safely gain access to the materials by themselves allows children to determine choices of materials and activities without the teacher having to worry about the safety of the child's independence. The layout of the classroom should also include interest or activity centers with discernible boundaries. Activity areas that are in spaces with clear paths that lead to them are areas that children will use. The layout of the classroom should also include some places that provide for the privacy of children.

There is considerable variation found between the physical spaces used for early childhood programs. The factors one would take into consideration beyond issues of size and shape of the space would include: location of doors and windows; the lead levels of wall and ceiling coverings indoors, and the lead levels of soil and any painted surfaces outdoors; asbestos; ambulatory accessibility; and whether the space is used by other groups, child or adult.

Implementation of the thematic integrated curriculum approach does not require special furniture or equipment. In an inclusive classroom, there are certain pieces of furniture and equipment that are necessary to have in order to accommodate the special positioning and support requirements of children with physical disabilities. The children who require the use of these special chairs, standers, or other adaptive equipment will either arrive with the equipment, or the appropriate pieces will be procured by the school system soon after the child arrives.

The essence of the developmentally appropriate, thematic, integrated curriculum is the provision of a variety of activities being offered to children in a related manner and at their developmental level. The most appropriate materials are open-ended materials that may be used for multiple purposes such as manipulative materials. Another type of material that is open-ended would be anything that can be used by children to engage in dramatic play. Materials that help children explore and find out about things are important materials to have. Materials for the sensory area, for art exploration, to support music and movement activities, and large motor play should also be as open-ended and exploratory as possible.

It is very important to consider what type of schedule lends itself to the purposes of the integrated learning experience. The schedule should allow the children to select and engage in meaningful activity. Children need appropriate amounts of time for play to develop. A schedule sensitive to development takes into account that a young child needs active periods and quieter periods, time to be part of a small group and time to be part of a larger group, time to be outdoors and time to eat. Schedules and routines are guidelines for the flow of activity during any given school day that respond to the quality of activity and the interests of the children.

The teacher as facilitator is also the teacher as role model. Teachers need to model courteous behavior and common classroom courtesies. Another way that teachers serve as models is to engage in activity with children, to serve as an assistant to the child to enhance, sustain, or extend the play experience.

Communication with parents allows the parents to become partners in your endeavors. Making parents your allies is critical to the success of developmentally appropriate practice and to the role of teacher as facilitator.

Facilitation of activity in the integrated curriculum classroom means that teachers encourage children to engage in activity and encourage children to feel good about their explorations. The teacher in an integrated curriculum classroom should be involved but mobile.

Each classroom should have a plan for supervising activity that makes sure that all areas in need have enough coverage. Teachers should be careful to make children their first priority while they are in the classroom. Without children in the classroom, there is no curriculum.

DISCUSSION QUESTIONS

1) After visiting two different early childhood programs, compare and contrast these programs for aspects of developmental appropriateness. Think about the issues of space, materials, furniture and equipment, schedule and routine, and the facilitation of activity.
2) You have been invited to visit a site that may possibly be developed into some kind of early childhood program. The site is a former factory location. What concerns will you bring to the site when you visit

that relate to the creation of safe, developmentally appropriate programs?

3) You are asked to help develop a list of materials that are absolutely necessary to start a mixed-age preschool program. The list should contain justifications for each of the items. The budget is limited.
4) What are some of the benefits of collaboration between early childhood teachers? Discuss both the pros and cons.
5) You are a teacher in an early childhood program that supports the guidelines of developmentally appropriate practice. You have the chance to observe a potential teacher in your classroom. The teacher candidate has been asked to participate during the free choice of planned activity period of the day. What will you look for as indicators of appropriateness of this candidate and why?
6) Discuss the possible adaptations most environments will need to make to accommodate children with disabilities.

REFERENCES

Bredekamp, S. (1987). *Developmentally appropriate practice in early childhood programs serving children from birth through age 8*. Washington, DC: National Association for the Education of Young Children.

Christie, J., & Wardle, F. (1992). How much time is needed for play? *Young Children, 47*(3), 28–32.

Crosser, S. (1992). Managing the early childhood classroom. *Young Children, 47*(2), 23–29.

Dodge, D. (1989). *The creative curriculum for early childhood*. Washington, DC: Teaching Strategies, Inc.

Eliason, C. & Jenkins, L. (1994). *A practical guide to early childhood curriculum*. New York: Merrill.

Essa, E. (1992). *Introduction to early childhood education*. Albany, NY: Delmar Publishers Inc.

Hendrick, J. (1994). *Total learning—Developmental curriculum for the young child*. New York: Merrill.

Jacobs, N. (1992). Unhappy endings. *Young Children, 47*(3), 23–27.

Kelman, A. (1990). Choices for children. *Young Children, 45*(3), 42–45.

Krogh, S. (1995). *The integrated early childhood curriculum*. New York: McGraw-Hill, Inc.

Peters, J., Bunse, C., Carlson, L., Doede, L., Glasenapp, G., Haydon., Lehman, C., Templeman, T., & Udell, T. (1992). *Supporting children with disabilities in early childhood programs*. Monmouth, OR: Teaching Research Publications.

Stipek, D., Rosenblatt, L., & DiRocco, L. (1994). Making parents your allies. *Young Children, 49*(3), 4–9.

Thomson, C., & Ashton-Lilo, J. (1983). A developmental environment for child care programs. In E. Goetz & K. Allen (Eds.), *Early childhood education: Special environmental, policy, and legal considerations* (pp. 93–125). Rockville, MD: Aspen Systems Corp.

Watkins, K., & Durant, L., Jr. (1992). *Complete early childhood behavior management guide.* West Nyack, NY: The Center for Applied Research in Education.

Wortham, S. (1994). *Early childhood curriculum—Developmental bases for learning and teaching*. New York: Merrill.

ADDITIONAL READINGS

Christie, J., & Johnsen, E. (1989). The constraints of setting on children's play. *Play and Culture, 2*, 317–327.

Ebensen, S. (1987). *The early childhood playground: An outdoor classroom*. Ypsilanti, MI: High Scope Press.

Kostelnik, M. (1992). Myths associated with developmentally appropriate programs. *Young Children, 47*(4), 17–23.

Schillmoeller, G., & Amundrud, P. (1987). The effect of furniture arrangement on movement, on-task behavior, and sound in an early childhood setting. *Child and Youth Care Quarterly, 16*(1), 5–20.

PART

2

CHAPTER 4

Planning the Integrated Curriculum

KEY TERMS

early childhood educator
consultation
curriculum webbing
child-centered curriculum
language and literacy
dramatic play
conversation
social development
solitary or isolate play
parallel play
cooperative play
physical development
cognitive development
activity-rich environment
sensory area
hollow-blocks
dramatic play
book area
small blocks
manipulative activities
music and movement

THE EARLY CHILDHOOD EDUCATOR AS THE KEY TO THE SUCCESS OF THIS APPROACH

The characteristics of a well-rounded, professionally oriented, early childhood educator are extremely varied. An **early childhood educator** is a person who is knowledgeable about typical and atypical child development, models of early childhood curriculum from historical to current times, the workings of families, the workings of schools, current issues in the field, the role of the teacher as the facilitator of development and learning, and the person who is able to apply all that information to the early childhood classroom. The early childhood educator may work with infants, toddlers, preschool age children, or children from kindergarten through grade three. The early childhood educator may work in a public school setting or in a program found within the community. The early childhood educator may work in a public program in the community or in a private program located in the community. Regardless of where this person finds employment, this person is certain to be involved with children, parents, other educators, specialists, social workers, therapists, and community agencies. The early childhood educator also wears many other hats. This person needs to be resourceful, organized and an organizer, a good listener, a keen observer, and an excellent manager. All of these qualities are also very important to the role of the early childhood educator as key to the implementation of integrated curriculum.

Early Childhood Educator as Key to Integrated Curriculum

The early childhood educator is key to the success of the integrated curriculum because this person knows best what transpires in the early childhood classroom. While those who are considered experts in the area of child development may be able to sit in quiet offices separate from early childhood classrooms and think about children, reflect on what children need, and how they think teacher should deliver what they think is critical for children to experience, it has been quite some time since some of those wonderful thinkers have actually worked with young children. While that may not negatively influence some writers and developers of a curriculum, it may make it difficult for others to actually see how their ideas will work. What is being advocated here is the notion that early childhood educators are the right people to be developing units of integrated curricula because they are the very people who will be implementing them, evaluating them on site, and modifying them to meet the needs of the children they teach.

The Role of Consultation

Certainly there are many times, no matter how long one has been teaching, that **consultation** is necessary. This consultation may indeed come from someone who is considered an esteemed professional in the field. Each group of children one teaches presents different challenges to the teacher due to the history and experiences the children bring to the classroom. The group may be a challenge due to one specific child or the group may be a challenge due to a particular set of behaviors exhibited by several children in the class. Sometimes the classroom teacher will really need the "expert" for assistance or inspiration. Other times, the teacher may need the support or advice of another teacher because the other teacher is right there in the same school building and has the opportunity to see more immediately what the teacher is talking about. Very often, when working with young children, seeing is believing and no matter how detailed the description of activity or behavior, the situation is something that must be seen in order to assist the teacher to come up with the solution to the problem.

Curriculum Packages Versus Classroom-specific Curriculum

Curriculum that is developed by someone on the East Coast of the United States may not be appropriate for implementation in the Southwest. Suppose a curriculum developer develops a unit of curriculum on the theme of seasons. This person may make the assumption that all children have the opportunity to experience four seasons with their associated changes in temperature, weather conditions, change of clothing, change in food availability, and school schedules. Now suppose that you are a teacher in a part of the country that does not experience seasons in this way. You receive an advertisement for integrated curriculum packages. The information uses all the "right" words: thematic, developmentally appropriate, activity oriented, "hands-on," etc. You order these materials and when you receive them, you find out that much of the information, and many of the activities, are not appropriate for your use. The inappropriateness of total application of this curriculum in your classroom situation is based primarily on the geographic differences between where you teach and where the curriculum was developed. Using this as an example, think of how many other situations may be different between classrooms from one classroom to another:

- the type of children
- the socioeconomic level of the children
- the quantity and quality of educational experience the children in your class had prior to entrance into your program
- the educational level of the parents
- the length of your school day
- the number of days the children attend school during the year
- the resources you have access to
- the number of teachers working in your classroom

The point being reiterated here is that early childhood educators, with the appropriate education, training, and supports, are the most appropriate persons to develop and implement integrated curriculum in their own classrooms.

The early childhood educator is the key to integrated curriculum because of his or her role as an observer, facilitator, organizer, and innovator. Since this person is the one to develop, implement, and evaluate what occurs in his or her own classroom, this educator is in the right place at the right time in order to see what is and what is not working. Success in the classroom according to this approach is measured by observing the following in the children: involvement, productivity, enthusiasm, self-esteem, social skills, literacy development, both oral and written communication skills, problem-solving skills, and independence in a social and learner sense.

Through the implementation of integrated curriculum, the early childhood educator is able to reach out to all children in the classroom. Through adaptations and modifications in the activities provided, all children may be involved within the range of their own abilities and styles. The teacher is right there to encourage, modify, support, assess children, and evaluate the success of the curriculum while it is ongoing. The teacher in this kind of environment does not need someone else to come into the classroom to assess children and evaluate the program. Tests should not need to be administered by others and scored by others for teachers to know how the children in their classes are doing. The teacher determines goals and objectives for the class and for all the individual children within the class. The teacher measures the success of the total program based on the progress children make against developed goals and objectives. This reiterates the role of the early childhood educator as key to the success of integrated curriculum.

WHAT ARE THE STEPS TO BE FOLLOWED WHEN PLANNING AN INTEGRATED CURRICULUM

Planning a new unit of study should follow this format:

- select a theme
- brainstorm ideas for activities and centers
- identify appropriate objectives
- research appropriate books to be shared with the children and to be used by the children independently
- obtain materials and equipment necessary to carry out the activities

Workman and Anziano (1993) present an approach to **curriculum webbing** that begins by identifying concepts from children's interests to serve as a starting point. What they suggest as the next step is for several teachers to get together to brainstorm each topic, listing as many headings and subheadings as their experience and understanding allows. Krogh (1995) also presents a rationale for the weaving of a web for curriculum development. She speaks to the process of integrating traditional subject areas into an integrated curriculum theme. Regardless of the approach taken, in order to follow the plan, the teacher sometimes must begin by researching the topic for the basic information that is lacking in order to begin the planning process. Without being familiar with the topic, there will be a lack of focus within the integrated curriculum theme. With little substance to the theme, the curriculum will not be successful. Teachers may need to conduct considerable research to able to present the best possible curriculum for some topics. This time will be well spent but the time factor involved will necessarily delay the introduction of that particular curriculum topic. That is why it makes sense to have several topics developed well enough so that the beginning of the school year will be a smooth one. The teacher will then be able to use the planned curriculum topic and activities as an opportunity to observe children and as a springboard for other topics. Planning an integrated curriculum is not difficult. It is time consuming and requires thought, but the results are well worth the labor. When teachers organize themselves to work as planning teams, the work of individual teachers is energized by the others, labor can be divided, resources may be shared and the children will certainly benefit from the effort.

PITFALLS AND PROBLEMS OF CHILD-CENTERED PLANNING

There might be a tendency when implementing a **child-centered curriculum** to focus too much on children's immediate interests and needs without focusing on the critical concepts and social goals of language and literacy. Taking all leads from children as to what to plan next without having a developmental framework within which to incorporate the interests and needs of the children might lead to large gaps between concepts. This would not be conducive to sequential learning and might leave some children very frustrated.

Learning is a continuum and as such must proceed along a logical path. Nachbar (1992) presents a model for including children in curriculum planning around a specific theme. The process for the involvement of the children included working through four stages:

1. What do you know? (a baseline of information);
2. What do you wonder? (for focus and direction);
3. Gather information (research); and
4. What did you learn? (Review of information.)

With the teachers taking the direction for the curriculum planning process as well as providing the guidance and support the children need, the quest will be interesting and exciting.

Role of the Teacher in Child-Centered Planning

In an effort to develop integrated curriculum that is beneficial for children on a variety of levels, expertise in child development as well as adult good sense must prevail. The adult in the setting is the one who is in the position to see what children need to be introduced to. That is not to say that the interests of the children cannot provide the vehicle for meeting the needs of the children but rather that sometimes the interests evidenced by the children, while genuine, are more sophisticated than what the children are able to handle prior to being introduced to other more basic concepts. Once those more basic interests are introduced, then the choice of interest indicated by the children will be more logical and more appropriate. The more appropriate a topic is for study by young children, the greater the likelihood of meaningful learning, and, in turn, there is increased probability of success of the integrated unit of study.

Using Broad Themes upon which to Base Curriculum

Another caution when planning integrated curriculum for young children centers on the fact that one cannot always wait for child ideas to surface in order to plan curriculum. One must have a storehouse of ideas to be able to introduce and develop should you find yourself working with a group of children who are very quiet, shy to warm up to this responsive environment, or so lacking in experiences that you will need to provide them with many experiences before they will be able to evidence their own interests. When this is the situation you find yourself in, you need to initiate the planning and present organized, whole learning experiences for children. These experiences will form the foundation upon which all future learning will take place.

An early childhood teacher in the process of engaging in this foundation planning needs to think about planning for continuity and building conceptual relationships for children. One way to accomplish this is to select organizers that are broad based enough to house children's ideas. Keeping in mind that continuity is critical, these broad organizers such as learning about "me," the family, the community, animals, etc. allows the teacher to build upon prior knowledge and connect concepts for children so that they are not learning about concepts in isolation. When the children are ready to initiate ideas of their own and the teacher begins to notice the children investing in particular ideas, the children's ideas then may be used as a springboard for broader based curriculum. Jones and

Nimmo (1994) present the concept of emergent curriculum as a way in which teachers and children can develop curriculum day by day and week by week. This approach emphasizes planning based on the daily life of those involved in the classroom rather than mapping everything out months in advance and then adhering to the plan regardless of whether children and teachers are enjoying it or learning from it.

Preparing to Meet the Interests of the Children

Another concern when planning child-centered curriculum is that teachers cannot possibly know about all topics that may be of interest to children. This translates into the fact that as a new teacher or a veteran teacher, being ready and knowledgeable in all subjects in order to be able to implement thematic ideas that are of interest to all children at all times may not be possible. The development of an interesting, developmentally appropriate, thematic integrated unit takes time. It makes sense to become aware of several sources of ideas and resources (Berry & Mindes, 1993; Deiner, 1993; Dodge, 1989; Dolinar, Boser & Holm, 1994; Kostelnik, (Ed.), 1991; Krogh, 1995; Trostle & Yawkey, 1990) for the development of new themes to be used as a springboard for your own theme which will be developed to meet the specific population and needs of the children in your class.

PEERS AS NURTURERS AND FACILITATORS

Children come to school for a variety of reasons. Certainly they come to school so that they can learn. One can certainly learn at home and it is without a doubt children do learn so much before they come to school. Once they begin to attend school, they continue to learn from their home environments. They learn from their parents, they learn from their siblings, they learn from members of their extended family, they learn from other adults who play major and minor roles in their lives, they learn from their experiences with toys and books, and they learn from the media.

Children Come to School for Socialization

Children also come to school for the experience of socialization. Some children are fortunate enough to have peer experiences prior to attending school. These experiences may have been gained through informal or more formal activities ranging from meeting families on the playground, attending library story hours, swim programs, fitness activities, or other activities of specific nature. Some children may have siblings close to their ages, and they may have long-lasting peer relationships either with children in their neighborhoods, children who are offspring of their parents' friends, or children within the extended family. Whatever the situation in which the child has enjoyed peer socialization experiences, development of social relationships with children seen on a daily basis for an entire year might be quite different. The social skills already developed may prove to be quite adequate or a new set of behaviors may need to develop.

Child Social Skills Related to Peer Nurturing

Children come to school with a variety of levels of social skills. Some children are extremely skilled in the many ways one is able to make social initiations and responses. These children have an intuitive sense of how to handle peers who are shy, peers who are overbearing, or peers who are negative or aggressive. They seem to be able to analyze the social situations, plan their mode of operation, and follow through with their plans. There are other children who come to school with few social skills or no social skills at all. It usually takes a combination of peers and adults to help these children to grow and develop into totally social beings. Some children are appreciative of differences in others and sensitive to the needs some individuals have. Some children have had little or no experience with individuals different from their own family experience and as such are initially a bit wary of some peers and adults in their classrooms.

Children have the powerful potential to nurture other children. There are many children who demonstrate a great degree of empathy at an early age (Doescher & Sugawara, 1989). These children are able to sense when their peers need comforting and they provide that comfort in a most nurturing manner. They are also able to sense when their peers do not want anyone around and will give them the time and space they need. They stay nearby in order to see if they are needed but they do not crowd the child with the problem. These children are usually also the children who are extremely sensitive to persons of color, older people, and individuals with disabilities. They have the innate ability, or an ability that was learned at a very early age from living in a very nurturing environment, to know how to nurture or help others. They are able to help without being overpowering and take pride in the new abilities of those they help. Sometimes, these children need some support from the adults in the environment in order to be able to nurture. Initially, they may be too overbearing and want to "do" for the child instead of help the child do for him- or herself. Sometimes, when the adults in the environment have not had too much experience with children with special needs and are themselves a "soft touch," there are children in the class who will remind the adults that the child with special needs ought to be encouraged to do that something without help.

Children with Disabilities Respond to Peers

Occasionally teachers find that some children with special needs respond much more positively to their peers than to adults. Adults do not provide the motivation for these children to engage in communication, either verbal, non-verbal, or both. Adults do not seem to be the primary motivation for children with special needs to engage in any activity. Face it! For some children, peers are much more interesting than adults. Adults have their purpose but these children are more interested in their peers. The following example of peers as motivators involves a child with multiple disabilities.

CASE STUDY

This child came to school with her own aide. This three-year-old girl was from a large family. She was used to having many children and adults around her. She was able to vocalize and had a most endearing smile. She was confined to a wheelchair for most of the time she was at home, and while in school she was in a modified stroller or special seat. She had cortical blindness. She was very responsive to several different kinds of music. One of the problem areas that needed addressing was her eating. She had a reflux problem, had endured several surgeries, and was still fed by a feeding tube at night while asleep if she did not have enough food intake by mouth during the course of the day. One day while attempting to feed her, one of the teachers was approached by one of the children in the class who wanted to know if she could feed her friend. Although hesitant, the teacher allowed the child to feed her friend. What do you think the teacher observed? The child being fed did not resist being fed the way she did when an adult attempted to feed her. The teacher carefully monitored the process making sure the child doing the feeding did not try to feed too much with each spoonful and was careful to allow enough time between spoonfuls so that the reflux problem was not aggravated. The child doing the feeding was proud and felt a great sense of reward from the experience. The child who needed to be fed was far more interested in the new arrangement than in the attempts any adult had made in the past. The child doing the feeding engaged in this behavior out of concern for her friend. She did not treat her friend as a plaything. She did not pity her friend. When the family of the child with special needs was informed about the new occurrence, the parents were quite excited. There were several other children in their family who could help with the feeding of this very special child. Hopefully these children would be as successful as the child in school had been. The "helping" was done by a child who had a real ability to nurture. The nurturing child came from a family in which there were two other children who were each nine years apart (children were 3, 12, and 21). This nurturing child was raised by her mother and her 21-year-old sister. In a sense she had double nurturing from two women who adored her and gave her considerable attention. She was not spoiled, she was nurtured.

Peers as Facilitators of Inclusion

Children who can nurture other children are able to serve as facilitators of inclusion. They help the teachers in the classroom to bring the curriculum to the children with special needs or bring the children with special needs to the curriculum. They are not afraid to help move the child around in the wheelchair or other adaptive equipment to the next activity. They take pride in doing so. They often do not need to be asked, they just do what they see needs doing. Their involvement with their peers with special needs is based on respect for their friends. They treat their friends with dignity.

The child in this next case serves as an example of how children with special needs have the potential to kindle the most positive behaviors in children and adults.

CASE STUDY

A four-year-old boy came to school from another culture. It appeared that he had little or no experience with children with special needs and cautiously watched a child with multiple disabilities from across the room. At the start of the school year, when invited to share an activity with the child with special needs, he flatly refused and stayed as far away from her as he possibly could. Over the next few weeks, the teachers noticed some dramatic changes in his behavior and attitude. He began moving closer to the child with special needs and began interacting with her on a regular basis. He would involve her in dramatic play, manipulative play, art activities, and sensory play. He would want to help move her from one area to another and be with her when it was time to go outdoors. He began to declare to the teachers in the classroom that he really loved her and that she was his special friend. Her response to him was always a big smile! As one can see in this scenario, both children as well as the adults involved all grew from including this special child in the classroom.

SUPPORTING THE DEVELOPMENT OF ALL CHILDREN

All children have the right to be educated in the most appropriate, stimulating, child-oriented environment possible. All children deserve the opportunity to explore and discover. All children should have the opportunity to have as many different experiences as possible in order to determine what is exciting to them and what is accessible or can be made accessible to them.

Designing the Universal Curriculum

When children are in environments where everything that will happen in the classroom is predetermined by someone who does not work within that environment, there is a great likelihood that the development of all children in that classroom will not be supported. There is no way that anyone can design a universal package that will be able to address the needs of all children in all schools. Long lists of identified skills are often found in packaged curricula. That is usually what curriculum packages are—long lists of skills. These skills are usually addressed in activities that may or may not be tied to a theme. These activities are presented in some type of format that would have the consumer, the early childhood educator, believe that there was a real design behind the order or sequence of the activity ideas. There may be no order at all but rather what you might find is one activity for each of three or four objectives with none of the activities or objectives relating to the others.

Curriculum Kits

The importance of relatedness of activities in the education of young children should not be underestimated. Many different kinds of instructional "kits" that were extremely popular in the 1960s and 1970s were supposed to be self-contained curriculum packages. Some had pictures to be used with language or concept lessons, some had beads or pegs, some had puppets, and some had sorting activities. There usually was a detailed manual for the teacher to use that was designed as a script for the teacher to follow when presenting all the lessons or activities to the children. The most important lesson many teachers learned from being given these kits was that the kits could not be used to address all the needs of all the children in their classes. Many teachers used the materials in the kits to teach other lessons or as the basis for other teacher-made games. Some of the pieces of these kits began to migrate to other classrooms to the point that the author, as a consultant, when going in to different classrooms in the same building would find these pieces spread across several rooms with the teachers in the classroom not knowing that what they were using had once been part of a much larger instructional kit. Obviously, over time, this costly instructional tool gave way to curriculum of one sort or another that was better suited to the needs of the children and more compatible with the personality and teaching style of the teacher.

Integrated Curriculum is Adaptable

When one thinks of taking a standard or published curriculum and feels the immediate need to make adaptations to that curriculum because one realizes it will not support the needs of all the children in the class, what becomes obvious is that the development and implementation of the integrated curriculum approach makes perfect sense. Integrated curriculum is adaptation oriented. The reason it is adaptation oriented is because the curriculum is fluid, open ended, child oriented, and allows the teacher and the children to determine the types of activities and centers that work well for individual children, as well as for the entire group. This approach to curriculum recognizes that there many ways to reach individual children and many ways to present concepts and skill opportunities that are dynamic and exciting for children, as well as meaningful and relevant to their lives.

LANGUAGE AND LITERACY DEVELOPMENT

Language and literacy development is an integrated process that does not happen just through special lessons and special times of the day. Language and literacy development is an ongoing process that happens because of all the other things that take place in the environment surrounding a child. Prior to entering the school environment, children should have had many different kinds of experiences that support the development of language and literacy. They have heard people speak using language to ask questions, make declarations, express concern, and share information. They have seen people write to leave information for someone else, to make lists for themselves, and to record important information for future use. Children see people read what they have written as well as read what other people have written that has been published in books, magazines, newspapers, and other printed matter. All of these experiences serve to set the foundation for language and literacy development. Not all children are fortunate enough to grow up in such environments. What this usually means is that there are many children who come to school with language development levels that are below their chronological ages. If a five-year-old comes to school with a functioning language level of a three-year-old, one cannot approach the child in the same way and with the same materials as one would approach a five-year-old with the language development of a five-year-old.

Integrated Curriculum Supports Language and Literacy

The classroom environment that is rich with resources and based on an integrated curriculum, is one that naturally supports the development of language and literacy. This kind of environment will include print at an eye level that children can see and centers of activity that include activity-related, meaningful print such as signs and labels, things to write with and write on, books, pictures, storytelling, fingerplays, puppetry, dramatic play prop boxes, and varied process-oriented art activities. Teachers need to recognize drawing as an early step in literacy development.

Remember that all integrated curricula should start from that which is meaningful and appropriate relative to the interests and ideas of the children in the class. From this stems the language that relates to the theme, books that relate to the theme, and all the related activities that can be developed as the integrated curriculum evolves. This is the chief means by which teachers are able to infuse language and literacy into the content in the classroom. When an integrated curriculum is used to infuse language and literacy, the language that is used becomes important to the children and this importance will enhance the probability of the children acquiring the language and internalizing it into their active vocabularies.

Importance of Reading to Children

Books are a very important part of any environment for young children. No matter what the age of the children in the program, no matter what the population of children, no matter where the program is located, books are critical to the development of the children. Books are important sources of literacy stimulation for children. Children are interested in books long before they are able to read. The more access children have to books, the greater the likelihood that children will develop a love of reading and experience the delight and learning that comes from reading. In addition to reading aloud to children at school, one way to encourage early literacy development is to start a family lending library (Brock & Dodd, 1994).

Reading to children is such an important part of the early childhood curriculum and the overall development of young children that one should not think of letting one day go by without reading to the children at least once. Some children have had the wonderful experience of being read to regularly since the time they were infants. They are well acquainted with many books, have favorites, and "read" to themselves on a daily basis. Children know what books are for and hopefully have established a bond with books and reading that should serve them well for the rest of their lives. They understand the mechanics of reading, even though they do not read yet themselves. Children know that books convey stories usually through the words on the pages of the book. They may already know that these stories may be about real people and real places or they may be stories about "pretend" people and "pretend" places. Elster (1994) discusses the influence of read-aloud sessions—including both reading and discussion—on the emergent readings of preschool children. He suggests the following ways that teachers can promote active involvement in read-aloud and emergent reading (pretend reading) experiences in preschool and primary-grade classrooms:

1. Invite children to participate actively in read-aloud sessions;
2. Provide frequent opportunities for young children to engage in book handling and emergent reading;
3. Read favorite books repeatedly to encourage emergent reading, then make these books available for children to look at on their own or with other children and adults;
4. During read-aloud and independent-engagement times, teachers have opportunities to observe children's emerging literacy in authentic situations; and
5. Educate parents about the ability of their child to "pretend read" books and to participate in reading through "completion reading."

Teaching Reading Skills

Many parents and teachers are extremely concerned about the teaching of reading to young children. This concern often translates into the teaching of reading skills to children at a very early age. Many preschool teachers are asked whether they teach reading. Some parents ask whether the children will be taught their ABCs. They often compare programs for preschoolers and evaluate them based on which program engages in the most direct instruction of reading skills. When the response to this type of parent revolves around the fact that everything within a teacher's program prepares children for reading (i.e., that all activities could be called reading readiness), that is not what some parents want to hear. They do not want to hear about "print awareness" because they think you are skirting the issue of the teaching of reading.

Sometimes what is behind the parent questions concerning the teaching of reading is the fact that friends of the parents may have a child who is an early reader and this parent needs to have a child who is also an early reader. There is a responsibility to educate parents even before their children attend these programs. When a parent asks a question, the response should include the most current information based on the most current research and practice. One must help parents understand that all children are different and that often when a child is an early reader, there is no explanation as to how or why the child became an early reader.

All teachers need to remember that reading is a communicative process and that to read for the sake of reading, so that someone can check off a skill on a skill checklist, will not make reading meaningful, life-long, and enjoyable. Teachers and parents all need to think about the fact that once a child is able to read unassisted, there is still considerable enjoyment in hearing stories read aloud. Often, children hold back from letting others know that they can read because they have an idea that if the adults in the environment know they are able to read, that the reading aloud times are over. This should not be what happens. Children as well as adults love to be read to and parents and teachers should continue to read aloud to children through all their school years. At home, reading to children is often the quietest, coziest time of the day. In some families, it is also a private time for each child in the family. There may be one group story for all the children in the family followed by individual stories for each child.

Importance of Dramatic Play for Language and Literacy

Dramatic play is a wonderful, active, engaging means of stimulating and reinforcing language and literacy development. All dramatic play offers opportunities for children to talk and listen as well as engage in "reading" and "writing" activities. Children play out roles during the course of dramatic play. They sort out their worlds during this play and use a lot of language while playing their parts. Depending on the theme of the integrated curriculum, the dramatic play can take the form of working in a store, restaurant, or office. The children may set up a police station, firehouse, construction site, or museum. They may make price signs or direction arrows, write out menus, take orders, total bills, and give receipts. All of this activity reinforces language and literacy skills as the children use their language and "print awareness" to invest themselves in their roles (Campbell & Foster, 1993).

Some children who have no language at all begin to develop language around the dramatic play activities within the framework of an early childhood program implementing a thematic integrated curriculum. These might be children with delayed language development who do not respond to direct language intervention from adults but who will thrive on the indirect language stimulation and modeling provided by peers through the dramatic play environment. The opportunities for social interaction created by dramatic play multiply the potential for language and literacy development because involvement with peers places children in closer proximity to conversation with peers than almost any other type of activity within the early childhood classroom environment. More information about the role of dramatic play in the classroom is found in Chapter 8.

Importance of Conversation for Language and Literacy

Conversation is so much a part of daily life that people sometimes do not understand how meaningful conversation is to the development of language and literacy. Often, you see people talking at children rather than speaking with them. Granted that early conversations with young children are often very brief, these conversations set the tone for meaningful interchange between adults and children. Conversations allow children to know that adults are interested in what they have to say and what they have experienced. Sometimes it may seem as though children are always talking and that there is no silent time when particular children are around. Although this may be annoying to some people, the alternative of hearing no language at all from certain children may be even more distressing. One can always modify the behavior of children who talk incessantly, but it is much more difficult to get language going for a child who has no language at all.

Children who receive authentic responses from adults when they ask questions in conversation are children who will become better thinkers and speakers. Also, when teachers demonstrate sincere interest in what children have to say, children come to understand that what they have to say is interesting. More information about language and literacy appears in Chapter 11.

SOCIAL DEVELOPMENT

In classrooms that are activity oriented and are based on the thematic integrated curriculum approach, **social development** is a far more natural outcome than in classrooms where children work on skill development in a far more individualized, do-it-by-yourself atmosphere. Social development is critical in the early childhood years. It is almost expected that children will have developed all the basic social skills necessary for life when they leave the early childhood years. Social development is centered on the child's growing ability to become a part of group interactions. Social development is the natural result of daily experiences with peers and adults. This means that children need to develop verbal social skills as well as nonverbal social skills. Verbal social skills involve skill in asking and answering questions, ability to join in conversations in a socially appropriate manner, and ability to follow conversations. Just as in any other area of development, social development needs to be planned for and begins by helping children to know about themselves and about those around them.

Children first begin to learn about the world that surrounds them by exploring space and materials. They initially engage in this behavior by themselves. This is what is called **solitary or isolate play.** Children engaging in this type of play spend their time figuring out how things work, making appropriate sounds of the toys and equipment they use. Adults who join in this play have the potential for encouraging further social development and the development of the next stage of play, parallel play.

Parallel play involves two or more children playing in close physical proximity to each other but often not even acknowledging each other. Children involved in parallel play often use the same or similar toys. There is the potential for encouraging cooperative play from parallel play situations but not before children are ready to do so. Sometimes adults are too eager to move children into the next phase of social development at a pace which has the potential for setting them back. When children evidence an interest in other children, in what they are doing and what they are saying, then the time is right for facilitating cooperative play if it does appear to be happening spontaneously.

Cooperative play is not something that just happens naturally for all children. For some children, cooperative play needs to be highly encouraged or almost taught. For other children, cooperative play is a normal, natural outgrowth of solitary (isolate) and parallel play. What influences this natural progression of play development varies from child to child but some commonalities are obvious across the development of most children. Opportunities to play near and with other children is one of the best ways to encourage the development of cooperative play for children with and without disabilities. Children with disabilities should be encouraged toward maximum independence but in a context of as much as they need in order to function socially as well as possible (Brown, Althouse & Anfin, 1993). Adults in close proximity to the play who serve as facilitators for the play without directing the play enhance the level of sophistication of the play.

Providing children with the materials appropriate to use in cooperative play situations makes it much easier for children to become really involved in cooperative play. These materials are simply things that may be used by more than one child at a time or things that set the tone for play that requires more than one child at a time. These are not necessarily expensive materials and equipment but something as commonplace as cardboard boxes that two or more children can get in at a time, materials that suggest everyday household activities, transportation themes, or favorite stories. These types of play situations encourage children to play with each other because children do not have to compete for the one piece of equipment or try to flip the one switch that makes something run or push the one button that activates the motor.

Play is part of the continuum of social development that starts when a child is born. Children interact with people in their environments from the moment of their births. They use all the skills that they have to communicate with us. They communicate with their voices, their bodies and their facial expressions. They progress to using words instead of always using vocalizations. Their communication and social interactions take on a more stylized form. They play, teachers observe or interact with them during their play and continue to learn more and more about these children. Play is a child-centered activity that allows children to come to terms with personal experience in and knowledge of the physical and social world (Scales, Almy, Nicolopoulou & Ervin-Tripp, 1991). Play is indeed a critical component of social development.

Some children do not have things to play with or people with whom to play. Some children grow up in environments in which the adults are much more interested in having them gain academic skills and demonstrate those academic skills rather than develop in a more age-appropriate fashion within areas such as social development. Although children do develop "skills" within the social interaction and social awareness areas, many people do not know that these skills are the basis for the social behavior all adults are expected to exhibit throughout their adult lives.

The social skills that children develop in the early childhood years are more appropriately developed if they are directed to meaningful lifelong activities such as nurturing and caring for others (i.e., family play, hospital play, school), working cooperatively with others (i.e., restaurant, library, supermarket, bakery), or following a plan (i.e., construction site, planning a trip, going on a picnic). There are many other themes which children can play but these themes may not relate to the everyday social skills children will need in their later years. Additional play themes will receive attention in Chapter 8.

PHYSICAL DEVELOPMENT

Physical development refers to both the gross motor and fine motor development of young children. Physical development occurs in predictable patterns and sequences. Teachers need to be able to recognize the stages of development so they can adjust the curriculum to provide a good balance between practice and challenge (Hendrick, 1992). So much of what children do in the early childhood years entails either fine or gross motor activity or both. Gross or large motor activities include: crawling, creeping, scooting; walking; running, galloping, skipping; jumping, hopping, leaping; balancing; throwing, catching; climbing; using wheeled vehicles. Fine motor activities include: pouring; cutting; zipping, buttoning, snapping, tying; twisting, turning; holding and printing, tracing, painting; inserting.

Need for Daily Physical Activity

The physical development of children is of much concern today. Teachers need to plan daily opportunities for physical activity. It seems as though the more that is known about prenatal and postnatal development, the more aware one becomes of the potential pitfalls and hazards that may be encountered in the early years. There are many positive and negative influences on physical development once children are born. The foods children eat, the places in which they live, the air they breath, even the people they live with have the potential for helping as well as harming children. One cannot assume that children will develop normally within the physical domain due to many reasons including current family life-styles, air pollution, lead levels in the water, lead paint, asbestos contamination, and so forth.

With so many families putting in long working days, many children do not have the time at home with their families to go on long neighborhood walks or even play outdoors. Teachers need to assist families in encouraging the physical development of their children rather than allowing children to become couch potatoes early in their lives. Habits formed in the early years often become lifelong habits, so putting the effort into developing good habits in young children is well worth the effort. Many families live in situations in which children cannot easily go outdoors to play. Children may not have access to stairs to climb or places in which to run around. Some children are physically contained most, if not all of the day. When this happens, their physical development may be severely delayed or retarded. The result of this is seen in children who are not physically agile, children who are not skilled motorically, and whose overall development and self-concept may be hampered. Children who are not able physically are often left out of normal everyday activities. They are often not chosen by their peers in games situations because children do not want to lose. When children with low physical ability do have a choice of activity, they are apt to choose more sedentary activities because they see that other children are more skilled and able than they are and they are embarrassed to join in the activity for fear of ridicule or being physically hurt.

Sometimes children do not develop well physically because their physical development does not receive the same attention as does their language, cognitive or social development. These children will often try to reason with their parents or teachers as to the many reasons why they should not go for a walk, kick a ball, jump on a trampoline, or walk across a balance beam. Their intellectual prowess may be extremely convincing but teachers must make sure they do not succumb to the argument. Physical activity is important for all. It is very important for children to engage in physical activity for the release of energy, for the potential for social interaction, for the change of pace it provides, and for the pure physical stimulation. Children who are apprehensive of physical activity need to be encouraged to try to engage in the activity without any fear of ridicule. This requires an attempt to prepare the environment in which the physical activity is attempted. Preparing the environment for physical success means that the teacher needs to set up a variety of physical activities ranging in skill difficulty from a very simple activity to a much more sophisticated one. Planned movement experiences enhance play experiences (Avery, 1994). The sensitive teacher will make sure that the simple activity does not appear to be very simple so that the skilled child will not be tempted to make a remark concerning the simplicity of the activity level.

Importance of Fine Motor Activity

When planning for fine motor activity, many of the considerations should be the same to ensure that a child will not shy away from the activity. Children who are highly verbal and highly social may not be very well developed in the fine motor area. Often when the language, cognitive, and social come so easily, the fine motor skill may be a struggle for a child. When a child who is used to getting something right on the first try attempts a fine motor task and is not able to do it immediately, the child may never want to try again. Again, this may be due to lack of opportunity or fear of failure. In some families, where there is a real fear of the child being hurt from the use of scissors or a plastic knife, the child is never allowed to use these materials. Lack of use and lack of exposure to any motor tasks results in an inability to engage in the activity.

Role of Play in Fine and Gross Motor Development

Play is a very important feature in the development of both fine and gross motor skills. Rather than give children "exercises" to follow in order to stimulate the growth and development of certain muscles, play provides the ideal opportunity for children to "practice" certain muscle skills in a developmentally appropriate, meaningful manner. Some forms of play are more physically active than others (Avery, 1994). When children use clay or work with dough, they are developing their fine motor muscles in a manner that is so much more meaningful to them than if you asked the children to open and close their hands over and over again. One approach has meaning and the other is just an exercise. Just think of which one you might be apt to do more willingly. Keep this in mind when thinking of fine motor activities for children.

COGNITIVE DEVELOPMENT: THINKING AND PROBLEM SOLVING SKILLS

In the early childhood years, young children are expanding their knowledge about the world around them. This knowledge comes from observation of events, hands-on experience with concrete experiences, listening to peers and adults, and other encounters with the world. Children need exposure to concepts in math and science, social studies, and the arts in order to broaden their horizons. They learn from looking at and listening to books being read to them and stories being told to them. Goldhaber (1994) challenges the early childhood educator to be serious about play. She points out that there is a resurgence of interest in science education that should afford educators the opportunity to use the vocabulary of developmentally appropriate practice to explain the open-ended, cognitively challenging learning experiences that characterize their play-based programs. Goldhaber suggests that by calling it science teachers might be able to let children play.

Learning through Doing

Optimal **cognitive development** in children just does not happen. As with other areas of development, cognitive development needs to be planned for and encouraged. Since teachers know that children acquire concepts through manipulation, observation, and discovery, the environments provided for young children need to be based on learning through doing. Children need to be active procurers of information rather than passive recipients of information.

Role of the Teacher

The teacher serves a very important function in assisting children in cognitive development. The teacher makes plans for including both teacher-directed and child-directed experiences. All of these experiences fit very nicely into a thematic integrated curriculum approach. Considering the understanding as to how young children learn, it is up to the teacher to organize the cognitive environment so that children go from the more concrete to the more abstract concepts. The teacher will need to organize the environment to include experiences that will allow children to make observations, manipulate concrete materials, discuss their observation, test hypotheses, and make inferences. The teacher, within the integrated curriculum, will provide children with a variety of experiences so that there will be something of interest to each and every child. There will be activities provided at different levels so that the child who already knows a lot of information concerning a particular topic can go beyond that learning and the child for whom this is a first exposure will be comfortable with the experience and activity without being overwhelmed. In thinking about how challenging this may appear to be to a teacher who has never provided cognitive experience in this way, one has only to think about the alternative to be encouraged to attempt the integrated curriculum. In a more traditional approach to the presentation of cognitive curriculum, when a child already knows what is being taught, there are few alternatives provided for the child. The child is often told to draw or read, basically to keep busy and quiet, until the teacher and the class are done with what needs to be covered. A "good" child may actually do this, read or draw, but more typically, most children in the early childhood years would be more apt to create their own activity. The nature of this activity would probably have great potential for disrupting the class and eventually labeling the child as a behavior problem or troublemaker. Children deserve a lot better than waiting for the rest of the class to "catch up" to them. What each child deserves is a stimulating conceptual environment in which there is the potential for continued cognitive development through discovery learning.

OVERVIEW OF APPROPRIATE ACTIVITY AREAS

Although there is no magic formula for the perfect early childhood classroom, there are many different types of activities which have great potential for stimulating development in several areas at the same time. The object of providing an **activity-rich environment** in the early childhood years is to be able to provide enough variety of activity within the classroom. The activity-rich environment provides children, all children, no matter what the developmental level or whether the child has special needs or is a "normal" learner, with the opportunity for hands-on learning in a socially stimulating and personally rewarding environment. Some of the activities areas to be presented might be offered on a rotating basis, depending on space and the potential to supervise all of these activity areas. All of these activity areas have social potential in that they can be occupied by more than one child at a time and as such place children in closer proximity to the potential for social interaction. Some of these activity areas have a greater need for supervision than others. In the chapters that follow, each of these areas will be presented and discussed in great detail.

This listing and definition of each activity area is designed as an introduction to the areas and is intended to serve as an overview of the variety of activity to be discussed.

Sensory Area

The **sensory area** is an area of the room that can be as large or as small as space allows. It is an area that requires a certain amount of supervision depending on the nature of the materials provided for the children to use. Some of the materials that can be offered for exploration are: water, colored water, soapy water, ice cubes, sand, wet sand, cornmeal, dry pasta, cooked pasta, raw rice, raw popping corn, popped corn, potting soil, seeds, gelatin, beans, and styrofoam. A more detailed list of appropriate materials and experiences for the sensory area is provided in Chapter 6. The sensory area is important not only for the sensory stimulation it provides but also for the opportunity for observation, manipulation, verbal and nonverbal social interaction, and creative play.

Hollow Block Area

Hollow blocks are a basic component of any early childhood program. Through the use of these blocks, children may build concretely or creatively, engage in pretend play, or be realistic. Children may use these blocks independently, with one peer, or with a small group of peers. These blocks are made of solid, natural color wood and come in several sizes. These blocks have the potential for stimulating several different behaviors. They are important for cognitive development, language development, social development, and physical development, both gross and fine motor. More information about large hollow blocks and block play may be found in Chapters 7 and 8.

Dramatic Play

Dramatic play is a fluid area found within early childhood environments. While there may be one or more designated areas in which this type of play usually takes place, in actuality, dramatic play may happen anywhere in the early childhood environment, both indoors and outdoors. Dramatic play is thematic play that allows children to sort out the world in which they live. Children begin dramatic play in the early years. Signs of dramatic play may be found in most toddlers who "pretend" cook, talk on the phone, care for babies, drive the car, etc. These early signs indicate that the child is aware of his or her surroundings and is playing out what happens in the environment. Dramatic play can be very helpful to children who need to reenact experiences from within their environments.

Children reenact experiences that are joyful as well as experiences that are unpleasant or problematic. While this type of play usually occurs naturally, such play should also be purposefully encouraged and enhanced in early childhood programs (Essa, 1992).

Observation of dramatic play can assist teachers in getting to know more about the kind of living situation a child in the class may be in. This is certainly helpful when there is little contact between the teacher and the family. While dramatic play can be extremely insightful, it can also cause unnecessary alarm. The following is an example of a play situation that had potential for serious alarm.

CASE STUDY

A three-year-old highly verbal boy was observed playing in the housekeeping corner. He was part of a small class of 3–5-year-old children. This boy was observed playing with a baby doll and was seen placing the baby doll in the oven and in the refrigerator. A teacher who was facilitating play in this area of the room was initially alarmed and spoke to the child about what he was doing. She reoriented the play to help the child engage in more caring, nurturing behavior with the baby doll. The teacher was able to help the child to develop more appropriate behaviors for which the family was ever so appreciative. The teacher found out shortly after the baby in the oven episode that the family was expecting a second child and this little boy had recently heard of the "good news." Evidently, this little boy had not been so sure that this news was so wonderful. By working through his apprehensions concerning the situation and being helped to find another way to respond to babies long before the baby was born, this wonderful little boy was quite ready to receive his sibling with a much more positive set of behaviors. His parents reported no attempts to harm the baby once the baby and mother were at home. This boy may not have been in love with the idea of a sibling but he did not respond to the sibling in a negative manner.

Dramatic play allows children to try out different roles. Through this play, children are able to work on the distinction between reality and fantasy (Read, Gardner & Mahler, 1987). The youngest child in the family may choose to be the older brother while a child who may be the older brother may choose to be the baby when engaging in dramatic play. Teachers as participant observers can learn a lot about the children being taught by providing opportunities for them to engage in dramatic play.

You might wonder about how dramatic play relates to thematically based integrated curriculum for young children. What better way to reinforce concepts introduced throughout the classroom than through providing the opportunity for children to play out the roles related to the people, places, and things about which they learn. Community helpers, storybook characters, family, friends, travel, communication, and many other themes may all be developed into dramatic play opportunities that will serve to stimulate and reinforce information gathered over time.

Dramatic play also provides opportunities for socialization and creativity. Children create settings in which to engage in dramatic play as well as costumes for the roles they play. Their language is stimulated by this type of play and their fine and gross motor abilities are stimulated by the behaviors in which they engage in order to carry out a role. More discussion concerning dramatic play may be found in Chapter 8.

Book Area

Every classroom needs a **book area.** Book corners may be portable and flexible to accommodate the integrated curriculum theme being developed and implemented at the time. One of the most important features of a book corner in an early childhood classroom is the "softness" of the area. This means that the area, if the children are to sit in it, needs to have floor space for reading. Pillows and carpeting are always a welcome addition to the area. The book area should be large enough to accommodate an adult as well as children.

Another important consideration when developing a book corner is to set out books at a variety of levels and to include books that may be used independently by the children without fear of destruction of the books. The way in which children learn about how to handle books and the appreciation of books is through teacher and parent modeling of book use and book enjoyment. Children with disabilities may need to have access to books with sturdier pages to enable easier page turning, and larger color pictures or photographs as illustrations to encourage better visual attention. The child with considerable visual deficit may need to have books on tape to encourage interest in books.

Small Blocks and Accessories

Through the use of **small blocks,** children may make observations, compare and contrast, manipulate, build concretely or creatively, pretend, and be reality based. Children play what they know. This "knowing" comes from a variety of sources including the curriculum ideas presented in the classroom, classroom materials, and suggestions from peers (Reifel & Yeatman, 1991). Children may use blocks independently, with a friend, or with a small group of peers. Blocks are available in a variety of substances. There are solid, natural color wood blocks in many shapes and sizes, colored wooden blocks, hollow wood blocks, and cardboard blocks. Each type of block has the potential for stimulating several different behaviors. Blocks are important for cognitive development, language development, social development, and physical development, both gross and fine motor. Blocks can be used in infinite ways and as such are favorite materials to use because they are open-ended. Each day, blocks may be used differently and with different peers. A variety of accessories may be used in conjunction with block play to enhance and extend the play. This is what continues to make these concretely shaped materials creative and exciting to use. More information about blocks and block play may be found in Chapter 7.

Manipulatives

Children learn through using their hands to explore their environments. One way to encourage manipulation of materials is to provide children with many different types of **manipulative activities.** One look through any comprehensive early childhood catalogue will provide the early childhood teacher with many choices as to manipulative materials. Manipulative materials range from large pieces that are easy to put together to items with many small pieces that require much more eye-hand coordination, finger strength, and dexterity. Many manipulatives may be used with other children as well as independently. When these materials are used with other children, conversation, observation, planning, comparing, and cooperation are just some of the behaviors one could observe the children engaging in. In mixed-age groupings, younger children are stimulated by the creative endeavors of the older children and are often encouraged to stick with something that is challenging because of the behavior modeled by the older, more skilled children. When children use these materials independently, they may be observed spending long periods of time working on basics or working on something with extensive detail. Children often incorporate the theme being studied within the integrated curriculum into their work with manipulatives. Further discussion concerning the use of manipulatives in the early childhood curriculum may be found in Chapter 7.

Music and Movement

Music and movement are also very important components of the developmentally appropriate curriculum for young children because both of these activity-based areas of learning serve many functions in the development of the young child. Many of the things that teachers ask children to do in their early years are very precise and exacting in nature. To master tying one's shoes, one must follow precise steps. When a child indicates that the process is completed, one may instantly see whether or not the child was successful because the shoe is either tied or it is not tied. Exploration takes place within the areas of math and language arts but when skills are being developed in the academic areas of math and language arts, there are certain structures and specifics that are expected. There is little opportunity for creative expression in math because math answers are specific. There is opportunity for creative expression when a child engages in the open-ended creative writing process, but reading is exacting. This means that much of the time that children spend in school requires attention to detail and performing up to expectations. This is not always easy for any child. It may be even harder for children with special needs. That is why the integrated curriculum must include music and movement activities. Within music and movement activities, children may express themselves, create new and different songs and physical responses to music, and move the way they feel like moving. There is considerable opportunity for open-ended responses in these two areas. Music and movement activities offer opportunities for considerable joy in the course of the day. Children may enjoy both of these areas by themselves or with other children. Music and movement offer opportunities for sharing cultural diversity in an almost effortless manner. Music and movement are universal in nature and require very little in terms of materials and equipment. Detailed attention to these areas is found in Chapter 10.

MEET THE CHILDREN

It is always difficult to put a new conceptual framework into place in one's mind when reading about a new concept without seeing it in practice. If you are able to locate a developmentally appropriate program that implements thematic integrated curriculum, plan to visit this early childhood program whether it is found in the public schools or in the private sector. It is possible that this program includes children with special needs. If the program does not include children with special needs or if you are not able to locate a program based on the integrated curriculum approach, the following information will prove very helpful to you as you continue to learn about the process.

The following cases are introduced here so that you will become acquainted with some personalities who have been included in early childhood programs based on the integrated curriculum approach. These cases are based on actual children but some details have been changed so as to preserve the privacy of the individual children and their families. The vital individual child characteristics that are important to conveying the message of this text have been preserved. Reference to these cases will be made throughout the remainder of this book as each area of activity is detailed. The purpose of including these cases is to allow the reader to develop a more realistic vision of what inclusion means and what the integrated curriculum approach has to offer a teacher working with a diverse group of children during the early childhood period. In some of the cases, there was little that needed to change in the environment in order to accommodate the individual child. The case will still be included in the discussion concerning content specific content areas to demonstrate that some children and some areas of curriculum need little attention in order to foster inclusion.

CASE STUDY

Meet Anthony

Personal and Family Characteristics: Anthony is a boy with fair skin and very blond hair. He is three years old. He attends a multi-age preschool. He has a younger sister. Both his parents attended graduate school. They live in a suburban community.

Behavioral Characteristics: Anthony has a very unusual attention pattern, never looking at books or other visual displays. He listens intently to verbal stimulation which means that conversations that surround him, whether offered by adults or peers, holds his attention. He often repeats phrases out of context that he has heard in the conversations of others. At home he is able to relate the stories read to the children at school during the course of the day even though he never looked at the book and did not appear to be paying attention during the time the story was read. Anthony does not relate to the other children. He responds almost too well to the routine and schedule in his school. If the routine changes even the slightest bit, he becomes agitated. If the room arrangement is altered it is very unsettling to him. His speech is almost robot-like. He has begun to eat only certain foods, peanut butter most often being the food of choice.

Meet Sharon

Personal and Family Characteristics: Sharon is an eight-year-old girl with blond hair and an infectious smile. She is the middle child of three children in an intact family. She has cerebral palsy with associated visual deficits and learning disabilities. She is a highly verbal, very social child who participates in school and community activities, sleeps over at the homes of her friends, and attends summer camp. She uses a wheelchair and has been in integrated settings since she attended preschool. She has had many surgeries at several different hospitals over the years. Some of these operations took place in another state which meant there was real disruption to the child and her family in terms of routine and parental roles.

Behavioral Characteristics: When she was in preschool she was slightly oppositional but her teachers and her parents worked cooperatively to help her learn another way of dealing with her feelings, her frustrations, and her environment. Now that she is in a totally integrated, public school setting, she receives help from the resource room teacher and needs to use the computer for her written work. She uses large-print materials for some of her work. Other work is reproduced for her on the computer using larger fonts and more space provided between lines of print. Accommodations need to be made for her academic activities and physical education activities. She is independent in her use of her wheelchair.

Meet Charlie

Personal and Family Characteristics: Charlie is a handsome child with dark hair and dark eyes who is slightly built. He is the middle child of three children. He is seven years old. He lives in a suburban town with his siblings and parents. His parents did not know of his diagnosis of Down's Syndrome until his first birthday. His family has always included him in family and community activities. He is a skilled swimmer.

Behavioral Characteristics: After an experience in an early childhood special education program, he was enrolled in an integrated setting and has been in integrated settings ever since. His language is well developed, and his social skills are close to age appropriate. Although he is a quiet child, he is often seen as a leader as well as a follower. He receives academic support assistance from resource teachers and participates in adaptive physical education activities.

Meet Sarah

Personal and Family Characteristics: Sarah is a child who would probably not be labeled as a child with special needs but her behavior pattern certainly presents a challenge to her teachers and parents. She is the youngest of five children in a blended family. Her oldest sibling is away in college. Sarah is four years old.

Behavioral Characteristics: Sarah speaks to her mother when her mother picks her up from school, but never speaks to anyone at school, neither adults nor peers. She participates in play with the other children but not with the same level of energy or commitment the other children evidence. She smiles occasionally and laughs when something appears funny to her. She does not go to other homes for "play dates" and other children do not come to her home to play. Her parents are concerned about her social development and location-specific use of language but they are not distraught over the situation.

Meet Martie

Personal and Family Characteristics: Martie is an African-American child who lives with a foster family. He is five years old, very tall, well built, and very strong. He is prone to acting out behavior which often follows weekends of canceled visits with his biological mother. He had a very disrupted life prior to coming to live with this foster family. His living situation consisted of several foster homes mixed in with some attempts by his mother to try to have him live with her. The current living situation is the best one he has ever had.

Behavioral Characteristics: Martie appears to be bright. His academic skills are uneven, probably due to his disrupted early history. His language is "streety" but he certainly makes everyone understand his needs. Since he has been enrolled in this educational program, his behavior has gotten in the way of anyone getting close enough to him to make an assessment of his abilities. He is getting to the point where teachers and his peers can get closer to him. He does participate in most activities quite readily. Sometimes Martie meets transitions and routines with opposition and strong acting out behavior. Since he is very large and very strong, his behavior outbursts need to be managed with verbalizations as much as possible. His early history consisted of considerable physical punishment and restraint. He told one teacher that he was afraid of belts and hangers. One can only imagine too well why he has that fear.

Meet Christina

Personal and Family Characteristics: Christina is a tall six-year-old girl. She is the only child in her family. She has visual impairments and must wear her rather thick glasses at all times. She has a strong personality and has a history of oppositional behavior. She and her mother participated in a parent training program from the time she was two to three years old.

Behavioral Characteristics: She needs large-print materials and needs to sit close to the location of the focus of visual attention. During her preschool years which were spent in an integrated setting, she evidenced herself to be quite social and a little domineering. Some of this same behavior still exists but it appears to be diminishing over time.

Meet C.W.

Personal and Family Characteristics: C.W. is a charming little four-year-old boy who lives with his mother in the city. They have been forced to move several times in his short life due to the condition of the building in which they were living or due to their financial situation. He is extremely social, very caring, and very polite. He is curious and an active participant in all aspects of his preschool program. He seems to be unaware of his disabilities which consist of mild cerebral palsy and visual impairments.

Behavioral Characteristics: He is very well liked by all the children in his class and loved by some of the children. He is often found hugging other children by his initiation and being hugged by other children by their initiation. He can be slightly oppositional at times but can be redirected to more positive behavior and activity without too much adult effort. His self-help skills appear to be developing well. He is toilet trained with only occasional accidents that appear to have more to do with his physical disability than his developmental level. C.W. is beginning to exhibit a longer attention span relative to books and large-group activities. He engages in longer conversations with peers and adults and sits for long periods of time working on puzzles and other manipulatives which really challenge his motor disability. He takes great pride in task completion and wants to do most tasks independently.

SUMMARY

An early childhood educator is a person who is knowledgeable about typical and atypical child development, models of early childhood curriculum from historical to current times, the workings of families, the workings of schools, current issues in the field, the role of the teacher as the facilitator of development and learning, and the person who is able to apply all that information to the public school or community-based early childhood classroom with infants, toddlers, preschool age children, or children from kindergarten through grade three. This may include work with children, parents, other educators, specialists, social workers, therapists, and community agencies.

The early childhood educator is key to the success of the integrated curriculum because this person is in the early childhood classroom. The early childhood educator is an observer, facilitator, organizer, and innovator. Success in the classroom according to this approach is measured by observing the following in the children: involvement, productivity, enthusiasm, self-esteem, social skills, literacy development, both oral and written communication skills, problem-solving skills, and independence in a social and learner sense.

Through the implementation of integrated curriculum, the early childhood educator is able to reach out to all children in the classroom. Through adaptations and modifications in the activities provided, all children may be involved within the range of their own abilities and styles. The teacher measures the success of the total program based on the progress children make against developed goals and objectives.

Planning a new unit of study follows the following format:

select a theme

brainstorm ideas for activities and centers

identify appropriate objectives

research appropriate books to be shared with the children and to be used by the children independently

obtain materials and equipment necessary to carry out the activities

When implementing a child-centered curriculum, focusing too much on children's immediate interests and needs without focusing on the critical concepts and social goals of language and literacy might lead to large gaps between concepts. Learning is a continuum and as such must proceed along a logical path. One way to accomplish this is to select thematic organizers that are broad based enough such as: learning about "me," the family, the community, animals, etc. that allow the teacher to build upon prior knowledge and connect concepts for children so that they are not learning about concepts in isolation.

One reason children come to school is for the experience of socialization. Some children have peer experiences prior to attending school that might have been gained through a variety of experiences. Development of social relationships with children seen on a daily basis over an entire year might be quite different. Some children have an intuitive sense of how to interact with peers with different personalities. They seem to be able to analyze the social situations, plan their mode of operation, and follow through with their plans. Some children come to school with few or no social skills. A combination of peers and adults can help these children to grow and develop into socially adept beings.

Children have the powerful potential to nurture other children. Because some demonstrate a great degree of empathy at an early age, some children with disabilities respond more positively to peers than adults. Children able to nurture others are able to serve as facilitators of inclusion.

There are several areas of development that should be addressed within the early childhood classroom. These domains include language and literacy development, social development, physical development, and cognitive development and are the focus of concern when developing individualized educational plans for children with disabilities. There are many different types of activities which can be provided to support development in all domains. These activity areas include: sensory, hollow blocks, dramatic play, books, small blocks and accessories, manipulatives, and music and movement activities.

DISCUSSION QUESTIONS

1) Discuss the role of the early childhood teacher with regard to the development and implementation of integrated thematic curriculum.
2) You have a small classroom. You want to provide a variety of activity areas but have limited space. Brainstorm ways to provide a variety of activity areas within the space constraints you have.

3) You are planning to have a parent meeting soon. It is the first one of the year. You want the program to inform parents about the integrated curriculum approach. What are the key elements you will stress in order to have parents understand what goes on in your classroom on a daily basis?
4) You observe a child being very responsive to a child with disabilities. The responsive child is eager to help and seems to have a sense of appropriate helping. How can you nurture the situation to the benefit of both children?
5) A salesperson calls and attempts to sell you a language development kit that contains books, puppets, picture cards, and a teacher's manual. What is your response to this salesperson? Why?
6) Is it vital to address all areas of development within the early childhood years? Is it appropriate to develop an early childhood program that specializes on one or more areas? Why or why not?

REFERENCES

Avery, M. (1994). Preschool physical education: A practical approach. *Journal of Physical Education, Recreation & Dance, 65*(1), 37–39.

Berry, C. & Mindes, G. (1993). *Planning a theme-based curriculum: Goals, themes, activities, and planning guides for 4's and 5's*. Glenview, IL: GoodYear Books.

Brock, D., & Dodd, E. (1994). A family lending library: Promoting early literacy development. *Young Children, 49*(3), 16–21.

Brown, M., Althouse, R., & Anfin, C. (1993). Guided dramatization: Fostering social development in children with disabilities. *Young Children, 48*(2), 68–71.

Campbell, E., & Foster, J. (1993). Play centers that encourage literacy development. *Day Care and Early Education, 21*(2), 22–26.

Deiner, P. (1993). *Resources for teaching children with diverse abilities—Birth through eight*. Fort Worth: Harcourt Brace Jovanovich Publishers.

Dodge, D. T. (1989). *The creative curriculum for early childhood*. Washington, DC: Teaching Strategies, Inc.

Doescher, S., & Sugawara, A. (1989). Encouraging prosocial behavior in young children. *Childhood Education*, 65, 213–216.

Dolinar, K., Boser, C., & Holm, E. (1994). *Learning through play: Curriculum and activities for the inclusive classroom*. New York: Delmar Publishers Inc.

Eliason, C., & Jenkins, L. (1994). *A practical guide to early childhood curriculum*. New York: Merrill.

Elster, C. (1994). "I guess they do listen": Young children's emergent readings after adult read-alouds. *Young Children, 49*(3), 27–31.

Essa, E. (1992). Introduction to early childhood education. Albany, NY: Delmar Publishers Inc.

Goldhaber, J. (1994). If we call it science, then can we let them play? *Childhood Education, 71*(1), 24–27.

Hendrick, J. (1992). *The whole child.* New York: Merrill.

Jones, E., & Nimmo, J. (1994). *Emergent curriculum.* Washington, DC: National Association for the Education of Young Children.

Kostelnik, M., (Ed.). (1991). *Teaching young children using themes.* Glenview, IL: GoodYear Books.

Krogh, S. (1995). *The integrated early childhood curriculum.* New York: McGraw-Hill, Inc.

Nachbar, R. (1992). What do grown-ups do all day? The world of work. *Young Children, 47*(3), 6–12.

Neuman, S., & Roskos, K. (1993). *Language and literacy learning in the early years: An integrated approach.* Fort Worth: Harcourt Brace and Jovanovich College Publishers.

Read, K., Gardner, P., & Mahler, B. (1987). *Early childhood programs: Human relationships and learning.* New York: Holt, Rinehart and Winston.

Reifel, S., & Yeatman, J. (1991). Action, talk, and thought in block play. In B. Scales, M. Almy, A. Nicolopoulou & S. Ervin-Tripp, *Play and the social context of development in early care and education* (pp. 156–171). New York: Teachers College Press.

Scales, B., Almy, M., Nicolopoulou, A., & Ervin-Tripp, S. (1991). *Play and the social context of development in early care and education.* New York: Teachers College Press.

Trostle, S., & Yawkey, T. (1990). *Integrated learning activities for young children.* Boston: Allyn & Bacon.

Workman, S., & Anziano, M. (1993). Curriculum webs: Weaving connections from children to teachers. *Young Children, 48*(2), 4–9.

ADDITIONAL READINGS

Christie, J. (Ed.). (1991). *Play and early literacy development.* New York: State University of New York Press.

Gallas, K. (1994). *The languages of learning: How children talk, write, dance, and sing their understanding of the world.* New York: Teachers College Press.

Goelman, H., & Jacobs, E., (Eds.). (1994). *Children's play in child care settings.* New York: State University of New York Press.

Jones, E., & Reynolds, G. (1992). *The play's the thing: Teachers' roles in children's play.* New York: Teachers College Press.

Klugman, E., & Smilansky, S. (Eds.). (1990). *Children's play and learning: Perspectives and policy implications.* New York: Teachers College Press.

Rogers, C., & Sawyers, J. (1988). *Play in the lives of children*. Washington, DC: National Association for the Education of Young Children.

Roopnarine, J., Johnson, J., & Hooper, F. (Eds.). (1994). *Children's play in diverse cultures*. New York: State University of New York Press.

Wassermann, S. (1990). *Serious players in the primary classroom: Empowering children through active learning experiences*. New York: Teachers College Press.

CHAPTER 5

Art

KEY TERMS

creativity
Reggio Emilia
stages of artistic development
process
appropriate art environment

IMPORTANCE OF ART ACTIVITIES FOR DEVELOPMENT

What is art is a question that has certainly been debated by artists, critics, historians, and collectors for thousands of years. When one thinks of art, one usually thinks of creative work or the making and doing of things that have beauty. What is then difficult to determine is the definition of beauty. Beauty is not perceived in a universal manner. What is beautiful to one individual is not always beautiful to another. If beauty were universal, there would be few colors, few styles, and far less variety in the world. The perception of beauty is also culturally based. Children from diverse cultural backgrounds have exposure to different art forms and different experiences during the course of their development. Diverse cultural experiences will impact on the art children produce. Teachers need to be sensitive to the personal nature of art that is created on the basis of what a child has seen, heard, touched, tasted, and smelled. To have expectations of what something should look like when it is completed is to ignore the nature of personal experience and individual differences.

Creativity in Art

Creativity in art is often defined as making something different, something that has not been created before. This creativity is evidenced in the form, line, color, use of space, composition, movement or motion, use of a variety of media, and many other factors. Creativity may also be looked at relative to the individual differences within children. Although children develop along similar paths, each child is unique and that which is new and different in the art an individual child creates can be defined as creativity for that particular child. Just as the concept of beauty may be defined by cultural differences, so may creativity be influenced by cultural differences. When teachers are sensitive to the fact that what children create in the process of using art materials need not conform to a predetermined standard set by the teacher, children will probably be more involved in art activity. At the **Reggio Emilia** schools in Italy a teacher who is trained in the visual arts works closely with the other teachers and the children in every preprimary school and visits the centers for infants and toddlers. A special workshop space is set aside in these schools and is used by all the children and teachers. The space contains a great many tools and resource materials along with records of past projects and experiences. In the view of the teachers who work in these programs, children's expression through many media is not a separate part of the curriculum but is inseparable from the whole cognitive and symbolic expression in the process of learning (Gandini, 1993).

Developmental Stages in Art

Much has been written about the artistic development of children by several authors considered experts in the field (Kellogg, 1970; Lowenfeld, 1947; Goodenough, 1926). These authors report that children pass through predictable **stages of artistic development** just as they pass through predictable stages of development in the physical, language, social, emotional, and cognitive domains. These predictable stages include:

- Stage One: Random Scribbling
  The child makes large arcs on the paper. The child has no visual control over where the marks go. The entire body moves as the

child paints or draws. This motor involvement is very important to development.

- Stage Two: Controlled Scribbling
  There is a greater variety of scribbles. The movements get smaller as the child begins to use the wrist. Visual control begins. The child maintains visual contact with the art work until it is completed.
- Stage Three: Named Scribbling
  At this point, children have in mind what the picture is. For the most part adults do not recognize what the child made. What the child draws is a symbol of something in the environment. This is evidence of abstract thought on the part of the child.
- Stage Four: Early Representational
  The drawings begin to look like the objects they represent. Objects are not proportional. The largest object is the one that is the most important to the child. The way the child handles the brush, crayon, or marker is more adult like than child like.
- Stage Five: Preschematic
  Objects are more proportional. There is a right side up to the paper and a base line develops. The child is using wrist and fingers and uses an adult grip on the drawing instrument. There is a relationship between the point at which a child uses closed forms in drawing and is ready to use closed forms in writing.

The Value of Art for the Young Child

One must also consider the contribution art makes to the development of the young child (Gardner, 1982). The recognition of the importance of art as it relates to the development of the young child dates back to the late 1800s when Froebel introduced art into the kindergarten classroom. In the 1920s, art teachers, who supported the ideas conveyed by Dewey began to recognize the worth of a child's self expression in art. No longer was it deemed necessary to only work on developing exacting representations in art. It was now beginning to be acceptable to consider something referred to as "child art." This "radical" concept did not become popular until after the Second World War. It is now recognized that authentic expression through art is rarely achieved without opportunity, active facilitation, and acceptance from adults (Chapman, 1978). Art activity provided within the framework of developmentally appropriate curriculum is not skill oriented or academic. It is process oriented and involves cognitive growth. It is critical that children have opportunities for cognitive growth that come from their own creation and design. Art brings the personal dimension of feeling, sensitivity, empathy, and expression to the education program. In this age of information explosion teachers must ensure that children are not bombarded only with words aimed at teaching them things. Children should be exposed to information through all of their senses. People send and receive information through all of their senses. These senses are used to interpret information. Therefore it is important to develop all sensory languages in children as well as the more typical written and verbal language. Art needs to be thought of as one of the basics of early childhood education and not one of the frills. Whether a young child is developing normally or has special needs, art activity has the potential to bring much joy and learning to the child.

The Value of Art in the Integrated Curriculum

Art activities play an important role in the integrated thematic curriculum. Through art, children are able to demonstrate what they learn about the themes they study. When children are given an opportunity to draw, paint, or collage they further develop their art skills while expressing their own ideas about concepts learned. Art may be used as a means of assessment and compared over time. More information about art as means of assessment may be found in Chapter 15.

OBJECTIVES OF ART ACTIVITIES FOR CHILDREN WITH AND WITHOUT DISABILITIES

An art program of quality should begin in the preschool years and continue throughout the school years. The art program during the early childhood period should provide for the developmental needs of young children regardless of their rate of development. These needs focus on the perceptual, emotional, aesthetic, and creative areas and can best be fostered through visual and tactile perceptual experiences, the production of art, opportunities for the aesthetic judgment and valuing of art, and discussions and activities focusing on the heritage of art (Herberholz, 1985). In order to accomplish these goals Herberholz suggests that teachers provide experiences in:

- examining intensively both natural and man-made objects from many sources and through a variety of means
- expressing individual ideas and feelings through the use of a variety of art media suited to the manipulative abilities and expressive needs of the child
- experimenting in depth with art materials and processes to determine their effectiveness in achieving personal expressive form
- working with tools appropriate to the students' abilities, in order

to develop manipulative skills needed for satisfying aesthetic expression
- organizing, evaluating, and reorganizing work-in-process to gain an understanding of the formal structuring of line, form, color, and texture in space
- looking at, reading about, and discussing works of art including painting, sculpture, constructions, architecture, industrial, and handcrafted products using a variety of educational media and community resources (Herberholz, 1985)

During the early years of development, children with and without disabilities encounter many experiences that require them to learn exact information. What is unique about the area of art is that what children create during art experiences is purely their own expression. There is really no right or wrong. An adult cannot say that the painting or drawing needs to be done over again because when a child declares the work to be complete, it is complete. It is important to allow children to talk about their art experiences. That is not to say that teachers should ask them to tell what they have just made but rather to invite them to talk about the **process** they used to create something or how they felt while they were creating their art. This sends a message to children that the process of the art experience is as valuable as the product produced. It validates the participation of the child and thus values the child. The product on the piece of paper is not critical. Kuschner (1989) shares the viewpoints of several professionals in early childhood (Klein, Kantor & Fernie, 1988; Spodek, 1986; and Suransky, 1982) who point out that the manner in which a child comes to believe what is important comes from the value messages delivered by adults. If teachers want to cultivate a child's interest in art activity, they must promote the child's interest in that art activity with language and behavior that indicates support.

There are many things one is able to learn from observing a child in the process of creating a work of art. One may assess a child based on the use of space, selection of color, control of paint or other media, or articulation about the creation. Just observing the child in the process of creation affords the opportunity to see whether the child is somewhat impulsive or more reflective. This observation may yield information concerning a child's comfort level, spontaneity, independence, or previous experience with art materials. Listening to what a child has to say about the process employed to create the work of art adds insight into the language and conceptual development of the child. It will also tell you about how the child feels about himself or herself and how comfortable the child is in sharing experiences. One must be careful about reading into what a child creates or says about what has been created.

CASE STUDY

An incident concerning the use of color occurred once when a parent called a teacher, obviously quite upset about all the black drawings her child had come home with over the last two weeks. The parent was ready to take the child to a psychiatrist to be treated for depression because she had read somewhere that the use of black in drawings is an indicator of depression. This surprised the teacher who thought of this child as a very happy, secure child. The teacher urged the mother to wait a few days before taking action so that a few classroom observations could be made. The mother agreed to wait. Several days later, the teacher reported to the mother. She had observed the child during art opportunities. Each day, the child waited until all the other children had gone up to the front of the room to select crayons from the cans in which they were stored. Each can held a different color. What the teacher observed was that this child went straight to the can of black crayons and selected one or two of these crayons to use. After observing this for several days, the teacher asked the child why she did not choose any of the other colors. The child replied that she liked crayons with points and wrappers. Since all the other children rushed to use all the other colors, those crayons no longer had points or wrappers. This child obviously knew what was most important to her and followed through on it. When the teacher was finished relating this story to the mother, the mother laughed and indicated that she had to agree that her daughter certainly did have a mind of her own and was not easily influenced by her peers. The mother thanked the teacher for her observations and support of the child being able to follow her own mind. Sometimes, the choice of color of paper or paint for a project is not made by a child but rather dictated by what is left in the supply cabinet by that time of the year.

Teachers must not jump to conclusions without gathering the facts. Conclusions made on the basis of one observation are often erroneous. A teacher became alarmed when talking with a child about the drawing she had made of her family. The teacher noticed that all the family members were represented except for the child. When the teacher asked the child why she had not included herself in the picture the child revealed that the picture was her "family" and she was "herself." To this child, the family was the rest of those people who lived with her. She did not feel the need to include herself in the picture because everyone knew she lived there too. After all, that was how they got to be her family! For this child there was no problem with self concept; just a matter of semantics.

DEVELOPMENTALLY APPROPRIATE ACTIVITIES AND MATERIALS

What needs to be considered when planning for developmentally appropriate art activities and art materials? Developmentally appropriate art implies that children can have a reasonable sense of freedom to explore the materials and activities without constant supervision from an adult in the environment. There are certain materials and activities that are not safe for young children. This requires knowledge by the teacher that the materials are non toxic and are "user friendly." Some examples of "user friendly" materials might be crayons, some markers, play dough, clay. It also means that the materials and activities are open-ended enough for children to explore and discover while being able to use the materials in an individual manner.

Creating an Appropriate Art Environment

An **appropriate art environment** for young children requires that the teacher(s) create an area of the room in which art materials and other related equipment and resources are available to the children with minimal teacher intervention. The art area, if at all possible, should include ready access to water, easel(s), and table art activities. There should be a variety of materials such as markers or crayons, easel painting, and possibly collage for children to use but all of the art materials in the classroom should not be available at the same time. When too many choices are available at one time, children might find themselves overwhelmed by the necessity of making a decision about the color paper to use or whether to use paints, markers, or crayons.

Demonstrations on Safe Use of Materials

Children may need demonstrations on how to use certain materials in a safe manner. Younger children may need to be told or reminded that paints and paste go on the paper and not in their mouths. They may need guidance in using scissors so that they do not cut themselves or their hair. Children need adults in the environment to facilitate their involvement in art activities without creating models that they are not able to reproduce. When a child sees a creation completed by an adult, that completed creation may serve as a model for the child to imitate. Even though the teacher may tell the child to use the materials in any way, the child may still try to reproduce what the teacher created. When this cannot be accomplished, there is bound to be frustration on the part of the child. There may even be an unwillingness to participate in the activity at all.

Art as a Process Not a Product

Providing an environment in which art activity is a process and not a product affords children the opportunity to engage in these activities to the best of their abilities and the extent of their interests. Children who are in environments in which there is a required daily project with the resulting projects looking the same, are often likely to be very disinterested in the art activities offered. Sometimes children wind up detesting these activities and thus they may lose out on several levels. They may lose out in:

developing a love for producing art

developing an appreciation of art necessary to be a current and future consumer of art

experiencing the potential that art activity has for enhancing the development of fine motor skills, language skills, social skills, perceptual skills, and

knowing the opportunity art provides for the expression of feelings and experiences.

This opportunity for expression is of critical value for all children but certainly for children with emotional difficulties. Often, children draw, paint, or sculpt what they cannot tell you. What a child creates through artistic activity cannot be censored, denied, or criticized.

Role of the Teacher

The role of the adult relative to the provision of a developmentally appropriate art program is to present the materials and activities in an inviting manner and to support and encourage children to become involved in the process. Once the involvement is established, the role of the teacher is to continue encouraging and supporting the child. Some of this encouragement is accomplished through feedback and some through appropriate questioning techniques that attempt to elicit discussion from the child without asking for exacting information. The role of the adult is not to tell the child that what has been created is "garbage" because the child colored outside the lines. Teachers should certainly support children through feedback about their artwork but the feedback must not be corrective or punitive in nature. The feedback also needs to be of such a nature that allows the child the license to continue with the creation without the burden of hearing that "this is the most beautiful painting I have ever seen." When a child hears that this work being created is the most beautiful, the most colorful, etc. the child may feel as though this is the last piece of artwork he or she will ever produce because there can never be anything better. Some children are sensitive to the fact that this particular adult says similar things to all children about all of their artwork and the insensitivity serves to turn the child away from artistic endeavors.

Questioning children about the art work they are in the midst of creating or have finished creating is also very tricky.

CASE STUDY

On a particular day, during the time that the easel was available, a child made several large circular strokes on the paper with the blue paint. A teacher asked the child what he was painting. After hearing this question the child appeared apprehensive. After several minutes and false starts, the boy told the teacher that what he made was a blue bagel. The teacher was wide eyed and asked the child to tell her more about the painting. The boy appeared unsure of how to respond and seemed to be thinking hard about what else he could tell the teacher about his work. After a while he continued with the story adding that the blue bagel was rolling down the hill to get away from the monster. The teacher did not press any further. The boy seemed relieved. One can argue that this interaction between teacher and child encouraged creativity on the part of the child. In actuality, the creativity was in the story the child developed in response to what he thought was a command to tell the teacher about his painting. What the child painted was large blue circular motions. He was experimenting with the paint, the brush, and the paper. He began to paint without a plan as to design, use of space, or idea of what the end product would look like. What he felt forced into doing was defending his actions. This does little to encourage further exploration. What might encourage a child to talk about what they have done is for the teacher to ask the child if there is anything he or she would like to tell about the drawing or painting in progress or just completed.

Some children stay away from art materials. They seem to think that the paint, markers, or crayons will permanently change the color of their skin or stain their clothing. Sometimes the child seems concerned about this permanent change to skin or clothing due to a voiced warning from the parent before starting the school day. A parent may mean well in cautioning a child to be careful about getting dirty with the reminder that dirty clothes means not being able to go out to dinner after school. The message serves to inhibit activity on the part of the child. A parent may remind a child to "make something nice for Mommy today!" The child may avoid making anything at all rather than make something that the parent might perceive as less than pretty. Some teachers relate that they occasionally encounter parents who throw the child's artwork in the trash while exiting from the classroom at the end of the day. This does little to encourage the child's exploration in the art area.

When a teacher encounters a parent who does not appreciate child art, it is critical that information be shared with parents concerning the importance of what the child is doing. In addition to the message being delivered to parents, the classroom environment should provide for a special place for the child to display and store artwork. Enabling a child to keep a portfolio of artwork in the classroom delivers the message to the child that this work is very special and should be kept in a special place. Children should be allowed to decide what will be kept in the portfolio. Maintaining a portfolio is an appropriate idea for all children. Often, teachers wish they could hold onto some artwork from each child to use as part of an overall assessment of the child. Establishing a process by which a child may decide what stays in the portfolio and what goes home will make this possible. Another way to establish maintaining some art in the portfolio is to declare that once a week, each child must put something in the portfolio. It may be exchanged with another creation at another time, but at least there will always be several items in there.

Displaying Children's Art Work

Children often want to take all their artwork home. They enjoy seeing their creations displayed in their homes. They enjoy the accolades they receive from their extended families. Other children often do not want to take their work home. Sometimes this is due to the fact that there is no space for displaying the art in the home. Other times, it is due to the fact that the artwork is not appreciated by the family. The family may not understand the importance and value of the work and they may ridicule the child by making comments about the work. Teachers should help parents understand the importance of the creations the children bring home. They need to help parents to value what the child does.

Regardless of whether the child wants to take artwork home or not, it is essential to display artwork within the classroom environment. Care should be given to rotating the display so that each child has an opportunity to be in the limelight from time to time. The work should be displayed at various eye levels so that all children, ambulatory or nonambulatory, have the opportunity to study what they have created as well as the chance to study the work of others. When artwork is displayed with children in mind, children are able to develop appreciation for art and begin to develop appropriate museum behaviors. Each work should have the name of the child posted next to it so that children receive proper credit for their work.

CASE STUDY

A first grade teacher with particular interest in art history introduced her children to the work of a famous impressionistic painter. All of this came about quite spontaneously. It was her practice each Monday morning to ask the children about their weekend activities. One Monday morning, one of the children asked this teacher about her weekend and whether she had done anything special. The teacher told the children about the special art exhibit she attended in a museum in another state. The children seemed interested and she promised them that the next day she would bring some of the prints and stationery she had purchased at the exhibit. After the children viewed these items the following day, they asked many questions about the techniques the artist used. They then began experimenting with impressionistic techniques as compared with the way they painted previously. While they were actively engaging in producing artwork, they spent time studying about the artist. They then planned and implemented an impressionistic museum, made invitations to be sent to their parents and important townspeople. They made programs, learned how to act as docents, and made refreshments to serve at the grand opening of their museum. What began as a simple question developed into a wonderfully enriching adventure. This course of study involved math, science, and social studies as well as language arts and the arts. This creative, resourceful teacher was sensitive to the level of interest and ability of her students. She was able to present sophisticated information to the children in a very age-appropriate manner. This is a wonderful example of the development of a thematic unit that stemmed from the interest of the children in the class. If the teacher had planned this unit based on her own interest in art history, it would have had a very different tone to it and might not have been enjoyed by all the children.

Appropriate Art Materials and Activities

The following materials and activities are most appropriate for children in the early childhood period. It is important to remember that children need teachers to help them learn appropriate ways of using materials. Teachers set the tone that encourages excitement about exploration without the exuberance turning into a big mess.

Painting

The process of painting allows a child to explore color, different strokes and shapes, the use of space, the creation of designs using different size shapes and strokes and the freedom to use large motions. Often, painting is taken for granted because it is a common activity. One must remember that painting at an easel or on other surfaces is not available to all children outside of the school experience. It is inappropriate to assume that with all the art supplies available in neighborhood stores, that families are making these materials available to their children at home. Some families find providing art activities in the home somewhat difficult due to time, space, or money constraints. Some people may think that art activities have the potential of creating a mess that is not easily cleaned up. Some people are uncomfortable with art because they have limited experience with it themselves. If this is the case, a "parent night" with opportunity to explore the media available to children might be just what is needed in order to remove the barriers that exist.

Painting may be done by children on an individual basis, with a friend, as a group mural, or in individual pieces and then put together as a story or in quilt fashion. Painting may be done to a musical background, a drum beat, with eyes open or shut. No matter how painting is introduced, the process of painting is one that provides opportunity for considerable growth on the part of the child. Observations of the process of painting will often reveal that there are several layers to a painting. Sometimes when children begin to paint very representational people, they begin each person with detail to the anatomy and then paint on clothing. If the teacher is not nearby when the painting occurs, the under layer might never be discovered.

Painting Liquids.
Painting may be done with a variety of liquids including tempera paints, finger paints, and water colors. In addition, painting may be done with food dyes, glue, and liquid shoe polish.

Painting Textures.
Different textures may be added to the paints to vary the experience. These textures may include sand, sawdust, powdered soap, or glue.

Painting Tools.
Painting may be done with a variety of brushes and other tools including long handled brushes, short handled brushes, wide tip brushes, thin tip brushes, foam brushes, tooth brushes, small rollers, feathers, feather dusters, cotton swabs, sponges, toothpicks, roll-on deodorant bottles, eye droppers, shoe polish applicators, blocks of wood, tongue depressors, popsicle sticks, branches, hands, feet, pipe cleaners, cotton balls, string, marbles, or straws.

Painting Surfaces.
Various surfaces may be used for painting. The following list offers suggestions as to what is commonly available and appropriate for children in

the early childhood period to use: newsprint, butcher paper, construction paper, textured paper, fingerpaint paper, paper bags, paper towels, cardboard, sandpaper, paper plates, wallpaper, wrapping paper, corrugated paper, shelf paper, cloth, paper doilies, acetate transparencies, cardboard tubes, bristol board, rocks or stones, and boxes of all sizes. Fingerpainting may be done directly on a washable table surface and prints may be taken from the table. This allows a child to experiment for a long time before making a print.

Printing.
Paints may also be used for printing activities. Vegetables and fruits are appropriate for printing. In addition, stamps, potato mashers, forks, erasers, clay designs, paraffin and soap printing, corks, spools, and other gadgets make for interesting prints. Sponges cut into shapes that relate to themes being explored are also appropriate for printing. Printing may also be done with buttons that have been glued to wooden dowels. Varying the size and shape of the buttons results in interesting prints.

Drawing
Drawing may be done with a variety of tools on a variety of surfaces. All of these possibilities afford children the chance to express themselves in ways that words may not allow at the time.

Drawing Tools.
Tools for drawing are also varied and may include crayons, craypas, chalk, colored pencils, and washable markers. Once again, varying the type of surface on which the drawing is done challenges the child and provides the stimulation necessary for extended exploration. When using chalk, wetting the paper or dipping the chalk in water, buttermilk, or a sugar-water solution makes the painting more vivid and helps the chalk to adhere to the paper.

Drawing Surfaces.
There is almost no end to the surfaces on which children are able to draw. Each surface type provides the child with another experience, another challenge. The variety of surfaces include newsprint, butcher paper, construction paper, textured paper, wax paper, crepe paper, tracing paper, steamed mirrors, fogged windows, fingerpaint paper, paper bags, paper towels, cardboard, sandpaper, paper plates, wallpaper, wrapping paper, corrugated paper, shelf paper, cloth, paper doilies, acetate transparencies, cardboard tubes, bristol board, rocks or stones, and boxes may be used for painting.

Collage
Collage is a very versatile medium for young children that involves pasting small objects, papers, fabric pieces, etc. down on paper, cardboard, or

another surface. Initially, children may make collages using materials collected or prepared by teachers. As children develop tearing and finally cutting skills, they may find and prepare their own materials.

Collage materials.
Materials to collage with may include nature objects, construction paper, ribbons, glitter, sequins, magazine pictures, tissue paper, recyclables, dried flowers, weed, seeds, wood shavings, sand, feathers, pompoms, paper scraps, old greeting card fronts, wrapping paper, fabric, yarn, eggshells, old jewelry, old puzzle pieces, buttons, keys, toothpicks, labels, foil, foil wrappers, wrappers, and cellophane. White glue or paste may be used to construct the collage.

Collage Surfaces.
Collage may be done on all sorts of papers, cardboard, boxes, cans, egg cartons, food trays, wood, vinyl, styrofoam, foam rubber, plastic lids from food containers.

Modeling and Carving
Children may experiment with modeling and carving using several different materials that can be used alone or with tools.

Modeling and Carving Materials.
Play dough and soft clay are ideal for young children because these materials are flexible and easy to manipulate. Children within the early childhood years also enjoy using wet sand to mold shapes. In addition to soft sculpture materials, assorted "junk" for sculptures including wood shapes and scraps may be used for making more stable sculptures. A collection of boxes of varying size, shape, and texture makes for interesting sculptures. Children may create these individually or as a group. After the sculpture is completed, the sculpture may be painted or used as a basis for collage.

Modeling and Carving Tools.
The tools appropriate to use for modeling and carving include tongue depressors, plastic knives, rolling pins, cookie cutters, pizza cutters, small bowls, and pans.

MODIFICATION OF MATERIALS OR ACTIVITIES TO INCLUDE CHILDREN WITH SPECIAL NEEDS

All of the materials discussed above can each be used by themselves or in combination with others. All of these materials can be made accessible to children depending on the needs of the individual child. Modifications

FIG 5.1 Children can enjoy art as a social experience.

will be listed by nature of what initially makes the experience inaccessible to a child:

Physical Considerations

When a child cannot reach an easel, modifications can be made so the child is able to be close to the easel. Sometimes, the barrier a child experiences that deters the child from experiencing art activities requires a modification as simple as a platform for the child to stand on that enables the child to reach the easel. The child may need the easel surface and paint well lowered so that sitting at the easel makes the easel accessible for a child with physical disabilities. The child may need a higher or lower chair to be able to reach the table. The child may need to stand in order to be able to participate in the art experience.

When a child cannot hold on to the paint brush, a lighter brush may make it easier for the child to have the experience of painting. If the lighter brush does not make painting accessible, the child may be able to work with a brush if an adaptive device is designed specifically for the size of the child's hand. This device may be something as simple as a small sponge ball with a slit in the center for the brush handle to fit into (see Figure 5.2). The sponge ball is then placed in the child's closed fist. The child may then be able to use paints with or without gentle adult support. The adult facilitating the activity may find it necessary to lend support by lifting the child's elbow.

FIG 5.2 A simple adaptation allows a child with a physical disability to handle a paintbrush.

FIG 5.3 Minor adaptations may allow for greater range of motion enabling a child with physical disabilities to engage in art activty.

If the child is in a wheelchair or other adaptive chair, providing a foam wedge (see Figure 5.3) to support the elbow in order for the child to be able to reach the paper on the easel is a simple modification. The gratification experienced by the child with special needs who is then able to paint at the easel just like the other children do, is well worth the effort necessary to make the modifications.

A child in an adaptive seat with a tray may need to have the art activity brought to the tray instead of attempting to move the child up to the table. If the child can easily be moved close to the table, the paper or other surface for painting, drawing, or collage may need to be taped to an inclined surface (a triangular hollow block or wooden wedge works well) for accessibility to the child. If collage materials are cut into very small pieces, the child with physical disabilities may simply need collage materials that are larger or thicker in order to be able to pick them up unassisted.

Visual Impairments

Children with mild to moderate visual impairments often require few modifications. For a child with minor impairments, allowing the child to work on a surface that brings the art materials closer to the child affords the child the opportunity to engage in the same activities as the other children. It may also be necessary to have the child work on a white or black background for contrast. It is important for the child to work in a well-lighted room to maximize the child's vision. This child may also need larger tools and surfaces to work with initially. Once the child is familiar with materials, tools, and surfaces, there are usually few modifications necessary. Often, children with visual impairments enjoy the whole body experience of art activities which by nature are very sensory in orientation. A vision specialist, physical therapist, or occupational therapist can offer suggestions for other modifications when necessary. Each child presents unique challenges to all working with the child. Teamwork makes the work much easier and the outcome more positive for the child.

All of these accommodations are not detrimental to the program or the environment. None of these modifications disturb other children. All of these accommodations demonstrate a willingness to enhance the developmental appropriateness of the environment based on the knowledge and understanding of what makes an environment and a program accessible and appropriate for children.

Social, Emotional, or Behavioral Disorders

Children who display behaviors that are challenging to peers or adults sometimes stay away from art activities. Often, these children do not engage in new activity because they are unsure of what to do. They do not yet understand the nature of the open-endedness of art activities. They should be provided with opportunities to watch others for quite a while before they are encouraged to attempt to try something themselves. What teachers need to do for them is allow them the time and space they need in order to feel comfortable.

Sometimes, a child with behavior problems will need support in the area of impulse control. Although art activities are ideal for helping such a child to move toward more control, initially, there may be many messes before the child begins to develop mastery over materials and tools.

A child who exhibits a profile of social immaturity will certainly benefit from art activities. Art activities are motivating, rewarding, and promote an atmosphere of socialization through the sharing of materials and the commenting on each others' art work. Both teachers and peers may be involved in the social growth that can take place through engagement in art activities. Teachers observing such a child will be able to document growth over time through what the child produces as more self–esteem and control is gained over his or her environment.

Learning Impairments

Some children are not able to learn at a rate similar to other children of the same chronological age due to retardation or related learning deficits caused by physical, visual, or other reasons. Modifications which would enable the child to participate in art activities along with other children might include stating instructions or procedures in a very simple manner, demonstrating techniques necessary to participate in the activity, or assistance to enable total participation as necessary. Experimenting without pressure to produce a specific product allows children to develop their own style, to take risks, and to take their time (Barbour, 1990). Development takes time and a variety of experiences. It is wise to avoid making assumptions about what children are and are not able to do. It is best to provide rich experiences to all children, that when coupled with support and encouragement, will maximize the child's potential.

Language and Communication Deficits

There are many reasons why children have delayed language development or experience communication problems. Regardless of the reason, art is of great importance in promoting growth in the deficit areas. As a means of nonverbal expression, art may become the vehicle for initiating communication with peers and adults. Engaging in art activities allows a child the opportunity to hear the language of the other children as well as the language of the teacher offering materials, asking questions and responding to questions posed by the children. By being part of the group in a safe, physical sense, a child with language or communication deficits will be encouraged to begin to speak.

CASE STUDIES DESCRIBING MODIFICATIONS

CASE STUDY

Anthony was reluctant to engage in art activities because of the fear of getting dirty. Since he was a child grounded in routine, the unstructured nature of art activities was initially unsettling to him. He would ask the same questions each day when approached with an invitation to participate in art activity. His questions revolved around whether the paint would come off if it got on his fingers, whether the smock would hurt him if he put it on, whether his mother would think it was OK to use the paints (markers, chalk, crayons, scissors, etc.). Daily, the teachers would reassure him that it was not dangerous to engage in art activity and that the art materials would not permanently change the color of his skin. He was also reminded that his mother in fact gave him permission to participate and wanted him to have fun at school. He would watch the other children enjoy their participation in the art area. Often during his observations, a teacher would approach him with another invitation to participate. He would refuse but continued to observe. Over a period of several months, Anthony came into closer proximity to the art activities. Occasionally he would ask if he had to wear a smock and be told the purpose of a smock as well as told that he need not wear one in order to participate. Eventually, he began to talk to the other children while they engaged in art activity. He tended to have more conversation with children who engaged in "drier" art projects (i.e., coloring, cutting, pasting) than with children who engaged in painting of any kind. One day, Anthony came in to school and announced that he thought he might make a picture for his mommy that day. As overjoyed as all the teachers were to hear the news, they were all careful not to overwhelm Anthony with their enthusiasm for his declaration. As the morning went on, he entered the art area, sat down, picked up a crayon and put it to paper. Not only did the teachers take note of this new behavior, but the children in the area remarked about how nice it was to see Anthony making a picture. This was the start of a slow, careful exploration of a wide variety of art activities. Anthony never did take to wearing a smock but he also never got himself dirty. He was careful and methodical in everything that he did and that behavior carried over to the art area as well. To the delight of the teachers, Anthony began to enjoy art activities and took great pride in making things that he could take home and hang up on the wall in his new house. This transformation took time and understanding. It took very minor modifications of the environment. The first modification was to inform Anthony that he did not have to wear a smock in order to participate. Often, a rule like wearing a smock becomes a strong deterrent to a child's participation in an area that would eventually bring the child much joy and afford the child the opportunity to explore unknown territory. Another modification was to make sure that there was always room adjacent to the art activity for Anthony to be able to sit and observe the activity without feeling crowded or too close for comfort. He was allowed to determine safe distances by his own standards.

If you recall from the description of Anthony in Chapter 4, he was a child who was not easily visually engaged. Having him participate in art activities heightened his visual awareness and ability and allowed him to see that attending visually was as rewarding as attending to auditory stimulation. As Anthony became more involved in a greater variety of art activities, an added bonus was his increased level of peer interaction both verbal and nonverbal. Art activity brought Anthony into closer proximity to peers and after his lengthy observation period, he was ready to participate. The unstructured nature of the medium of art no longer bothered Anthony and in fact allowed him to become more flexible in general. His parents noted related changes at home as well. Anthony began to look at books when read to and seemed to take notice of household furnishings that had never previously grabbed his attention. For Anthony, art was an empowering experience.

Sharon, a child with physical disabilities, requires few modifications in her school environment relative to the art area. Sharon is a very social child and eager to do what other children do. She attends art classes with her classmates. She needs to be able to work at a table which can accommodate her wheelchair. She may need help obtaining materials and putting them away. Otherwise, Sharon is able to manage all art materials and tools. When Sharon and one of her teachers attended her neighborhood public school for her first transition visit (moving from preschool to kindergarten), one of the activities of the morning was art class. The art teacher had never before worked with a child with special needs. She had no idea how to approach this child in a power wheelchair. Sharon was so excited about the whole day she was not in as much control over her motorized chair as she usually was. When she approached the long work table, she did not disengage the power switch and began to move the table across the room! While the other children were fascinated with her ability to move furniture, the teacher did not share the same sentiment. This episode made for interesting discussion at school and at home later that day. Sharon was reminded about being a responsible "driver" and most people involved had a good chuckle. The art teacher also asked the transition teacher what the child's name was and how to spell it. The transition teacher told the art teacher to ask the child herself. Naturally, Sharon stated her name and spelled it for the teacher too! What the teacher learned immediately was that although Sharon might need a wheelchair for mobility, there was nothing wrong with her mental abilities. The visit was a successful one. Sharon learned about her neighborhood school and what to expect when she attended the next fall, the classroom teachers and the art teacher learned about her needs and the stereotypes they held. Sharon has been in that school since kindergarten and is a participating member of each class.

Charlie might have required assistance with socialization and language production but the only kinds of assistance he needed in the art area was with scissors, smocks, obtaining some materials, and hanging things up to dry. His hands and fingers were pudgy and not as well developed as those of the other children during his preschool years, thus tasks requiring fine motor expertise were challenging. Charlie enjoyed working on challenging tasks and willingly practiced tasks that were difficult for him to accomplish. Charlie participates in all aspects of his art program in his school. He does not require support in these activities anymore. It is gratifying to see the engagement of this child in an area that provides him with opportunities for socialization and language within the context of a preferred activity.

Sarah, a totally silent child at school, required no modifications in the art area. She was very interested in all art activities and was very skilled. Her mother, a self-taught sculptress, invited the whole preschool class to visit her house to see all her sculptures and to see where she did her work. The teachers discussed the idea of the field trip and decided that even though Sarah might find it difficult to have all the children in her house, it would be worth the risk. Sarah was quiet during the whole visit and listened to all the questions the children asked her mother. After the trip, the class returned to school and had snack. During the snack, Robert (known to be fairly oppositional himself) complimented Sarah on the work that her mother did. He told her that the trip was the nicest one he had ever taken and thanked her profusely for allowing him to come. He told her that he liked it so much that he was going to bring her a present in two or three more "sleeps" (his term for days). After a few minutes, he jumped up and said he did not have to wait that long because he had something special in his cubbie that he could give her right then! Robert returned with some artwork he had made and gave it to Sarah. Sarah was all smiles. He asked her if she would come to lunch at his house and she said YES!! This was the start of a wonderful friendship as well as the start of verbal interaction with Sarah initiating to children and teachers. The children responded to her with great enthusiasm. The teachers and her parents could not have been happier.

Martie is the type of child who is afraid of failure so he exhibits opposition to activities with which he has no previous experience. Martie stayed away from art activities for this reason. Martie also attempted to intimidate other children who wished to participate in art activities telling them that painting is for sissies. It was important for Martie to see that men can be artists too. Teachers placed pictures of male artists around the art area and also introduced prints of the work done by male artists. After some initial indifference to these exhibits, Martie was seen to show interest in them when he thought there was nobody watching him. After some time, Martie began to use art materials. His drawings and paintings often were negative in nature but his involvement in the art area did allow him to express himself and begin to relax. He also began to relax relative to his peer interactions while engaged in art activities. One can only hope that he will continue to find art a positive and appropriate release of emotion and tension.

Christina, a child with visual deficits and oppositional behavior, was always eager to be involved in art activities and enjoyed using a wide variety of media and tools. Christina did not require any modifications in the art area. She seemed to enjoy working on larger surfaces but worked equally as well on smaller surfaces. In other settings, Christina often tried to control the activity and her peers. In the art area she was so involved with the materials she did not feel the need to control. For Christina, this was very important to her social and emotional growth and development. For the teachers it was important to see another side of Christina. Seeing Christina engage in positive behavior with peers and adults without any oppositional behavior demonstrated that certain situations set off or maintained the oppositional behavior in which she usually engaged.

C. W. found art activities to be very gratifying. He had no access to art materials at home and since he and his mother moved quite often, producing art work that was his and could be put up on the walls was important to him wherever he happened to be living at the time. His mild cerebral palsy affected one side of his body so during art activity he was encouraged to try to use the hand that was weaker. Cleanup after an art activity was also very beneficial for this child because scrubbing the table with a large rag or sponge required that he use both hands, thus providing him with additional exercise for his muscles. Art activity afforded the teachers the opportunity to reinforce important skill development in a manner that was meaningful as well as fun for C. W.

SUMMARY

Art activity is an essential component in a developmentally appropriate early childhood program. Art activity promotes growth in physical, cognitive, language, social, and emotional areas. Art activity may be planned to support the theme of the integrated curriculum being implemented in the classroom. Children may enjoy art for the sake of the artistic experience, for the release of emotion experienced, or for the discovery involved in the use of color, shape, texture. Regardless of the disability, children can experience great joy in participation in the process of creating art. Art can be made accessible to all children with the materials usually found in every early childhood classroom.

DISCUSSION QUESTIONS

1) Discuss the benefits of open-ended art activities for the development of young children.
2) Collect samples of artwork over a period of time. Compare the samples looking at the use of color, shape, the area of the paper used, the degree of representation identified. Discuss your findings with another student who has completed the same collection process.
3) You read an article in the local newspaper that highlights an early childhood teacher who speaks to the importance of coloring in the lines. Prepare a response to the article to be sent in the form of a letter to the editor.

4) A child is ready to be picked up from your kindergarten class. The child is holding a lunchbox and carrying three pieces of artwork completed recently. When the parent leaves with the child, you notice that the parent takes the artwork and deposits it in the trash can near the door to the classroom. What can you do in the future to prevent this situation from happening again?
5) Select one of the child cases in this chapter. Brainstorm activities you think would be appropriate for the child you choose. Identify any modifications you think would be required in order for the child to carry out the activity.
6) Think back to your early school years. List the art activities you remember doing. Compare your list with that of another student in your class.

REFERENCES

Barbour, N. (1990). Whose creation is it anyway? *Childhood Education, 66*(3), 130–131.

Chapman, L. (1978). *Approaches to art in education*. New York: Harcourt Brace Jovanovich.

Chenfield, M. (1983). *Creative activities for young children*. New York: Harcourt Brace Jovanovich.

Cherry, C. (1990). *Creative play for the developing child: A teacher's handbook for early childhood education*. Carthage, IL: Fearon Teacher Aids.

Edwards, L., & Nabors, M. (1993). The creative arts process: What it is and what it is not. *Young Children, 48(3)*, 77–81.

Eliason, C., & Jenkins, L. (1994). *A practical guide to early childhood curriculum*. New York: Merrill College Publishing Company.

Gandini, L. (1993). Fundamentals of the Reggio Emelia approach to early childhood education. *Young Children, 49*(1), 4–8.

Gardner, H. (1982). *Art, mind, and brain*. New York: Basic Books.

Goodenough, F. (1926). *Children's drawings as measures of intellectual maturity*. New York: Harcourt Brace Jovanovich.

Haskell, L. (1979). *Art in the early childhood years*. Columbus, OH: Merrill Publishing Company.

Herberholz, B. (1985). *Early childhood art (3rd ed.)*. Dubuque, IA: William C. Brown Co. Publishers.

Jenkins, P. (1980). *Art for the fun of it—A guide for teaching young children*. New York: Prentice Hall Press.

Kellogg, R. (1970). *Analyzing children's art*. Palo Alto, CA: Mayfield.

Klein, E., Kantor, R., & Fernie, D. (1988). What do young children know about school? *Young Children, 43(5)*, 32–39.

Kuschner, D. (1989). "Put your name on your painting, but . . . the blocks go back on the shelves". *Young Children, 45(1)*, 49–56.

Lowenfeld, V. (1947). *Your child and his art*. New York: Macmillan.

Spodek, B. (1986). Development, values, and knowledge in the kindergarten curriculum. In B. Spodek (Ed.), *Today's kindergarten: Exploring the knowledge base, expanding the curriculum* (pp. 32–47). New York: Teachers College Press, Columbia University.

Suransky, V. (1982). *The erosion of childhood*. Chicago: University of Chicago Press.

Swanson, L. (1994). Changes—How our nursery school replaced adult-directed art projects with child-directed experiences and changed to an accredited, child-sensitive, developmentally appropriate school. *Young Children, 49(4)*, 69–73.

Van Hoorn, J., Nourot, P., Scales, B., & Alward, K. (1993). *Play at the center of the curriculum*. New York: Merrill College Publishing Company.

ADDITIONAL READINGS

Gallas, K. The languages of learning: *How children talk, write, dance, draw, and sing their understanding of the world*. New York: Teachers College Press.

Golomb, C. (1992). *The child's creation of a pictorial world*. Berkeley, CA: University of California Press.

Jolongo, M. (1990). The child's right to the expressive arts: Nurturing the imagination as well as the intellect. *Childhood Education, 66*(3), 195–203.

Szekely, G. (1990). An introduction to art: Children's books. *Childhood Education, 66*(3), 132–139.

Thomas, C. (1990). "I make my mark": The significance of talk in young children's artistic development. *Early Childhood Research Quarterly, 5*, 215–232.

CHAPTER 6

Sensory

KEY TERMS

sensory activities
substances
experiences
therapeutic value
safe practices

IMPORTANCE OF SENSORY ACTIVITIES FOR DEVELOPMENT

Sensory activities include experiences that provide children with the opportunity to use one or more of their senses to explore their environments. Children are surrounded by sensory opportunities at home and at school. Why then is it appropriate and important to provide daily sensory experiences? Though children may be surrounded by sensory opportunity, they may not be in a position to take advantage of these experiences due to accessibility, safety, the sensitivity of those caring for the children, and the time factor. While children may live near a park or have a sandbox in the backyard, the child may not be at home during daylight hours and thus be unable to take advantage of the opportunity inherent through sand play. Other children may not be able to use the sandbox near their home because animals use it regularly or adults use it to extinguish cigarettes. Most people have access to running water and should be able to provide water play for children but there are many people who feel water is for washing and not for playing. In thinking about all of the sensory experiences that can be provided for children within their daily lives, it is often just not feasible to provide these activities.

Importance of Sensory Experience for Development

The importance of sensory experiences lies in the development that takes place in young children when they have the opportunity for free exploration, under supervision, of a variety of substances. Each of these substances with differing properties including different textures, different temperatures, different consistencies, and different weights allows children to come to discover facts through their own observations. These observations come from the child seeing, feeling, smelling, tasting, and listening. While many of the **substances** and **experiences** introduced in the sensory area may be considered ordinary rather than extraordinary, what is extraordinary about developing a sensory area is the time and opportunity it affords children to explore with few constraints. Through sensory experiences, children learn about comparing and measuring in addition to learning about characteristics and properties. Establishing a sensory area allows children to explore in cooperation with other children, to share ideas and experiences. Language shared, close physical proximity, and simultaneous discoveries add to the individual knowledge acquired by each child.

Children Learn Through Repeated Explorations

Children learn best through repeated explorations and the sensory area affords children this type of repeated exploration. Children are active learners in their own experiences. They are not placed in early childhood classrooms to be filled up with facts that we tell them. They are naturally like sponges and learn best when they can "dip" into the environment with guidance and support but without being told everything teachers think they need to know (Bredekamp, 1991). What is also very special about sensory experiences is that children do not tire of them because each time the child experiences sand or water, the child discovers something new or is able to exercise greater control over the medium. This is due to experience and maturation. Children need to have some of the same experiences repeated over time because they are not initially able to glean the maximum potential the activity has to offer the first few times they have the experience.

Teachers need not be afraid to repeat experiences during the year or over the early childhood years. Each time a child explores a pumpkin, opens seeds, tastes apples, or smells different spices or extracts, the child has a greater body of knowledge to which to relate the experience. A child smelling cinnamon for the first time may not be able to relate it to anything in the environment. If the class bakes cinnamon buns later during the year or the child goes out to the shopping mall with his parents and passes a bakery that has just made a fresh batch of cinnamon rolls, the next time you have cinnamon for the children to smell during a sensory activity, the child will have something to relate it to and the connection will be made. In a preschool classroom, a teacher was interested in providing several milk-like liquids for children to smell and then taste. Included in the group of liquids was whole milk, skim milk, evaporated milk, sweetened condensed milk, chocolate milk, and eggnog. All of these liquids were placed in the same kinds of containers so that packaging would not influence the child while the child smelled and attempted to label each of the liquids prior to tasting a sample from a small clear plastic cup. When a particular child came to the eggnog, he smelled it several times, smiled, and then told the teacher it was Christmas! As you can see, smells do have particular family, holiday, or cultural associations for some children. For some children, being able to taste the samples allowed them to identify an event associated with it rather than come up with a label. For other children, tasting the item cemented the identification. Adults often have the experience of smelling a familiar scent and enjoy the associated memory. This supports the notion that sensory experiences are a very important part of a child's development.

Sensory Activities Introduce New Experiences

Another important reason for including sensory activities is to provide children with experiences they might not ever have if they did not have them at school. Certain foods are not commonly used in some households. When a child tastes them in school surrounded by peers and supportive teachers, the child should find this to be a positive experience. For a child who does not live near the beach or a park with a sandbox, providing sand play simulates those natural experiences. For urban children, providing chicken feed, other seeds, and hay to touch and smell brings a bit of the farm to the city.

Sensory Experiences Are Accessible to all Children

Sensory experiences are very accessible to all children. Very often, children with special needs gravitate to sensory activities because of the ease with which they are able to be involved, because they might contain familiar elements and because they are able to exercise some control over the activity without becoming frustrated. Aside from the safety limitations associated with using sensory materials, these activities have no right or wrong. The satisfaction a child receives from involvement in these activities is of his or her own doing. What the child does within the sensory area is fine. There is no finished product and few, if any, formal expectations. The materials are soothing and provide a child with considerable feedback. Involvement with these materials in close proximity to other children is often the first introduction a child with special needs may have to the world of peer social interaction. Standing near a child who is describing what he or she is doing allows the child with special needs to hear some new language or have some previously heard language reinforced. Concepts discussed by peers with the facilitation of a teacher present something for a child to think about. After having heard the words heavy and light for example, a child can experience what these two words really mean through lifting different size containers of sand, water, or feathers. A child with poorly developed fine motor skills will more readily work on further developing those skills through sensory play than through pure, prescribed exercise. A child with emotional problems will be able to relax in the sensory experience and be comfortable because there is no exacting conduct expected. There is considerable opportunity for growth and development within this activity area.

Sensory Experiences Provide Opportunities for Dramatic Play

Williams and DeGaetano (1985) suggest using the sensory area for dramatic play as well as for the sensory experience. With the addition of transportation vehicles, small figures, rocks, shells, or small plants to the sand or water, children can create environments that may be familiar or unfamiliar to them. A child who has never been to the beach will have the opportunity to learn about the beach from a child who is busily creating a beach in the sensory table. The vocabulary and concepts pertaining to the beach will be shared. Children will relate stories about the times they shared with their families at the beach. The experience will be much more meaningful than just hearing about it without exploring the sand, water, and shells. When children come to school in a different part of the country than they are used to living in, they bring their experiences with them. Children who have family members who work in construction may create construction sites in the sand or dirt while children who have been camping may recreate a lake they visited. Children from different cultural backgrounds will be able to share their interests and experiences.

OBJECTIVES OF SENSORY ACTIVITIES

Establishment of a sensory area affords children the opportunity to safely explore their environments, one or more elements at a time. The major objectives of sensory activities are:

- to introduce different textures and fluid media to children
- to provide for the exploration of these materials
- to explore the familiar
- to explore the unfamiliar
- to make predictions about transformations
- to develop concepts based on explorations
- to introduce related vocabulary within the area
- to provide for shared language experiences
- to introduce textures and smells of different cultures
- to develop fine motor skills through pouring, scooping, sifting, squeezing, transferring materials from one hand to another or from one container to another
- to engage in dramatic play in a smaller, more controlled environment than that of typical dramatic play areas involving furniture, props, dress-up clothes, and possibly more children
- to have fun while exploring materials that will build a frame of reference for future scientific discovery
- to be involved in activity that has tension reduction potential

DEVELOPMENTALLY APPROPRIATE ACTIVITIES AND MATERIALS

The sensory area can be as exciting and stimulating as teachers want to make it. This area can also be calming and soothing. For a long time, it has been acknowledged that certain substances such as sand, water, and mud have **therapeutic value** for young children (Hill, 1977). Hendrick (1994) points out the many benefits of sensory materials and sensory play. She reinforces the notion that it is within these activities that a child may "relax and mess about to their heart's content (p. 235)."

Materials that are appropriate to use in the sensory area typically may be used and re-used many times during the school year. Some of these materials may be saved to be used from year to year. What actually happens with the materials and the plans the classroom teacher has for these materials once they are made available to the children will vary with the interests and the abilities of the particular children in the class. Children will use the variety of materials provided in ways which are meaningful to them as they begin to explore and make comparisons.

Safety Concerns in the Sensory Area

When planning for this area, safety is of utmost concern. Young children have a tendency to put small things in their mouths, in their ears, and up their noses. Therefore, extreme caution should be exercised and close supervision provided when initially implementing sensory activities. Children need to be reminded that while they may be exploring substances which are normally eaten, the substances in the sensory table are not to be eaten. Sometimes teachers and families are uncomfortable with the notion of using food for exploration. Remember to be sensitive to this concern. There are many non-food substances such as sand, cedar shavings, fabric strips, ribbon, seeds, cotton batting, etc. to explore without exploring food. Teachers must always respect the values and traditions of the children and families they work with.

As the teacher and the children are more comfortable with the materials in this area, children may be given more independence with the materials. With younger children and certainly at the beginning of the year, using simple sensory materials, such as sand or water that do not require as much supervision as some other materials makes sense. This approach will allow the teacher to establish **safe practices** in the sensory area while introducing children to the wonderful experiences that can be made available.

Guidelines for Management of the Sensory Area

There are certain guidelines which should be implemented in the sensory area. It is wise to limit the number of children from four to six. There are several reasons to limit the number of children in the area. Children really need space when exploring a variety of substances and fluids. If they feel cramped or crowded, they may begin to use the materials in an inappropriate fashion with the result of someone getting hurt, very wet, or dirty. Being crowded diminishes the extent of exploration in which a child may engage, thus limiting the potential impact of the sensory experience. Children should be protected by a smock when using sensory materials so that they do not have to worry about getting dirty and can fully enjoy the experience. If wearing a smock becomes a barrier to engaging in the sensory experience, it is up to the teacher and the child to determine whether not wearing a smock is a viable option. When one is dedicated to meeting the needs of individual children, one must be prepared to bend the "rules" to meet the needs of the individual child.

Parents need to understand the importance of sensory experiences in order to be supportive of children who may come home with visible signs of having been involved in sensory exploration. Once children are comfortable with the idea of the limited number of children who may be in the

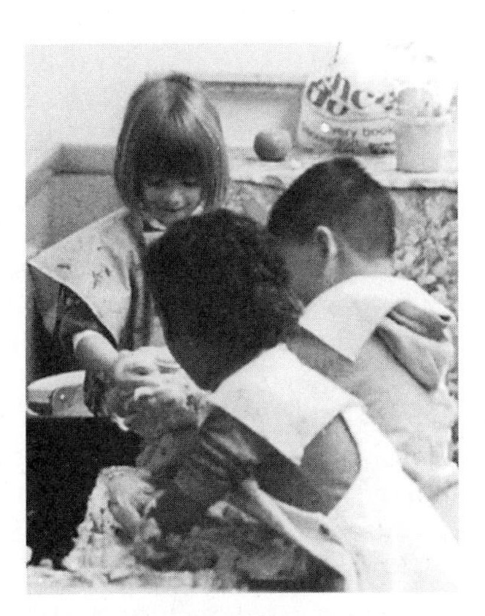

FIG 6.1 Children engaged in sensory experience grow in many ways.

area at one time and the appropriate use of materials, you may safely graduate to sensory materials requiring more supervision.

Substances and Materials Appropriate for the Sensory Area

Water and appropriate accessory materials include the following:

plain water

water with food coloring (care should be taken to use just a little food coloring to avoid staining skin and clothing)

water with shampoo

soapy water with bubble wands

soapy water with straws

water with dish detergent

water with baby dolls adding small bars of soap for washing the dolls or shampoo for washing the hair

water with plastic sea animals

water with small plastic cars

water with kitchen utensils (i.e., sieves, funnels, whisks, slotted spoons, ladles, cups, measuring cups, strainers)

basters, measuring spoons, ice cube trays, small pitchers

water with squirt bottles

ice cubes

colored ice cubes

snow in the winter

Crosser (1994) points out the many wonderful things children may learn from water play experiences. Water play promotes problem-solving and thinking skills and is particularly well suited to the development of concepts in math and science. Children further develop large and fine motor abilities, engage in socialization, and learn language. Crosser discusses the role of the teacher in the water play area as one of being an enabler as well as being ready to communicate to parents the value of this developmentally appropriate activity. The article also includes 25 ideas for promoting discovery learning in water play. York (1991) suggests that when exploring liquids with children it might be interesting to add a scent to the water. She further suggests introducing essential oils that come in a variety of scents such as herbal, floral, wood, or citrus.

Sand and appropriate accessory materials include the following:

sand

sand with water

sand with shovels and buckets

sand with shells

sand with powder tempera paint

sand with small plastic dinosaurs

sand with plastic desert animals

sand with small plants

sand with glitter.

Other solids and appropriate accessory materials include:

cornmeal

rice, colored rice

unpopped popping corn, popcorn, Indian corn, unhusked corn

beans of all sizes, colors and shapes

tissue paper

cotton balls

styrofoam "peanuts"

bubble wrap (popping the bubbles is wonderful activity for strengthening small muscles)

fabrics of all types: satin, tulle, silk, cotton, velour, fake fur, wool, flannel, corduroy, jersey, leather

sandpaper

colored cellophane
streamers
cedar chips
seeds
bird seed
potting soil
pasta
cooked pasta
ooblick (4 parts cornstarch to one part water)
goop (equal parts of white glue and liquid starch)
gelled clear gelatin, colored gelatin
feathers
cotton batting
polyester batting
dough
pumpkin pulp
leaves
hay
seaweed
dry oatmeal
oatmeal with water
shaving cream
wood chips
bark
lambswool
wax paper
different foil papers
elastic
flour
containers of spices
cotton balls which have been soaked in different extracts

Use of Sensory Materials with Dramatic Play Materials

All of the materials listed above can be used in conjunction with some dramatic play materials. If children were exploring oatmeal in the dry state and later were offered the opportunity to add water to some of the dry

FIG 6.2 Sensory play can also be social play.

oatmeal, it would be appropriate to place some oatmeal in a bowl and allow the child to get some water in a measuring cup or pitchers and with a spoon or whisk, mix the oatmeal. You might even offer cooking aprons and chefs' hats to add to the pretend element of the play. Sometimes, children will ask for additional materials to be added while they are in the process of exploration. As long as it is not a ploy to once again play with the plastic dinosaurs, and it is deemed safe by the teacher, it should be allowed. Sometimes children have the best ideas of all.

MODIFICATION OF MATERIALS OR ACTIVITIES TO INCLUDE CHILDREN WITH SPECIAL NEEDS

As mentioned earlier, all of the materials discussed above can each be used by themselves or in combination with others. As was pointed out in the discussion on accessibility in the art area, all of these materials can be made accessible to children depending on the needs of the individual child. Modifications will be listed by nature of what initially makes the experience inaccessible to a child:

Physical Considerations

When a child cannot reach the sensory table or whatever is being used to contain the sensory materials, modifications can be made to enable the child to be close to the table or bin or to find a way to bring the sensory experience right up to the child. Sometimes, the barrier a child experiences that deters the child from experiencing sensory activities requires a modification as simple as a platform for the child to stand on that enables the child to reach the table. The child may need to be on his or her knees on a chair that is backed up to the sensory area. A child who is not able to stand independently may need to use a stander in order to be able to participate. If a stander is not used, an adult sitting behind the child may provide support.

If the child is in a wheelchair or other adaptive chair, a simple modification is to provide a foam wedge to support the elbow to enable the child to reach out to the sensory materials placed on the work tray attached to the chair. The gratification experienced by the child with special needs who is then able to explore the sensory materials just like the other children do, is well worth the effort necessary to make the modifications. It is preferable to position the child at the sensory table with the other children because then the child is in closer proximity to social interaction and there is a greater likelihood that interaction will take place than when the child in the adaptive chair sits apart from the other children.

Sometimes, a child with motor problems might find it difficult to explore the materials because the hand is closed tightly. What might need to happen prior to sensory exploration is a brief session of relaxation exercises as prescribed by the occupational therapist. After these exercises, the child is often relaxed, open handed, and ready to go. The teacher in the area or the paraprofessional working with the child is the one to engage the child in these prescribed activities in order to allow the child to gain maximum potential from the experience.

Visual Impairments

Children with visual impairments are often very interested in the experiences provided in the sensory area and require few modifications. For a child with minor impairments, allowing the child to get as close to the substances without getting into the substances works best. This child may need to initially work with larger spoons, bowls, cups, etc. Once the child is familiar with materials, tools, and substances, there are usually few modifications necessary. Often, children with visual impairments enjoy the stimulation of sensory activities which by their nature provide immediate feedback in addition to being easily managed.

None of these modifications interfere with the exploration of the other children. All of these supportive interventions enhance the developmental appropriateness of the environment for any child, regardless of whether the child has special needs or not.

Social, Emotional, or Behavior Disorders

Children who display behaviors that are challenging to peers and adults often take great pleasure in sensory activities. While these children are sometimes afraid to engage in new activities because they are unsure of themselves and fear rejection by adults and children, the familiarity of some substances placed in the sensory table makes the area a more inviting and secure place to explore. Sometimes they may need to watch others for quite a while before they are comfortable enough to play but much learning takes place from watching and listening to others.

As was pointed out in the discussion on art activities, a child with behavior problems will sometimes benefit from guidance in the area of impulse control. Although sensory activities are also ideal for helping such a child move toward more control, initially, there may be many messes before the child begins to develop mastery over substances and materials.

The exploration of sensory experiences affords the child who exhibits a profile of social immaturity many opportunities to grow. Since there are few instances where there is a right and a wrong when engaging in sensory play, a child will have considerable time to engage in play that meets the needs of the child at that time. A socially immature child may also be language delayed and will benefit from being surrounded by the conversation that often takes place around the sensory area. Not every day is a high language day in the sensory area. Some days can be extremely quiet as children become totally involved with their hands and their minds. What is unique is the manner in which each child approaches and becomes involved in the area. Since many sensory substances provide a therapeutic value, it is not unlikely that a child who is experiencing a generally difficult morning or a difficult transition from home to school will find great release of tension within the sensory area. Sometimes, a parent walking a child into school, finding it difficult to separate, will be able to do so after the child is engaged in sensory exploration. It is important for the teacher to facilitate this transition from parent to sensory exploration so the parent and child may more easily separate.

Learning Impairments

Modifications which would enable the child to participate in sensory activities might need to include stating and restating instructions or procedures in a very simple manner, having a chart or a photograph indicating sequence or process of appropriate behaviors, demonstrating techniques necessary to participate in the activity, or assistance to enable total participation. Sometimes children with learning difficulties wait to be invited to the area each time they approach. A child might also wait to be told that it is OK to begin to play. Children with learning difficulties often need frequent reassurance and invitations to continue their involvement with activity. The benefits gained from the sensory experience focus on opportunities for development in the areas of language, socialization, cognitive and physical growth, and development.

CASE STUDIES DESCRIBING MODIFICATIONS

CASE STUDY

You will recall that **Anthony** was reluctant to engage in art activities because of the fear of getting dirty. Since he was a child grounded in routine, the unstructured nature of art activities was initially unsettling to him. He would ask the same questions each day when approached with an invitation to participate in art activity. His questions revolved around whether the paint would come off if it got on his fingers, whether the smock would hurt him if he put it on, whether his mother would think it was OK to use the paints (markers, chalk, crayons, scissors, etc.). Understandably, his behavior was quite similar related to sensory materials. His concerns about getting dirty and the permanence of the substances that he might come in contact with precluded his participation in sensory activity. As was done with art activities, Anthony was also reminded that his mother in fact gave him permission to participate and wanted him to have fun at school. He would watch the other children enjoy their participation in the sensory area. He stood closer to this area than he did to the art area while he made his observations. Since the sensory substances were in a contained area, he might have felt more secure being in closer proximity to them. It took Anthony less time to become involved in the sensory area. He would occasionally ask if he had to wear a smock in order to play in the sensory area and be told that he need not wear one in order to participate. Involvement in this area promoted growth in language and social interaction. He tended to have more conversation with children when the activity involved the use of more familiar substances. Once again, the teachers were careful not to overwhelm Anthony with their enthusiasm for his activity involvement. As the year went on, he became more and more involved in a wider variety of sensory activities with increased confidence and enthusiasm. As was seen in terms of his behavior pattern in the art area, Anthony was careful and methodical in everything that he did in the sensory area. To the delight of the teachers and his parents, Anthony began to verbally share his experiences at dinner time. He talked about how much fun it was to play in the sand, water, or whatever else was available that day. For Anthony, sensory experiences were also liberating.

Sharon requires some modifications in her school environment relative to the sensory area. Since it is preferable to be in a standing position to engage in sensory experience, she needs to be able to be in her stander or have someone physically support her at the hips so that she may stand at the sensory table. She often needs help obtaining materials and putting them away. Once all these accommodations are in place, Sharon is able to manage all sensory substances and materials. In her preschool years, Sharon thoroughly enjoyed sensory experiences. Unlike children who are totally mobile, a child like Sharon must often rely on adults to bring certain experiences to her. She cannot change her physical position without the assistance of an adult. She cannot engage in shifting from her adaptive equipment to the floor or ground without assistance. Therefore, she cannot be spontaneous about getting down on the ground to dig in the dirt, feel the grass, or smell the flowers. She always enjoyed these activities and never seemed to care about how dirty she got. Her parents also did not care about what she looked like when she came home as long as they knew that what she looked like was a reflection of her involvement in appropriate activities.

In the sensory area, **Charlie** needed assistance with getting his smock on and off, obtaining some materials, and washing up after he finished playing. Charlie was usually concerned about his clothing staying clean and dry so for most sensory activities, he preferred to wear a smock. Involvement in the sensory area afforded him increased opportunity to strengthen his fine motor skills. As you may recall, his hands and fingers were pudgy and not as well developed as those of the other children in his preschool, thus tasks requiring fine motor expertise were challenging. Charlie enjoyed working in the sensory area because although he was fairly quiet, the small number of children in that area, coupled with the nature of the activity allowed him to engage in verbal interaction with his peers. His mother indicates that Charlie still enjoys sensory type activities even though they are not a regularly scheduled activity in his second grade classroom. During recess, he can be found in the sandbox engaged in some serious digging and dramatic play.

Remember **Sarah**, a totally silent child at school? She required no modifications in the sensory area. She was quite interested in all sensory activities and it seemed as though the messier it was, the better she liked it. You may recall that her mother was a self-taught sculptress. Sarah was quite used to seeing someone involved with squishy, pliable substances as well as wood, marble, and stone. Sarah lived in a very sensory world. Her mother told the teachers that while she worked on a sculpture, she would often give Sarah clay or other substances to work with so that she could work alongside her. It seemed as though this modeling of behavior on the part of the mother paid off in Sarah's extreme interest in sensory activity. It is probable that another reason for the sensory area being of great interest to Sarah is that one can participate fully in these kinds of activities without talking!

Martie initially indicated that playing in the sensory area was for wimps. Martie said that he stayed away from these activities for just this reason. Martie could be seen watching other children having fun and being excited about their sensory explorations. It was important for Martie to see that other boys thought it was fine to engage in this kind of activity. He needed to be introduced to the fact that many occupations involve working with sand, water, mud, fabric, etc. Once this was pointed out to him and reinforced with pictures from magazines as well as books involving these professions, he showed an interest in the sensory area. After some time, Martie began to be involved with sensory activity on a regular basis. His involvement in this area allowed him to physically relax. He also began to relax his image of who should be involved in these activities. He no longer felt he always had to be a macho man. He no longer worried about getting dirty and started to be comfortable being a child.

Christina, a child with visual deficits and oppositional behavior was always eager to be involved in any activity and enjoyed every sensory activity presented. Christina did not need any modifications in the sensory area. Christina often tried to control the activity and her peers. She soon learned that all the other children were so involved with the materials that they did not respond to her control attempts. For Christina, this was very important to her social and emotional growth and development. Over time, she made fewer attempts at control and engaged in more positive interactions with her peers.

C. W. found sensory activities to be very exciting. He had little access to anything like this at home. He lived in an impoverished neighborhood where parents did not feel safe allowing their children to play outdoors. Therefore, he had no access to a neighborhood sandbox or any other source of sensory activity. His mild cerebral palsy affected one side of his body so during sensory activity he was encouraged to try to use his weaker hand. Clean up after sensory activity was also very beneficial for this child because washing his hands or helping to empty the sensory table required that he use two hands, thus providing him with additional exercise for his muscles.

SUMMARY

Sensory activity is an integral part of an early childhood classroom. Within this area, children experience the freedom to explore within their own time frame following their own ideas. Children benefit from the relaxing atmosphere promoted by the materials provided in the sensory area. Social interaction and language abound when children become absorbed in play that is both relaxing and absorbing. Cognitive learning and imagination have the opportunity to develop through the hands-on discovery undertaken in the sensory area. Teachers need not be afraid of potential mess created in this area because sensory play can be extended through the cleaning up that takes place when the play is completed.

DISCUSSION QUESTIONS

1) You are a new first grade teacher in a school where teachers are beginning to embrace the developmentally appropriate approach to planning environments for young children. You have volunteered to help the early childhood teachers develop sensory areas and activities for their classrooms. What will you suggest as appropriate for the younger and older children?
2) Get together with a classmate and brainstorm ideas for varying experiences with sand that could relate to a specific theme of your choice.
3) Develop a column for a parent newsletter that explains the importance of sensory experiences for children. Include a few suggestions for parents to implement in the home.
4) The person who maintains the building in which you teach voices concern about the "mess" that your sensory activities create. Brainstorm ideas of how the activities can be cleaned up by the children and adults in the room so the custodian will be content and the materials will not attract bugs, etc. to your room.
5) In your room you have a child with physical disabilities who is always exceptionally clean and beautifully dressed. While your intent is not to cause the child to get dirty, you wish to have the child engage in sensory activities to the fullest potential of the child. What can you do to communicate your intent to the parents and prevent the child from becoming covered with whatever substance the child will use in the sensory area?
6) Think about how sensory exploration relates to the world of work. Discuss with a classmate the similarities between these activities and the many careers individuals have in which they work with the same substances on a regular basis.

REFERENCES

Betz, C. (1992). The happy medium. *Young Children, 47(3)*, 43–45.

Bredekamp, S. (1991). Guidelines for appropriate curriculum content and assessment in programs serving children ages three through eight. *Young Children, 46(3)*, 21–38.

Crosser, S. (1994). Making the most of water play. *Young Children, 49*(5), 28–32

Hendrick, J. (1994). *Total learning—Developmental curriculum for the young child.* New York: Merrill.

Hill, D. (1977). *Mud, sand, and water.* Washington, DC: National Association for the Education of Young Children.

Williams, L. R., & De Gaetano, Y. (1985). *Alerta: A multicultural, bilingual approach to teaching young children*. Menlo Park, CA: Addison-Wesley.

York, S. (1991). *Roots & wings—Affirming culture in early childhood programs*. St. Paul, MN: Redleaf Press.

ADDITIONAL READINGS

Broekel, R. (1988). *Experiments with water*. Chicago: Children's Press.

Dinwiddie, S. (1993). Playing in the gutters: Enhancing children's cognitive and social play. *Young Children, 48*(6), 70–73.

Lewis, J. (1989). *Learn while you scrub: Science in the tub*. New York: Meadowbrook Press.

Wyler, R. (1989). *Raindrops and rainbows*. Englewood Cliffs, NJ: Julian Messner.

CHAPTER 7

Manipulatives and Small Blocks

KEY TERMS

manipulative materials
small blocks
problem solving
gifts
occupations

IMPORTANCE OF MANIPULATIVE AND SMALL BLOCK ACTIVITIES FOR DEVELOPMENT

Manipulative and small block activities are implemented with materials that by their very design invite children to use them in ways that have great potential for promoting development across a variety of areas. Access to **manipulative materials** and **small blocks** will help children increase their fine motor skills, cognitive skills, language skills, and develop skills in the social and emotional areas. Such activities also promote creativity when used independently or with peers and social interaction skills when these materials are used with peers. The natural curiosity of children makes the open-ended nature of manipulatives and small blocks very attractive. The hands-on experiences provided through the use of these materials provide children with the background they need to acquire mathematical concepts, attach language and symbols to these concepts, and grow in their ability to learn new concepts (Kostelnik, Soderman & Whiren, 1993). Manipulative and small block play encourages new exploration while repeated activities reinforce skills already acquired.

Small blocks are probably one of the oldest manipulative materials we know in early childhood. The potential contributions of blocks for early childhood curriculum are many and as such, small blocks will be handled as a sub-topic of manipulatives.

Manipulative Play

Initially, the nature of activity in the manipulative area might focus more on **problem solving** about how to put pieces together to construct something, complete a pattern or work a puzzle. For younger children or children whose fine motor skills are not well developed, puzzles with separate, noninterlocking pieces allow the child to gain dexterity in holding onto and moving pieces into appropriate places. A child working on a

FIG 7.1 Manipulative play promotes problem solving.

FIG 7.2 Manipulative play promotes physical proximity.

puzzle has a very different experience than a child who is working with Legos or other more complex manipulatives that have the potential for creative construction.

It may appear obvious that certain manipulative materials are an inherent part of any early childhood classroom. It is hard to imagine a classroom without puzzles, pegs, beads and the like. The history of some manipulative materials dates back to the time of Friedrich Froebel, the originator of the first kindergarten, in Germany. This first kindergarten started around 1837 was based on a curriculum which recognized that young children had innate gifts that needed to be developed. Froebel felt that these innate gifts could be developed if children engaged in tasks which were of interest to them (Osborne & Osborne, 1991). His "**gifts**" (objects) consisted of blocks and other shapes while his "**occupations**" (activities) consisted of activities such as modeling with clay, drawing, mat weaving, and paper folding. What was viewed to be important then is still important now. Children benefit from hands-on exploration of materials and activities of their choice. Whether the child has special needs or not, all children have the potential to benefit from these experiences. Some children will have had many of these experiences prior to entering school while other may have had lots of experiences with toys that "entertain." Some children have never worked a puzzle, placed pegs or strung beads but they are reading. Teachers and parents must not be falsely impressed by the early reader. Often, this type of learner exhibits major holes in his or her learning. Providing stimulating choices of manipulative play for the child with a wide range of skills encourages that child to engage in meaningful play. This meaningful play does not take away from the child whose skills are already developed.

CASE STUDY

Parents visiting a preschool program asked what there could possibly be at the school that would interest their child because after all, he was already reading at age three. They were shown all the materials that were available and it was explained to them that the children were able to choose the activities they wanted to do. When they were listening to this information, they looked over at their child, and saw that the child had chosen large wooden beads to string. The child was totally engaged in the task and was humming a little sea chantey while he worked. The parents were quite surprised that something so simple would engage their child who was of superior intellect. While they had been busy reading to him, filling his head with facts as well as spending a lot of time with him teaching him to read, they had not been aware of the importance of manipulative activities. When the child attended that school, he spent a vast amount of his time with blocks, beads, pegs and puzzles. What can be learned from this anecdote is that teachers need to take the lead from the children in every classroom. Teachers need to respect the right of children to engage in activity meaningful to them, and they need to respect their right to play.

From time to time, as technology becomes more prominent and inviting as a tool for learning, the question remains whether educators remain convinced that it is appropriate to have puzzles and other manipulatives in classrooms for young children. The opportunity to observe children at play with manipulative materials provides teachers, among other things, with information concerning a child's attention span, whether the child is able to work successfully, or whether the child needs assistance. What is critical is that a child be observed in the process of problem solving, creating, constructing, and following patterns. These observations will show whether a child seeks assistance at all or just attempts to leave the area if working on a specific manipulative task proves to be too difficult for the child to complete. Teachers are also able to learn about the manner in which a child obtains assistance; whether the child asks a peer to help or always seeks out an adult. This type of observation and assessment is both a necessity and a luxury. Assessment of completed tasks alone does not inform about the process by which the child developed a creation.

FIG 7.3 Manipulative play provides opportunities for shared decision making.

OBJECTIVES OF MANIPULATIVE ACTIVITIES

There are several objectives to be accomplished through manipulative activities. These objectives are:

- to provide opportunities for children to explore materials that can be put together in a variety of ways
- to provide children with the chance to strengthen their fine motor muscles
- to provide children with opportunities to solve problems
- to provide children with opportunities to work on the math related skill of directionality
- to provide children with opportunities to work independently
- to provide children with opportunities to work cooperatively
- to provide children with opportunities to develop social skills
- to provide children with the opportunity to create something that can be extended over time
- to provide children with opportunities to engage in creative tasks
- to provide children with opportunities to work with materials that enhance the imagination
- to provide children with the opportunity to create something that can be saved to be observed and admired by others thus enhancing their self-esteem

- to provide children with the opportunity to follow patterns
- to provide children with opportunities to develop self-discipline
- to provide children with the opportunity to complete designs
- to provide children with opportunities to complete a task
- to provide children with the opportunity to sort and classify objects
- to provide children with the opportunity to talk about their constructions
- to provide children with the opportunity to engage in pretend play based on their constructions

Small Block Play

Play involving small wooden blocks provides multiple opportunities for children to involve their entire bodies from their fingers that move and place the blocks, to the conceptual activity necessary to plan and execute the construction, to the social interaction that takes place in the block area. Blocks are essential "hands-on" materials (Hirsch, 1984).

While wooden blocks do not provide children with weaker muscles as much success-oriented opportunity as other manipulatives that have magnets or knobs or other adaptive devices, these blocks are still appropriate equipment for many children with special needs. These blocks are sturdy and are thus appropriate for stacking, filling, spilling and activity that involves lining blocks up along the floor.

Small Blocks—Materials with History

Through the use of blocks, children engage in experiences which have the potential to extend their knowledge and skill development in the following areas: physical development, language development, social development, science, social studies, math, and art. It is difficult to imagine an early childhood classroom without wooden unit blocks. The design of unit blocks has been around since they were introduced in 1914 by Caroline Pratt, founder of the City and Country School in New York. Children have been making roads and bridges, houses, office buildings, farms, garages, and the like in classrooms all over the world. The constructions children make are enhanced by all types of appropriately sized vehicles, people, furniture, paper and pencils or markers to make signs and addresses, small road signs, town map mats, natural materials for "cargo" for vehicles, colored cubes for decorating buildings, or magazine pictures of all sorts of buildings for inspiration.

Storage and Accessibility of Small Blocks

Storage and accessibility of blocks is an important consideration. Blocks need to be stored on shelves that are sturdy, in the area designated for

FIG 7.4 Manipulatives may be shared by children with and without disabilities.

block building, and in a manner that makes them inviting to use. This means that all of the same shape blocks should be stacked together so that children are able to see what is available to them. Blocks that are appropriately stored help to foster organization skills in young children. Blocks stored in this manner are also blocks that are safe to use. There will be no need to fear blocks falling down on children and causing them harm. Shelving for blocks will need to accommodate the various sizes and shapes contained in the block collection.

One of the nicest things about blocks is that with proper care, they will last a lifetime and can always be added to in order to enhance the collection. Children who are physically unable to reach blocks due to their special needs, may be able to work with blocks if the blocks are brought to them. If this is the case, other children may be encouraged to share in their block play with their peers with special needs. A child who cannot manage blocks may be able to share ideas with a child who can do the placing of the blocks. Blocks have great potential for cooperative play.

Learning from Observing Children Use Small Blocks

Observations of children during block play will yield interesting information about all aspects of a child's development. Of great importance will be the information gained concerning a child's cognitive ability. It is obvious that children engage in serious thinking while playing with blocks (Reifel, 1984). This has been known since the time of Froebel but not as much attention was always paid to this aspect of block play.

Safety in the Block Area

Safety in the block corner needs to be ensured for typical children and children with disabilities. To accomplish this, simple rules should be established concerning how high one may build, as well as when and in what manner blocks may be knocked down. The size of the block area will help determine an appropriate number of children for the area at any given time. In addition, it may become necessary to establish a traffic pattern so that children using the blocks will not interfere with other children using blocks who wish to build something by themselves.

OBJECTIVES OF SMALL BLOCKS ACTIVITIES

The most important thing that children do with blocks is play with them. Block play is absorbing and entertaining. Block play is flexible and open-ended. In addition to the pure play value of using blocks, there are many things that children can experience and accomplish through the use of small blocks:

- to provide opportunities for children to explore materials that can be put together in a variety of ways
- to provide children with the chance to strengthen their fine motor muscles
- to provide children with opportunities to solve problems
- to provide children with the opportunity to create interesting patterns and arrangements of blocks without much adult intervention (Reifel, 1984)
- to provide children with an opportunity to develop a sense of pattern and symmetry (Day, 1994)
- to provide children with opportunities to work independently
- to provide children with opportunities to work cooperatively, and share ideas
- to provide children with the opportunity to create something that can be extended over time (if space allows)
- to provide children with the opportunity to develop genuine respect for the work of others
- to provide children with the opportunity to sort and classify blocks according to shape and size
- to provide children with the opportunity to explore the dynamics of balance through construction (Day, 1994)
- to provide children with the opportunity to learn to express oneself nonverbally and release emotions in an acceptable form (Day, 1994) and to provide an acceptable outlet for aggressive behavior (Bailey & Wolery, 1992).

- to provide children with the opportunity to talk about their constructions
- to provide children with the opportunity to role play with small block accessories
- to provide children with opportunities to engage in dramatic play if vehicles, people, and animals are included in the block area
- to provide children with the opportunity to use materials to create the world as they see it (Day, 1994)
- to provide children with the opportunity to play out social studies concepts
- to provide children with the opportunity to develop self awareness
- to provide children with opportunities to explore spatial relationships
- to provide children with the opportunity to develop concepts such as big and little, more than and less than, equal to
- to provide children with the opportunity to learn about geometric shapes (properties and names)
- to provide children with the opportunity to gain an understanding of area and volume (Trawick-Smith, 1994)
- to provide children with the opportunity to develop numerical concepts

DEVELOPMENTALLY APPROPRIATE ACTIVITIES AND MANIPULATIVE MATERIALS

The manipulative play area can provide a variety of activities that cover the range from simple to complex, structured to creative. Temptation abounds when looking through the multitudes of early childhood catalogues currently available. If one is fortunate enough to be able to attend regional conferences or the national early childhood conferences, the abundance of manipulatives displayed at these conferences astounds and baits all teachers! These materials are colorful, range in size from small to large, are hand made or factory mass produced. These materials are made from wood, plastic, foam, fabric, metal, or combinations of substances. It is difficult to determine what a basic set of manipulatives might look like due to age and ability differences in groups of children and the age range that exists in early childhood. Obviously, one would not have the same materials in a second grade classroom as one would have in a toddler classroom. Some of the manipulatives for older children are merely more sophisticated versions of manipulatives that are appropriately introduced in toddler classrooms. The major differences in the two different levels of manipulative tasks focuses on the size of the pieces and the number of pieces a child needs to deal with at the older, or more skilled stage of development. It is wise to have a variety of materials at varying levels of difficulty in each classroom, regardless of the age range. The range of manipulatives appropriate for play in early childhood includes, but is not limited to the following:

beads, spools, buttons—wooden; plastic; all one color or multi–colored; bead pattern cards; shoelaces, strings, or yarn

sewing cards—durable cards with holes punched out around shapes; safe needles and yarn

dressing frames—wooden frames with fabric containing either a zipper, buttons, snaps, laces, buckles, hooks and eyes, velcro tabs

lock board—wooden board or box with various real locks and latches

bolt board—wooden board or strip with large bolts and nuts in graduating sizes

faucet board—large wooden board with various faucets mounted on board

mazes—wooden with beads that follow wire tracks or carved paths; magnetic with shapes that move along roadways on top of the maze when guided by magnets from underneath the maze

pegs—wooden or plastic; large or small; plastic; wood or foam pegboards which can be large or small; peg pattern cards

puzzles—wooden, foam, or plastic; with knobs or without; isolated shapes or interlocking; concept oriented or design; from small to floor sized

interlocking blocks—wood or plastic; in squares and rectangles; varied shapes; varied colors; with accessory pieces such as wheels or connectors; with dramatic play accessories such as people, vehicles, work-related items

stacking shapes—wood or plastic; varied colors or plain wood; geometric shapes; cylinders to stack on or shapes to stack on each other; pattern cards

stacking pegs—plastic with wood, plastic or foam peg board

shape sorters—shapes may be sorted and placed on cylinders or sorted and placed into a shape box with two dimensional cut-outs that correspond to the three-dimensional shapes; pattern cards for shapes that are sorted onto cylinders

sequential tasks—pattern cards that follow a sequence; story sequences; size sequences; tasks may be found on cards or puzzle type pieces geoboards—plastic or wood boards with pegs or nails and elastics to outline shapes; pattern cards

pattern blocks—wood or plastic; children can create their own patterns or follow established patterns

table set of blocks—set of small wooden blocks in natural wood or colors which can be used on a table top instead of the floor; can be combined with other small accessories for dramatic play

attribute blocks—wood or plastic; three colors; geometric shapes in two thicknesses; two sizes; designed to provide experiences with concepts that are basic to all math study

marble rollway—plastic or wood blocks, chutes and tubes which can be combined to create a roadway for marbles

matching tasks—manufactured matching tasks come in all kinds of formats and require that children make pairs based on exact matches, relationships; before and after; inside and outside; opposites; mothers and babies; fronts and backs; parquetry blocks and pattern cards

graded size tasks—pegs; cylinders, shapes, or blocks; range in size from large to small; fit inside a shape or are free standing

lids and jars—plastic jars with corresponding lids can be put out for manipulative tasks that involve the opening and closing of the jars as well as the matching of corresponding sized jars and lids

dominoes—wood or plastic; appropriate for matching quantity to quantity; can be used as manipulative to build buildings; some dominoes are based on matching textures, shapes, animals or people

flower arranging—may be done with plastic, silk, or real flowers; flower arranging foam; containers in which to place foam

MODIFICATION OF MATERIALS OR ACTIVITIES TO INCLUDE CHILDREN WITH SPECIAL NEEDS

As was pointed out in the discussion on accessibility in the art and sensory areas, many manipulative materials (including small blocks) can be made accessible to children depending on the needs of the individual child. General modifications will be listed by nature of what initially makes the experience inaccessible to a child:

Physical Considerations

When a child cannot reach the manipulatives table or the floor area on which these materials are placed, environmental modifications can be made as indicated:

work standing up—this may seem like a very simple modification but it is one that may make all the difference in the world to some children. Greater dexterity may be achieved by standing because the standing position allows a child to exert greater pressure on the manipulatives as the child attempts to put them together. A child who is small in stature or who has weak muscles may find that standing affords him or her greater range of motion.

work on the tray of stander or adaptive chair—this is a logical working situation for children who require the use of this type of adaptive equipment. While it is preferable that children with special needs work on the same surfaces as all the other children in the class, it may not always be possible. If the tray of a stander or adaptive chair is used, other children should be encouraged to share manipulatives with the child with special needs on the tray of the adaptive equipment. When a stander is used, peers may need to stand on a block or chair in order to reach the stander tray.

Visual Impairments

Children with visual impairments are often very interested in manipulatives and require few modifications. For a child with minor impairments, allowing the child to get as close to the materials as possible works best. This child may need to initially work with larger manipulatives. Once the child is familiar with these materials, there are usually few modifications necessary. Puzzles may be modified by coloring in the "board" of the puzzle with a dark color and outlining the puzzle pieces with dark color. This helps the child make the visual discrimination more easily. Often, children with visual impairments enjoy the stimulation of manipulative materials that by nature provide immediate feedback in addition to being fairly easily managed.

Once again, none of these modifications interfere with the exploration of the other children. All of these supportive interventions enhance the developmental appropriateness of the environment for any child, regardless of whether the child has special needs or not.

Social, Emotional, or Behavioral Disorders

Manipulative activities are sometimes frustrating for children who display behaviors that are challenging to peers and adults. Often, these children have developed few coping skills and if something does not fit together perfectly at the first try, the child may at one extreme wind up quietly leaving the area, or at the other extreme throw the manipulatives around the area and need to be removed from the area. Sometimes, children with social and emotional problems may not be comfortable engaging in manipulative play because they are unsure of themselves and fear

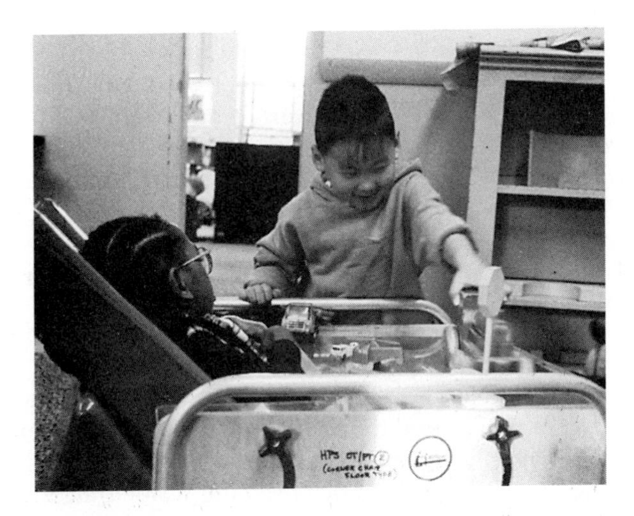

FIG 7.5 Adaptive equipment enables children with and without disabilities to be where manipulative play happens.

rejection by adults and children. Sometimes they may need to observe others using the manipulatives before they are comfortable enough to use them themselves. Observation provides children with considerable opportunity for learning about how materials go together but observation does not strengthen the muscles necessary to manipulate the materials. Once a child begins to work with the manipulatives, the child may need adult assistance in addition to encouragement in order to succeed. As a child becomes more skilled and less frustrated with the materials, the child will, with great pride, inform the adult that assistance is no longer needed. Limiting the number of blocks children work with may initially help to make the experience more positive. The number of blocks available to use should be in direct relation to the size of the area the child will play in. Some children with social and emotional problems engage in more appropriate behavior the more space in which they have to build. They easily feel crowded and might refrain from engaging in block play if the area is too crowded.

A socially immature child who is also language delayed will benefit from being surrounded by the conversation that often takes place around the manipulatives area. Although some days may find little conversation and much concentration in the manipulative area, this remains an area with high potential for language involvement. As children build and create with a variety of manipulatives, they use a wide variety of vocabulary. In addition to real words, they may invent words to describe their creations. For a child with social or emotional problems, seeing other children have fun with language has the potential to be an extremely freeing experience. What the child may learn is that every word uttered need not be perfect or real in order to join in a conversation. The role of the teacher relative to encouraging language is to interject appropriate thought provoking questions and appropriate vocabulary. This is not something the teacher can plan as in a lesson plan but comes from on-the-spot judgments about what the nature of the play needs in order to enhance the play and learning taking place (Jones & Reynolds, 1992).

Learning Impairments

Modifications which would enable the child to participate in manipulative activities might need to include several demonstrations of techniques necessary to use the materials, or assistance to enable total participation. If a child with learning difficulties typically waits to be invited to the area each day then the teacher might want to establish a routine with that particular child which starts the child out at the beginning of the day in the manipulative area. The teacher might ask the child what he or she plans to do in the manipulative area so as to avoid having to tell the child it is alright to use the materials and it is alright to start. The child may benefit from having the teacher begin an activity with the child so the child may be involved from the beginning rather than waiting for the child to make a decision about what to make or which manipulatives or blocks to use.

Analyzing Existing Materials for Use with All Children

Children with disabilities may benefit from the use of some modified materials made available to them in order to participate in manipulative play. Before attempting to modify existing materials for the child with disabilities, the manipulative materials within the classroom collection should be surveyed and analyzed for the potential they hold for children with special needs. Educators may overlook certain materials because they have not been used in a while or because they might be too simple or too complex for the group of children who are being taught. When looking at manipulatives with an eye as to possible modifications of the material for use by a child with disabilities, teachers may begin to think differently about the material for all children. Sometimes, the manufacturer includes guidelines for use that if implemented exactly would preclude use by many children in the class. Looking at materials with a new eye usually opens up minds to the additional functions materials may serve.

Materials Not Requiring Modification

Some manufactured materials lend themselves quite well to children with deficits in the areas of visual, motor, language, cognitive, or social and emotional development. The following materials are readily available. The reasons they are accessible to children and do not need modifications to be used are described below:

Magnetic blocks—are appropriate for children who do not have the fine motor dexterity to use other kinds of blocks that require fine motor ability and the ability to balance things. They are also useful for children with visual deficits because they are typically larger and multicolored and are more easily seen. For a child with cognitive deficits, using these kinds of blocks allows the child to make progress in planning and problem solving without the frustration of stacking blocks that may not stay where you place them. When children use magnetic blocks, the success they experience buoys the spirit and encourages the child to further pursue the task, thus enhancing skill and development in the area. Once the child masters the skill of building, the skill may be applied to building things like cars, houses, etc. to which a child may add either people or furniture. Peers who observe a child playing at this level are often found to join in the fun! This then enhances the potential of the child for language growth as well as social and emotional growth. A child with social and emotional issues often frustrates quite easily. When a child meets with success without frustration, the child personally begins to feel very differently and becomes more appealing to the peer group.

Puzzles with knobs—are very helpful for children with fine motor deficits and visual deficits. When a child can grasp the knob of a puzzle piece, the child can more feasibly accomplish puzzle completion independently. The potential for self-concept benefits in addition to fine motor enhancement are abundant. Children often engage in conversation while working on manipulative tasks and thus the child who is able to meet with success at a manipulative task is to be found in a high language potential area, thus enhancing the language potential of the child with special needs.

Large piece puzzles—puzzles with larger pieces are useful for children with visual, motor or cognitive deficits. The larger pieces afford the child the ability to pick up and replace pieces independently. Again, this adds to self–esteem.

Modifying Manipulatives to Make Them Accessible

There are other means of modifying manipulative tasks that make materials accessible to children with special needs.

Modified knobs—while puzzles with knobs may be accessible to some children, the knobs may be too small for other children. This means that you may need to find puzzles with larger knobs or switch the knobs on the puzzles to larger knobs. Some puzzles that do not have knobs can be enhanced with the addition of large knobs.

Work on a mat or tray or dysum—a child may be able to work with materials already in your classroom if they can keep the materials in place. Materials placed on a mat or tray or dysum (a blue tacky surface available through adaptive materials catalogues) diminish the potential level of frustration encountered by some children who do not have the dexterity to manage materials that may move around the table.

CASE STUDIES DESCRIBING MODIFICATIONS

CASE STUDY

Anthony loved manipulative activities for many reasons. One reason was that manipulative materials did not make him dirty. As you may recall, he was reluctant to engage in art or sensory activities because of the fear of getting dirty. Since he was a child grounded in routine, the structured use of many manipulatives brought him great delight. He did not need an invitation to use manipulatives. Involvement in this area promoted growth in language and social interaction. He tended to have more conversation with children when the activity involved the use of more familiar materials, materials he had at home. Teachers were careful not to intrude in the play in which Anthony engaged but they were sure to praise his creations, his language and interactions. As the year went on, he became more and more involved in a wider variety of manipulative materials with increased confidence and enthusiasm. As was seen in terms of his behavior pattern in the art area, Anthony was careful and methodical in everything that he did with manipulatives. Anthony talked to his parents about how much fun it was to play with manipulatives. For Anthony, manipulative activities extended skills he already possessed while opening up opportunities for him in the social and language areas.

Though **Sharon** is able to sit at a table she still requires some modifications in her school environment relative to the use of manipulatives. She needs to be in a sitting position that allows her elbows to be above the table surface. When she sits in this position, she has much more mobility and dexterity in the fine motor area. She often needs help obtaining materials and putting them away because containers with manipulatives are often heavy and managing such a container while attempting to use a walker or trying to obtain such a container from a shelf that may be a little too high or a little too low may prove to be difficult. Once all these accommodations are in place, Sharon is able to manage all manipulative materials. In her preschool years, Sharon thoroughly enjoyed manipulative experiences. Sharon is not totally mobile and must often rely on adults to bring certain experiences to her. She cannot change her physical position without the assistance of an adult. She cannot engage in shifting from her adaptive equipment to the floor or ground without assistance. Therefore, manipulative materials, such as small blocks placed on the floor, are not as accessible to her as manipulatives that can be used at a table. As mentioned earlier, she cannot be spontaneous about getting down on the floor so teachers must remember to place materials on the table for her to use or make sure that there is a table available for her to use when she selects manipulative activities.

In the manipulative area, **Charlie** needed considerable assistance when he first entered preschool. He needed assistance obtaining some materials because they were too large or too heavy for him to carry to the table or to the floor. He was always eager to explore everything and using manipulatives often required that he use both hands in order to put pieces together. This afforded him increased opportunity to strengthen his fine motor skills. As you may recall, his hands and fingers were pudgy and not as well developed as those of the other children in his preschool, thus tasks requiring fine motor expertise were challenging. Charlie enjoyed working with manipulatives because he enjoyed the interaction with his peers. He loved to build roads with small blocks and to drive cars and trucks back and forth on these roads. His mother indicates that Charlie still enjoys manipulative activities at school and at home as well. Charlie is a middle child and plays well with his older brother and younger sister.

Sarah was quite interested in all manipulative materials and required no modifications in order to work in the area. Sarah was one of several children and was quite used to seeing someone involved with some type of manipulative play. It is probable that another reason for manipulatives being of great interest to Sarah is that once again, one can use these kinds of materials without talking! Sarah enjoyed building houses or rooms with small blocks and decorating them with furniture, people, flowers, and fabrics. Skill in building and creating with manipulatives brings much peer attention and praise from teachers. Although very quiet, it was obvious to all who observed her that Sarah really enjoyed the praise of others.

For **Martie**, manipulative play was a natural activity. Martie could be seen at the manipulative table with other children having fun and being excited about his creations as well as their creations. It was important for Martie to see that both girls and boys thought it was fine to engage in this kind of activity. He needed to be introduced to the fact that many occupations involve working with manipulative type concepts. Once this was pointed out to him and reinforced with pictures from magazines as well as books involving these professions, he showed an even greater interest in manipulatives. When Martie used manipulatives he was usually very relaxed. He was strong and had a good sense of design. These two strengths were applied to the creations or "inventions" on a daily basis. Based on feedback to his foster family, the family purchased some manipulatives for Martie to use at home. Being able to use these kinds of materials gave Martie something to do at home that brought admiration from his foster family and brought people in the family to Martie to share in the activity in which he was perceived to be a leader or model.

Remember **Christina**, a child with visual deficits and oppositional behavior who was always eager to be involved in any activity? Christina did not need any modifications in order to work with manipulatives. She did not have a fine motor problem and could put things together with ease. What she did have trouble with was executing her concepts. When Christina had difficulty making something go together the way she wanted it to, she would try to enlist her peers to do it for her. She soon learned that all the other children were either not interested in executing her designs or not able to do so. She usually had difficulty in explaining what she wanted and if it did not look exactly the way she wanted it to, she became very angry and yelled at the child who was trying to help her. This was a very important lesson for Christina, one that was very important to her social and emotional growth and development. As she gained skill in carrying out her own designs, she made fewer attempts at control and engaged in more positive interactions with her peers. Some of these positive interactions involved planning something with a peer and combining forces to create what they designed together.

As with everything else at school, **C. W.** found manipulatives to be very exciting. As was mentioned in reference to art and sensory activities, he also had little access to anything like manipulatives at home. Although he lived in an apartment with his mother and had the space for manipulatives, they had barely enough money for rent and food. C. W. always looked clean and neat and usually wore very fashionable clothes. His young mother placed more value on how C. W. looked than what he had to play with. Play with manipulatives as opposed to activities during which C. W. had the potential to get dirty, respected the values his mother had of keeping C. W. clean and neat. C. W. was a very playful child and could make something out of nothing. He made things out of cardboard tubes, boxes, bags, etc. These things did not even have to be decorated for him to be able to use them in his play in some way. The use of manipulative materials helped C. W. to use both his hands so that the mild cerebral palsy that affected one side of his body was challenged. Even cleaning up after using manipulatives was beneficial for this child because he used both his hands to put things back in the appropriate containers and both his hands to place the containers back on the shelves. Due to his physical difficulties, it was more difficult for him to use small blocks with great success when he first entered school. As the years went on, he became more adept at using both his hands and more skilled in maneuvering his body in the space allocated for small block play. As his skill level increased, his time in the area increased as well. He no longer knocked things down as quickly as he built them because he was able to move around the structures without accidently knocking them down.

SUMMARY

Play with all kinds of manipulatives is an integral part of an early childhood classroom. Within this area, children experience the freedom to explore materials and follow their own ideas. Through the use of manipulatives, children come to understand mathematical concepts. They are able to work out designs and figure out principles while they add and remove pieces as they see fit. Children benefit from the atmosphere of experimentation promoted by the kinds of materials provided in the manipulative area. Language and social interaction become spontaneous as children become absorbed in the play of their peers as well their own play. Children bring their own experiences to their manipulative play. Stories they have read, movies, or TV programs they have seen, places they have visited all have an influence on what they create in the more open-ended manipulative play. Cognitive growth and the further development of the imagination flourish when children create, talk about their creations, observe the creations of others, and join creations to make even more involved constructions. Teachers often do not need to spend a lot of time with children to initiate manipulative play. Children usually appear to take to it naturally and have usually had experience with manipulative play prior to coming to school. Manipulative play changes in nature over the early childhood years but the need for and the appropriateness of manipulative play in the early childhood years never diminishes.

DISCUSSION QUESTIONS

1) Select two manipulatives from an early childhood catalogue. Compare and contrast them noting their size, color, the material they are

made from, the number of pieces in the manipulative, the cost, and the flexibility with which the manipulative may be used with a variety of children. Discuss the results of your comparison with a classmate.

2) A parent informs you that the first thing her child talks about each day after school is what was created with the manipulatives made available to the children that day. The parent indicated that they do not have any of these kinds of materials at home. It appears that the mother would like to be able to provide this type of experience for the child at home. What can you suggest to the mother that would be inexpensive, safe, and developmentally appropriate for the child to use?
3) A child always wants to use certain manipulatives independently and you are attempting to build in a socialization component to the use of these manipulatives. What can you do to move the child more in your desired direction without having the child leave the area entirely?
4) A child in your class, if allowed, will remain working with manipulatives or blocks during the entire play period. How can you arrange the environment to interest the child in other areas so the child will be able to take advantage of a broader range of experiences?
5) Prepare information concerning the use of blocks and manipulatives for volunteers who work in your classroom on a regular basis. This information should be general enough to serve the purpose for the entire year but specific enough to answer most questions that these people might have.
6) A child builds a complex structure with the small blocks. The child worked on the structure during the entire play period. When it is time to clean up, the child asks if the structure may remain standing so his mother may see it at the end of the day and so that he may play with it and add to it the next day. What will you say to the child and why?

REFERENCES

Bailey, D., & Wolery, M. (1992). *Teaching infants and preschoolers with disabilities* (2nd ed.). Columbus, OH: Merrill.

Day, B. (1994). *Early childhood education—Developmental/experiential teaching and learning* (Fourth edition). New York: Merrill.

Eliason, C., & Jenkins, L. (1994). *A practical guide to early childhood curriculum.* New York: Merrill.

Hirsch, E. (Ed.). (1984). *The block book (rev. ed.).* Washington, DC: National Association for the Education of Young Children.

Jones, E., & Reynolds, G. (1992). *The play's the thing: Teachers' roles in children's play.* New York: Teachers College Press.

Kostelnik, M., Soderman, A., & Whiren, A. (1993). *Developmentally appropriate programs in early childhood education.* New York: Merrill.

Osborne, D. (1975). *Early childhood education in historical perspective.* Athens, GA: Education Associates.

Osborne, D., & Osborne, J. (1991). *Early childhood education in perspective* (3rd ed.). Athens, GA: Daye Press.

Reifel, S. (1984). Block construction—Children's developmental landmarks in representation of space. *Young Children (40)*, 61–67.

Trawick-Smith, J. (1994). *Interactions in the classroom—Facilitating play in the early years.* New York: Merrill.

ADDITIONAL READINGS

Cartwright, S. (1988). Play can be the building blocks of learning. *Young Children, 43*(5), 44–47.

Provenzo, E., Jr., & Brett, A. (1983). *The complete block book.* Syracuse, NY: Syracuse University Press.

Reifel, S. (1982). The structure and content of early representational play: The case of building blocks. In S. Hill, & B. Barnes (Eds.), *Young children and their families: Needs for the nineties.* Lexington, MA: D. C. Heath.

Reifel, S., & Greenfield, P. (1982). Structural development in a symbolic medium: The representational use of block constructions. In F. Forman (Ed.), *Action and thought: From sensorimotor schemes to symbolic operations.* New York: Academic Press.

CHAPTER 8

Dramatic Play in the Large Block and Housekeeping Corners

KEY TERMS

dramatic play
themes
fantasy play
sociodramatic play
dramatic play equipment

INTRODUCTION

In the early childhood period, **dramatic play** serves as the demonstration of the growing awareness of the social environment of the child. Pretend behavior becomes obvious in the normally developing child in approximately the second year of development. This early dramatic play imitates certain gestures and people in the child's surroundings. Children may be observed to pretend talking on the phone, feeding a baby, reading a book, or cooking a meal. The nature of the play in which a child engages depends on the activity surrounding the child at home, in the community, and at school. A child growing up in the city will observe many activities and events not available to the child growing up in the suburbs or in a rural area. A child living in a rural area will be part of activity not readily available to children in the city.

Dramatic play may involve materials and objects but it may also exist in a very sophisticated manner without any props at all because it is person oriented. Dramatic play may be verbal or nonverbal or both. It is the kind of play that may involve few or many children at a time. The dramatic play abilities of individual children develop over time. Opportunities for dramatic play within the early childhood setting become even more important for children with limited previous experiences. One of the factors that influences dramatic play is access to other children. When a child grows up isolated from other children, it is possible that the child may not develop the same kind of play skills as do children who have access to peers. Parents who are sensitive to play development often provide stimulation for dramatic play for children without siblings by engaging the child in pretend play. While this is very helpful for the development of play skills, it may not help the child to be prepared for the realities of playing with other children. When that child encounters a peer group, the need to share materials, wait turns, and follow as well as lead in terms of ideas might prove to be difficult at first.

Nature of Play Changes during the Course of the Year

During the school year, as groups of children become more involved with each other, the nature of the play will change. The **themes** children choose to play will become more sophisticated as the experience base is enlarged and the children are exposed to more and more literature. Some themes will be played on a regular basis and will unfold as stories unfold and develop. Additional children will be worked into the play and roles will be expanded as the children's command of language and interaction skills are enhanced. Some groups of children play the same theme each day when they play outdoors. Often they can be heard planning what will transpire once they get outdoors as they put on their outer garments in preparation for going outdoors. Other times the planning for what is to happen actually takes place outdoors. The planning is so involved and so time consuming that by the time the children actually begin to play, the time for play has elapsed and it is time to return indoors. Undaunted, this procedure will often be followed day after day. As children become more verbally sophisticated and more aware of planning, the fun appears to be as much in the planning as in the doing.

Sometimes towards the end of the day in a full-day, early childhood setting, as the group of children present becomes smaller, children may engage in play that continues from where it left off the day before. Not unlike a soap opera, the play may repeat a bit of the story from the previous play session and move on. The observer may see or hear hints about what will transpire in the next play session through a bit of forecasting by the players.

Dramatic Play Takes Place in a Variety of Activity Areas

Dramatic play may take place in a variety of areas within an early childhood environment. Indoors, one would find dramatic play in the housekeeping corner, the large block corner, in the sensory area, and in the small blocks and accessories area. The nature of the play observed in each of these areas may be different due to the differences in allocated space, the permissible number of children in the area, the materials and equipment found within the area, and the time children actually have to spend in the area. Outdoors, dramatic play takes on a different look due to the nature of the play facilities, equipment, and the number of children outdoors at one time. The nature of teacher role in each of these areas may differ. Teachers certainly have a role to play in encouraging and maintaining dramatic play.

Role of Teacher in Dramatic Play

The role of the teacher in dramatic play is to arrange the environment to be conducive to this type of play and to support children who choose to develop their own theme for play. In the first type of play, the teacher serves as a facilitator, the one who sets up the area to suggest a certain theme and supports the theme with the addition of props where appropriate. With children who have special needs, the teacher may have to take a more active role and encourage the child to participate or model the role for the child. In situations where children have already determined the theme of their play, the teacher again serves the role of facilitator by bringing props, making suggestions of ways to extend the play, or opening up some additional space to allow the play to extend and become more creative. A good example of teacher as facilitator may be found in the following scenario.

CASE STUDY

Children were playing fast food restaurant one day. The dramatic play area was set up with large hollow blocks defining the outer wall of the food preparation area and the housekeeping area serving as the kitchen. Children took on roles as the order takers and order fillers. Other children with money in hand were the customers. The teacher was in the area facilitating the play. When one of the servers somewhat rudely put the food in front of a customer, the customer remarked that he would bust the place up because the people were so rude. The other "customers" supported the notion of wrecking the place. The teacher quickly stepped in and suggested that while that certainly was one way to handle the situation, another way might be to stage a protest! The children quickly asked what that meant. She explained that they could inform the management that they did not like the service and they would take their business elsewhere if the service did not change. They made picket signs and marched chanting "We don't like the service!!!" The children who were working the food area cleaned up the restaurant, apologized to the customers and promised to do a better job of serving the food. This quick thinking teacher did far more than salvage the play. She taught children about positive change efforts and helped them to see that destruction and violence were not the only response possible. In addition, the children learned some new vocabulary and concepts.

Another important role played by the teacher in the dramatic play area relates to time. When schedules are rigidly adhered to and dramatic play is available for 45 minutes, wonderful opportunities for extended or enhanced play may be lost. It is always wise to see how the play is progressing in order to determine if the time should be shortened or lengthened. Play that is positive and creative deserves additional time. Play that is falling apart should be terminated in a positive manner so that children do not develop negative attitudes about certain themes or children. Some groups of children enjoy very positive play relationships the majority of the time. All groups are prone to have a negative day from time to time. Children may be set off by interruptions or a slow start to the day due to delayed school opening on a snowy day. Some children may be a bit under the weather and be tired or irritable. Extremely hot and humid weather can produce short fuses in all people. Under these conditions, it is wise to monitor both quality of activity and the time factor. No schedule should preclude modifications if the modifications will enhance the experience children will receive.

What Teachers Can Learn through Observing Dramatic Play

One of the most exciting things about dramatic play is the spontaneity of language and interaction within the play episodes. The teacher is able to learn so much about children through observations made during this spontaneous play. As children play, they define themes and declare roles (Smilansky & Shefatya, 1990). Children narrate their actions as well as have conversations with each other.

Some children always play the same type of role regardless of the theme of the play. If the children are playing zoo, family, or school there is usually one child who plays the role of the smallest, or the youngest. The child may actively choose the role or be relegated to this role by default. There are many reasons why this behavior may occur. One reason may be that the child is less experienced than the other children and feels safe playing a role closer to his or her own real life situation. Playing another role may involve some risk taking and the child may not be ready.

CASE STUDY

In a kindergarten classroom in a middle class neighborhood, a girl was observed to be crawling around on the floor barking like a dog. The teacher and the school social worker were very concerned about this behavior. When they met with the mother, they discussed the experiences the child had prior to entering that school. This child did not attend preschool, lived with her mother and grandparents and spent no time with other children. During the day in the two years before she entered school, she helped her grandfather with his hot dog stand. The mother worked third shift so she could be with her child during the day. All the other children in that particular class attended early childhood programs for one or two years before entering the public school. Several of them were in the same programs. By the time they entered the kindergarten, they had play experience and a shared play history. This one little girl who had no such experience and shared history wanted to be part of the play in the classroom. Quite on her own she figured out how to become part of the play scenario. She played a role that no other children appeared to want to play. By playing the part of the dog, she placed herself in the heart of the action and was able to learn a lot about dramatic play by observing the other children from the inside rather than from the outside. Not all children are able to do this for themselves. If they are able to get this far into the dramatic play situation, they may need adult assistance to move on to other roles within the same play theme. These new roles may include higher level nonverbal behaviors and finally appropriate verbal interaction. The role of the teacher is to provide the support necessary to children in order to encourage growth without being intrusive and without pushing children beyond what they are able to handle comfortably at that time.

Creating Opportunities and Space for "Fantasy" Play

Fantasy play has its beginnings in the toddler period with imitative play with "things" on a solitary basis and later moves on to much more sophisticated play with others. The height of this type of play is often in the kindergarten year. Unfortunately to date, few data are available beyond the kindergarten period because in many communities, play and especially fantasy play is seen as counterproductive to schooling so the time children spend in this kind of play is greatly diminished by the first grade (Pelligrini & Dressden, 1992). Hopefully as the work of the National Association for the Education of Young Children guidelines for developmentally appropriate curriculum and practice make inroads in the public schools, young children will have more access to and spend more time in **sociodramatic** play during the school day.

The housekeeping area is not the only area in which dramatic play takes place. Many classrooms have large hollow blocks made of wood or bricklike blocks made of corrugated cardboard. The substance of the blocks is not as critical as the use of the blocks. Children enjoy creating enclosures and vehicles that they are able to go inside of. The enclosure might be a house, an apartment, a condo, a hotel, an office, a library, a cave, a museum, a school, or any other structure they can think of. What is important to the children is that they plan it and execute it. Some groups of children recreate the same structure every day they come to school. The structure may look the same to the teacher but it is not called the same thing by the children. The enclosure will often relate to the integrated theme being implemented in the classroom. If the children choose to create a vehicle, it might be a car, a train, a bus, a limo, an airplane, a spaceship, or a truck. Again, it may look the same to the teacher but it is very different to the children.

In a second grade classroom where the teacher did not have large blocks for creating enclosures, she introduced a tepee to the classroom environment. As the integrated themes were changed each month, the tepee became something else from a house to a school to a store to an Indian museum. Different activities and items were placed in the tepee according to the theme and the children never tired of having this enclosure in their room. Some teachers who do not have large blocks use refrigerator or other appliance boxes to achieve the same effect. The children decorate the boxes according to the theme being covered and enjoy the enclosed space within their classroom.

Large blocks and boxes are wonderful additions to dramatic play that may begin in the housekeeping area. Children pretending to go on a family picnic might create a vehicle to use to drive to the park or the beach. Children playing out a favorite book or story told to the class may use

FIG 8.1 Children take on a variety of roles during dramatic play.

whatever is available to create an enclosure that supports the story. A food store may be set up using the blocks as shelves and counter while the housekeeping area remains the place where the family lives and takes the food they purchase at the store. It is important to have a second space in close proximity to the housekeeping corner that allows for the extension of the sociodramatic play. Having this additional space allows more children to be involved in the play while it enhances and diversifies the play. Having double the space assures enough room for children with special needs in adaptive equipment to be included in the play without crowding out the other children. The teacher can help procure the materials the children need to enhance and benefit the play.

IMPORTANCE OF DRAMATIC PLAY ACTIVITIES FOR DEVELOPMENT

Benefits of Dramatic Play

Play for the integrative function of play is a major reason to ensure opportunities for dramatic play in an early childhood program. There are many other benefits including the fact that when children play, they are free to be themselves more than at most other times. There is little that is

FIG 8.2 Adults can facilitate dramatic play through involvement in the activity.

required of a child except to express ideas and to play safely. During play, children make choices, communicate those choices, and follow through on their plans. In all areas of development, dramatic play provides the stimulation and opportunity for potential growth and development. Dramatic play affords children the opportunity to work out problems in their own way and in their own time. Children may take on familiar roles in order to problem solve or they may experiment with different roles in order to help themselves figure things out. This kind of problem solving usually involves nonverbal play and is of critical importance for young children whose verbal skills and problem solving skills are not well developed enough to allow them to pinpoint the problem and discuss it with someone else.

In the area of social development a child has the potential to learn to negotiate, to wait, to trade, and to make substitutions when the desired item is in use by others. Cooperative skills, which are so desired in the workplace can be developed through dramatic play. Children learn to listen to ideas, offer their own ideas, compromise, and combine ideas. They learn to share materials and space through a productive process (Cartwright, 1993). They learn that they do not always have to be the leader. They learn about different social roles. They learn about other cultures through sharing experiences via play. They learn how to observe a group and grasp the opportunity to move into the group when the time is right.

Children Get in Touch with Their Feelings through Dramatic Play

Social interaction provides opportunities for emotional development. Children have the potential to get in touch with their own feelings through dramatic play. More experience with their own feelings affords children the opportunity to control their feelings. When a child experiences something in the family situation, dramatic play often offers the child the chance to work out feelings about this event or sequence of events in a safe and supportive environment. An example of this can be found in the following scenario.

CASE STUDY

A boy in a child care center located within a low-income housing community came to the center in an agitated mood each morning for several mornings. The director greeted him noting that it was not one of his parents who dropped him off. She tried to find out why someone else dropped him off and what was bothering him. She determined that he needed space and quiet and decided to observe him closely. Each morning he went to the dramatic play area and began fussing over one doll. He seemed to be giving the doll medication, placed "bandages" on the doll, and cradled the doll. While all this was done in a nurturing manner, it was done with a sense of urgency and seriousness that made it appear quite different from what is commonly played out in a "take care of baby" dramatic play episode. After a few days of observing this episode being repeated daily, the director was able to get in touch with the family. They reported that their baby had been very sick and had required emergency medical treatment at home a few times over the last week or so. The treatment was required during the night and they thought that the little boy had remained asleep during the ordeal. They were unaware of the fact that not only was he awake but that he had crept out of bed and had observed the whole thing. He was sensitive enough to see that everyone was very upset and fearful but was not able to ask questions or get the reassurance he needed from his parents. When the parents learned that their son was reenacting the events that had taken place at home, they promised to sit down with him and explain what had transpired. They had been so absorbed by their own feelings that they were unaware that their other child needed support. After a few days, the boy stopped playing his morning "emergency" episode and became part of the regular play. His needs had been met. His play was a signal and a way of expressing himself. Close observation of dramatic play allows teachers to support the emotional development of young children by responding to any red flags a child may raise.

Children Develop Physically through Dramatic Play

Development in the physical domain occurs through the encouragement of using newly acquired or emerging physical skills. Children involved in dramatic play will often repeat certain behaviors many times over thus setting up their own practice of a task that may not be as enjoyable to practice if presented in a non-play-based situation. Children can learn self-help skills as well. Imagine asking a child to button and unbutton a shirt three times just for practice. Now picture a child dressing and undressing a baby doll in the housekeeping area. Children can learn visual discrimination skills by matching and grouping dishes, dolls, types of clothing, etc. in the dramatic play housekeeping area. The task that is self motivated and self directed has greater potential for absorbing the interest of the child. Outdoor dramatic play has the potential for challenging children to try out new behaviors while enacting a role. Children also have a chance to practice already developed skills in much the same way as they do fine motor skills.

Children Develop Cognitive Skills through Dramatic Play

There are many ways that children demonstrate cognitive growth. They use language to express their ideas. They extend and expand on ideas, whether the idea was theirs or anothers. They make signs and labels for things or respond to existing signs and labels. They can learn to problem solve. They show signs of advanced planning such as "When you come home say that you're home and that you want to go to the park before we eat and then I'll say OK".

Several studies note that children who often engage in pretend play score higher on IQ tests or other measures of intelligence than children who do not engage in this form of play (Christie, 1983; Johnson, Ershler & Lawton, 1982; Rubin, Fein & Vandenberg, 1983). Effects of this kind of play also appear to have an effect on language and literacy abilities (Pelligrini, 1985).

Creativity Can Be Demonstrated through Dramatic Play

Children demonstrate creativity and intelligence in many ways (Gardner, 1983). Observations of children during dramatic play affords the opportunity to see another kind of creativity. While a finished product in the art area may be a prime example of creativity, the process involved in creating the art work may be the real demonstration of creativity. The process of dramatic play is where more creativity can be found. There is no product in dramatic play unless you tape the ongoing interaction and role play between children but the observations made during the process will inform

FIG 8.3 Language can flourish through dramatic play activity.

you about the creativity of those involved. When a child desperately wants to join in the play and all traditional roles have been spoken for, the child may invent a new role and gain access to the situation. This is certainly demonstration of creativity! Unique use of familiar items is another way children demonstrate their creativity. The greater the variety of themes made available to the children, the greater the opportunity for creative development.

Recent research by Lieber (1993) compared the social pretend play of children with and without disabilities. Critical to this study is the implication of these findings for those involved in the integration of children with special needs. Lieber points to the differences in the entry behavior of children and the limited exposure of the children with disabilities. This supports the importance of facilitating play within the regular classroom environment instead of providing training sessions for children outside of the classroom with the expectation that the child will be able to transfer skills to the normal peer group. Rehearsing children without the benefit of peers does not prepare the children for the spontaneity of responses from normal peers. This type of preparation is similar to learning a prepared dialogue in a foreign language. When placed in an applied setting, an appropriate initiation might be made but if the response is different from the one anticipated, the person does not know what to do next. Foreign language experts know that the best place to learn a foreign language is in the country where that language is spoken. This is also the case with dramatic play in naturalistic social settings.

OBJECTIVES OF DRAMATIC PLAY ACTIVITIES

When children engage in dramatic play they use creative thinking while playing roles with which they are familiar. Participation in dramatic play enables all children to experience growth in all areas of development. Specifically, the provision of dramatic play enables the teacher to provide children with opportunities:

- to share and plan with others
- to learn to cooperate
- to engage in routine family activities that are of a positive nature
- to engage in family activities that might provide for the release of fear, anger, hostility, and aggression
- to learn about other families and their practices
- to learn about other cultures and cultural practices
- to express their thoughts through play
- to experiment with different roles through play
- to experiment with language through play
- to use small muscles through play
- to use large muscles through play
- to develop solutions to their own problems they encounter in school or at home
- to escape problems they may have by engaging in pleasurable activity for a period of time
- to plan play episodes with their peers
- to explore notions of good and bad through play
- to explore their own likes and dislikes through play
- to demonstrate empathy for others through role playing

DEVELOPMENTALLY APPROPRIATE ACTIVITIES AND MATERIALS

Dramatic Play Equipment and Materials for Indoor Play

Currently there are many pieces of furniture and equipment for dramatic play which were not available in previous years. As technology changes the look of the modern home, particularly in the area of the kitchen, changes are reflected in the pretend equipment marketed for dramatic play. While it might be fun to have one of everything that might be found in a modern home from a washing machine and dryer to a microwave oven, not all children have homes that reflect these modern conveniences. In order to encourage positive dramatic play opportunities, these pieces are not critical. Children use equipment with which they are familiar. They more readily play themes with which they are familiar (Howe,

Moller, Chambers & Petrakos, 1993). While they can gain information about items they do not have in their own homes through the play in which they engage in school, it is possible to make some of the "extras" from cardboard boxes with the children having input into the creation of these items.

What follows is a list of appropriate large pieces of **dramatic play equipment.** Space always influences what one is actually able to include in a dramatic play area but this list reflects an assortment of equipment appropriate for the range of early childhood dramatic play from the toddler period through grade three.

Appropriate dramatic play furniture

stove
refrigerator
cabinet(s)
sink, cupboard
doll bed (large enough to be used by children)
high chair
"arm chair" or rocking chair
workbench
desk
bench/cot
tables and chairs.

In addition to all of the items mentioned above, it is necessary to have adequate shelving or other storage for dramatic play materials not in use on particular days. All hats, dress-up clothes, kitchen utensils, etc. need not be available each day. Children respond well to variety. If the area remained the same each day, the children might tire of the area, thus not taking advantage of all that dramatic play has to offer.

Dramatic Play Equipment and Materials for Outdoor Play

Equipment appropriate for outdoor areas depends on the climate and the terrain of the outdoor play space as well as the age and size of the children. Since the beginning of time, children have played whenever and wherever they have been able to do so. The nature of the play has been greatly influenced by the play environment. When there are hills, the children engage in play that involves crawling over the hills or rolling down the hills. The roles children play may take a more adventurous nature such as explorer, pirate, cowboy and Indians, etc. than if the terrain is flat and there are no places to hide behind or crawl into. If equipment is available, children will tend to use it. If the equipment is static, meaning it can only be used in one way and does not support the use of imagination, it may be used for a short while and then abandoned for more adventurous play that is conjured up by the children themselves. Several manufacturers are currently showing equipment conducive to dramatic play. Much of the equipment available for outdoor play consists of riding toys or large transportation vehicles such as a truck, fire engine, or train locomotive. The riding toys should include a variety if possible. Some toys should be adaptive or adaptable for children with disabilities. Some toys should be for use by individual children and some toys should accommodate more than one child at a time. The riding toys that accommodate more than one child at a time naturally encourage socialization, albeit at the nonverbal level to start with. For safe use of riding toys, it is preferable to have a hardtop surface on which to use the riding toys. When children attempt to use riding toys on a grassy surface, there are often rises and small depressions in the surface that make safe riding very difficult. For a child with special needs, riding the wheel toy may be difficult enough on a flat hardtop surface. Adding obstacles makes the task almost impossible to master.

It is nice to have a seating area with tables outdoors as well. This area may of course be used for snacks, lunch, or art activities but it may also be used by children during outdoor play as part of whatever theme the children may develop. It is also nice to have a place to sit outdoors when a child may not be up to playing actively but may want to watch what the other children are doing. There are many reasons for children to need to sit out while other children play. Some children may begin to feel comfortable with dramatic play indoors where props support the play and where the space is more defined. The same kind of thematic play taking place outdoors may be too open ended for that same child due to a lack of props and defined space.

Storage of Dramatic Play Materials

In addition to consideration of the types of equipment appropriate for dramatic play, another important consideration concerns having enough storage areas for dramatic-play materials and dramatic-play theme boxes. Dramatic-play materials can be as detailed and as varied as space and funds allow. Many of these materials may be collected over time or purchased in the kitchenware sections of discount stores. Other materials are more appropriately purchased through early childhood educational materials companies because of size, safety, and durability issues. The following list of materials is not meant to mention each and every item that may be collected but to represent a list of materials that would be important to have as a basic core:

- pots and pans made either of plastic or metal
- plates and cups made either of plastic or metal
- silverware made either of plastic or metal
- ironing board and iron, laundry basket
- rack or set of drawers for dress-up clothes
- mirror
- dish rack, towels, sponges
- dolls which reflect gender and ethnic diversity as well as special needs, doll stroller, doll high chair, doll bottle, doll feeding dishes, and spoons
- doll bed which should be large enough to accommodate a child
- dress-up clothes, hats and jewelry which reflect different genders and ethnic diversity
- briefcase, umbrella, lunch bucket
- blankets and pillows
- phones
- housekeeping tools
- message board and appropriate writing tools
- phone book

Creating Theme Boxes

For theme boxes, the potential is unending as to what can be collected and organized according to different themes. When these boxes are developed, it is much easier to implement different themes more often because one does not have to gather the requisite materials each time the theme is to be set up in the dramatic play area. The following is a list of themes and appropriate items to support those themes:

business office: paper, envelopes, pencils, pens, stamps, stamp pads, erasers, typewriter, calculator; ruler; phone, stapler, hole punch, carbon paper

post office: telephone, stamps, envelopes, paper, mailbox and mail pouch, rubber stamp, packages, postcards, letters, money, cash register, scale, signs

hospital or doctor's office: white shirt, cots, gowns, bandages, elastic bandages, stethoscope, syringes, tubing, masks, empty medicine containers, fever strip, clip board, phone, magazines for waiting room area, chairs, eye chart, scale, tape measure, medical kit.

Variations on this play can be a veterinarian's office with the inclusion of stuffed animals as patients or children playing the roles of the animals, or an eye doctor's office with a selection of empty frames or inexpensive sunglasses for the customers to choose their new glasses.

service station: tools, overalls, rags, small (empty) oil cans, foot operated air pump (appropriate for inflating air mattresses), rubber hose, box to use as a gas pump, sponge, window wiper, bucket, old tire, flashlight, spark plugs, keys

fire station: hats, hose, badge, boots, telephone, vehicle, walkie talkie, megaphone, bell, flashlight

restaurant: napkins, paper plates, menus, cups, silverware, plastic or silk flowers, vases, tablecloth, aprons, order pads, pencils or pens, music appropriate for dining.
Variations on this theme can be fast food restaurant and items appropriate to each specific setting (including caps, paper bags, napkins, signs, etc.) may be obtained from different fast food enterprises. Area may be set up to reflect the fast food logo appropriate to the one being played.

ice cream store: scoops, cups, sundae dishes, spoons, napkins, price charts, pictures, ice cream containers ranging from single serving to gallon container size, different colored pom poms to represent ice cream scoops, different size pom poms to reflect cherries, chips, other toppings, hats

flower shop: silk, plastic, and straw flowers which can be supplemented by real flowers if appropriate to the theme being implemented, vases, florist foam blocks, arrangement containers, cards, ribbons, cash register, pricing chart, money, adding machine or calculator, phone, order forms, pens, pencils, hats

shoe store: different pairs of shoes, slippers, boots, different size footwear, socks, foot measuring device, shoe advertisements, purses, mirror, shoe boxes

clothing store: shirts, pants, skirts, blouses, jackets, socks, underwear, gloves, hats, scarves, clothing advertisements, tape measure, hangers, price charts, money, cash register, credit cards

food store: empty food boxes and containers, store ads, money, cash register, food posters, plastic fruits and vegetables, aprons, caps, food store bags, shopping list paper, pencils, food coupons

book store: books, magazines, money, cash register, posters depicting different types of books (adventure, mystery, cookbooks, etc.)

toy store: selected small toys, puzzles, manipulatives, toys from shelves may be added when the play area is set up, money, toy ads and catalogues, cash register, bags sporting goods store: balls, gloves, bats, rackets, pennants, jackets, team caps, sneakers, cleats, flippers, masks, money, ads, cash register

music store: records, tapes, record player, tape recorder, pictures of all types of music stars, ads, money, cash register, bags

library: books, records, magazines, newspapers, cards, pockets, date stamp, stamp pad, paper, pencils

museum: rocks, shells, small artifacts, pencils and pens for making labels, sturdy paper for making labels, reference books on rocks, shells, etc., phone, brochures (which can be made by the children), money, tickets, guide hats.
This dramatic play may be incorporated into whatever theme is being implemented, i.e., circus, apples, community helpers, farm, etc.

detective agency: flashlights, magnifying glasses, microscope, phone, pads, paper, "clues" items, hats, raincoat, badges, identification cards, tape recorder

travel agency: brochures, tickets, phone, money, clipboards, paper, travel posters

train station: engineer caps, tickets, timetables, ticket punch, stopwatch, bell, suitcases, cargo

bus station: timetable, tickets, ticket punch, suitcases

airplane: food trays, small pillows, "movie" for in-flight entertainment, host/hostess uniforms, suitcases

space station: "space food," microphones, helmets, spacesuits, airpacks

ship travel (could be a fishing boat, a ferry or a cruise liner): rocking boat or large blocks to make boat, fishing rods, fish, sunglasses, sun hats, music, "entertainment," books, food, uniforms

picnic: basket, plasticware, tablecloth, plastic jug, plastic ants

puppets: puppet stage, puppets depicting people of different gender and ethnic diversity, animals, tickets, money, programs

pajama party: pajamas, pillows, backpacks, sleeping bags, blankets, snacks, stuffed animals, games

camping: sleeping bags, pillows, food, tent, flashlights, canteens, firewood, tape of nature sounds

school: books, notebooks, pencils, rulers, erasers, slates, chalk, charts, backpacks, lunch boxes

construction workers: hard hats, tool belts, tools, construction blueprints, pictures of completed buildings, gloves bakery: baker hats, aprons, bowls, whisks, measuring spoons, measuring cups, recipes, rolling pins, cookie cutters, plastic knives, bakery pictures, posters

factory: depending on the theme being implemented, the factory may be set up to make applesauce, gift items

television or radio station: microphone, charts, flannel board and flannel weather cut outs, papers, pointer, camera

birthday party: plates, cups, "cake," candles, wrapping paper, cards, presents, games, favors, balloons, hats, dress ups so children can be in "party" clothes

infant child care center: dolls, food, plates, spoons, bibs, high chair, cradle, carriage or stroller, blankets, clothes, diapers, lotion, wipes, bathtub, soap, shampoo, towels, aprons

Dramatic Play in the Small Block or Hollow Block Area

Dramatic play also takes place in the block corner with either small blocks and accessories or in the hollow block area. Appropriate small block accessories include trucks, cars, planes, people, trains, small farm, zoo, domestic, sea or wild animals, small dinosaurs, small village scenes, city play mats, farm play mats, small wooden farm set, small wooden school set. There are many other materials available and many other materials that can be made to add to the diversity of small block dramatic play. Careful observation of what the children like to construct will provide you with the information you need in order to provide appropriate supplemental materials.

In the large hollow blocks area, a steering wheel, dowels to support signs children make to identify their constructions, and sheets or other large pieces of fabric to use as a roof, grass or the ocean floor would also enhance the play. Sometimes providing large sheets of cardboard to use as a roof makes it easier for children to secure their constructions. All the theme boxes described earlier can be appropriately used within the large block area.

One last idea about theme boxes pertains to the space necessary to store all these boxes. It is unlikely that any one classroom has the space necessary for these boxes but what teacher would not want access to all of these resources? Ideally, whether in a public school or private early childhood setting, all the teachers could get together to contribute resources to these boxes. The boxes could be distributed among all the classrooms. A comprehensive list of all theme boxes, their contents, and locations could be developed and copies made for all teachers. In this way, all teachers and children would be able to benefit from the tremendous resources gathered by all the teachers.

FIG 8.4 Children enjoy creating enclosures while engaged in dramatic play.

MODIFICATION OF MATERIALS OR ACTIVITIES TO INCLUDE CHILDREN WITH SPECIAL NEEDS

So many of the materials and activities found in the dramatic play area are familiar to children. If a child has some special need it is quite possible that either the family or the therapist(s) working with the child addressed the issue of how to make the materials and activities available to the child. Adaptive devices, adaptive furniture and a realistic approach to the feasibility of the child engaging in certain activities at that time have possibly been addressed. General modifications will be listed by nature of what initially makes the experience inaccessible to a child:

Physical Considerations

When a child cannot reach the table or the floor or shelves in the dramatic play area, environmental modifications can be made as indicated:

- Engage in play standing up—Once again this may seem like a very simple modification but it is one that may make considerable difference to the child. When choosing roles to play, the child needs to be encouraged to select roles that do not require sitting down or getting from a standing to a sitting position. Greater mobility may be achieved by standing because the standing position (if the child is in a mobile stander) allows a child to be moved to another part of the dramatic play area more easily by a teacher or a peer.

- Work on the tray of stander or adaptive chair—Incorporating this piece of equipment into the play makes sense when playing certain themes. If the children are playing restaurant, bakery, library, or store, this surface becomes a logical part of the play. While it is preferable that children with special needs use the same surfaces as all the other children in the class, the other children may use the tray surface as well.

Visual Impairments

Children with visual impairments are usually very interested in dramatic play and require few modifications. For a child with minor impairments, allowing the child to get as close to the materials and the play situation as possible works best. This child may initially need help in finding the materials and learning cues as to where they belong. Once the child is familiar with these situations, there are usually few modifications necessary. Children with visual impairments enjoy the stimulation of dramatic play because it is not exacting and does not tax them visually.

Social, Emotional, or Behavioral Disorders

Dramatic play activities are sometimes frustrating for children who display behaviors that are challenging to peers, adults, or both. Often, these children have developed few coping skills. In other activity areas, if something does not fit together perfectly at the first try, or the child has not had prior experience with the activity, the child may react negatively. This may also happen in the dramatic play area. This happens because the child does not have the social skills or the emotional stamina to take a risk in social interaction or role play. Children who are emotionally fragile may not have the correct perceptions of peer responses to their behaviors or dress up clothes choices. Sometimes, the very unstructured nature of dramatic play that appeals to many children is exactly what frightens the child with special social or emotional needs. Sometimes it is best to create a situation where the teacher and the child spend some time observing the play and commenting on it prior to any attempt to join in. Once the child appears to be ready to enter the play, the teacher needs to facilitate the entry and remain involved or supportive until the child is really comfortable. If the teacher exits prematurely, the child is bound to follow the teacher and the play episode will be over for that child.

Regardless of whether the child is one who is prone to acting out or is usually withdrawn, the same supportive facilitation may be necessary to ease the child into a positive play situation.

CASE STUDY

A child with a very disturbing, hoarse quality to his voice and some fairly extreme acting out behaviors had difficulty getting children to pay positive attention to him. Although he was very bright, highly verbal, and skilled in describing how he felt when he was rejected by his peers, he was not aware of the impact of his behavior on the peers in the class. His teacher worked slowly and carefully to point out instances where he could join in the play and exactly what he might say and how to say it so as to receive positive responses from children. He was supported to use a "sweet voice" instead of his usual "rough voice" with the result being that the children welcomed him to play. His family was very supportive about reinforcing the concept of the sweet voice and found that they all loved listening to him. Not only did the reminder to use a different voice alter the voice quality but it also altered the nature of what he said. His verbalizations became more positive, less accusing, and more loving.

As was pointed out in the discussion about manipulative materials, the socially immature child who is also language delayed will benefit from being surrounded by the conversation that takes place in the dramatic play area. Although this type of child may not yet play cooperatively, the child may engage in solitary play in the proximity of children who provide high potential for language involvement. As children engage in dramatic play, whether it is parallel or cooperative, they may narrate their activity and use a wide variety of vocabulary. In addition to real words, they may invent words to describe their actions.

Learning Impairments

Modifications which would enable the child with learning impairments to participate in dramatic play activities might include having a teacher situated within the activity area in order to model appropriate play behaviors and to support the development of interaction between the child and the other children in the area. Demonstrations of the use of materials may be of benefit to the child because the child may have limited exposure to certain materials and experiences due to developmental delay. A child with learning difficulties may not have the entry behaviors necessary to begin to interact with others. The child may not know how to play a certain role. If this is the case, the teacher might want to establish a routine with that particular child which starts the child out at the beginning of the day in the dramatic play area. This may be very helpful because if the child is the first or one of the first children to enter the area, it is not as overwhelming as attempting to join play in progress. The teacher might ask the child what he plans to do in the dramatic play area as a means of prompting behavior. If the teacher can support a peer being the one to initiate to the child, teacher dependency can be diminished or avoided.

Children with special needs may need to have some modified materials made available to them in order to participate in dramatic play. If a child cannot manage the small play dishes, cups, and silverware these should be replaced with regular-size, plastic picnic dishes that are larger and easier to grasp. If the dolls are heavy, one or two lighter dolls may need to be added to the family. If all the dolls are of hard plastic, a cloth doll or rubber doll would also be a welcome addition. Some of the dress up clothes need to have velcro fasteners instead of small buttons or zippers. Play fruits and vegetables may need to be collected in several smaller baskets instead of one large basket. If a child cannot manage the large wooden blocks, the addition of a wagon may allow the child to transport blocks to the "construction" site. You may also develop the guideline of two children carrying each large wooden block as a safety precaution. These are simple modifications to make.

CASE STUDIES DESCRIBING MODIFICATIONS

CASE STUDY

Anthony had a most difficult time in the dramatic play area. Since he was a child grounded in routine, the unstructured nature of many of the dramatic play activities were unsettling to him. He did not respond well to invitations to enter role play. Involvement in this area initially consisted of observing children from clear across the room. He tended to have a concerned look on his face when watching the other children. When a teacher attempted to engage him in conversation about the play he was observing, he found it difficult to describe what he saw. Since he was not able to predict what the children would do next, he found it difficult to talk about it. As the year went on, he became more and more involved in solitary play with dramatic play materials. As time passed, his solitary play took place in closer proximity to the children. As themes were repeated, Anthony began to reach a comfort level not seen before. He seemed to be most comfortable with activities that most closely resembled family routines. He began to ask the teachers questions about what the other children were doing. His observations began to leave him with a smile on his face rather than the worried look he had early in the year. As was seen in terms of his behavior pattern in most areas, Anthony was careful and methodical in everything that he did in the dramatic play area. Anthony began to relate dramatic play episodes to his parents. Initially he talked about what the other children did. As the year went on, he started to tell them about what he said and what roles he took on. Sometimes he asked to play these things at home. At first he became upset if the play was not repeated in the exact same manner as it had been played at school. This was actually very helpful for his development because it forced him to become more flexible and accepting. This was a slow process but one that was very worthwhile.

Sharon loves dramatic play! She is a very dramatic child! She needs to be in a proper sitting position that allows her elbows to be above the table surface. Once in this position, she has the mobility and dexterity she needs to use materials and engage in role play. She often needs help obtaining materials and putting them away but her peers help her with these tasks. She is not at all shy about asking others to help her. In her preschool years, Sharon thoroughly enjoyed social interaction and role-playing experiences. Sharon cannot change her physical position without the assistance of an adult but she is still able to be in the center of a sustained dramatic play episode with a variety of children.

In the dramatic play area, **Charlie** needed assistance when he first entered preschool. The assistance focused on obtaining some materials for him because they were too large or too heavy for him to carry. He was always eager to explore everything and using materials that related to transportation thoroughly engaged him while requiring that he use both hands in order to play. Once again you may recall, his hands and fingers were pudgy and not as well developed as those of the other children in his preschool, but that did not stop him from being the driver of whatever vehicle the children built. His favorite piece of dramatic play equipment was the steering wheel. Just as he loved to build roads with small blocks and to drive cars and trucks back and forth on these roads, he was also determined to build roads with the large blocks. Although the blocks were large and heavy for him, his determination and the admiration of the other children were enough to sustain his efforts. His mother indicates that Charlie still enjoys dramatic play activities at school and at home as well.

Sarah was quite interested in observing dramatic play activities. Sarah was reported to engage in active dramatic play at home with her siblings but was purely an observer at school. You may recall that Sarah did not speak at school. As the year went by, Sarah began to follow other girls in their actions within dramatic play. She dressed up and mimicked their actions but did not say anything! Sarah seemed to enjoy building houses or rooms with large blocks and followed the other children in filling the rooms with dishes, food, babies, and flowers. It took quite some time and the subtle support of the teachers and her peers but eventually, Sarah spoke quietly to her peers within the dramatic play context. Occasionally this verbal interchange was prompted by her peers directing her as to what to say but the most important thing was that she was participating and growing!

For **Martie**, very active outdoor dramatic play was a natural activity. Martie could be seen outdoors with other children having fun and being excited about the "games" they created. Once indoors, Martie did not seem comfortable with dramatic play that centered around family and friends. This became quite understandable to his teachers as the year went on and they learned more about his family and living situations. Martie did not easily relate to the scenarios being played out by the other children. The nurturing and tenderness displayed to baby dolls and family roles seemed to make him uncomfortable. When other teachers developed themes that implemented more of a community helper focus, if Martie was familiar with the role, he would participate. He could direct his peers in those situations and liked being in a leadership position. Martie used dramatic play activities to work out some of his family problems but usually not through actual family play. Martie became more comfortable with all themes except for family as time went by. Although a big strong child, he could be gentle and nurturing when playing veterinarian or firefighter. This kind of play was responsible for a lot of his maturing in the social/emotional area during the course of the year.

Remember **Christina**, a child with visual deficits and oppositional behavior who was always eager to be involved in any activity? Christina did not need any modifications in order to engage in dramatic play. Although she did have trouble convincing her peers to carry out her ideas, mostly because her most favorite theme to play was "getting married," she did enjoy a wide circle of friends. She would enlist her peers to participate in weddings and one day went off on her honeymoon! She was very persistent in her pursuit of a groom on a daily basis. She was able to enlist the interest of some of her female peers in "designing" wedding dresses and veils. She spent considerable time in front of the mirror getting ready for the big event. As the year went by, with encouragement from her teachers, she was more willing to try other roles and involve herself with other scenarios. This was a very important lesson for Christina, one that was very important to her social and emotional growth and development. She made fewer attempts at control and engaged in more positive interactions with her peers. She became comfortable with following and leading.

As with everything else at school, **C. W.** found dramatic play to be very exciting. C. W. was a very playful child. He was very resourceful. He related to all the children and was a much sought–after playmate. The girls loved and nurtured him. He was a hugger and hugged at all the appropriate times.

Few children ever noticed his special needs because he was so much a part of everything that went on at school. He thoroughly enjoyed dressing up and was partial to hats and vests. If he could not manage a "costume" by himself, he did not hesitate to ask an adult for assistance. He took his roles seriously and used his whole body in his play. His imagination was very obvious through these activities.

SUMMARY

Dramatic play is an integral part of an early childhood classroom. Within this area, children experience the freedom to explore materials and follow their own ideas as well as the ideas of their peers. Through dramatic play, children apply mathematical concepts. They are able to work out problems, play out roles, and use language to express themselves. Language and social interaction become almost spontaneous as children become absorbed in the play of their peers as well their own play. Children bring their own experiences to their dramatic play. Stories they have read, movies or TV programs they have seen, places they have visited all have an influence on what they play out in the more open-ended dramatic play. Cognitive growth and the further development of the imagination flourish when children create scenarios, talk about their actions, and observe the interactions of others. Teachers often do not need to spend a lot of time with children to initiate dramatic play but they may need to be around to facilitate and support the positive nature of the play. Dramatic play changes in nature over the early childhood years but the need for and the appropriateness of dramatic play in the early childhood years never diminishes.

DISCUSSION QUESTIONS

1) There are no dramatic play materials in your kindergarten classroom which is one of four rooms slated to undergo a transformation from academic focus to developmentally appropriate focus. How will you acquire what you wish to have in the room? Is there any way you may work cooperatively with the other teachers?
2) Think about the themes you used to play when you were a young child. What do you think influenced those themes? What themes do you observe children playing when the theme is of their own choice? What do you think motivates those choices of theme?

3) You observe children playing a theme you think has potential to become negative in terms of scaring some children, excluding some children, and becoming too loud and rowdy for indoor play. What will your response as teacher, facilitator and overall classroom "manager" be to the situation? Why?
4) At the start of the school year, the parents of your first grade students seemed to be supportive of the children playing in the classroom. Now it is close to mid-year and several of the parents have asked when the children will stop playing and begin doing some real work. What will you say to these parents to explain the reason the children are playing and what it is that they are learning through play?
5) With a classmate, brainstorm some ideas for dramatic play activities appropriate for an integrated theme you mutually select. Think about the materials you would like to have to support the dramatic play.
6) You observe over a period of time that there is a child with disabilities in your class who engages in dramatic play for very brief periods of time. This is a concern you wish to address. What ideas do you have to involve the child in more sustained play?

REFERENCES

Abraham, M., Morris, L., & Wald, P. (1993). *Inclusive early childhood education—A model classroom.* Tucson, AZ: Communication Skill Builders.

Bredekamp. S. (1990). *Developmentally appropriate practice in early childhood programs serving children from birth through age 8.* Washington, DC: National Association for the Education of Young Children.

Cartwright, S. (1993). Cooperative learning can occur in any kind of program. *Young Children, 48(2),* 12–14.

Christie, J. (1983). The effects of play tutoring on young children's cognitive performance. *Journal of Educational Research, 76,* 326–330.

Day, B. (1994). *Early childhood education—Developmental/experiential teaching and learning* (Fourth edition). New York: Merrill.

Dimidjian, V. (Ed). (1992). *Play's place in public education for young children.* Washington, DC: A National Education Association Publication.

Dodge, D. (1989). *The creative curriculum for early childhood.* Washington, DC: Teaching Strategies, Inc.

Dolinar, K., Boser, C., & Holm, E. (1994). *Learning through play: Curriculum and activities for the inclusive classroom.* New York: Delmar Publishers Inc.

Eliason, C., & Jenkins, L. (1994). *A practical guide to early childhood curriculum.* New York: Merrill.

Gardner, H. (1983). *Frames of mind: The theory of multiple intelligences.* New York: Basic Books, Inc.

Hendrick, J. (1994). *Total learning—Developmental curriculum for the young child.* New York: Merrill.

Howe, N., Moller, L., Chambers, B., & Petrakos, H. (1993). The ecology of dramatic play centers and children's social and cognitive play. *Early Childhood Research Quarterly, 8(2),* 235–251.

Johnson, J., Ersler, J., & Lawton, J. (1982). Intellectual correlates of preschooler's spontaneous play. *Journal of General Psychology, 106,* 115–122.

Kostelnik, M., Soderman, A., & Whiren, A. (1993). *Developmentally appropriate programs in early childhood education.* New York: Merrill.

Krogh, S. (1990). *The integrated early childhood curriculum.* New York: McGraw-Hill Publishing Company.

Lieber, J. (1993). A comparison of social pretend play in young children with and without disabilities. *Early Education and Development, 4(3),* 148–161.

Pelligrini, A. (1985). Relations between preschool children's symbolic play and literate behavior. In *Play, language and stories,* edited by L. Galda and A. Pelligrini. Norwood, NJ: Ablex.

Pelligrini, A. & Dressden, J. (1992). Play in school? Yes, we're serious. In *Play's place in public education for young children,* edited by Victoria Jean Dimidjian. Washington, DC: A National Education Association Publication.

Rubin, K., Fein, G., & Vandenberg, B. (1983). Play. In E. Hetherington (Ed.) & P. Mussen (Series Ed.), *Handbook of child psychology: Vol. 4. Socialization, personality, and social development.* New York: Wiley.

Seefeldt, C. (1989). *Social studies for the preschool-primary child.* Columbus, OH: Merrill.

Smilansky, S., & Shefatya, L. (1990). *Facilitating play: A medium for promoting cognitive, socio-emotional and academic development in young children.* Gaithersburg, MD: Psychosocial & Educational Publications.

Trawick-Smith. J. (1994). *Interactions in the classroom—Facilitating play in the early years.* New York: Merrill.

Van Hoorn, J., Nourot, P., Scales, B., & Alward, K. (1993) *Play at the center of the curriculum.* New York: Merrill.

Wortham, S. (1994). *Early childhood curriculum—Developmental bases for learning and teaching.* New York: Merrill.

ADDITIONAL READINGS

Christie, J. (Ed.). (1991). *Play and early literacy development.* New York: State University of New York Press.

Fein, G., & Rivkin, M. (Eds.). (1986). *The young child at play: Reviews of research, volume 4*. Washington, DC: National Association for the Education of Young Children.

Gallas, K. (1994). *The languages of learning: How children talk, write, dance, and sing their understanding of the world*. New York: Teachers College Press.

Goelman, H., & Jacobs, E., (Eds.). (1994). *Children's play in child care settings*. New York: State University of New York Press.

Jones, E., & Reynolds, G. (1992). *The play's the thing: Teachers' roles in children's play*. New York: Teachers College Press.

Klugman, E., & Smilansky, S. (Eds.). (1990). *Children's play and learning: Perspectives and policy implications*. New York: Teachers College Press.

Morris, L., & Schulz, L. (1989). *Creative play activities for children with disabilities: A resource book for teachers and parents*. Champaign, IL: Human Kinetics.

Rogers, C., & Sawyers, J. (1988). *Play in the lives of children*. Washington, DC: National Association for the Education of Young Children.

Roopnarine, J., Johnson, J., & Hooper, F. (Eds.). (1994). *Children's play in diverse cultures*. New York: State University of New York Press.

Wassermann, S. (1990). *Serious players in the primary classroom: Empowering children through active learning experiences*. New York: Teachers College Press.

CHAPTER 9

Large Motor Development

KEY TERMS

physical development
physical activities
large motor activities
developmental milestones
accessible playscape
adaptive physical education
play environments

INTRODUCTION

Large motor development is something that so many teachers and parents take for granted. When children follow normal paths and rates of **physical development,** teachers tend to prepare environments that will be safe for children, play with them in a normal fashion, and think little about what actually happens on a daily basis to perpetuate this growth and development. In fact, almost everything that is done for and with the infant and toddler helps to promote physical development. The daily care routine of feeding, burping, changing, dressing, placing, playing, singing, and talking to the young child plays a very important role in large motor development. Parents and teachers are well aware that physical change in size and ability of children takes place very rapidly. This is what often makes it appear that it all happens by itself.

Some children do not develop as normally. Some are born with or are predisposed to conditions which interfere with the development that takes place so easily in other children. This makes teachers aware of the fact that children are often assessed based on their physical abilities because this is what is noticed first. Physical abilities or motor development almost serves as the casing in which the whole child dwells. Teachers must certainly encourage large motor development in children. If large motor development is going to be a slow and difficult process or almost non existent, teachers must not abandon the physical child but must also look beyond the exterior to nurture and develop other parts of the child which are not disabled. Large motor development and activities have an impact on all other aspects of the child and the program. Large motor activities are inherent in much of early childhood education and need to be planned for, as with other activities.

IMPORTANCE OF LARGE MOTOR ACTIVITIES FOR DEVELOPMENT

The early childhood years are important ones for physical development. During the infant and toddler period, many motor skills emerge and are later refined and improved during the preschool years through the variety of active play activities in which children engage. The active play that young children enjoy takes place both outdoors and indoors. Further refinement takes place during early school years if children are provided with adequate physical activity opportunities. This translates into children having planned opportunities to move around in their classrooms instead of sitting at their desks all day. Sometimes there is a tendency to gear physical activity for children beyond the preschool years into a more competitive, sports-oriented direction. Physical development contributes to positive development in other areas. **Physical activities** should not take a back seat to cognitive activities. In order for children to be active and physically healthy, they need to have daily physical activity. Some children enjoy this kind of activity in the natural course of events. They have access to a safe outdoor play space where they can run, roll, climb, and slide. This space may be as close as their own backyard, a housing complex recreation area, or a neighborhood park. In some cities, indoor play spaces are being developed as an alternative to city parks. This is not only due to safety issues but due to the recognition that children of families living in small apartments need to engage in large motor activity on rainy,

FIG 9.1 Many outdoor activities promote physical development.

snowy, or extremely hot and humid days when the outside air is unfit to breathe.

While it is agreed that children require large motor activity for pure exercise as well as continued whole child development, there are many programs that do not provide adequate planned large motor components on a regular basis. In the course of natural activity, children use their whole bodies or as much of their bodies as they are able. Children with special needs may require assistance in utilizing their bodies. Specialists such as physical therapists and occupational therapists work with teachers and parents to teach the appropriate way to achieve maximum results from children. Peers do a lot to encourage this type of activity as well.

Some children seem to be more sedentary in nature. Often that happens because the family tends to be sedentary. Children do not need to go "work out" in order to be active. If left to their own devices, children can usually think of many ways of moving around and spending energy.

Components of Large Motor Activities

There are many components to **large motor activities.** Throwing, catching, kicking, jumping, and swinging involve the use of locomotor skills. When planning for large motor activities, teachers may select from the following list that provides for variety and range of motion: walking; throwing and catching; balancing; hopping, jumping and leaping; running, galloping, skipping; climbing; crawling, creeping, scooting; using wheeled vehicles (Beaty, 1992).

Many large motor actions occur during the course of the regular play activities that are an integral part of the classroom. When children walk, pretend to be an animal, carry large blocks, help move chairs or tables, or reach to put things away, these are all examples of large motor involvement that is not planned for as a separate part of the activity of the day. During the day children typically bend, stretch, twist and turn, and jump. Children with disabilities benefit from assisted physical activities that stretch their muscles to help them to be more flexible without stretching them beyond what is appropriate and healthy for them.

OBJECTIVES OF LARGE MOTOR ACTIVITIES

The major goal of large motor activities is to assist children in the achievement of physical competence. In addition, other goals focus on helping them to develop the knowledge, attitudes, skills and behaviors necessary to develop and maintain a healthy lifestyle.

Large motor activities allow teachers to provide children with opportunities:

- to develop eye-hand coordination
- to develop eye-foot coordination
- to develop body awareness—to know about the body as it moves
- to develop endurance
- to develop flexibility
- to develop muscle strength
- to develop balance
- to develop ability to relax the whole body
- to use their whole bodies in a purposeful manner
- to do work
- to use their physical skills in cooperative play
- to use their physical skills in social interaction
- to express themselves
- to enhance self-esteem by learning to use their bodies in a competent fashion
- to demonstrate knowledge of spatial relationships
- to engage in motor planning (figure out how to get from one place to another without bumping into objects, people, or furniture)
- to play games
- to demonstrate ability to follow directions
- to lead
- to follow
- to develop a sense of accomplishment

DEVELOPMENTALLY APPROPRIATE ACTIVITIES AND MATERIALS

Safe, Age-appropriate Physical Activity

While many large motor activities simply require the child and no additional materials, a very important consideration is the safety of the child. Teachers must remember that young bodies can be taxed very easily. This means that movements requiring more strength and endurance than is normal for the young child and games requiring extreme skill development are not developmentally appropriate for young children. There are so many things that children can do in the large motor domain that are appropriate, there is no need to rush them and place the wrong emphasis on physical activity. All people need to engage in physical activity to stay healthy and alert. There is no need to engage in competition each time children engage in physical activity. Teachers should promote developmentally appropriate activities for children which help them feel good about themselves and their bodies.

Children Who Are Large in Stature

Some children inadvertently mislead teachers into thinking they are more physically capable than they really are. This often happens when the child is large in stature and appears more mature. Be careful to remember that the physically large child is not necessarily equally physically advanced or cognitively advanced. Often this very large child develops more slowly. The child may begin to crawl and walk at a later point because there is just that much more body to maneuver.

Importance of Knowing about Developmental Milestones

Teachers and parents need to be knowledgeable about **developmental milestones** in the physical domain in order to know if a child is progressing within normal parameters. When children are in the infant or toddler stage of development, physical milestones seem to be what parents use to compare children. You will often hear parents talking about the fact that their child already crawls or walks. It may appear to the listener that these parents are rushing children into these behaviors. What it really turns out to be is the way in which parents boast about accomplishments the child has already achieved. As children mature and their behavioral repertoires expand, parents include information on vocabulary, daily antics, and whatever else they are able to relate to willing listeners. For a child at the infant through toddler stage, motor abilities and food consumption are logical points of observation. While development is taking place in the cognitive and in the social and emotional domains, much of this other development may not be as obvious to parents.

The most appropriate way to know whether an activity or material is developmentally appropriate and thus safe for a young child is to regularly review developmental milestones in the physical domain. In this way, teachers will not rely on the memory of accomplishments of previous students as their guideposts for development. The following list contains highlights of physical development for children between three to eight years of age. This list is useful as a check point for teachers and parents who have questions about the development of a specific child or who just wish to refresh their memory.

Physical Development: Three- and Four-Year-Olds

rides a trike; pushes a wagon
runs smoothly and can stop easily
climbs jungle gym ladder
walks stairs with alternating feet
jumps with two feet
high energy level
does a running broad jump by age four
begins to skip alternating feet, one foot ahead of another
balances on one foot
keeps good time in response to music
fine motor skills developing: works zippers, can do some buttons
scissor control—cuts paper in half; some cut on a line
holds paper with one hand while writing with the other
night control of elimination

Physical Development: Five- and Six-Year-Olds

well controlled and constantly in motion
often rides bike as well as trike
skips with alternating feet; hops
greater fine motor control: uses toothbrush, hammers, saws, scissors, pencils, needles for sewing
handedness well established
dresses self but may need help with shoe tying
starts to lose teeth

Physical Development: Seven- and Eight-Year-Olds

variation in height and weight; rate of growth slows
masters skills for game playing; enjoys team sports

greater fine motor control: draws diamond and forms letters well
willing to repeat skills to achieve mastery
has sudden spurts of energy
continues to lose baby teeth; permanent teeth appear
body more proportionate; facial structure changes

Encouraging Healthy Physical Activity

Some children need to be stimulated and encouraged to participate in physical activity even if the activity is developmentally appropriate. This may be due to the fact that the child has limited experience with the equipment or the nature of the activity. Once introduced to and encouraged to participate, the child may appear to be immediately comfortable. One might question why children would need to be introduced to an activity if it is appropriate for them. An established pattern of behavior may already exist and will continue to exist until a teacher intervenes and through participation with the children, encourages the child to become involved. The established pattern of behavior may consist of hanging back and appearing fearful. If teacher encouragement is effective and involvement is found to be rewarding, the children will continue the activity.

Encouraging the Fearful Child

Once in a while, a teacher may encounter a child who is genuinely fearful of some physical activities. The child may be afraid of heights and thus avoids climbing of any kind. Demonstrations of safe climbing techniques as well as teacher proximity to the climbing apparatus may be all the child needs to encourage participation. Sometimes a child who does not respond to the encouragement of a teacher may be encouraged through the use of a peer model. Children observing other children enjoying an activity or the challenge of a piece of equipment might be stimulated to join in the fun even if it is a little scary at the start. Other times, this may not work because the fear may be reinforced by overly cautious adults who provide graphic daily reminders about the perils of climbing too high. This is not as easy to overcome because teachers do not always know about these messages. Reassuring parents about the safety of the equipment as well as the level of teacher supervision provided may calm their fears. Sometimes parents are fearful due to their own personal experience. Teachers must work with parents to help them see that voicing their own fears on a regular basis may be detrimental to the child.

The child may be afraid of running outdoors but will run indoors.

CASE STUDY

A lively, tall, apparently well-developed two-year-old girl evidenced this problem. While active indoors, she spent most of the time outside attempting to climb up the teacher's body. Careful observation of this girl from the time her father parked the car and carried her into the school building until the time the father physically picked her up and carried her to the car at the end of the session, led the teachers to ask the father why he did not have her walk with him. He told the teachers that she fussed so much about putting her feet down on the sidewalk that it was easier for him to just carry her. The teachers were quite curious as to whether this was now a bad habit or whether there was actually a problem. They took stock of what was outdoors. Each piece of portable equipment was brought indoors one at a time. The child played on the equipment when it was indoors. It then appeared that something about the outdoors was problematic. The next day, as the group was headed through the sliding door to the playground, a stiff wind stirred up the dry leaves piled up in the corner of the yard near the door. The leaves began to blow into the classroom. The child began to scream. She was afraid of the leaves against her ankles and legs. This is what had kept her from walking outdoors. This incident was shared with the father at dismissal. He began to recollect that she started to walk in the fall of the previous year. She was a little unsteady on her feet but was fiercely independent and wanted to walk alone. One day when the wind picked up, she fell over in a pile of swirling leaves and began to scream. He recalled picking her up and telling her not to worry, she was safe. The windy fall was followed by an icy, snowy winter. The child spent both of those seasons being carried around outdoors and walking around quite capably indoors. The mystery was solved. It was not a motor problem at all. It was a fear that could be handled. By bringing piles of leaves into the classroom and occasionally having a slow-moving fan gently blow the leaves around on the floor, the child began to lose her fear of walking around where there were leaves on the ground. Though cleaning up leaves from the floor added to the daily routine for teachers, it was well worth the effort to see this child enjoy the outdoors with her whole body!

Creating Healthy Caution in the Young Child

Some children appear to be fearless when it comes to engaging in physical activity regardless of whether equipment is involved. While parents and teachers should not undermine this fearlessness, they should responsibly educate these children about issues of safety. Children nonchalantly walking off the edge of a pool or releasing their grip from the top of a high climber may not always come to a positive conclusion. A child with attention deficit disorder (ADD) may appear fearless and unaware of danger because of the distractibility and impulsivity that often accompanies the ADD. Teachers should not show children that they are afraid they will hurt themselves but rather teach them appropriate caution.

Safety of Space and Equipment

One critical factor that serves to allay the fear of adults relative to the antics of young children is the safety of the space and the equipment in which children play. Young children need to play in space that is appropriate for them. This translates into space that is clean, well built with that age group in mind, and well monitored to make sure that nothing in the space has changed which would render it unsafe or inappropriate for that age group. Some school and public playgrounds have large playscapes which pose grave potential danger for young children. The danger may be in the height, the distance between steps or bars, the slope of the slide, the design of the structure or the material from which the equipment is made. The playground would need adaptive equipment for children with physical challenges. As public schools include groups of younger children, it is critical to ensure that the school playscape is appropriate for the younger child. If this is not a possibility, another area should be designated and developed for younger children.

There is much more known now about playground safety than when many of these structures existing today were erected. Communities are becoming more aware of how dangerous these structures are. Unfortunately, this knowledge sometimes comes as a result of tragedy. Another reason for concern focuses on equipment that is designed so that adults cannot access certain parts of the equipment. This means that if a child is in danger because he or she panicked, got caught on something, slipped, or was being crowded by other children, there would be no way in which an adult could come to the aid of the child. This kind of situation may have long-lasting effects on a child with the result being that the child might never go near large muscle equipment again. Even with appropriate space and appropriate equipment, children need adequate, involved adult supervision. They move quickly and situations can change from moment to moment.

Developmentally Appropriate Equipment

While the best resource for activity remains the child's own body, the following equipment is very appropriate for large motor activity because the items are not part of a static structure and can be arranged in a variety of ways: tires, barrels, crates, boards (Hendrick, 1994). With portable equipment one must make sure that the pieces are level and balanced. This is not always easy to do because some yards have a sloping surface. If this is the case, portable equipment may not be an option.

A clean, good size sand box is an important piece of equipment in a play yard regardless of whether the yard consists of mostly portable or permanent equipment. In addition to the sensory value of sand play, the sand box provides large motor opportunities for children with limited skills and abilities. Simply getting in and out of the box may prove to be a challenge for a child. Sitting up in the box may also be difficult but the nature of the material and the proximity to other children may be enticing enough to make it happen.

Permanent Playground Structures and Spaces

The cost of some of the more beautiful, versatile, permanent, outdoor, large motor equipment is often prohibitive for centers, school, and communities. Often, these structures are also inaccessible to children with special needs. In an attempt to provide something for children that is within the financial means of a program and also accessible, structures are often built by community volunteers. There are many positive outcomes of such building but often these structures require considerable maintenance and may not follow all the basic safety guidelines.

Each outdoor play space has assets and deficits. Some yards are totally paved and others are totally unpaved. While the paved yard yearns for some green grass, the totally grassy yard may be under water much of the year. Keeping children safe and dry when you have to contend with water is always a challenge. Playgrounds in city schools must make do with what is there. There is just so much that can be done with a yard that is bound by brick wall. However, if you did not have a brick wall, then you could not "paint" the wall with water and brushes. For every minus you can usually find a plus, if you look hard enough (Hendrick, 1994).

Planning for Variety

It is important to think about the range of motion in which a child can engage when involved in physical activity. Wheel toys, ladders, slides, balance boards, rocking boats, and balls all provide for a variety of exercise and can be used both indoors and outdoors.

As children master certain skills and movements they can be challenged to enhance their skills in those areas by having them engage in variations of those behaviors. The following list contains a few examples of skills and variations. The age and skill level of the children will determine which of the many large motor skills and possible variations can be implemented in the classroom:

FIG 9.2 Outdoor time provides opportunities for physical activity and development.

Skill	Variation(s)
▮ walk a straight line	walk backwards
	walk around a circle
	walk on tip toes
	walk on heels
	walk with toes pointing out
	walk with toes pointing in
	walk a balance beam
	follow the leader
	walk like an animal
▮ walk in one direction	walk, stop and change direction
▮ balance on one foot	walk across balance beam
	follow the leader
	move from footprint to footprint
	use varied heights balance boards
▮ climb stairs	climb jungle gym
▮ throw or catch a ball	use beanbags
	ring toss
▮ crawl over surfaces	crawl through a tunnel
	crawl through a defined course

These activities can certainly be presented to children as isolated activities or they may be incorporated into whatever integrated theme is implemented. Trostle and Yawkey (1990) in their book rich in integrated learning activities, point out some of the logical ways in which large motor skills can be developed and enhanced through the variety of activities provided for children within an integrated unit. Other authors (Berry & Mindes, 1993; Abraham, Morris & Wald, 1993; and Kostelnik, (Ed.), 1991) also provide excellent examples of how young bodies can be challenged through thematic activity.

Materials for Indoor Large Motor Play

Simple materials to enhance indoor large motor experience might include: balance boards and beams, hoops, ring toss, indoor appropriate-size golf equipment, velcro balls and catching mitts, soft rubber balls, foam balls, cloth tunnel, small round or square trampoline (not high off the ground), exercise mat, rocking boat (with stairs on the reverse side), bean bag toss, small parachute, and fabric streamers.

Games and Large Motor Play

Games can play an important role in large motor activity. For young children, the games must not be too organized with several rules. If there are too many rules, the children will either not want to play the game, or attempt to play it but be easily frustrated by having to remember too much. Sometimes children wind up making up their own rules in order to get through the game. If the game is designed so that there is always a winner, the game may have great appeal to the child with a more competitive and aggressive nature but may not have any appeal for the child who likes to play for the sake of playing. Emphasis should be placed on cooperative games and individual achievement (Kostelnik, Soderman & Whiren, 1993). Children need to have positive models in play. It is therefore necessary for teachers to participate until children are comfortable with the game, their peers, and, of course, themselves (Poest, Williams, Witt & Atwood, 1990). In addition to learning structure, routine, and turn taking through play, children are exposed to certain concepts such as direction (e.g., up-down, forward-backward, right-left, far-near, over-under, in-out). These concepts are much easier to learn through large motor play than through other means. As children mature and skills become refined, games such as hopscotch may be added to the repertoire.

Teachers as Models for and Participants in Physical Activity

In modeling physical activity, it is critical to remember that children are not able to do what an adult can do in terms of strength and endurance but may be able to do things that adults cannot do relative to the flexibility and limber quality of the young child. You may hear exercise experts suggest that the greatest way to keep physically fit as an adult is to imitate each movement a toddler executes during the course of the day. Now that is real exercise! When adults want children to engage in physical activity, one of the greatest motivators may be to participate with the child in a partnership, not in competition. The object is not to "beat the time" or "do the most" but to share the fun of the activity.

Obstacle Courses

Whether indoors or out, children enjoy obstacle courses. The course can be as simple or as complex as the group is able to handle. When it is too simple, children might suggest more challenging enhancements. As children master the course, they might want to go through it with a partner. This would require that they organize and synchronize their movements. As physical skill progresses they may want to go through with one hand behind the back or go through backwards. Another way to vary an obstacle course is to place a number card at each different part of the course. At each of these "stations" the child would have to do what the card says. The movements indicated at each station could be varied so that over time the full range of movements would be included (Day, 1994).

As can be seen from these examples, there are many things that teachers can do to enhance the development of large motor skills as well as encourage children to become more interested in physical activity as a rewarding part of daily life.

MODIFICATION OF MATERIALS OR ACTIVITIES TO INCLUDE CHILDREN WITH SPECIAL NEEDS

All of the activities and equipment already mentioned, while developmentally appropriate, may not be accessible to children with special needs. The range of special needs children may have precluded designing one particular large motor plan that would meet the needs of all children. The play environment must be adapted to meet the needs of each child. Adults in the environment must be prepared to make modifications in equipment or activities or design alternative activities for children with special needs. General modifications will be listed by nature of what initially makes the experience inaccessible to a child:

Physical Conditions

Children with physical disabilities involving the use of adaptive devices may pose circumstances that require consultation from specialists who work with the child on a regular basis. Questions teachers might have about a child with this kind of special need might concern the suitability or adaptability of activities and equipment within the classroom or school environment. Even if a teacher has considerable experience working with children with physical disabilities, it is always wise to consult with specialists who work with a particular child and with the family. As a teacher, you would not want to attempt to implement an activity or a program with a child that would be counterproductive to the therapeutic efforts already being directed to this child. Working with specialists such as the physical therapist and occupational therapist is a critical component of planning for any child with special needs. It is even more critical with regard to a child with physical disabilities.

Children with severe physical disabilities that affect their mobility might still be able to participate in some physical activities if the environment in which the activity is to happen is accessible. If the activity involves the use of a parachute and the child uses a wheelchair, the child may be able to hold onto the parachute and help to lift it up and down so that other children may run under it. If the child uses a motorized wheelchair, the child may be able to be of the ones who runs under the parachute. If the child uses a walker, an activity using a parachute may not be accessible to the child because it requires using one or both hands to hold onto the chute or the ability to move quickly to get under and out from under the parachute. This does not mean that the child cannot be in the area of the activity. It is possible to have the child call out the names of children who will run under the parachute. In that way, the child will feel as though he or she is participating and playing an important role in the play, even though it may not be the same physical role other children are playing.

CASE STUDY

A child with muscular dystrophy who was able to move his hands and slightly move his head and slightly raise his shoulders was integrated in a preschool class. This child was highly verbal, very social, and fairly petite. He sat in a padded molded vinyl seat and had no independent mobility. Children would gravitate to where he was and worked with manipulatives with him on a regular basis. He was not at all shy about asking for teacher assistance and making his needs known. When it came to large motor activities, he was very happy to be an active observer. He would be in the center of circle games as well as on the circle with the other children. He enjoyed singing along with the other children as part of the game. If appropriate, a teacher would carry the child around as part of the circle game. When other children were engaged in active play outdoors, he was an avid observer to the point of sweating if they were running. One day he told his teacher that his friend was coming over after school. The teacher asked if they were going to watch a movie. He said they were not. She asked if they were going to read books. He said they were not. She asked him what they were going to do and he replied that they were going to fight! He then gave the teacher a demonstration of fighting. He moved his shoulders up and down and shouted fighting noises with great dramatic flair! While you might discourage this behavior in most children, it was not discouraged in this child. Since the teacher knew he could not really fight, she allowed him to maintain the concept that he could.

When outdoors, a teacher would be able to hold him on her lap so that he could experience the sand box and occasionally a teacher would hold him closely and run or jump with him in her arms. On those days he would go home after school and tell his mother that he jumped and ran at school. His manner of speech and description of experiences made his stories quite believable. In fact, he had run and jumped in the arms of a teacher. This is a good example of a simple modification to the environment. A much physically larger child might not be able to share the same experience in the same way. Another adaptation would need to be created.

For outdoor play, physically disabled children with adaptive equipment needs may not be able to have access to the large equipment. Currently there are some manufacturers making equipment that is accessible with ramps, wide pathways, and supported sides to the equipment. Even this type of equipment may not be accessible for all children using adaptive equipment because the child may not have the stamina to access the equipment. One community was very proud of the **accessible playscape** it built at a neighborhood school. When a child using a wheelchair went outdoors to use the equipment for the first time, the equipment was still not accessible due to the surface that existed between the school exit and the playscape. Everyone had spent so much time focusing on the playscape, they never looked at the path between the school and the playscape site. The committee was extremely upset when they heard that piece of news and went back to the drawing board to see what could be done to make the modifications necessary to render the area totally accessible.

The important point to remember is that while other children are engaged in physical activity, the child with adaptive equipment should also engage in some form of physical activity that is developmentally appropriate for that child. There are many things children might be able to do from a wheelchair or stander depending on the type and severity of the disability. They might be able to throw balls, kick balls, or hold one end of a jump rope for someone who is jumping. One just needs to look at the environment to explore the possibilities. Sometimes the peer group can be enlisted to come up with new ideas for the child or new ways of facilitating inclusion in large motor activities.

To accommodate the very special needs of some children with physical disabilities, some modifications or a special program made need to be made available. If an **adaptive physical education** program is required according to the individualized educational plan (IEP) developed for the child, a specialist will be made available to the child. It is important to coordinate with that specialist and ask that person any questions you might have about activities you provide on a regular basis. The specialist may also be able to suggest other activities that could be incorporated into the daily routine that would benefit not only the child with physical disabilities but all the children in the class as well.

Block (1994) presents a checklist to determine curricular adaptations in the area of physical education for individuals with specific limitations. The checklist is divided into five major questions concerning the limitations of strength, speed, endurance, balance and coordination, and accuracy. Within each area of limitation there are things to consider with regard to modification of the environment, allowances for the child to attempt the task from a different physical position and the use of modified equipment. These are important considerations for teachers in early childhood classrooms. Answers to these questions help to support the inclusion of children with physical disabilities.

Visual Impairments

Children with visual impairments can be oriented to space and equipment and thus may not require many modifications. For a child with minor impairments, allow the child to get as close as possible to the materials and the play situation. This child may initially need some assistance from adults to learn about the equipment or the location of the equipment so that they may access it safely. After that orientation, they may not need any further assistance. An outsider observing the children may not detect any impairment at all because the child may be so acclimated to the situation.

Children with visual impairments enjoy the stimulation of physical activity using large motor skills. As long as they feel safe, they will participate fully. Some slight modifications to equipment might involve painting the stairs or handrails of the equipment with a color that is visible to the child. It is best to consult with the vision specialist working with the child and the family before any painting or taping of equipment is done because as the expert in the field, the vision specialist will know the best technique to implement in order to have the child be safe and secure.

Social, Emotional, or Behavioral Disorders

Children with social, emotional, or behavioral disorders engage in a wide range of behavior that may or may not influence large motor activity. A child who is withdrawn emotionally and socially may be very inactive physically. The child may be afraid of failure and stay away from activities which are personally intimidating. That is not to say that the child is not skilled motorically but the child does not willingly engage in large motor activity. If the teacher can slowly begin to reassure the child that it is physically and emotionally safe to become involved in physical activities, the child may find a release of emotion and an accepting peer group. Physical activity may then become a source of praise from peers and adults.

Children with a repertoire of acting out behavior often have few coping skills. If they are not able to follow a direction or carry out some physical activity perfectly at the first try, the child may at one extreme, wind up quietly leaving the area or at the other extreme, act out and need to be removed from the area. Sometimes a child with these problems may need to observe others engaged in the physical activity before being comfortable enough to join in. The child may benefit from adult assistance in addition to encouragement in order to succeed in a game or learn a new skill.

A socially immature child may just need more time before venturing to try some physical activities. Since most physical activities require that a child be away from furniture and materials, this type of child may feel vulnerable just being out in the middle of open space. The child may not feel ready to hold a hand or be in close proximity to another child. Teachers must move slowly with children who are cautious. The objective is to encourage rather than discourage participation.

Learning Impairments

Modifications which would enable the child to participate in large motor activities might need to include demonstrations of the process or sequence of steps to be followed, or assistance to enable total participation. Visual cues may be appropriate to assist the child in remembering what to do in an activity. Special practice sessions might be arranged so that the child has time to build skill prior to needing to use the skill to join in the activity.

If a child with learning difficulties typically waits to be invited to join in physical activity then the teacher might want to establish a routine that pairs a peer with that child for physical activities. It would be important to have a small group of peers rotate playing the role of "inviter" so that it did not become the responsibility of one specific child.

Design of Play Environments for all Children

Frost (1992) presents considerable information and designs for **play environments** suitable for all children. Within this information is a list of the areas that need to be thought about when planning such a facility. They include: special planning; mobility, accessibility, and challenge; play leaders with special skills; and special attention to safety. The special planning involves looking at the design of the play space before any site preparation or construction begins. This cannot be a "create as you go along" project due to the special nature of wheelchair access. Planning for the focus on disabilities should not preclude excitement and challenge from the space.

Important considerations concerning mobility and accessibility necessitate thinking about ramping. Since many activities such as sand and water play can be presented at ground level, ramps are essential only when children cannot come out of a wheelchair. A well designed play environment might afford a child the opportunity to get into some other seat or to be in a horizontal position to pull through a maze or path.

As teachers are most usually the play leaders on school playgrounds, it is important to learn about the play environment and the expectations for use of all the pieces in the environment. Sometimes when you walk onto a playground with separate pieces of equipment, it is difficult to know what each piece is for. In previous years there may have existed connectors that were dismantled rather than refurbished. Children are very resourceful and most usually can create a use for something. While each remaining piece may work by itself, it would be nice to know the original design.

Safety is a concern for all play environments regardless of who will use them. While children without special needs may be able to deal with less than totally safe conditions such as a splintering surface or a weak board, children with special needs and their special equipment require well maintained play environments. A fall for any child is less than desirable. A fall for a child with special needs may be devastating. A child with physical disabilities often cannot brace a fall and falls very hard. This sometimes makes the child extremely fearful of using any play equipment at all. If the playscape is not 100 percent secure, the child may be traumatized. A child with mental retardation may be fearful or unaware of potential danger. For this type of child, the more secure the environment, the more successful the experience.

CASE STUDIES DESCRIBING MODIFICATIONS

CASE STUDY

Anthony was reluctant to engage in large motor activities. His reluctance did not appear to have anything to do with his concern about getting dirty or his extreme need for routine. It appeared that his concern focused more on his perceptions of the potential danger of large motor activity. His mother told the teachers that she gave him her permission to participate but she was a bit unsettled about his involvement. She told the teachers that she and her husband were not very physically adept and she was afraid that if Anthony "played rough" he would wind up getting hurt. In her mind, physical activity was synonymous with rough play and physical injury. In other areas of activity in the classroom Anthony came into closer proximity over the next few months. It was more difficult with regard to large motor activity. What finally did appeal to Anthony were large motor activities with a more cognitive component. If the activity required taking a certain number of steps, jumping three times before saying the name of an animal, or hopping from one color to another, Anthony would be motivated to participate. Once this was discovered, teachers planned carefully to ensure that with each integrated theme, there were a certain number of activities that were cognitive based and large motor oriented. Anthony never became a very physically active child but he did engage in enough physical activity to allow teachers to see that he had fairly well developed skills and would participate if the activity appealed to him. It was hoped that over the years, he might find physical activity rewarding enough to engage in it just for the intrinsic pleasure involved.

Sharon requires considerable modifications in her school environment relative to the area of large motor activity. She attends adaptive physical education classes with some other children who do not share the same physical disabilities but who also benefit from a special program. Sharon engages in her large motor activities from her wheel chair. These activities focus on the upper body. Some of these activities involve group cooperative games which capitalize on her mobility. During recess, Sharon is out on the playground with her peers. They plan games they can play together. The playscape at her school is not handicap accessible so Sharon cannot use it at this time. The school is planning adaptations for the playground to make it accessible as mandated under the Americans with Disability Act, 1990 (ADA). Until these modifications are accomplished, she still manages to enjoy being outdoors, wheels herself all over the yard, and sometimes chooses to spend time willingly turning rope for the others who are able to jump.

Sarah, a totally silent child at school, required no modifications in the large motor area. She was very skilled motorically. It was reported that at home she engaged in very active play with her siblings. While her play was not as physical at school as it was at home, she did engage in physical activity more readily than many of the other areas provided to her. Once again, she felt comfortable with large motor activity because she did not have to engage in any conversation to be able to participate. Sarah could be seen with a smile on her face during large motor activities. Although she might change her expression if she found an adult observing her, it was obvious from body posture that she was enjoying herself. Large motor activities placed Sarah in close proximity to her peers and for that alone, they were important activities for Sarah.

Martie had a very high level of skill in the area of large motor development. His body was large and strong. He enjoyed large motor activity and received much praise from peers and adults for all the things that he could do. This was very important for Martie because it was the one area in which it was guaranteed that he would outperform his peers. While his skill made him a "star" it also gave him something that he could help other children to learn. As it turned out, Martie was very patient with other children who wanted to know how to throw a ball better, do flips, or jump as high as he did. He usually did not use his skill and strength in a negative manner but occasionally he would use his strength against an adult who he perceived to be threatening. His involvement in physical activity allowed him to release energy, express himself, and to relax. He also began to relax relative to his peer interactions while engaged in large motor activities. One can only hope that he will continue to find large motor activity an appropriate activity and a means of releasing emotion and tension.

Christina was as eager to be involved in large motor activities as she was just about everything else in her school environment. Initially it appeared that due to her visual deficits, she might benefit from some modifications in her large motor activities but after some orientation to location of furniture and objects, she needed no modifications at all. Christina who often engaged in oppositional behavior, did not try to control the activity and her peers. In physical activities where it was necessary to follow directions, Christina listened to teacher input and caution, and did not argue or attempt to change the "rules" to suit her needs. For Christina, this was very important to her social and emotional growth and development.

C. W. found large motor activities to be somewhat challenging. His mild cerebral palsy made his gait slightly awkward but he never let that stop him. He wanted to try everything no matter how challenging it might be. When the school bus brought him to school, he would hop off the bus with little regard to the fact that this act might prove dangerous to him. He was not opposed to receiving adult assistance to get him started or in terms of a demonstration of how to do something but once shown, he wanted to do it all himself.

SUMMARY

Large motor activity is an essential component in a developmentally appropriate early childhood program. This type of activity promotes growth not only in the physical area but in cognitive, language, social, and emotional areas as well. Large motor activities may be integrated into the thematic curriculum being implemented in the classroom. Since we know that this is a critical activity for whole child development it is important to maintain the momentum of engagement in physical activities beyond the preschool years regardless of whether there is a formal program of physical education or not. Regardless of the disability, children can experience great joy in participation in some form of large motor activity.

DISCUSSION QUESTIONS

1) The weather prevents being able to go outdoors for days on end. Brainstorm with a classmate what you can do to substitute for this activity, thinking about variety and appropriateness.
2) Parents of a child in your classroom inform you that they are signing their child up for two sports teams as well as gymnastics lessons. They want to know what you think of all this wonderful activity. What will your response to them be? Why?
3) Observe one child during play activities and list all the physical actions you observe the child engage in during that time. Compare your list with the list of a classmate comparing activities present during the observation, the number of children in the program, and the ages of the children observed.
4) A child in your room appears to fall for no apparent reason. When the path is clear, with no materials, equipment, or furniture in the way, the child occasionally hits the floor making contact on the knees. The knees are consistently bruised. What can you do to determine the cause of the problem? What modifications might be made to program an environment to remedy the situation?
5) A child in your room is never observed using the climbing apparatus available in the playground. What resources do you have to encourage the child to participate?
6) There is a child with disabilities in your class who does not seem to understand or want to heed your message about the danger of jumping down stairs. What can you do to create a safer situation for the child without making the child fearful of other physical activity?

REFERENCES

Abraham, M., Morris, L., & Wald, P. (1993). *Inclusive early childhood education—A model classroom*. Tucson, AZ: Communication Skill Builders.

Avery, M. (1994). Preschool physical education: A practical approach. *Journal of Physical Education, Recreation and Dance, 65*(1), 37–39.

Beaty, J. (1992). *Skills for preschool teachers* (4th edition). New York: Macmillan.

Berry, C., & Mindes, G. (1993). *Planning a theme-based curriculum: Goals, themes, activities, and planning guides for 4's and 5's*. Glenview, IL: GoodYear Books.

Block, M. (1994). Including preschool children with disabilities. *Journal of Physical Education, Recreation and Dance, 65*(1), 45–49.

Bredekamp, S. (1987). *Developmentally appropriate practice in early childhood programs serving children from birth through age 8*. Washington, DC: National Association for the Education of Young Children.

Day, B. (1994). *Early childhood education—Developmental/experiential teaching and learning (Fourth edition)*. New York: Merrill.

Dolinar, K., Boser, C., & Holm, E. (1994). *Learning through play: Curriculum and activities for the inclusive classroom*. New York: Delmar Publishers Inc.

Eliason, C., & Jenkins, L. (1994). *A practical guide to early childhood curriculum*. New York: Merrill.

Frost, J. (1992). *Play and playscapes*. New York: Delmar Publishers Inc.

Hendrick, J. (1994). *Total learning: Developmental curriculum for the young child*. New York: Merrill.

Kostelnik, M., Soderman, A., & Whiren, A. (1993). *Developmentally appropriate programs in early childhood education*. New York: Merrill.

Kostelnik, M., (Ed.). (1991). *Teaching young children using themes*. Glenview, IL: GoodYear Books.

Krogh, S. (1990). *The integrated early childhood curriculum*. New York: McGraw-Hill Publishing Company.

Poest, C., Williams, J., Witt, D., & Atwood, M. (1990). Challenge me to move: Large muscle development in young children. *Young Children, 45* (5), 4–10.

Shipley, D. (1993). *Empowering children: Play-based curriculum for lifelong learning*. Scarborough, Ont.: Nelson Canada.

Trawick-Smith, J. (1994). *Interactions in the classroom—Facilitating play in the early years*. New York: Merrill.

Trostle, S., & Yawkey, T. (1990). *Integrated learning activities for young children*. Boston: Allyn & Bacon.

Wortham, S. (1994). *Early childhood curriculum: Developmental bases for learning and teaching*. New York: Merrill.

ADDITIONAL READINGS

Allen, K., & Marotz, L. (1990). *Developmental profiles: Birth to six*. Albany, NY: Delmar Publishers Inc.

Greenberg, P. (1992). How much do you get the children out? *Young Children, 47*(2), 34–37.

Wortham, S., & Frost, J. (Eds.). (1990). *Playgrounds for young children: National survey and perspectives*. Reston, VA: American Alliance for Health, Physical Education, Recreation and Dance Publications.

CHAPTER 10

Music and Movement

KEY TERMS

music
movement
music aptitude
creative dance

INTRODUCTION

A very close relationship exists between **music** and **movement.** It is not that it is not possible to have one without the other, but one enhances the other. Much of the music by and for young children naturally incorporates movement. Both music and movement are to be valued as critical components of early childhood curriculum.

IMPORTANCE OF MUSIC AND MOVEMENT ACTIVITIES FOR DEVELOPMENT

What is Music?

Music is a vital part of daily living. Music surrounds everyone while they shop, ride the elevator, wait for an appointment, or to be connected to the person they telephoned. Music sells products and services. Music can be heard not only from the car radio but from that of the person driving alongside. Children listen to their own music from cassette players with or without headphones. Is this all important? What do children get out of all of this musical bombardment? If teachers are careful and facilitate all of this exposure, children may become actively involved in music. They will have the potential to learn about the great variety of music available and they will hopefully develop musical skills. All of these aspects of music involvement have the potential to bring joy to the lives of those involved, may provide a great release of tension, serve as a healthy form of expression, and may develop into a career for some. Music enhances life. It is something to be enjoyed by all and not only by those who have specific talent.

What educators add to an environment has the potential to enhance the environment and those within the environment. Music is an important addition to the environment of an early childhood classroom. It can be woven into the thematic integrated curriculum and add to the diversity and multiculturalism of what is offered to children. Music is culture and language. It is history and art. It is creative and disciplined. It is simple and complex. It is thoughtful and fun. Whatever it is, music has the potential to enhance learning and access learning.

It is in the early childhood years that children have the potential for the optimal growth of their musical ability and intelligence. Regardless of the level of musical aptitude one is born with, that level will never be realized in achievement without positive musical experiences during the early years (Gordon, 1979). The early childhood period is as critical for **music aptitude** as it is for all other development.

Brand and Fernie (1983) advocate an emphasis on vocal development, instrumental skills, and music appreciation in early childhood curriculum. Children use their voices from the time they are born. All the sounds they make mean different things. Each cry and coo communicates a need or a response to something in the environment. These sounds are presinging behaviors. Children used to be exposed to chanting and singing on a regular basis as part of their daily routines. There was a time when parents and grandparents had a whole repertoire of folksongs and rhymes they would sing to children while they played with them, fed them, bathed them, and dressed them. Somehow, over the years, the practice of singing these kinds of songs or any songs to very young children seemed to fade away. In fact, these songs and chants seemed to almost disappear. With the work of Feierabend (1986), these songs have been recorded and are being shared with parents and young children. What was at one time a fairly natural behavior on the part of parents and grandparents is now presented to parents and their children in early childhood music classes. In this way, the tradition will once again flourish. Children who were exposed to these chants and songs early on were hearing language as well as feeling rhythm while they were rocked and bounced and while they clapped their hands. All of these activities contribute to the language and cognitive growth of the child. In addition, this contributes to the natural singing voice of the child. Casual observation of young children at play will show them singing their way through many play actions. They often create songs that narrate their activities.

Music can enhance the affective climate of an early childhood environment (Van Hoorn, Nourot, Scales & Alward, 1993). While music has this power, if it used only to distract, manage, and entertain, both children and adults are missing the many opportunities music is able to provide.

Often, music is used only at group times or to organize children through transitions. While these are two important times to use music, they are not the only times. Music should be listened to but it should also be created for children, with the children, and by the children. Whatever other reasons may exist, music is a pleasurable and natural part of children's lives.

What is Meant by Movement?

Movement is active learning. Movement is an important nonverbal tool for learning. Moving brings pleasure to children. Movement is a necessary part of each day. It is not just something children do when they are supposed to be sitting down. Movement is creative expression and expending energy using the entire body. Movement activities provide opportunities for problem solving and allow children to develop critical thinking skills. While children may have adequate opportunities to engage in movement activities at the preschool and maybe kindergarten levels, all too often by the time children reach the first grade, these opportunities are greatly diminished. If a school does not schedule kindergarten and first grade children for physical education classes due to budget considerations, these children may have no opportunity for movement education or exploration. It is then up to early childhood educators to integrate movement activities into the thematic curriculum.

Initially, movements are based on the child's own body. To ask a child to move like a particular animal or element of nature is to assume that the child has the experience and cognitive basis for knowing how to move.

Movement experiences must relate to the learning that has or is taking place. As there is an appropriate sequence of concepts to present to children that build upon one another, there are appropriate sequences of movement experiences as well.

What is the Relationship Between Music and Movement?

In the minds of young children, music and movement are often the same thing. Music supports movement and enhances it. Music can be taught through movement and movement through music. Music and movement in the integrated curriculum function to support the more academic components of study as well as the other arts.

What is Creative Dance?

One of the freest methods of providing experiences that use a child's motor abilities is **creative dance.** This requires some open-ended suggestions from the teacher with spontaneous activity generated by the children (Hendrick, 1994). A truly free experience can only be implemented if the teacher feels free and is not self-conscious about engaging in this type of activity. While many of the elements of creative dance are similar to those of movement activities, the movements that are created by the children are more expressive. The emphasis is not so much on learning about how the body moves as it is in movement education but in using the body for self-expression of ideas and feelings. An appropriate plan for this kind of dance starts with some warm-up activities that set the tone for the creativity as well as the safety and management of the group. Teacher participation will encourage child participation. Children do not look for teachers to be dance experts but do look for enthusiasm and spontaneity. There are those in the field who feel that it is critical to establish creative movement first before exposing children to music so that the music does not dictate the movements. A simple drum beat may be more appropriate to establish creative movement and may have a wider appeal than some musical selections. If music is to be used, tapes of instrumental multiethnic or folk music are more conducive to movement than vocal music recordings. A combination of "on the floor" and "in the middle of the room" activities will help to encourage appropriate physical activity and social behavior children need in order to work within the framework of a much freer activity.

OBJECTIVES OF MUSIC AND MOVEMENT ACTIVITIES

Although music and movement are so closely related, rather than think in terms of combined objectives, it is important to recognize the objectives of each area independent of the other before combining them for activity development and program implementation.

Music Goals for the Early Childhood Years

Objectives for music in early childhood are many and allow teachers to provide children with opportunities:

- to express themselves freely through music
- to derive pleasure from musical experiences
- to develop an understanding of the elements of music
- to experiment with creating and performing music
- to broaden their knowledge of music
- to experience and respond to a wide variety of music (Day, 1994)
- to learn that music is worth knowing—for every member of society
- to learn that a glorious part of our cultural heritage is passed on through music
- to test the limits of their potential in music
- to use music as an outlet for creativity and self-expression
- to learn about other cultures through music
- to be successful in music for some children who may not find it in other curricular areas
- to increase musical concepts and skills
- to derive more enjoyment from making and listening to music
- to experience music as a powerful symbol system that is important to learn along with verbal and mathematical symbols
- to learn that music is more subjective than quantifiable, thus it is more like real life than are most other curricular disciplines (MENC, 1986)
- to experience music through a variety of activities, materials, instruments, and movements
- to become acquainted with a variety of types of music
- for listening activities to foster music understanding
- to become aware of contrasts in music such as fast and slow, high and low, loud and soft
- to be responsive to simple rhythms through locomotor movements, body movements such as clapping, or the use of rhythm instruments
- to sing a variety of songs
- to express the mood or feelings of a musical selection through body movements and the opportunity to express emotion through music (Eliason & Jenkins, 1994)

Movement Goals for the Early Childhood Years

Early childhood movement programs have traditionally focused less on performance and competition and more on creativity and games. The current goals of movement education are fairly broad and afford children many opportunities to grow. These objectives allow teachers to provide children with opportunities:

- to feel good
- to develop self-discipline and self-reliance
- to develop self-expression and creativity
- to become physically fit and skillful in a variety of situations
- to develop confidence in meeting physical challenges
- to look good and to carry themselves well
- to do better
- to get along in close proximity to one another
- to develop cooperation and sensitivity to others (Kirchner, 1978)
- to get excited about movement activity
- to understand the principles of movement and become aware of what their bodies can do
- to survive other physical activities by learning about body alignment and injury prevention (Riggs, Dodds & Zuccalo, 1981).

DEVELOPMENTALLY APPROPRIATE ACTIVITIES AND MATERIALS

Planning for Music

Music activities can be implemented with or without the addition of materials. Many music activities are very portable. If you have children and a teacher and a bit of floor space you can have a music activity. Music activities and materials do not have to be costly in order to be developmentally appropriate. The materials used do need to be quality materials so that children hear true sounds. Whether listening to a recording or using instruments, the quality of the sound does make a difference in what children learn.

Children certainly benefit from exposure to a wide range of music and musical activity but one must pay careful attention to the words in unfamiliar songs. If a child brings a record or tape to school, listen to it before sharing it with the class. Sometimes children are so anxious to bring something from home, they bring some music with lyrics inappropriate to an early childhood population. They may have taped from the radio or from the tapes of an older sibling, aunt, or uncle. While the children may not really understand the lyrics and just be responding to the beat, it would be inappropriate to share with the class. The teacher would need to explain to the child that the words in the songs are words that are too grown up for children to hear and that it is best to leave the tape at home from now on.

Music Appropriate for Young Children

There is a wide range of music appropriate for children. Some of it is found on tapes specifically prepared for the early childhood population. Other sources of music are to be found on the radio, in the library, or from the families of the children in the class. If you ask parents to share music, be specific about the type of music you want to present to the children. If you have a child in your class from another country, folk music native to that country would be a welcome addition to your offerings. If these same people have instruments from their country, the children would have an additional positive experience.

Planning for Movement

Movement activities that are developmentally appropriate are those that recognize the physical capabilities of the children and use those capabilities for movement exploration. Movement activities require space with safe flooring. The manner in which children respond to the activities presented will allow you to know whether the activities are developmentally appropriate. Teachers need to take the lead from the children as well. Children will verbally or nonverbally suggest activities or extensions of the activities presented. This would be a clear indicator of developmental appropriateness. Occasionally a child may suggest something that sounds exciting but you know is not safe for children to do. It is up to you to suggest the child come up with an alternative after explaining why it is not possible to do what the child suggested.

Singing

One of the most natural activities for music for young children centers on singing. Children sing naturally while they play, walk, or engage in daily routines. Children have a repertoire of imitative behaviors that allow them to imitate the sounds, words, and actions of songs. Listening to good singing greatly influences a child's vocal development. Feierabend advocates singing for children and not with them. He contends that the teacher should introduce a song by singing it for the children, first asking them to listen to the singing. The teacher sings the song several times before the children sing the song. The presentation of the song by the teacher may be done over a period of several days. When you then allow children to sing by themselves, they are able to hear themselves sing and will not need to feel as though they must try to match the teacher. The teacher playing the role of the listener, is able to take the opportunity to observe the children, listen to the words they use, and assess the quality of their singing.

The most appropriate songs for children to learn are those that contain words the children will understand. The songs should have simple and clear melodies. As children master these songs, more complex material may be introduced. Research on song acquisition suggests that there is a sequence for learning songs: words, rhythms, phrases, melodic contour, or shape (McDonald & Simons, 1989). As the child learns the song, the child become more accurate in terms of melody. This happens as the words are retained. Simple songs such as question and answer songs or name games can help children make the transition from speaking to singing. Children enjoy motion songs. There are many songs which have simple motions that support the words of the song. These are very appropriate for young children. As children gain mastery over language and singing, songs with more complex motions can be introduced. For a child with a language deficit or physical disability that interferes with language production, being part of a singing circle can still be appropriate and a source of real joy to the child. The feelings evoked, the fun to be had from listening to the language, and the opportunity to select a song from a picture choice board can make the child very much part of the activity.

Expandable songs (where children add a word or a phrase of their own thinking), nursery rhymes, traditional songs, folk songs, lullabies, ballads or story songs, songs that relate to the integrated theme being implemented, and rounds are all appropriate for the early childhood years. There are also many lovely song picture books that can be the impetus for extended learning. The song can be sung, the book read, and related activities developed to expand the learning to the areas of art, dramatic play, science, field trips, or any other areas that relate in a meaningful and age-appropriate way (Barclay & Walwer, 1992).

Listening to Music

If music surrounds a child from birth there are two possible results. Either the child responds by tuning it all out or the child responds by listening. The listening may lead to an early preference for one type of music over another. The listening may be learned over time through exposing the child to carefully planned listening activities. There is an important difference between hearing and listening. A child may hear music but not listen to it at all. Listening to music fine tunes a child's ability to listen to language and literature. Some children are able to listen to a piece of music by sitting quietly. While it may appear that the child is being passive, the child's mind is active and the imagination is being stimulated according to the kind of music being listened to. Other children will need to move

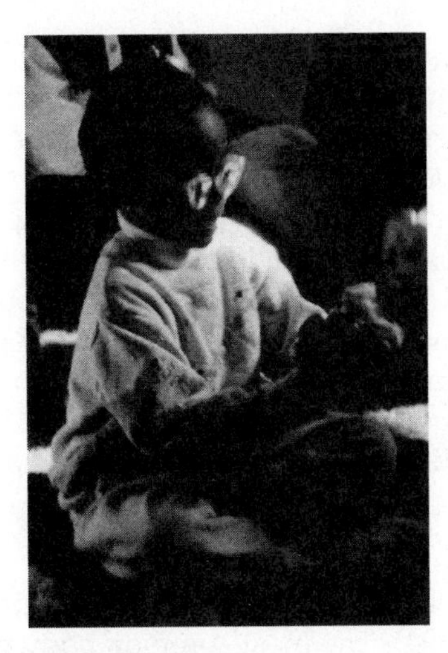

FIG 10.1 Circle time is a good time for music.

around and respond to the music in an active way. Some musical selections for children incorporate movement into the music. The instructions may be verbal or musical.

Promoting Good Listening

There are many conditions that promote good listening. Children need to be physically comfortable. There should be no or few distractions. Children need a good reason for listening. They need to be told what to listen for prior to the start of the music. Good listening on the part of the children flows from the children having a good listening model. A teacher who asks children to listen and then spends the listening time doing something else, sends the wrong message to the group (Bayless & Ramsey, 1991).

Describing Music

Describing music refers to the demonstration of the attention paid during the listening process (Krogh, 1990). Children can describe what they heard through the use of their bodies, through art, through words, and through the use of instruments or through song.

Rhythm Instruments

The resources available for rhythm instruments are extensive. The variety of rhythm instruments appropriate for the early childhood years include: bells, clappers, cymbals, drums, gongs, rhythm sticks, shakers, triangles, wooden blocks, xylophone, and recorders. Instruments afford children the opportunity to reproduce and create music. They offer an outlet for expression. Any instrument serves as an extension of the body, a step beyond movement (Krogh, 1990).

While quality instruments should be used if at all possible, homemade instruments are purposeful in providing children with the opportunity to make sounds and add those sounds to a song, a poem, a story, or folk tale. Children and teachers can make shakers, wood blocks, rhythm sticks, gongs, drums, maracas, and other percussion instruments. Krogh (1990) and Bayless and Ramsey (1991) provide excellent information on the construction of several different kinds of homemade instruments.

Body Instruments

There are many parts of the body that can be used as appropriate instruments (Eliason & Jenkins, 1994). The most common body part used as an instrument is the hands. Hands are used for clapping and fingers are used for snapping. You can slap your thighs, tap your head, and nod to a beat. You can click your tongue and stamp your feet. You can whistle, hum, and hiss. All of these are available to most children all the time. A child with a disability that prevents certain kinds of body part responses can often nod or smile in response to the music. The teacher needs to specify when it is appropriate to respond using one or more of these body parts. Sometimes, it is more appropriate to listen and participate without engaging in one of these.

Musical Games

There are many musical games appropriate for the early childhood years. Some of these games are simple enough for children to follow along by carrying out the instructions couched in the words of the song. Others are more complex and require role play or practice before actually playing out the entire game. Many of these games are available on records and supply instructions for learning the song that supports the game. Once learned, they can be played by singing the song and carrying out the actions. Some musical games are easier to learn if you are able to watch them being played or are able to participate in the play when they are introduced.

Rhythm Activities

All musical activities provide rhythm experiences for children. Many children demonstrate a natural sense of rhythm. There are other children who have a difficult time sensing the rhythm pattern of music. During an activity, a teacher can help to identify the rhythm of the music by beating the rhythm out on the child's knees or his or her own knees. This may serve to cement the pattern for the child because the child can hear it, see it, and feel it. Chants are appropriate for developing rhythm in children. Chants are almost a natural behavior for children and can often be heard while they are at play. Sometimes chants are used in a negative way between peers, "You can't come to my birthday!" Using chants as a rhythm activity would modify the content of these negative chants for the young child. It is the responsibility of the teacher to listen carefully to the words children use and to redirect their language and intentions to more sensitive and appropriate language and action.

Elements of Movement upon Which to Develop Activities

There are many elements of movement upon which appropriate activities may be developed. These elements are described as follows:

Body Awareness

In the movement area this refers to awareness of the shape of the body in space, where the different parts of the body are, how the body moves and rests, the body's behavior when combined with other bodies, and how the voice is a part of the body (Sullivan, 1982). Regardless of the cognitive or physical ability of the child, all children need to develop body awareness. Rather than teaching about the body while children are in a sitting position, it makes much more sense to use the body as the main material for learning.

Force and Time

Children can also learn about force and time by making their bodies limp, being energetic, being light, being fluid, being slow, and being quick.

Space

Space refers to the knowledge a child has of where his or her body is located in a room, the level of the room the body is in (high—standing straight or being in the air; middle—crawling, walking or standing in a stooped position; low—on the floor), the direction the body is moving in (forward, backward, sideways), size of the body (big or small), and the extension of body parts into space.

Locomotion

Locomotion refers to the ways in which children engage in movement through space at various levels. This involves facilitating children to move across the room in a variety of positions at the lowest level (lowest—wriggling, rolling, scooting), at the middle level (middle—crawling, crouching, doing the ape walk), and the highest level (highest—walking, running, skipping, galloping, leaping, sliding, hopping, jumping). An obstacle course is an appropriate way to practice these movements and reinforce spatial relationships.

Weight

The understanding of weight in a movement sense refers to the relationship of body to ground, ways to manage body weight in motion as well as in relation to others. This also refers to the body in collapse and understanding body momentum.

Working with Others

This movement concept refers to children combining with others to solve problems, to develop trust, to explore strength and sensitivity, and to feel a sense of union with others.

Isolations

This area of movement knowledge focuses on children knowing how various individual body parts (head, shoulders, arms, hands, elbows, wrists, neck, back, upper torso, ribs, hips, legs, knees, ankles, feet) can move (swinging, jerking, twisting, shaking, lifting, tensing, relaxing, becoming fluid, pressing, gliding, floating, flicking, slashing, punching, dabbing).

Repetitions

This concept refers to getting to know a movement and how it feels when repeated often. It also refers to being able to repeat a shape or action (Sullivan, 1983).

All of these motions can be done for the sake of movement alone but they can also be incorporated into other thematically integrated activities. An example of this might be having children engage in isolations as they play the role of robot or they become puppets in a live puppet show. They might act out the story of the doll maker and the dolls that come to life at night when the doll maker goes to sleep. Repetitions might be incorporated into an activity during a theme that explores machines. What better way to understand the repetitive nature of machines than by becoming one for a while.

Role of the Teacher in Movement Activities

The first role of the teacher in the movement area is to model without being overbearing. The teacher can also describe and label the child's movements and describe their relationship to musical ideas. While the teacher can also suggest movements, care should be taken to make sure that the teacher is not directing or imposing movements on the children (Andress, 1991).

Movement Activities Use Thinking Skills

Movement activities that use thinking skills can be divided into six categories: Categorizing; comparing; contrasting; hypothesizing; extrapolating; and problem solving (Gabbard, 1993). Categorizing or sorting by class could involve asking children to group body parts into those that can bend and those that cannot. Comparing or finding similarities and differences might involve having children move like animals and then think of those that move alike and those that move differently. An example of contrasting or discovering degrees of difference would involve children observing and reporting on what they noticed when people of different sizes jumped on a trampoline or jumped on the floor. Hypothesizing or making a tentative assumption might involve having children think about different kinds of movements and how they might work or not work in certain situations. Extrapolating which involves predicting from past information and experience might ask children to predict how far they can jump or roll within a specific time period. Problem solving or seeking solutions could ask children to figure out different ways to get across the room without walking.

Creative Dance

Creative dance as an extension of movement education activities is appropriate for young children. It allows the child to have a means of demonstrating interpretations of experiences he or she has had. Since all of these activities build on the elements of movement mentioned previously, it is more appropriate here to mention the experiences that can be acted out through creative dance.

Growth Cycles

Children can move to represent any growing thing as it develops. It is, of course, most appropriate to present these opportunities to children after they have observed the actual growth process themselves. The possibilities are endless but may include growth of plants, trees, animals, humans, insects, and birds.

Elements of Nature

Children can interpret wind, rain, snow, and sun. After the children have experienced movement interpretations in this theme and the growth theme, they could be combined to allow children to demonstrate their interpretations of the effects of the elements of nature on growth.

Daily Routine

Children can creatively express daily routine personal care activities such as bathing, eating, sleeping, and shaving, as well as household routines such as doing the laundry, ironing, and washing dishes. Training specific movements for children with disabilities can be accomplished by making these movements part of another activity. Fine and large motor practice performed by pretending to bathe oneself, iron, or wash dishes are some good examples of the way to fold practice into natural activity using everyday activities.

This is by no means an exhaustive list. It is meant to stimulate thinking about the range of possibilities for creative expression. It is important to allow children to choose some themes to dance. The value of these kinds of activities cannot be underestimated.

CASE STUDY

A three-year-old boy in a child care center who had made an adequate but not outstanding adjustment to his new routine greeted his mother with considerable enthusiasm at the end of the day. When she asked what had made him so happy he told her that they danced during the day and he loved it!! The mother shared this information with the director the following day. The director was pleased to hear that the child had discovered the joy of creative movement. The child was much more eager to get to the center after that, hoping that each day would be a dancing day!

MODIFICATION OF MATERIALS OR ACTIVITIES TO INCLUDE CHILDREN WITH SPECIAL NEEDS

All of the activities and materials already mentioned, while developmentally appropriate, might not be accessible to all children with special needs. The range of special needs children may have necessitates designing a program for music and movement that would take into account the needs of all children. As each of the other areas of the curriculum must be planned to meet the needs of individual children as well as to be integrated into the theme being implemented, music and movement must be planned for in the same way. Teachers must be prepared to make modifications in some materials or activities or possibly design alternative activities for children with special needs. General modifications will be listed by nature of what initially makes the experience inaccessible to a child:

Physical Considerations

Music activity is something in which all children can participate whether with their voices, their bodies or both. A child with severe physical disabilities may not be verbal but may be vocal and able to use that vocal ability to respond to music heard. Children with physical disabilities and limited or no communication ability are able to demonstrate recognition of music heard previously through eye contact, a smile, or a nod. This demonstrates that while the physical child may be disabled, the music child is not disabled. This concept has been reported and discussed in music therapy literature since the 1970s by authors such as Nordoff and Robbins (1970, 1977, 1983). They contend that music involvement by children with severe physical disabilities is one way to assess the intelligence of the child. Music activity that responds to the uniqueness of each child provides stimulation and satisfaction for the child while providing much information about the potential of the child that has yet to be tapped.

Making music with typical rhythm instruments may not be available to a child with physical disabilities but switch-operated instruments may be appropriate substitutes. Teachers and therapists need to work together to develop possible adaptations that allow the inclusion of the child in a great variety of music activities. Being in the midst of music can have therapeutic value for a child with physical disabilities. Music with the right rhythm and tone has the potential to energize or relax a child.

CASE STUDY

A very petite, almost three-year-old child with physical disabilities finds music very calming. Her mother learned the value of music for this child very early in the child's life and is rarely without a portable cassette player for the child to use when she becomes anxious. A new social situation for this child produces a certain level of anxiety and she typically asks for her music. Now that the child is to be included in a preschool program, the teachers will need to figure out a way to provide this support for the child without it attracting too much attention or distracting the other children. After observing the child in the new environment for a few days, the teachers will meet to develop a way to handle any necessary transition of the music support.

Children with physical disabilities involving the use of adaptive devices may pose circumstances that require creative planning relative to movement activities. When planning movement activities, it is important to keep in mind that children with physical disabilities are not always totally disabled. This means that the child may be able to move a limb, fingers, or the head and neck. This allows the child to engage in certain activities with no modifications necessary. The only difference in some movement activities between the child with physical disabilities and the child without is that the child with the physical disability might need to engage in the activity from a wheelchair. Once space is organized so that all children have the room they need in order to do the activity, all may participate. If locomotion is part of the activity, the child using a wheelchair may need a peer or adult to move the wheelchair around. An example of this may be an activity that asks the children to move around the room like birds. The child in a wheelchair with limb mobility can either move around the room with assistance (if the child cannot manage the chair independently) or be a stationary bird flapping its wings. Even if a teacher has considerable experience working with children with physical disabilities, it is always wise to consult with specialists who work with a particular child and with the family to describe the kinds of activities you are thinking about to make sure they are appropriate for the child. Since working with specialists is a critical component of planning for any child with special needs, the specialist will prove to be an asset to your planning process.

If the planned activity involves the use of scarves and the child uses a wheelchair, the scarf may be tied onto the child's arm if the child cannot hold on to things. If the child uses a walker, using scarves in a movement activity requiring children to move around the room will not be feasible. What will be appropriate for that child is to use the scarf while sitting down. This way, the child will reap the benefit of the upper torso movement even though the element of locomotion is eliminated from the activity. What is important in planning adaptations for any motor activity is to think about having the child participate in some way and on some level. That way, the child will feel part of the activity, even though he or she may not be doing exactly the same thing as the other children. One needs to look at the environment to explore the possibilities. Once again, the peer group can be enlisted to come up with new ideas for the child or new ways of facilitating inclusion in movement activities.

Visual Impairments

Children with visual impairments can certainly participate in music activities. Regardless of how severe the visual deficit, the child can hear and feel the music and respond to it with voice or body. In a situation where instruments are being presented to or used by the children, a child with visual impairments may need to get as close to the instruments as possible. This child may initially need some guidance from an adult to learn how to use the instrument without damaging it. This will also help the child to engage in the activity in a safe manner. Children with visual impairments enjoy the stimulation of music activity. Very often, these children are very rhythmic and respond to music in a very relaxed manner.

In movement activities, a child with visual impairments may need to hold on to the hands of an adult or another child in order to feel safe in an activity that requires locomotion in an open space. If the child feels comfortable in the space, it is possible that no modification is necessary. Some children with visual impairments do not cross boundaries. This means that they do not cross thresholds, walk through doorways, or step onto a slightly different level surface unless they are assisted by someone they trust. Once they have mastered this task, they will be comfortable repeating this by themselves. When planning a movement activity, if a child exhibiting this behavior is in the classroom, care should be taken to minimize the barriers (different surfaces) the children cross during the activity until the child with visual impairment is acclimated to the environment.

Social, Emotional, or Behavioral Disorders

Music has a calming effect on many children. Children with social, emotional, or behavioral disorders of an acting out nature may find that music calms them down. Once calmed down, they can then engage in the other activities provided. A child who is withdrawn may be very inactive. Music that serves to calm children down may be inappropriate to use with this child. This child may need music of a more energizing nature. In selecting music for background listening, it is important to take stock of the types of children in the group at the time. An overly active child certainly does not need "buzzing" music. This might further energize the child beyond the point of manageable behavior.

The child who may be afraid of failure who stays away from activities which are personally intimidating may find music the kind of activity that is not at all demanding. If the child does not want to sing or move, just being part of the group can give the child a sense of accomplishment and belonging. In time, the child may engage in hand motions of songs or appear to mouth words but not offer to sing. Each child should be able to respond at his or her own level and within a framework that is personally rewarding. The child with emotional or social problems may find a release of emotion through music. Once the child begins to actively participate in music activity, it may be that these activities become the core of the socialization process and the source of bridging school to home. The same pattern may hold true for movement activities as it does for music activities. Since the two areas are so closely related, this makes perfect sense. The one thing that may take longer to accomplish is a comfort level with movement activities that pair children together.

What teachers look for in providing music activity for any child is joy in participation and increasing interest, not perfection. A child with a repertoire of acting-out behavior and few coping skills needs to participate in activities which do not require exacting responses. A child with this behavior profile may at first be apprehensive and cautious about participation because music is not something the child has had a lot of experience with. Over time, maybe after careful observation from a distance, the child will move closer to the activity and begin to reap the benefits of joining in.

With movement activities, the same caution that keeps the child away, will probably prevail. The goal for movement activities for this type of child is to have the child experience the joy of movement and the sense of accomplishment that comes from having control over your own body in space. Dance therapy uses dance movements as a means of nonverbal communication, emotional release of hostile and tender feelings, physical relaxation, and increased self-awareness (Toombs, 1968). Many overcontrolled children who perform well in academic areas reveal their loss of spontaneity and developing inability to express emotion by their inhibited response to dance. Dance then becomes a means of assessment of children. Espenek (1981) observed that certain moods or attitudes are expressed through characteristic postures used in dance:

dejected attitude—slumped shoulders, head on chest, fumbling steps

retiring attitude—inward drawn shoulders, head lowered

heightened tension—shoulders lifted to ears, head in neck, elbows tense, hands nervous

aggressive attitude—strutting chest, swagger, accent on heels

While early childhood teachers may not feel comfortable making assessments based on these movement types, it provides examples of how movements children engage in might be more telling than previously imagined. It could help teachers look beyond the more traditional means of assessment to use the natural behaviors children provide to better understand them.

A socially immature child may need more time before venturing to try some music activities. Often, this is the presenting pattern for all activity areas for this type of child. Since some music activities can be implemented sitting on the floor rather than being out in the middle of open space, there may be a security factor that affords the child the opportunity to participate more readily than might happen in something like a movement exploration activity. Since the child may not feel ready to hold a hand or be in close proximity to another child, care needs to be taken in planning appropriate activities that would facilitate the inclusion of this child.

Learning Impairments

Music needs little introduction in order for children to participate. Very few modifications are necessary to include the child with learning impairments. The child may need encouragement and an adult nearby to facilitate participation but since there is little that needs to be learned in terms of process, music is a natural activity. If the child has trouble remembering words to songs, humming along is appropriate. If the child expresses an interest in working on remembering songs, special practice sessions might be arranged so that the child has time to build skill prior to the next time the skill is needed.

Initially the teacher may want to sit near the child during music in order to provide the best model for the child. The language of an adult has greater clarity than that of the peer group regardless of how skilled the peer group language is. This pattern should not be maintained for the whole year because the child may then develop the feeling that teacher proximity is necessary for successful participation. Children need to become independent of teachers during the course of the year. Teachers need to facilitate the process of independence building.

In movement activities, children with learning impairments may need a teacher or a peer to assist with directionality and the presentation of an appropriate model to imitate. Rather than have the child collide with the peer group because they are going in one direction and the child is going in another, a little facilitation goes a long way. The child may also need reassurance to be able to work in the middle of open space. Working with a partner may work well for this type of child. The child will probably not be intimidated by another child and will learn the joy of participation and gain a sense of mastery over his or her body.

Caution about Prevention of Falls

A fall on the playground can be devastating but a fall indoors can also cause great harm. Typically movement activities are implemented on wood or tile floors. A fall on this type of floor can produce considerable injury for any child. Any precautions that can be taken should be taken. Some children should engage in movement activities with their sneakers on to avoid slipping. Some children trip easily in their sneakers and should work in their bare feet. This means that they need to take their socks off in order to feel the floor beneath them. This should help to make the activity more successful and produce less anxiety for all.

CASE STUDIES DESCRIBING MODIFICATIONS

CASE STUDY

Anthony was not reluctant to engage in music activities but he was reluctant to engage in any kind of movement activities. His willingness to participate in music activities was somewhat selective. The selectivity centered on his apprehension of being involved in whole group activity. If an instrument or a listening activity was available for independent or very small group use, Anthony was interested. It might have been that he was most interested in the mechanics of the instruments and the record player or tape player used for listening activities. He was very interested in real instruments and shared the knowledge he had about string and brass instruments. He listened to these instruments while his parents watched concerts on television. He was not interested in watching the concerts himself but did stay in the proximity of the TV so he could hear the music. He developed a very good ear for identifying specific instruments and later on he began to identify specific composers. His parents assured the teachers that they were not working with him on these activities. This knowledge was coming from critical listening. Seeing that Anthony was able to handle music activity in a small group setting, teachers set up singing activities with a few children at a time. Initially, he treated these as listening experiences but after a few of these sessions, he began to engage in the motions of the song and later on he would sing some of the words. It was obvious that he was sharing this with his family when his mother came to school one day and asked for the words to some of the songs he was trying to teach them at home. His reluctance to be involved in movement activities seemed to be related to his feelings about the potential danger of large motor activity. He saw whole body movements in movement activities in the same way that he saw any motor activity. Again, while his mother told the teachers that she gave him her permission to participate, she was a bit unsettled about his involvement in movement activity. Once more, the mother voiced her own feelings of inadequacy about her physical abilities and added to this that she was not a very creative person and thus felt sure that Anthony would not feel free enough to be creative in his movements either. While she did not seem to think that movement activities were rough, she was still concerned that he might fall and hurt himself. Anthony watched movement activities and became somewhat interested and motivated to participate when the creative movement activities focused on more scientific and cognitive areas. Moving like a plant or a tree in a rainstorm had a certain appeal for him. Once this interest was noted, teachers planned carefully to make sure that when activities like that were implemented, Anthony had a special invitation to participate early in the activity so he would not be overwhelmed by the other children or feel as though he did not have enough room in which to move. While Anthony would probably not choose to be involved in movement activities if something else were available, he did at least try some of them and stayed with the activity for at least 10–15 minutes before moving on to something else. New avenues had been opened to him. New experiences were conquered.

Sharon requires no adaptations for music activities that do not require whole body movement. She loves to sing and is able to join in all types of songs and most musical games. She is not a shy child and offers suggestions when the class sings expandable songs. When it comes to movement activities, Sharon does not require modifications as much as she requires a little more space in which to maneuver herself. Sharon is able to engage in movement activities from her wheelchair. She can work with other children in small groups in movement and creative movement activities that involve the upper body. Some of these activities involve small group problem solving that focuses on things such as moving like an airplane or some type of machine. Her peers usually find a way to have her be the core of the movement effort with the remainder of the children attaching themselves to the wheelchair in order to be part of a unified moving force. The children are clever enough to capitalize on her mobility. Though she cannot execute every movement her peers can do, she is most eager to be part of the action and usually finds a way to fit in. She really enjoys these activities.

Sarah participated in many music activities as long as they did not require her speaking or actually singing out loud. She imitated gestures, played musical games that required her to follow instructions, and seemed to love listening activities. As long as she did not have to talk to participate, Sarah was there. She required no modifications in the area of movement and creative dance. Since she was very skilled motorically and if movement activities required no verbal communication on her part, she was eager to participate in them. It was reported that at home she and her sisters danced around the house and had lots of costumes to wear for their dances. While her involvement at school did not appear as free and creative as it was reported to be at home, she did engage in movement and dance activity more readily than many of the other areas provided to her. Once again, she felt comfortable with movement activity because she did not have to engage in any conversation to be able to participate. Sarah smiled her way through movement activities. She seemed to enjoy the close proximity to her peers that was involved in movement activities and this proximity contributed to her socialization and her happiness quotient.

Martie enjoyed singing and listening to music. He preferred more active, louder, bolder music but would listen to all kinds of music. He liked to sing expandable songs so that he could add his clever responses. Music was quite pleasurable for him and was a time that he shared eagerly and cooperatively with his peers and teachers. You may recall that Martie had a very high level of skill in the area of large motor development. His body was large and strong. Although he enjoyed large motor activity and received much praise from peers and adults for all the things that he could do, this was not translated to the area of movement and creative movement activity.

He would watch other children engage in movement activities and look at them with a puzzled expression. He would not allow himself the freedom of letting go of his inhibitions long enough to let his guard down in order to try the activity. He saw himself as a "macho" man and hinted that this movement stuff was not for him. No manner of convincing enabled him to be comfortable about becoming involved. The closest he ever got to the activity was to watch. He did not tease the other boys who did participate but even his peers' invitations to join in did not encourage him to try.

Christina was eager to be involved in music and movement activities. Her visual deficits did not interfere with her participation in music and movement activities. Her enthusiasm for these activities created such pleasure in her life that her predisposition to engage in oppositional behavior was greatly diminished. She needed no modifications in the music area and had a wonderful memory for lyrics. She would also remind teachers that it had been a long time since a particular song had been sung and urged them to sing the song she requested. Initially it appeared that there might need to be some modifications in order for her to participate in movement activities but after some orientation to the space allocated for movement, she needed no modifications at all. Christina did try to control access to the scarves and bells that were sometimes offered to enhance movement but when it was obvious that she could not have them all, she did not try to control the activity or her peers. This was very important to her social and emotional growth and development.

C. W. loved music activities. He had a wonderful sense of rhythm, was a good listener, responded very positively to expandable songs, and went full speed ahead into musical games. Sometimes he had slight difficulty in participating in musical games because of his awkward gait but that did not keep him from joining in. C. W found movement activities to be somewhat challenging. Since his mild cerebral palsy made his gait slightly awkward, freer movements were sometimes difficult for him. Sometimes he resorted to executing all his movements on the floor which provided him with the stability he seemed to need. C. W. made these modifications himself. No teacher needed to do this for him. He wanted to try everything no matter how challenging it might be. He was not opposed to receiving adult assistance to get him started or in terms of a demonstration of how to do something but once shown, he wanted to do it all himself.

SUMMARY

Music and movement activity are very important components in a developmentally appropriate early childhood program. Both music and movement promote growth in the whole child. Since music surrounds children, it is a natural activity for children and requires very few materials. Movement activities also require very little in terms of materials. While children are not necessarily surrounded by movement activities in their homes, they have a natural predisposition to move. Teachers have a responsibility to encourage both music and movement in the early childhood classroom. Both music and movement are easily integrated into most themes being implemented in an integrated curriculum. Music and movement support physical, cognitive, language, social, and emotional development. Regardless of any disability, children can experience great joy participating in some form of music and movement activity.

DISCUSSION QUESTIONS

1) Teachers in your school get together to plan thematic integrated curriculum. When they plan they brainstorm ideas for books, art activities, dramatic play, and sensory science opportunities. You are new to the team and want to suggest that planning for music and movement should be an integral part of the planning. What can you offer to the team to make this planning happen?
2) Space is a problem in your classroom. You want to include movement activities in your program but feel you do not have the space. What can you do to create an atmosphere that will promote movement activities? What can you do to rearrange the physical space in the classroom?
3) You do not know many songs and feel the need to build your repertoire. How will you go about learning more songs and develop them into a workable collection that you can use in planning integrated curriculum? Get together with a classmate to share song collections.
4) There are a few children in your class with low level language ability. You notice that these children have a strong interest in music and movement activities. How will you work within the framework of music and movement to enhance the language level of these children?
5) Brainstorm resources for music and movement in your community that are appropriate for young children. Discuss these findings with a classmate.
6) A child in your class is very withdrawn. The child has not connected with any of the other children in the room but has connected with you. Is there any way you think that music and movement activities might help the child to become less withdrawn? Develop a plan for facilitating this happening. Discuss the plan with a classmate.

REFERENCES

Abraham, M., Morris, L., & Wald, P. (1993). *Inclusive early childhood education—A model classroom*. Tucson, AZ: Communication Skill Builders.

Andress, B. (1981). *Music experiences in early childhood*. New York: Holt, Rinehart & Winston.

Andress, B. (1991). From research to practice: Preschool children and their movement responses to music. *Young Children, 47*(1), 22–27.

Barclay, K., & Walwer, L. (1992). Linking lyrics and literacy through song picture books. *Young Children, 47*(4), 76–85.

Bayless, K., & Ramsey, M. (1991). *Music, a way of life for the young child*. New York: Macmillan.

Brand, M., & Fernie, D. (1983). Music in the early childhood curriculum. *Childhood Education, 59*(5), 321–326.

Bredekamp, S. (1987). *Developmentally appropriate practice in early childhood programs serving children from birth through age 8*. Washington, DC: National Association for the Education of Young Children.

Day, B. (1994). *Early childhood education—Developmental/experiential teaching and learning* (Fourth edition). New York: Merrill.

Eliason, C., & Jenkins, L. (1994). *A practical guide to early childhood curriculum*. New York: Merrill.

Feierabend, J. (1986). *Music for very little people, Music for little people* (with cassette). New York: Boosey & Hawkes.

Gabbard, C. (1993). Learning to think through movement activities. *Day Care and Early Education, 20*(4), 18–19.

Gardner, H. (1983). *Frames of mind: The theory of multiple intelligences*. New York: Basic Books, Inc.

Gordon, E. (1979). *Primary measures of music audition: Test manual*. Chicago: G. I .A. Publication.

Haines, B., & Gerber, L. (1992). *Leading young children to music*. New York: Macmillan.

Hendrick, J. (1994). *Total learning—Developmental curriculum for the young child*. New York: Merrill.

Hitz, R. (1987). Creative problem solving through music activities. *Young Children, 42*(2), 12–17.

Kirchner, G. (1978). *Introduction to movement education*. Dubuque, IA: W. C. Brown.

Kostelnik, M., Soderman, A., & Whiren, A. (1993). *Developmentally appropriate programs in early childhood education*. New York: Merrill.

Krogh, S. (1990). *The integrated early childhood curriculum.* New York: McGraw-Hill Publishing Company.

McDonald, D., & Simons, G. (1989). *Musical growth and development: Birth through six.* New York: Schirmer.

Nordoff, P., & Robbins, C. (1970). *Therapy in music for handicapped children.* London: Gollancz.

Nordoff, P., & Robbins, C. (1977). *Creative music therapy: Individualized treatment for the handicapped child.* New York: John Day.

Nordoff, P., & Robbins, C. (1983). *Music therapy in special education.* St. Louis: MMB Music.

Riggs, M., Dodds, P., & Zuccalo, D. (1981). *Early Childhood.* Reston, VA: American Alliance for Health, Physical Education, Recreation and Dance.

Shipley, D. (1993). *Empowering children: Play-based curriculum for lifelong learning.* Scarborough, Ont.: Nelson Canada.

Sullivan, M. (1982). *Feeling strong, feeling free: Movement exploration for young children.* Washington, DC: National Association for the Education of Young Children.

Toombs, M. (1968). Dance therapy. In E. Gaston (Ed.), *Music in therapy.* New York: Macmillan.

Trawick-Smith, J. (1994). *Interactions in the classroom—Facilitating play in the early years.* New York: Merrill.

Van Hoorn, J., Nourot, P., Scales, B., & Alward, K. (1993) *Play at the center of the curriculum.* New York: Merrill.

Wolf, J. (1992). Let's sing it again: Creating music with young children. *Young Children, 47*(2), 56–61.

Wolf, J. (1994). Singing with children is a cinch! *Young Children, 49*(4), 20–25.

ADDITIONAL READINGS

Gunsberg, A. (1991). Improvised musical play with delayed and nondelayed children. *Childhood Education, 67*(4), 223–226.

Hammett, C. (1992). *Movement activities for early childhood.* Champaign, IL: Human Kinetics Publishers, Inc.

Kahn, A. (1978). Focus on movement: Practice and theory. *Young Children, 34*(1), 19–26.

Kruger, H., & Kruger, J. (1989). *The preschool teacher's guide to movement education.* Baltimore: Gerstung Publications, Inc.

Pica, R. (1990). *Preschoolers moving & learning.* Champaign, IL: Human Kinetics Publishers, Inc.

Pugmire-Stoy, M. (1991). *Spontaneous play in early childhood*. Albany, NY: Delmar Publishers Inc.

Sanders, S. (1992). *Designing preschool movement programs*. Champaign, IL: Human Kinetics Publishers, Inc.

Stinson, W., Mehrof, H., & Thies, S. (1993). *Quality daily thematic lesson plans for classroom teachers: Movement activities for pre-k and kindergarten*. Dubuque, IA: Kendall Hunt.

CHAPTER 11

Language and Literacy

KEY TERMS

language development
speech
language
vocabulary
semantics
syntax
phonology
morphology
pragmatics
literacy
whole language
emergent literacy

WHAT IS LANGUAGE?

Language is what we use to translate experiences into a means of communication and thinking. **Language development** begins in infancy and continues throughout life. Language is received by the eyes and ears. Children learn language through listening to models, imitating those models, receiving feedback, refining their language, and using their language to share ideas. Language is critical to all learning and as such is a very important part of early childhood environments. Language is something that is inherent in all activities and should be integrated into all activity areas in an early childhood classroom. Language is also a critical component of every interaction between peers, between children and adults, and between adults. Language is being modeled, listened to, and imitated at all times. It must be remembered that to hear appropriate language from children, language-rich environments dense with interesting words that express interesting ideas as well as routine events must be provided for them.

It is important to understand the semantic difference between **speech** and **language.** Speech is defined as the faculty or power of speaking—the ability to express one's thoughts and emotions by speech sounds. Language is defined as communication using a system of arbitrary vocal sounds, written symbols, signs, or gestures in conventional ways with conventional meanings; both spoken language and sign language communicate ideas. Language is therefore a complex system involving several components. Learning and understanding words is referred to as **vocabulary,** knowing the meanings of words is **semantics,** knowing grammatical structure of sentences is **syntax. Phonology** is the sound system of the language, and **morphology** refers to the rules governing words. **Pragmatics** refers to the appropriate usage of words contingent on the social context in which the child must operate. This means that children must learn to whom they may speak, how they are to respond, under what circumstances they may speak, in what tone of voice, and which movements are appropriate (Essa, 1992). The following list summarizes milestones in language development which should be helpful to the teacher new to this age group.

Language Development Milestones

12–18 months	uses words intentionally; first words are really sentences; vocabulary of 3–50 words; uses consonant plus vowel; points to objects and body parts
18–24 months	responds to simple directions; points to two to three body parts; names objects and pictures; uses "what?"; vocabulary of 50–75 words
24–30 months	uses egocentric speech; refers to self by name; identifies pictures and objects; asks simple questions; vocabulary of 12–200 words; uses two to three word sentences
30–36 months	talks to self (narrates); uses "I" and "me"; recognizes action in pictures; recognizes objects by their use; vocabulary of 250–500 words; obeys commands with prepositions in them

3–4 years	remembers simple songs and nursery rhymes; vocabulary of 800–1,000 words; uses three to four word sentences; speech is fairly intelligible; is at "why" stage; relates experiences; uses plurals; holds up fingers to signify age
4–5 years	speech is more social and less egocentric; vocabulary of 1,500 words; frequent use of "how" and "why"; states age and sex; uses six to eight word sentences that are compound and complex; completes three-step commands; continuously asks questions; talks a lot; tells tales; "reads" aloud using pictures
5–6 years	reasonably accurate grammar and sentence structure in longer sentences; vocabulary of 2,000–2,500 words; intelligible speech; socialized conversation; speaks of self; primitive argument emerges; symbolic language emerging

What Is Literacy?

Literacy involves all forms of language: speaking, listening, writing and reading. Literacy is built on the foundation of language. Literacy begins with print awareness long before children begin to attend school. Interest in reading and writing begin when children are introduced to books, other forms of print, literature, and drawing. The environment plays a key role in the stimulation and maintenance of literacy skills. When materials, activities, and people in the child's environment demonstrate interest in literacy and literacy skills, this provides motivation for children.

Developmentally appropriate environments should include playful experiences with materials that promote literacy (Campbell & Foster, 1993; Christie, 1991; Neuman & Roskos, 1993). Each incident of pretend reading and writing is an indicator of emergent literacy and a valuable sign of the child's potential. Rather than think in terms of reading and writing as subjects that need to be taught to children, those involved with the education of young children are coming to recognize and value the benefits of print-rich environments. Teachers in these environments use what is within the classroom to promote values about and interest in reading and writing. All types of play and reading wonderful literature to children forms the basis for encouraging literacy.

What Is the Relationship between Language and Literacy?

Language is the beginning of the process that connects children to the printed page and ultimately to reading. Since reading is an important school skill, parents and teachers are often very anxious to establish this skill very early in the child's life. There are many prerequisite experiences children need prior to beginning the formal reading process. Language-rich experiences and environments geared to the promotion of literacy are ideal settings for the language and literacy linkage that will lead children to formal reading and writing. **Whole language** is the use of all aspects of language—reading, writing, listening, and speaking—in the process of becoming literate. Children learn about reading and writing by speaking and listening; they learn to read by writing and they learn to write by reading (Morrison, 1995).

Integrated Activities Support Language and Literacy

Language and literacy development can be encouraged through integrated activities in many areas of the early childhood classroom. Experiences within all the activity areas provide ample avenues for promoting language and literacy. Whether it be during sensory activities, using manipulatives, enjoying dramatic play, participating in music or movement activity, using their entire bodies in large motor activity, building with blocks, participating in circle or group time, eating and chatting during snack time, following the routine at different times of the day, or participating in field trips, children are exposed to words and ideas that stimulate their language development.

IMPORTANCE OF LANGUAGE AND LITERACY ACTIVITIES FOR DEVELOPMENT

Language is a critical basis for learning. It is often taken for granted that spoken language will develop within each child. There is also the expectation that all children will develop increasingly more complex language skill and proficiency as they move through developmental ages and stages. Language needs considerable attention from parents, teachers, and peers to be nurtured and maintained. Children need good language models to imitate. They need other sources of language stimulation. One of the most treasured ways to engage children in the pleasure of language is through sharing literature with them. The language children produce also serves as a means of assessing what children know and how they feel about themselves and others. While language is inherent in all activities within an early childhood environment, it is critical to pay substantive attention to the language learning and reinforcement possible within each activity presented to children. Too often adults assume that children understand all the vocabulary that surrounds them. Some children seem to be so sophisticated in the language they use and the manner in which the language is presented, adults have no idea that they really do not understand all of what they are saying. Some children do not understand all the language around them in the classroom because it is not their native language. Early childhood programs increasingly include children for whom English is not the primary language. Awareness of bilingualism as well as sensitivity to the cultural and family values associated with the speaking of another language is key to the inclusion of children with developed language skills in a language other than English.

Emergent Literacy

Emergent literacy is based on the assumption that children construct an understanding of literacy as a result of their own experiences with language. Some children come to school with a variety of literacy experiences and are well on their way to reading. Other children have not had as many experiences and thus are at the beginning of the process of understanding written language. The importance of providing literacy activities cannot be underestimated. If literacy is not well established, as the child moves from one grade to another, efforts to develop reading skills will not be as effective or develop as naturally. When a child has developed literacy skills, reading flows naturally and skills can be nurtured. The teacher's role relative to literacy development in the classroom is to read to the children, engage in conversations about the integrated curriculum being introduced, involve children in adding their contributions to language-experience charts and class books or big books, share and discuss books and stories, read poetry, sing songs, and perform finger plays with the children. The role of the child is to engage in all of these activities, play actively and enjoy their experiences.

Curriculum to Meet the Developmental Age of the Child

When the language development of a child does not match the chronological age of the child, the child will not be ready to take advantage of much of the curriculum opportunities typically offered to children in early childhood settings. Even when curriculum is developmentally and individually appropriate, the child with immature or delayed language is at a disadvantage. The most advantageous way to enhance the language level of a child with this kind of profile is through language-rich play opportunities. The more experiences provided for children, the richer the language opportunities. The richer the language opportunities, the greater the language base a child may draw upon. Since language is a necessity and not a luxury in this world, it is important to spend as much energy as possible to ensure that language develops. Children learn from their environments

FIG 11.1 The book corner provides experience that stimulates literacy development.

that words mean something. They look at books and ask what the words or the letters say. They ask what signs around them say. Often, they tell the adult with them what certain familiar signs say. They recognize the logos of stores and restaurants in their neighborhoods. When this type of learning does not take place naturally, it is important to create these kinds of learning situations in the early childhood classroom. Making signs to use in dramatic play areas simulates the outside community and allows teachers the opportunity to facilitate language learning within the play context. Since all parts of language are related, listening, speaking, reading and writing need to be integrated within the learning environment.

Field Trips

Field trips provide a wonderful opportunity for language and literacy enhancement. Taking children on a trip away from the school environment provides a common experience for all children. Preparation for a field trip involves considerable language learning, possible role play, dramatic play scenarios, sharing related poems and songs, and the reading of related books. The time spent in transit to the site of the field trip provides opportunities for further language reinforcement about the trip and the introduction of language concerning the mode of transportation taken. During the trip, teachers and chaperones are able to reinforce language and concepts while adults and children explore what the trip site has to offer. Some field trips involve a presentation by a specialist, and thus provide for further language opportunities. When the trip is concluded and the class returns to school, all the children can contribute to a shared language experience story about the trip. The story can then be copied to be added to the next newsletter that goes home to families. The story can be posted in a strategic location where all can "read" it. The children can also compose a thank you letter to the people who facilitated the trip. If they are not yet writing, they can contribute drawings to the letter. The children may also write individual books or a class book about the trip. If photographs were taken during the trip, they may be added to the class book. Children often refer to a shared field trip during casual conversation. If they have a class book to refer to, their recollections may be reinforced and the integrated language experience further enhanced. If all the language experience stories written are saved during the year, they may be reviewed at the end of the year. The children will be able to see how their stories changed and developed during the course of the year. The teacher will be able to assess the collective language growth of the children in the class.

Creating a Positive Language Environment

Experiences need not be expensive or fantastic in order to stimulate language and literacy development. Good language models, interest in children, interesting things for children to do, and good conversation create the important language environment that is the basis not only for language learning but for all learning during the early childhood years. When children get excited about language, that excitement stays with them. They tune in to the environment, they listen and learn. This learning helps children make further connections and builds the learning chain.

OBJECTIVES OF LANGUAGE AND LITERACY ACTIVITIES

Although language and literacy are so closely related, it is important to recognize the objectives of each area, independent of the other before combining them for activity development and program implementation. Objectives for language in early childhood are separated here into expressive and receptive language. Objectives for *expressive language* (Morrow, 1989) suggest teachers should provide children with opportunities:

- to use language as a tool for communication at their appropriate level
- to pronounce words correctly
- to extend their speaking vocabularies
- to speak in increasingly fuller sentences
- to use adjectives, adverbs, prepositional phrases, dependent clauses, plurals, past tense, possessives

- to communicate in such a way that allows them to be understood by others
- to use language socially and emotionally by interpreting feelings and points of view
- to solve problems by generating hypotheses, summarizing events, and predicting outcomes
- to develop language that involves mathematical and logical relations, including describing size and amount, making comparisons, defining sets and classes, and reasoning deductively

Objectives for *receptive language* suggest that teachers should provide children with opportunities:

- to use all kinds of language
- to listen to stories
- to listen to songs
- to listen to rhymes
- to develop appropriate listening behaviors such as looking at the speaker, sitting relatively still, waiting for a turn to speak, and responding to oral cues (Kostelnik, Soderman & Whiren, 1993)
- to attend to and follow directions
- to be exposed to meaningful conversation that engages their interest
- to hear a variety of vocabulary
- to notice how appropriate inflection, intonation, volume, and speed aid the listener in understanding messages (Kostelnik, Soderman & Whiren, 1993)

The overall objectives for developing *literacy* skills suggest that teachers should provide children with opportunities:

- to use writing tools
- to make records of their ideas through drawing
- to make records of their ideas scribbling for writing
- to make records of their ideas through making things that look like letters
- to make records of their ideas through using invented spelling
- to make records of their ideas through using standard spelling
- to recognize own name in print (using a variety of print forms)
- to become familiar with print
- to become familiar with print-meaning associations
- to use picture books to "read" a story
- to use pictures and print to "read" a book
- to choose stories of their preference
- to recall details from familiar stories

- to become aware of story sequences
- to practice handling books properly
- to explore reading
- to regularly use the classroom and school library
- to explore writing
- to "read" their writing
- to develop stories
- to tell stories
- to retell stories
- to join in meaningful conversation

DEVELOPMENTALLY APPROPRIATE ACTIVITIES AND MATERIALS

Any activity or material within an early childhood environment has potential for use in language and literacy development. There are some materials that lend themselves more directly to the development of language and literacy and are listed below:

General Materials Appropriate to Language and Literacy

listening center with headphones
tape-recorder/player
filmstrip projector
computer and software
flannel board and easel
magnetic board
chalkboard
bulletin boards
book shelves
cushions for creating a soft area for reading
carpeted area
children's books:
- picture books
- nature books
- reference books
- dictionaries
- cookbooks
- phone books

- joke books
- big books
- children's magazines
- poetry books

phones

Things to Write and Draw With

thick and standard size pencils
felt-tip pens
pens
drawing or painting tools
chalk, crayons, craypas
erasers

Things to Write and Draw On

paper—lined and unlined; white and colored
sentence strips
heavy stock paper appropriate for book covers
cards
child size clipboards
chalkboards

Supplies for Organizing and Compiling Children's Work

stapler and staples
paper clips, brads
erasers
tape
"stamps"
scissors, hole punch
envelopes
stamp pads and stamps
materials for hanging children's work (tacks, tape, etc.)

Charts and Pictures

maps
graphs
photographs

pictures of animals of all kinds, foods, flowers, occupations, household objects, etc.

labels

recipes

directions

signs

Audiovisual Materials

flannel board stories

taped stories

filmstrips and tapes of children's books

films

Literacy Support Materials

all dramatic play materials

finger puppets

puppets

letters

templates: letters, numbers, shapes, seasonal

story sequence puzzles

story sequence cards

computer software

Activities Appropriate for Language and Literacy

Listening

In developing activities that are meaningful for language and literacy, it is important to remember that listening activities are as important as speaking activities. More learning situations are presented to children as they get older so it is critical to firmly establish listening as a strong avenue for learning. Good listening influences good reading and good speaking influences good writing (Eliason & Jenkins, 1994).

One technique that encourages children to listen is random selection of children to respond to questions or share experiences. In circle time, randomly choosing children to select a song to sing, a book to read, or to share with the class an event that took place over the weekend will encourage children to listen for their names.

Other ways to encourage listening include music listening and singing activities, participating in organized games, following directions in an exercise session, and following directions in cooking activities.

Speaking

Show and Tell

Many programs have regular show and tell times which are theoretically designed to offer opportunities for children to listen and speak. Some teachers refer to these times as "bring and brag" instead of show and tell. Children may feel pressured to find something to bring to school when they really do not have anything at all to bring. What should be a pleasant experience may turn out to be a stressful one. Rather than always asking children to bring something from home to talk about, the teacher might ask the children to select something from the classroom to talk about. The children could be encouraged to describe the item using color words and other descriptors. They could tell the class why they like the particular item and what the item is used for. This would relieve the burden of bringing something from home. While it would take away the responsibility of remembering an instruction, it would provide equal opportunity for all children. If the goal is to have children talk, what they talk about is immaterial. If the goal is developing responsibility, there are many other ways to nurture that.

Conversation

Conversation is one of the most appropriate ways to engage children in language activity. There are many topics that are appropriate for developing conversations with children. It is important to periodically introduce new topics with the understanding that children with limited experiences will still have access to familiar topics in order to be included in conversation.

Guessing Games

Any game that affords children the opportunity to listen to clues and make a guess is appropriate for supporting the development of speaking skills. Mystery boxes and feely bags are good examples of this type of game.

Reading Aloud

Reading good literature to children is one of the most pleasant ways to encourage listening. Elster (1994) points out that when adults read aloud they not only promote listening but reading as well. The more often a book is read aloud to a child, the greater the likelihood the child will retrieve the story language. It appears that children familiar with book reading at home pick up more story language than children who have had little or no previous experience. Sharing books in a way that includes discussion of words and pictures also promotes good listening development.

FIG 11.2 Sharing books promotes good listening.

Family Lending Library

A family lending library is another way to promote early literacy development while opening up opportunities for listening in the home environment (Brock & Dodd, 1994). The selection of books to go home with the children can become a regular activity during the school day. The books can be reviewed with the children, they can spend time browsing and then make their selections. The lending library may be organized with books that relate to the integrated theme being covered at the time or with books relating to the previous theme. Selections that support the previous theme allow families to reinforce thematic concepts as well as promote literacy.

Literature Means More than Reading to Children

It is important to provide a variety of literature-based activities that promote literacy and help to support the positive emotional climate of the classroom. This means that the books selected to read to children should have the potential to promote healthy attitudes towards all types of children, families, and activities. Some children live in communities that may be insular. They do not come into contact with a variety of people living various lifestyles. They may only know people who do the same kind of work their parents do. Through sharing quality literature, children will be able to develop personal responses to the information contained in the books. They will be able to question, respond, express their fears, and share their experiences. They hear their peers' and teachers' points of view. Hopefully all of this activity can help children come to be more accepting and understanding. These feelings should lead to the acceptance that supports inclusion (Gross & Ortiz, 1994). Gross and Ortiz (1994) propose that one good book, possibly featuring a character with a disability could become the core of many learning activities in many curriculum components. If the early childhood classroom is one that practices inclusion, this type of activity will reinforce the essence of the program. If the classroom does not yet include children with special needs, but is preparing for inclusion, this type of activity will help to prepare children, teachers, and parents for the time when it happens. If inclusion is not in the immediate picture, the children will still have the opportunity to be sensitized to the issues and situations involved in including individuals with special needs.

Dramatic Play

Dramatic play activities provide children with ample opportunities for listening, speaking, reading, and writing. These play activities create the most naturalistic environment for literacy to develop. As children go about engaging in role play, they bring what they experience in their lives to the play situation. Social interaction between children enhances literacy but what further enhances literacy is the adult-child interaction that takes place when adults facilitate dramatic play activities (Williams & Davis, 1994).

Prop boxes are a very important component of dramatic play and literacy development (Soundy & Gallagher, 1992; Soundy, 1993). A prop box may contain articles of clothing, signs, writing implements and other thematically appropriate items. Prop boxes may be labeled with pictures and words. All of this promotes literacy as children "read" what is contained in the box and associate it with the theme being played. Each time the theme is played during the year, the children become more sophisticated at "reading and writing" as it relates to the roles they are playing. They may begin to make their own signs or dictate what they want the teacher to write on a sign, menu, or recipe. Soundy (1993) suggests that prop boxes be developed that support specific stories. These prop boxes are designed to support the reading or telling and retelling of the story. Campbell & Foster (1993) detail the benefits and several suggestions for themes for play centers that help to promote literacy. The shoe store, fix-it shop, florist shop, old-fashioned school, great-grandma's attic, camping in a national park, and the travel agency are the play centers they describe in such a way as to make it easy for the teacher to implement in classroom.

Reading and Writing

Reading is more than skill acquisition. Kontos (1986) points out that before children can read, they must develop print awareness. This means that they must become aware of why people read and what people do when they read. These experiences form the cognitive maturity necessary to create the desire to read. Continuing to read to children and extending the variety of literature and literature-based activities, (i.e., acting out stories, retelling stories, flannel board stories) will contribute to a meaningful vocabulary and the mechanics of reading. The many readiness skills that come about from learning within a literacy-oriented environment include letter recognition, letter sounds and names, recognition of some sight words, connecting speech and print, recognizing the relationship between letters and words, recognizing the relationship between words and sentences, and knowing the direction of reading (left to right and from top to bottom).

All activities developed for children in early childhood classrooms are important for reading readiness. Once children are ready to read, there are many approaches available to use in teaching skills. Skills should not be taught in isolation. They should be taught in ways that allow children to apply them immediately to their own daily activities and routines.

Word Collections

Some children enjoy collecting their own words each day. In this approach, the teacher would ask the child what word the child wanted to learn that day. The child could draw a picture about the word, copy the word, collect the words in a book, and begin to use these words to build sentences.

Reviewing Plans

Children "read" the plan of the day with the teacher. They begin to recognize words used on a routine basis. They may take turns reading the plan with the teacher.

Journal Writing

Children use a journal to record their ideas. Initially they may draw their ideas and as they begin to engage in emergent writing, words will be added to their drawings and eventually entirely replace their drawings.

Big Books

Big books bring children physically closer to the printed page. They can see letter and word patterns. They can develop an appreciation for sentence formation. They will see punctuation marks. As the story is read and reread, the children will be able to get into the pattern of the language and feel part of the reading process. Big books may be selected from those already published or a teacher may develop big books specific to the experiences of the class.

Class Books

The entire class may develop a class book that is started with a sentence written by the teacher. When the book is completed, the children may create the illustrations. The book could be laminated and bound and then sent home to each family on a rotating basis. Parents and children could compose a response to the book to be shared with the teacher and classmates. Class books may develop as an extension of language experience stories based on class activities.

Individual Books Based on Predictable Books

Children may write books based on predictable books shared with the class. Each child writes a story based on the patterned language of the book, illustrates it, binds it, and then reads it to the class. The book can be taken home to share with the family and then placed in the class library.

MODIFICATION OF MATERIALS OR ACTIVITIES TO INCLUDE CHILDREN WITH SPECIAL NEEDS

What is most critical to develop language and literacy skills in children with special needs is a realistic approach to facilitation and inclusion of the children in all activity areas. Language is most effectively acquired when it is presented within a related context. As an example of this, the best time to introduce or reinforce food vocabulary would be at snack time, during cooking activities, or in the dramatic play area.

So many of the materials and activities used to promote language and literacy are familiar to children. If a child has some special need related to language and literacy, the child is probably receiving some specialized help. The child may be receiving services from a speech and language therapist. The speech and language therapist may be working in conjunction with an occupational therapist to help the child achieve maximum mouth and tongue function to produce the best development or enhancement of speech and language possible. The child may be using some assistive technology or modified materials in order to communicate with family and peers. To make the early childhood environment accessible in terms of language and literacy, adaptive devices will probably include some alternate communication systems. These alternate communication approaches might include a computer-based communication system that uses software appropriate for supporting the language of a young child or a switch-activated apparatus for children who are not able to use the keyboard to activate the system, a tape recorder with loop tapes that the child can activate through a switch device, or a photograph board with photographs that identify items and activities within the classroom the child may choose to play with or go to. The child may also use manual language (sign language) to communicate. Sign language is often used in combination with the development of spoken language to give a nonverbal child as many tools as possible in order to initiate language and the process of communication.

Universal Techniques to Facilitate Language Development

There are some universal techniques appropriate for the facilitation of language development. These techniques are appropriate for all children but are even more important when dealing with children with language delay. The first technique involves being sincere in language interactions with children. A sincere attitude towards what children have to say lets children know that they are respected as persons and that their initiations and interactions are valued by others. The second technique involves a certain amount of patience. Teachers need to wait for a short period of time after posing a question to a child. This affords the child time to formulate an answer. All too often, in an attempt to elicit a verbal response from a child, the adult in the situation keeps asking the question when the child does not immediately answer. Each child has a unique response pattern. Some children are impulsive and speak first and think later rather than think for a while and then respond. In order to maximize a child's language potential, teachers need to be sure that the child has a chance to speak. The third technique involves modeling and maintaining eye contact. When adults make eye contact with children, it not only serves as a model for the children but it demonstrates to children that the adult speaking with them is genuinely interested in them. Eye contact encourages the child to continue attempted communication.

When a teacher models language for children, the modeling may involve narration or repetition of key concepts. The narration approach to modeling involves the teacher giving a running commentary on what the child is doing or what is taking place. When narration is used, it is important to leave spaces for the child to interject or language may be inhibited rather than encouraged.

CASE STUDY

A mother and a child were part of a playgroup for children between the ages of two and four. This mother was very concerned that her child who appeared to be very bright did not speak. The mother was sure that the child understood everything that was said to her. The child followed directions and instructions but did so silently. When the mother's pattern of speaking to the child was observed and analyzed it was determined that she spoke so much and so fast that the child never had a chance to speak. When this was pointed out to the mother, she acknowledged that it would be difficult to change her own language pattern. She found that once she did speak less and left openings for her child to speak, the child spoke quite readily. The child had all this language stored up that was just waiting for an opportunity to be heard. This situation is a good example of how too much is not always a good thing.

When using repetition of key concepts, the teacher makes statements about what the child is doing and states the action in several different ways. This provides the child with models to imitate or comment on. Teachers can also use expansion to add meaning to what a child has said. When this happens, the teacher expands on a one or two word utterance or brief statement the child makes. The teacher might add adjectives and adverbs. The teacher might also add a comment that qualifies what the child is doing. Sometimes what a child needs is a prompt from a teacher to help the child recall a word. Some children respond well to this type of hint while other children find this very disturbing because it interrupts the flow of their thinking. Prompting for word retrieval might involve gestures (teacher gives a visual sign that demonstrates the word) or verbally providing information about the function of the word or the category of the word. Prompting involves providing the context in which the word may be used giving information that describes attributes of the word, or giving the child a choice of two words, one appropriate and one not. The teacher might also employ synonyms when describing actions so that the child learns more than one word for an action. Asking open-ended questions is the most appropriate way to attempt to elicit more than a one word answer. Varying questions with who, what, when, where, and why will broaden the range of a child's responses. The technique of literal interpretation places the teacher in the position of following a child's language or description literally. The teacher does exactly what the child says. If the child says put the egg in the bowl, the teacher does exactly that. If the child actually meant, crack the egg, put the yolk and white in the bowl, and throw away the shells, the child will then need to explain that to the teacher. The final technique involves relational modeling in which the teacher describes the relationships between objects, actions, people, and events over time and through space (Abraham, Morris & Wald, 1993).

There are many ways to modify activities and materials to include children in language and literacy based activities. General modifications will be listed by nature of what initially makes the experience inaccessible to a child:

Physical Considerations

Physical disabilities do not always interfere with language and literacy development. Sometimes the disability causes a language delay or prevents spoken language from being established. This necessitates the development of alternative communication approaches which utilize the range of motion within the child's physical repertoire. When a child cannot reach materials or equipment, needs to go to the bathroom, or wants to communicate another need or idea, these alternative means of communication become critical. It is important to continue to ask the child questions but also to make it possible for the child to answer those questions. Non-standard responses might include an eye gaze, a nod, a smile, an arm raised up, a thumb up, a look away, or a standard sign used in manual language. If it is possible to establish use of switch-operated equipment or the use of a computer or other tool, the possibilities for communication increase considerably. What is important to remember is that while a child with physical disabilities may not be able to speak, the child is still able to and has a strong need to communicate. The strongest motivation to communicate comes from involvement with activities and with peers. This means that all the modifications pointed out in previous chapters are appropriate for promoting language and literacy development as well. The correct physical position has a very strong impact on a child's ability to communicate and on the child's interest in literacy activities. Whether the child is in a sitting or standing position, consideration needs to be taken to ensure that the child is not barricaded from proximity to other children. Proximity constitutes a large motivation factor.

Visual Impairments

Children with visual impairments may benefit from some accommodations to maximize their experiences in the area of language and literacy development. When a child is not able to see the printed word or has difficulty seeing what everyone else is able to see, the environment is not as print rich for that child as it is for other children. The child with visual deficits may benefit from assistance in the form of some special materials or adaptive equipment. The special materials may consist of large print books, large picture puzzles, large piece manipulatives, or in the case of a child with no vision, braille materials. In addition, the classroom teacher might need to be sure that the child sits close to any visual materials such as books, big books, filmstrips, language experience charts, chalkboard, or flannel board. For a child with minor impairments, allowing the child to get as close to the materials and the play situation as possible serves to increase the likelihood that the child will become involved with the materials and activity. This child may need help in identifying materials.

Once the child is familiar with the materials and the play situations available in the classroom, the level of language development and literacy ability should increase because the level of comfort relative to the visual environment is increased. As new items and activities are introduced into the environment, there is a need to introduce the child to the new items while pairing the appropriate vocabulary with the items. Children with visual impairments enjoy language and literacy activities when the visual stimuli associated with the activities are of the appropriate size, color, and intensity. The adaptive equipment for a child with special visual needs may take the form of eyeglasses or as the child matures and becomes a reader, a page magnifier. If the child has no usable vision, the child may need a braille reader/writer system. Technology makes constant advances with systems to support children with visual deficits. It is important to maintain awareness of new developments in the field and to consult with specialists in the field for the most current information and equipment.

Social, Emotional, or Behavioral Disorders

Language and literacy activities are sometimes frustrating for children who display behaviors that are challenging to peers, adults, or both. Often, these children have developed few language skills that allow them to mediate social interactions. Since they may also have few coping skills, the lack of language ability compounds the social and emotional problems. In all activity areas, inability to communicate with peers or teachers negatively impacts on the experience the child receives from participation in the activity. The lack of language ability can also have an effect on role play in the dramatic play area. When the child does not have the language skills to participate in social interaction or role play, the child may not participate at all. Peers have certain expectations of what children will say and do within a role play situation. If a child does not have adequate language or stereotypical language, the peer group may not know how to respond to the child and wind up leaving the child out of the play. This further reduces the child's chance of developing language. In the role play situation, a child with a language deficit needs an adult to facilitate the language interaction that needs to transpire. When this happens, the child is accepted by the peer group, the child hears appropriate language models and learns what to say when playing certain roles. For the child with stereotypical language, some amount of pre-teaching might be necessary in order to prepare the child for specific dramatic play activities. It is the give and take of the play situation that will really cement the language for the child. One of the problems with more clinical approaches to developing language is that a child needs the spontaneity of peer play to stimulate and motivate language. On-site language facilitation works more effectively to develop and enhance language because the motivation is real and peer related.

Children who are emotionally fragile, may not have the correct perceptions of peer responses to their language. If a child laughs when a child with fragile emotions says something, the fragile child may think that the peer is laughing at him or her and not with the child or about the situation. This may result in the fragile child never returning to the play situation or ever attempting to communicate with that particular peer. Sometimes, the child with language delay needs a little more structure added to any play situation or routine part of the day in order to know what language to use under certain conditions. It is best not to make assumptions about a child's ability to use words rather than actions when negotiating a situation. When a child with a language deficit is involved in social interaction and is having an altercation, it is far more meaningful to remind the child to tell the other person what is wrong or what he or she does not like that to remind the child to use words. The child may not know what words to use. Sometimes it is best to create a situation where the teacher and the child spend some time observing the play and talking about what could be said to the peer group if the child were involved in the play. The teacher and the child may even need to role play so the child has a chance to practice the language involved before starting to play. Once the child appears to be ready to enter the play, the teacher needs to help the child make the entry and remain involved or supportive so that language facilitation can take place. If the teacher exits prematurely, the child may feel at a loss for words and the situation may deteriorate rapidly.

Whether working with a child who is prone to acting out or is usually withdrawn, the same supportive language facilitation may be necessary to encourage the use of situation appropriate language.

CASE STUDY

A boy with Down Syndrome with a limited vocabulary and an extremely quiet voice enjoyed being part of dramatic play activities. He was liked by his peers but could not be heard very well by them when he spoke to them.

After a period of time straining to hear him, the peer group gave up trying. His teacher was very perceptive and worked with him to increase the volume of his voice. This work was done throughout the day during activities and routine times as well as in private conversations. His parents were very supportive of the efforts to increase the volume of his voice as long as he did not become a very loud child. The whole family was soft spoken but this child was at the extreme end of the scale. Once his voice was more audible, his peers responded more positively to him. Once he received such a positive reaction from his peers, natural reinforcers took over and maintained the volume of his voice. The more he played with other children, the greater his vocabulary became. The more he interacted, the greater his self-esteem.

As was pointed out in the discussion about manipulatives, the socially immature child who is also language delayed will benefit from being surrounded by the conversation that takes place in the dramatic play area. Although this type of child may not yet play cooperatively, the child may engage in solitary play in the proximity of children who provide high potential for language involvement. As children engage in dramatic play, whether it is parallel or cooperative, they may narrate their activity and use a wide variety of vocabulary. In addition to real words, they may invent words to describe their actions. A teacher facilitating activity and language in the area would do a lot to influence language growth in a naturalistic manner.

Learning Impairments

Modifications which would enable the child with learning impairments to participate in language-based play activities might include having a teacher situated within the activity area in order to model appropriate language and play behaviors and to support the development of verbal interaction between the child and the other children in the area. Modeling the language that corresponds to the materials related activity serves two purposes. The first is to introduce the actual vocabulary appropriate to the materials and the situation and the second is to demonstrate the use of these materials while carrying on a conversation about them.

The child with delayed language may be severely delayed in language production and only mildly delayed in language reception. Through careful teacher observation and facilitation, the receptive language can serve as the basis for growing language production. It is always important to remember that all children have different levels of language production within the classroom environment. Some children will use their language skills on a regular and almost constant basis. Other children will demonstrate language competence but are basically quiet children. They use language appropriately and effectively. Their language is in no way delayed or impaired. They just choose their words carefully and engage in play and work on a quiet basis. This is acceptable behavior and indicative of their own unique personality.

CASE STUDIES DESCRIBING MODIFICATIONS

CASE STUDY

Anthony evidenced considerable language delay. His language delay appeared to be due to some early inner ear difficulties as well as his lack of interest in the social environment. Premature diagnoses suspected deafness, autism, pervasive developmental delay, and other labels. To his parents and grandparents he appeared to be aware of his environment and interested in mechanical and mobile objects. He had difficulty in expressing himself verbally and seldom made eye contact with either peers or teachers when he first started coming to school. His vocabulary was not extensive and his sentence structure was a little immature. Though the etiology of his delay was not certain, it was agreed that it was not due to his intellectual capacity. Since he was a child grounded in routine, the non-routine nature of many aspects of language were unsettling to him. His language was often repetitive and he might pick up on an expression that he heard at home and repeat it many times at school the following day. That was exactly how the teachers knew his parents were exploring home mortgage possibilities. The day after he accompanied his parents to a few banks, he was observed playing with manipulatives creating a little chant about fixed rate mortgage! When the observation was shared with his parents, they realized that he listened to and recalled just about everything he heard. It was determined that what he then needed was some help in putting what he heard into appropriate perspective. You may recall that Anthony tended to have a concerned look on his face when watching the other children engaged in play. When a teacher attempted to engage him in conversation about the play he was observing, he found it difficult to describe what he saw. Since he was not able to predict what the children would do next, he found it difficult to talk about it. It was determined that what he needed was language facilitation. He needed someone to help him understand the behavior he observed and pair appropriate vocabulary with the action. His home environment was not very social but it was very task oriented. He was not very social but he was task oriented. As the year went on, he moved from solitary play away from peers to solitary play in closer proximity to peers. As themes were introduced and then repeated, and planned language facilitation was implemented, Anthony began to reach a comfort level. He seemed to be most at ease with language linked to family routines. He began to pose questions about what the other children were doing. As was seen in terms of his behavior pattern in most areas, Anthony was careful and methodical in everything that he said. Initially, his language was almost mechanical sounding like it was produced by a robot. At home, he talked about what the other children did. He referred to himself using his first name and as time passed, he started to tell his parents about what he said and what roles he took on. His language grew and developed but still had a mechanical nature to it. One very interesting behavior related to literacy skills. Anthony came willingly to story time but spent the entire time facing outside the circle with his back to the book. His location in the circle was changed but it appeared that location had nothing to do with it. The teachers were sure that he was not paying attention to the story but was so grounded in routine that he would not leave the area. When his mother came to school one day asking for the name of the book read the previous day, knowing the entire story line, it became obvious that he was able to listen to and absorb a story without needing any picture cue.

Sharon loves to talk and engage in literacy activities! She is a very verbal child! She needs to be in a good sitting position to maximize her breathing but there is little that stops her from talking. She is not at all shy about asking others to help her or fetch for her. In her preschool years, Sharon thoroughly enjoyed social interaction and role-playing experiences and was often the biggest talker in the group. Sharon enjoys books and stories, participating in plays based on literature read in the classroom and now that she is in public school, she uses a computer to carry out her writing assignments. She needed assistance to begin the process of using the computer but is able to handle most things independently at this time. She has a slight vision deficit, wears glasses, and uses large print books. Some work sheets or assignments are printed out in larger print for her. This is only a slight modification of her environment.

In the area of language and literacy, **Charlie** needed some special attention when he first entered preschool. He had a limited vocabulary and used very short or incomplete sentences. He had an unusually quiet and somewhat breathy voice that made it difficult to understand what he was saying. Since he was always eager to explore everything, it was very easy to engage him in activity. While he was engaged in activity, he listened attentively and responded to invitations to expand his language production. He also tried very hard to speak in a louder voice. Peer reinforcement of his language usage pleased him very much. You may recall that his favorite piece of dramatic play equipment was the steering wheel. If someone tried to preempt his use of the steering wheel, he used as loud a voice as possible to stake out his claim. He also began to use his developing language to organize certain dramatic play activities. He once set up a "movie show" and told the children where to sit, how much the tickets cost, and when the show would begin. After a while, he also told them the projector was broken and he would have to fix it! The children sat in their seats and waited! Charlie learned the power of using language and the joy of peer interaction. His mother indicates that he continues to grow in language, loves books and tapes and has a much louder voice.

Sarah was not at all interested in participating in activities that were largely language based. Sarah was reported to speak at home and use language effectively with her parents and siblings but she did not use language at all at school. She usually spent an active day, responded to questions by nodding, and followed directions in a nonverbal manner. Nobody tried to force language out of Sarah because it was already known that she had the capability of using language but was choosing not to use it. It took quite some time and the subtle support of the teachers and her peers for Sarah to eventually speak quietly to her peers within the context of dramatic play. The content of her verbalizations was often prompted by her peers who would tell her what to say. The most important factor was that she was using her language skills and appearing to enjoy herself at the same time! Sarah appeared to enjoy literacy activities that did not require speaking. She enjoyed books and listening to flannel board stories. She would use puppets and make them do things but not say anything. She enjoyed using writing tools and made books for her family members. She engaged in pretend writing and made illustrations for her books. She did not talk about her books but was very proud of them and showed them eagerly to her mother at dismissal time.

For **Martie**, language was not a problem but using language to communicate was problematic for him. Martie was not comfortable with sharing his feelings through conversation. Due to his unstable early family history, he was cautious about sharing his experiences and usually had his guard up when activities or conversations centered around family and friends. Martie responded thoughtfully to books and stories that were sensitive and family oriented. He engaged in literacy activities by reading books, writing letters and lists. When a restaurant or store was set up in the dramatic play area, he enjoyed roles that required writing or reading. He was a very competent child. During the course of the year, he became more comfortable with the idea of using his language skills to share his feelings and ideas. He shared some very critical issues with his teachers but seemed to feel as though he could not say anything to his peers. His language and his literacy skills continued to develop as the year progressed.

Christina, had absolutely no trouble with language ability and no difficulty in language activities. She was quick to respond to questions and had opinions about everything which she was most eager to share with anyone who would listen. She told stories with great detail. She sometimes attempted to use her language ability to win arguments and coerce children into doing things they would not normally want to do. She used language in a very clever manner. During one period covering several weeks, a boy who was approximately a year younger than Christina seemed to be smitten by her. He followed her around much of the day and tried to sit as close to her as he possibly could. These two children sat at the same snack table each day. One day, he kept asking her if she would marry him. After he asked her the same question for about the twentieth time, she turned to him and said with a straight face, "Of course I will—when all the people in the world die!!" The teacher in charge of the group had a most difficult time containing herself. The young boy had a confused look on his face. On the one hand she had said yes, but something did not seem right to him about the way she said it. Christina simply continued to eat her snack. At the end of the school year when the teacher shared this story with Christina's mother, her mother almost died of embarrassment. She could never understand where her daughter got these expressions from. The reason the teacher decided to wait until the end of the school year to share the story with the mother was because the mother was a very shy, proper woman who would have been unable to face the teachers at school if she had known what the child said. Her embarrasment would have kept her away from the school and detracted from the positive relationship she had developed with her daughter relative to school.

In terms of literacy activities, Christina needed large-print materials and worked with large picture puzzles. She used large pencils and large pieces of paper. When she was in preschool, there were no big books so Christina always sat closest the book being read at story time. Other children did not appear to have a problem with this.

As with everything else at school, **C. W.** loved to talk. C. W. was a very playful child and was playful with language also. If no teacher or peer attempted to engage him in conversation, he would walk right up to them and ask what was new. He liked to tell stories about what he did on the weekend and often embellished these stories. He did not always have the correct word for what he wanted to talk about but could describe the situation well enough to get his idea across. In the process he usually learned new vocabulary words while the teacher reinforced his language. He was very interested in books and writing. Initially, he gravitated to books with photographs or very large illustrations. It was not clear whether this was due to his visual deficit or if it was easier for him to physically handle a larger book due to his cerebral palsy.

SUMMARY

Language and literacy development play an integral part of an early childhood classroom. When children experience the freedom to explore materials and follow their own ideas as well as the ideas of their peers, they continue to be curious. This curiosity brings them richer language experiences and richer literacy experiences. Through play, children apply mathematical concepts, work out problems, play out roles, and use language to express themselves. Language, social interaction, and literacy become almost spontaneous as children become absorbed in the play of their peers as well their own play. Children bring their own experiences to their dramatic play. The richer the dramatic play and other play experiences, the richer the experience the child will have and the greater the language and literacy base. Stories read, movies or TV programs seen, and places visited all have an influence on what children play out in the more open-ended dramatic play. Cognitive growth and the further development of the imagination flourish when children create scenarios, talk about their actions, and write stories about their experiences. Teachers sometimes need to spend a lot of time with children to initiate language and literacy activities and they may need to be around to facilitate and support the established effort. The early childhood years are a time for great growth in both language and literacy. Once language and literacy are both established, they need to be nurtured with exciting, creative experiences and lots of good literature.

DISCUSSION QUESTIONS

1) Develop a list of words for activities and objects commonly used during the course of a morning at school. Think of ways to explain or demonstrate the definitions of those words to children so all children will be able to understand regardless of their language level.
2) Discuss the role of the teacher in the integrated curriculum with regard to language development and enhancement. Specify behaviors a teacher should engage in to facilitate language while childen are engaged in activity.
3) Prepare information to share with parents about the importance of reading to children as a strong foundation for language and literacy. With this information include some ideas for books, alternative materials, and activities to encourage literacy at home.
4) A child in your class tends to be very quiet. When the child speaks, the child uses very appropriate language. The teachers are pleased with the progress to date. One day, the child's mother comes to school and informs the teachers that she is concerned about the bad

words the child has been using at home. She is quiet and shy herself and does not feel comfortable sharing the words of concern with the teachers. The teachers put their heads together to brainstorm what the child might be saying considering all the "richness" of possibilities that a child could learn from in the classroom. When the teachers talk to the mother and express their shared concern about the level of discomfort the mother feels, she tells the teachers that the child was calling them "stupid" at home. The teachers were relieved that the word of concern was not stronger but they realized that the mother had a valid concern and needed assistance with the elimination of language that was distasteful to the family to exhibit support for her feelings. What can you say to the mother to help her and to validate her feelings? What can you do at school to help with the problem?

5) A parent comes to you to express concern over the fact that the children in the school do not learn how to spell. When the parent went to school, learning 10 spelling words per week was an important part of the curriculum. What will you tell the parent to explain why this is the not the focal point of the curriculum in your school?
6) A child comes to your kindergarten class without any preschool experience. The child is the appropriate chronological age for school but as you get to know the child, it appears that the child is not at the same age developmentally. You are concerned about the child's language level and feel the need to develop a plan of action to enhance the language level of the child. Your plan should include individualized attention, group activities as well as home activities.

REFERENCES

Abraham, M., Morris, L., & Wald, P. (1993). *Inclusive early childhood education—A model classroom*. Tucson, AZ: Communication Skill Builders.

Bredekamp, S. (1990). *Developmentally appropriate practice in early childhood programs serving children from birth through age 8*. Washington, DC: National Association for the Education of Young Children.

Brock, D., & Dodd, E. (1994). A family lending library: Promoting early literacy development. *Young Children, 49*(3), 16–21.

Buchoff, R. (1994). Joyful noises: Facilitating language growth through the rhythmic response to chants. *Young Children, 49*(4), 26–30.

Campbell, E., & Foster, J. (1993). Play centers that encourage literacy development. *Day Care and Early Development, 21*(2), 22–26.

Christie, J., Ed. (1991). *Play and early literacy development*. Albany, NY: State University of New York Press.

Clements, N., & Warncke, E. (1994). Helping literacy emerge at school for less-advantaged children. *Young Children, 49*(3), 22–26.

Day, B. (1994). *Early childhood education—Developmental/experiential teaching and learning* (Fourth edition). New York: Merrill.

Edwards, L. (1994). Kid's eye view of reading—Kindergartners talk about learning how to read. *Childhood Education, 70*(3), 137–141.

Eliason, C., & Jenkins, L. (1994). *A practical guide to early childhood curriculum.* New York: Merrill.

Elster, C. (1994). "I guess they do listen": Young children's emergent readings after adult read-alouds. *Young Children, 49*(3), 27–31.

Essa, E. (1992). *Introduction to early childhood education.* Albany, NY: Delmar Publishers Inc.

Gross, A., & Ortiz, L. (1994). Using children's literature to facilitate inclusion in kindergarten and the primary grades. *Young Children, 49*(3), 32–35.

Hendrick, J. (1994). *Total learning—Developmental curriculum for the young child.* New York: Merrill.

Juliebo, M., & Edwards, J. (1989). Encouraging meaning making in young writers. *Young Children, 44*(2), 22–27.

Kontos, S. (1986). What preschool children know about reading and how they learn it. *Young Children, 42*(1), 58–66.

Kostelnik, M., Soderman, A., & Whiren, A. (1993). *Developmentally appropriate programs in early childhood education.* New York: Merrill.

Krogh, S. (1990). *The integrated early childhood curriculum.* New York: McGraw-Hill Publishing Company.

McMackin, M. (1993). The parent's role in literacy development—Fostering reading strategies at home. *Childhood Education, 69*(3), 142–145.

Morrison, G. (1995). *Early childhood education today.* Englewood Cliffs, NJ: Prentice-Hall, Inc.

Morrow, L. (1989). *Literacy development in the early years.* Englewood Cliffs, NJ: Prentice-Hall.

Neuman, S., & Roskos, K. (1993). *Language and literacy learning in the early years—An integrated approach.* Fort Worth: Harcourt Brace Jovanovich College Publishers.

Roskos, K., & Neuman, S. (1994). Of scribbles, schemas, and storybooks: Using literacy albums to document young children's literacy growth. *Young Children, 49*(2), 78–85.

Salyer, D. (1994). Noise or communication? Talking, writing, and togetherness in one first grade class. *Young Children, 49*(4), 42–47.

Sawyer, W., & Sawyer, J. (1993). *Integrated language arts for emergent literacy.* New York: Delmar Publishers Inc.

Schuele, C., Roberts, J., Fitzgerald, J., & Moore, P. (1993). Assessing emergent literacy in preschool clasrooms. *Day Care and Early Education, 21*(2), 13–21.

Shipley, D. (1993). Empowering children: Play-based curriculum for lifelong learning. Scarborough, Ont.: Nelson Canada.

Soundy, C., & Gallagher, P. (1992). Creating prop boxes to stimulate dramatic play and literacy development. *Day Care and Early Education, 20*(2), 4–8.

Soundy, C. (1993). Let the story begin! Open the box and set out the props. *Childhood Education 69*(3), 146–149.

Trawick-Smith. J. (1994). *Interactions in the classroom—Facilitating play in the early years*. New York: Merrill.

Van Hoorn, J., Nourot, P., Scales, B., & Alward, K. (1993) *Play at the center of the curriculum*. New York: Merrill.

Whitin, D. (1994). Literature and mathematics in preschool and primary: The right connection. *Young Children, 49*(2), 4–11.

Williams, R., & Davis, J. (1994). Lead lightly into literacy. *Young Children, 49*(4), 37–41.

Wortham, S. (1994). *Early childhood curriculum—Developmental bases for learning and teaching*. New York: Merrill.

ADDITIONAL READINGS

Daniels, H. (1994). *Literature circles: Voice and choice in the student centered classroom*. York, ME: Stenhouse Publishers.

Dolinar, K., Boser, C., & Holm, E. (1994). *Learning through play: Curriculum and activities for the inclusive classroom*. Albany, NY: Delmar Publishers Inc.

Witmore, K., & Crowell, C. (1994). *Inventing a classroom: Life in a bilingual, whole language learning community*. York, ME: Stenhouse Publishers.

CHAPTER 12

Sample Integrated Themes

DEVELOPED INTEGRATED THEME

This chapter includes a developed integrated theme (how things work, move, and change), a resource of ideas for another integrated theme (homes) and a list of topics for themes that are appropriate for the early childhood years. This list is not an exhaustive one but a sample of what may be developed. Remember that the children you teach will be the source of very appropriate themes. Some themes make sense due to the geographic region in which the program is located. Other themes may be appropriate due to a major national event taking place at the time. Often integrated themes evolve as a result of commonly shared experiences.

This chapter does not contain a calendar of themes presented in a workbook or recipe approach. It would be inappropriate to develop such a calendar and still work within the framework of implementing developmentally appropriate curriculum because the nature of where you begin and where you conclude at the close of a school year will be determined by the following elements: the children, the resources available to you, the length of the school day, the number of adults working with the children, the geographic location, etc. Presenting a curriculum that appears to be logical and complete is risky because there is the temptation to attempt to implement what exists in that curriculum as a package for a particular classroom. What exists on paper may not meet the needs of the children and teachers in the class. There are many published early childhood resources rich in ideas that may serve as a starting point for teachers looking for ideas and formats for organizing age appropriate curriculum. Several of these resources may be found in the references at the end of this chapter.

The theme "how things work, move, and change" is presented in considerable detail. It is recognized that the implementation of this theme would probably be different from one classroom to another depending on the age and experiences of the children and the resources available to the teacher. The activity ideas are presented as a resource of ideas from which to choose those activities that are the most appropriate to the population you are currently teaching.

The theme is first introduced by title, then by a listing of the overall content objectives of the theme. What follows are many detailed activity plans. Along with the title of each activity, the highlighted activity area or areas are indicated. Developmental objectives, materials, procedures, and modifications are described. Modifications are noted for physical, visual, social, emotional, language, and learning impairments. These modifications are presented not by specific disability label but by more global deficit areas. There are many ways in which disabilities manifest themselves. The degree to which the disability might impede full integration into activities will vary from child to child. Some disabilities are so mild as to be hardly noticeable. A child with mild disabilities may benefit from considerable assistance within some kinds of activities but needs little if any assistance with other activities. There is no universal formula or recipe for facilitating the participation of all children in all activities. Children with and without disabilities have different interests and the right to reflect those interests in their own choice of activities. Some of the modifications presented for each individual activity may appear to be repetitious. The reason they are listed within each area rather than in a general section on modifications is so that if a teacher chooses to use some activities from this list of activities, the teacher would not have to go back to another section of the chapter to read about what to do to modify the activity. The role of the teacher is to introduce activities to children, facilitate their participation, and modify the material or activity to meet the needs of individual children.

GUIDELINES FOR GENERAL MODIFICATIONS OF ACTIVITIES

It is recognized that there are some general modifications which can be planned on for each of the disability areas according to the nature of each of the activities. One major modification for all children, regardless of type of disability, relates to the expectation that all children will participate in all routines and activities in the classroom. For example, this means that when it is time to clean up, the adults need to find something for each child to do to help in the process according to the ability of the child. In the classroom, children without disabilities may have a tendency to want to help too much. They may take over responsibilities for the child with disabilities. In setting the tone for inclusion, it is important to explain to all the children why participation is required of all children in the class. After the explanation, adult modeling of the practice will reinforce the concept for the children. Creating an atmosphere of acceptance and nurturance of all children may require modifications, but elimination of expectation should not be substituted for these modifications. General information pertaining to each disability area is included here while specific information appropriate for individual activities is included in each of the activities detailed within the developed theme: How things work, move and change.

Physical Disabilities

Children may experience temporary physical impairments as well as lifelong impairments. A child with temporary impairments may require as many modifications of the environment and activities as do children with permanent physical disabilities. In general, children with moderate to severe physical disabilities will need assistance in moving around and through activity areas. They might also need an adult to help them handle the materials. Children with mild physical disabilities may require some assistance on an occasional basis depending on the type and size of materials being used. Regardless of the severity of the physical disability, adult facilitation will help the child to be as much a part of the socialization, language, and flow of activity as possible. A child with physical disabilities may need adaptive equipment brought to the activity area and an adult to assist the child getting into the adaptive equipment. The child may always require adaptive equipment and assistance with correct positioning in the adaptive equipment. These modifications will be necessary regardless of the nature of the activity. Many physically disabled children are able to engage in far more productive activity when they are positioned correctly. Often, this is one of the first needs to be addressed when a child is new to a setting. Positioning is not something that can be addressed only once. It requires ongoing attention because as the child physically grows and changes developmentally, the size of the child and the nature of the activities the child is able to do require adjustments or substitutions in equipment. Consideration given to modifications for activities and equipment enables the child to gain maximum access to all that the environment has to offer.

To motivate children with physical disabilities, give them tasks they can accomplish as well as tasks which challenge them. If a child does not appear to be interested in something, demonstrate how it works and what it will look like after use. This may be all the motivation the child needs.

Provide ample space for the adaptive equipment the child uses. Since most early childhood settings never seem to have enough space, accessible storage of adaptive equipment not currently in use may be necessary. For some children, moving things onto the floor makes them accessible. For other children, placing activities on the floor renders them inaccessible. Leaving materials on the floor created hazards for some children. This reinforces the point that planning cannot be universal in nature. One size does not always fit all, but with modifications, most children can certainly be included. It is not only materials and equipment that may need to be scrutinized but the classroom itself may need some modification. If a child is ambulatory, care needs to be taken to ensure that ramps (temporary or permanent) are in the classroom if the child will benefit from their use. Floors should not have a highly waxed finish nor should the floor be covered with scatter rugs that are not firmly attached to the floor.

Visual Impairments

There are different conditions which come under the heading of visual impairments. Children may be considered to have low vision and are partially sighted with enough usable vision for learning with the help of magnification and large-print materials. Other children may be considered legally blind. These children will learn using the auditory and tactile modes rather than relying strictly on their visual ability. Some children will wear glasses from an early age while for other children, it will be determined that glasses will not make a difference. The classroom teacher plays an important role in creating an atmosphere that supports the wearing of glasses. If glasses are a critical modification for a child, supporting the wearing of those glasses may be the only major modification required for the child.

Depending on the degree of visual impairment, children may need assistance in locating and identifying materials and equipment. An adult facilitator will help the child to work with the materials in any of the activity areas. Adult facilitation will also help the child identify the details of the materials which may not have been noticed by the child if they were not specifically pointed out. A child with severely limited visual ability and special mobility concerns will need to be watched carefully without being hovered over. The child will need to develop independence in the classroom environment. This independence can be nurtured within a classroom that is designed and maintained to facilitate safety for all children. If a room is rearranged, the child with considerable visual deficits will need an orientation to the redesigned space.

Regardless of the level of visual disability, children may find greater success working with larger materials or materials that have adaptation built into them. A good example of this would be puzzles with knobs which make it easier for children with low vision to complete a puzzle. Big books, books with photographs, and books with vivid colors make for much more meaningful involvement for these children. Take into consideration the degree of light in the classroom. Try not to use materials that create glare. Create a need to see. If a child can obtain all the information to engage in activity by just listening, the visual ability the child does have will not be challenged. When a child is listening, encourage the child to look at the speaker regardless of whether the child can see the speaker or not. This helps to open the channel of communication for the child. The more hands-on activity a child with limited visual ability can be involved with, the greater the likelihood the child will learn. Materials with texture will enhance learning and help children to discriminate between items. While the computer can be an excellent tool for learning, some modifications for the computer that make this approach to the presentation of information more meaningful incorporate the use of a voice synthesizer. This modification will allow what is printed on the screen to be fed back to the child in synthesized speech.

Social and Emotional Impairments

Children may experience temporary social and emotional impairments as well as long term impairments. Temporary problems may be due to life-cycle events which have a great impact on the child. The birth of a sibling, the illness of a family member, or the death of a family member, neighbor or friend may cause tremendous pain for a child. Sometimes teachers are not made aware of the event so it is difficult to know how to help a child or even that the child is in need of help or extra concern. All children are entitled to have difficult days from time to time. When a teacher notices that a child experiences several of these days in a row, it is critical that the teacher assess the situation and modify the environment and the activities to include the child. Some children are extremely sensitive and a comment made in passing by a child or an adult may have been the source of the child's discomfort.

Other children may have more long-term problems that are a result of abuse or neglect. Some inappropriate behavior patterns result in aggressive behavior while others result in withdrawn behavior. The aggressive behavior may be directed towards materials or persons. The behavior may be displayed in the form of temper tantrums or biting. Withdrawal or shyness may be displayed. Refusal to eat or sleeping problems may also be displayed. All of these behaviors may be seen in most children from time to time as changes occur in their lives. What is different is the intensity, duration, and frequency of these behaviors in children for whom these behaviors are part of everyday life. For the child with the short-term problem, extra attention, comforting, and nurturing will serve to help the child through the difficult period. Creating opportunities for the child to share feelings about the situation will help the child learn ways of coping so that in the future, the child may be able to identify the problem and discuss it before developing an inappropriate behavior pattern. For children who engage in inappropriate behavior patterns for long durations, modifications will require paying careful attention to the conditions under which the behaviors occur as well as peer and adult reactions to these behaviors.

The adult in the classroom can assist children with getting into the play and activity in the different areas in the room. Adult facilitation will help the children learn what behaviors are appropriate for different areas. Many times, children with social and emotional impairments are not able to read social cues consistently. They may have difficulty controlling their feelings or expressing their feelings. They may have limited social knowledge because their behaviors have excluded them from group experiences. Modifications may include cueing appropriate behavior by narrating what is happening in an activity area for the child prior to having the child enter the area so the child "knows the story" before attempting to join the play or conversation. Some children act first and think later. Adults may be able to help children by modeling appropriate "think first" behavior as well as helping them to think through the consequences of their actions. Teachers can look at the environment and analyze whether the arrangement of furniture, equipment, and materials prevents or encourages negative behavior patterns. A good balance of activities will serve to modify an environment to create a calmer atmosphere more conducive to learning and engaging in new, more socially appropriate behaviors. While it is important to help children let go of negative behaviors that interfere with positive social interactions, it is also critical to simultaneously help children develop new, more appropriate behaviors to replace the inappropriate ones. Within each activity offered in an early childhood program, children have opportunities for social and emotional learning. It is up to the teachers with support from the peer group to facilitate this happening.

Language Impairments

Language impairments interfere with a child's ability to communicate. Therefore, the major focus of modifications for children with language impairments needs to be directed to opening up channels of communication. This may be accomplished through assisting children with learning new vocabulary associated with each activity in which they engage. Children will also benefit from having an adult facilitate communication between children in the activity. Adult facilitation will help the child to be included in the play regardless of the language level. While creating opportunities to speak may require asking questions of the child, asking these questions during larger group activities places high demands on speech when the yield is small. Creating language-rich activities where children and adults are able to share experiences provides for considerable growth opportunities.

When language does not seem to be developing, providing alternatives to spoken language in the form of augmented communication or sign language may remove the pressure the child may be feeling. Once the pressure is removed, communication may begin with an alternative mode. Augmented communication plans should attempt to make the communication device as portable and user friendly as possible. The system developed should be able to be with the child in as many activity situations as possible. It should be able to travel home with the child as well as be used in school. In this way, the child will only have to use one system and will be able to focus on the words or phrases being introduced rather than the technique required to access the system.

Sometimes for children with delayed language, the emphasis seems to be on speaking. Listening activities are just as important for the nurturing of language. Activity modifications should focus on creating listening opportunities. While peer produced language may be at a high level in an activity, the quality of the language may not afford the child with a language deficit a high enough quality model to listen to and then to imitate. This is where the adult may intervene with repetitions of what children say so that opportunities for appropriate listening may prevail. If a child will not respond to adults in the classroom, the child may respond to peers or to puppets. This is another way any activity may be modified to encourage maximum language opportunity.

Learning Impairments

In order to help children who have problems with learning, teachers need to interact with children in the learning environment in a way that encourages maximum growth. While each child presents a very different learning profile, teachers may modify activities to accommodate these children. One way to assist learning is to provide demonstrations of how materials can be used to assist the child with learning the function of the items in each of the activity areas. It is also important that while implementing activities teachers do not assume a child knows the sequence in which things should be done. Adult facilitation can help children to be integrated into play. Children with learning impairments may need motivation to pay attention in an activity area or to directions. While other children may jump into the activity, these children may need to hear all about the activity before they will enter into the play. They may need to watch for some time before they begin. They may benefit from having a peer "buddy" to perform an activity with so that the peer will serve as a facilitator. Instructions may need to be repeated. Demonstrations may need to be performed more than once to maximize the benefit of the activity for the child. Children with a short attention span need to have activity modifications that encourage their participation and attention. Teacher attention needs to be directed to the development of awareness in all activity areas for children with learning impairments.

Hearing Impairments

Modifications for hearing impairments were not included in each activity because the modifications necessary for a child to be included in different activities in an integrated classroom are similar from one activity to another and will be described in general in this section.

Modifications for activities to include children with hearing impairments involve paying careful attention to the physical placement of the child. The child will need to be near the adult in the activity and at the same eye level so as to be able to hear appropriate language, and to be able to closely watch the adult's mouth during conversation. The child may need to be involved in quieter activities at first because the noise might be too distracting for the child. To minimize distractions for the child, it may be necessary to ensure that there is no music in the background. Alternative modes of communication may need to be established until the child is comfortable with the environment or the child acquires enough language to communicate. Use as many visual aids as possible so if the child misses the spoken language related to making choices or understanding what is going on in an activity, the visual cues will support the inclusion of the child. Use an overhead projector instead of a blackboard. Do not talk when the room is dark during the showing of a filmstrip. Understand also that a child will only get the visual part of a filmstrip even if the volume is turned up really high. Call names during activities so the child will know who will be speaking next and can turn attention to that person. For whole-group activities it is best to seat the children in a circle so everyone is visible (Deiner, 1993).

RESOURCE OF IDEAS FOR DEVELOPMENT OF A THEME

The second part of this chapter presents a resource of ideas for the development of a theme on homes. With the identification of the many ideas contained in this resource, the teacher is able to identify concepts to cover that are appropriate to the children in the classroom. Each time a resource of ideas such as this is used, it should be used keeping in mind the children in the class for whom planning is being done. Their specific needs and interests will determine the direction taken in developing the integrated theme.

There are many ways to develop integrated themes. One way is to identify key concepts and then develop activities to support them. Sometimes this can be limiting because all the potential resources available to support activities and experiences have not been explored. Thus, listing key concepts may somewhat curtail the planning, limiting it to the knowledge the teacher has about a subject at that point in time. Another way to plan is to identify a rich resource of ideas from which the concepts will flow. This resource of ideas can then be used over time as it can contain many ideas for activities appropriate for various developmental levels. This chapter contains an example of each.

TITLE OF THEME: PROCESSES—HOW THINGS WORK, MOVE, AND CHANGE

Overall Theme Objectives:

a) Children will become familiar with how things work
b) Children will explore sequences that facilitate making things work
c) Children will explore the roles people play in making things work
d) Children will learn related vocabulary

ACTIVITIES

Title of Activity: Dramatic Play—Florist Shop

- Content Objectives:

The children will label items in a florist shop

The children will learn how individual flowers can be put together to make arrangements (how things change)

The children will discuss what happens in a florist shop

The children will role play as they work in the flower shop

Dramatic Play—Florist Shop **continued**

- Developmental Objectives:
  language
  cognitive
  social
  fine motor
  creative
- Materials:
  real, plastic, or silk flowers
  floral containers
  floral foam for floral arranging
  gloves
  photographs of floral arrangements
  paper and markers to make signs
  cash register and money
  small boxes to put floral arrangements in
  phone, paper and pencils
  refrigerator to keep flowers cold
- Procedure:
  The children will take on the roles of florist and customer as they work in the florist shop. They will make arrangements, make transactions, and "manage" the shop. They will transform individual flowers into arrangements.
- Modifications:
  Physical impairments: assist child with handling the materials. Adult facilitation will help the child to be as much a part of the socialization, language, and flow of activity as possible through setting materials up so the child will be a central figure in the play.

  Visual impairments: Adult facilitation will help the child work with the flowers and other materials in the dramatic play situation. Facilitation will also help the child to identify colors, shapes, textures and sizes.

  Social and emotional impairments: assist child in getting into the role play in the area. Adult facilitation will help the child learn what behaviors are appropriate for each role played in the area. Adult facilitation will also help the child learn appropriate vocabulary to use and the sequence in which events should take place.

  Language impairments: assist child with learning vocabulary specific to the activity (flower, florist, arrangement, etc,) and facilitate communication between children in the activity.

Dramatic Play—Florist Shop **continued**

Learning impairments: assist child to learn the function of the items in the area (flowers, containers, florist foam, etc.) as well as the sequence in which things are done.

Title of Activity: Dramatic Play—Appliance Store

- Content Objectives:
  The children will label items in an appliance store
  The children will see how appliances work
  The children will discuss what happens in an appliance store
  The children will role-play as they work in the appliance store
- Developmental Objectives:
  language
  cognitive
  social
  fine motor
  creative
- Materials:
  small appliances: toaster, toaster oven, blender, iron, microwave oven, mixer, hand mixer, food processor
  appropriate food items to prepare in and with these appliances
- Procedure:
  The children will explore each of the small appliances with adult supervision. The teacher will provide demonstrations of how the appliances work with the children assisting the teacher in preparing the food items set out to use with the appliances.
- Modifications:
  Physical impairments: assist child in moving from one appliance to another or bring the items to the child. Help the child in handling the materials. Adult facilitation will place the child in the center of the socialization, language, and flow of activity.
  Visual impairments: assist child in locating and identifying food items and other materials. Adult facilitation will allow the child to work with the food items in the dramatic play situation. Adult facilitation will also help the child to identify shapes and sizes of the items.
  Social and emotional impairments: assist child in getting into the role play in the area. Facilitation will help the child to learn what behaviors are appropriate for

Dramaitc Play—Appliance Store **continued**

each role played in the area and what is appropriate play with each of the items involved in the play. Children will also be helped to learn appropriate vocabulary to use (appliance, machine, switch, power, on, off, etc.).

Language impairments: assist child with vocabulary (as indicated above) and create motivation for communication between children in the activity. Create listening opportunities by encouraging peers to give narrated demonstrations of appliance use.

Learning impairments: assist child to learn the sources of the items in the area as well as the the things that should be prepared prior to using the appliances. Provide models of behavior for the child to imitate.

Title of Activity: Dramatic Play—Shopping at the Grocery Store and Preparing Food at Home

- Content Objectives:

The children will label items in a grocery store

The children will discover how some machines in the supermarket work to keep foods fresh and some machines process sales (how things work)

The children will discuss what happens in a grocery store

The children will role-play as they work in the grocery store

The children will help to prepare food "transformations" by cooking applesauce, making butter, etc. in the housekeeping area (how things change)

- Developmental Objectives:

language

cognitive

social

fine motor

creative

- Materials:

food containers demonstrating the different food items that stem from the same source (i.e., cream into butter and cheese)

food items that are the source of other foods (food clusters, i.e., apples into applesauce and apple juice; milk into cream, ice cream)

cash register and money

brown paper bags

shelves

Dramatic Play—Shopping at the Grocery Store and Preparing Food at Home **continued**

photographs or food ads that show sources of and transformations of foods

equipment used to change foods from one state to another (i.e., cooking surface, pot and lid; pot holder; bowls; food mill; jars; spoons; spatulas)

appropriate food items (i.e., apples to applesauce, cream to butter) to prepare "transformations"

- Procedure:

A food store will be set up for children to explore the activities of shopping and bringing food home. The children will role-play customer and employee in the food store. The children will take turns being involved with what happens to the food once it is brought "home." Over several days, the children will explore different food clusters with adult supervision. The teacher will provide demonstrations of how the foods change from one state into another with the children assisting the teacher in preparing the food items. This activity can continue as long as there is interest in food preparation or the activity can be reintroduced periodically during the implementation of the theme.

- Modifications:

Physical impairments: assist child in getting around the activity area and in processing the foods. Help child to be part of a cooperative venture between two or more peers.

Visual impairments: assist child in locating and identifying foods and supplies. Adult facilitation will allow the child to work with the food items and in the dramatic play situation. Adult facilitation will also help the child to identify the state of the foods (i.e., solid, liquid).

Social and emotional impairments: assist child in getting into the role play in the area. Adult facilitation will help the child with learning to be patient, wait turns and help peers. Adult facilitation will also help the child learn appropriate vocabulary to use when asking for things to be passed.

Language impairments: create opportunities for the child to learn new vocabulary (names of foods, items associated with a food store, etc.) in order to facilitate communication between children in the activity.

Learning impairments: assist child with learning the names of the food items as well as learning about different food states.

Title of Activity: Dramatic Play—Tailor Shop

- Content Objectives:

The children will label items in a tailor shop

The children will discuss what happens in a tailor shop

Dramiatic Play—Tailor Shop **continued**

The children will role-play as they work in the tailor shop using burlap and plastic needles and other "sewing " materials (how things work)

- Developmental Objectives:

language
cognitive
social
fine motor
creative

- Materials:

self-help dressing boards: zipping, buttoning, lacing, snapping
lacing cards and shoelaces
burlap, plastic needles, yarn
embroidery hoops
thimbles
pin cushions
clothes
cash register and money
clothing ads
pictures of sewing machines
"mannequins"

- Procedure:

The children will explore each of the sewing items with adult supervision. The teacher will provide demonstrations of the process of "sewing" using the variety of materials provided. The children will explore the dressing frames, attempting to work each of the frames independently or with help if necessary. The children will dress the "mannequins" using the clothes set up in the tailor shop.

- Modifications:

Physical impairments: assist child in working with the sewing and self-help dressing boards. If the standard dressing boards are not an appropriate size to allow manipulation by the child, boards with larger buttons, zippers, etc. should be provided. Adult facilitation will allow the child to be part of the socialization, language, and flow of activity including dressing the "mannequins."

Visual impairments: assist child in locating and identifying each of the sewing and dressing items. Adult facilitation will allow the child to work with the sewing items. Again, if larger button, zipper, and snaps will facilitate the inclusion of a child, they should be provided.

Dramatic Play—Tailor Shop **continued**

Social and emotional impairments: assist child in getting into the role of playing tailor. Adult facilitation will help the child with socially appropriate behaviors and language as well as coping strategies if "dressing" the mannequin becomes too frustrating.

Language impairments: assist child with vocabulary such as button, yarn, material, pattern, etc. In addition to helping a child to learn labels, the adult can help the child learn verbs (i.e., sew, lace, snap, button, zip).

Learning impairments: assist child to learn the processes involved in working in a tailor shop. Adult facilitation will help the child to be integrated into the activity and to be knowledgeable about what happens in a tailor shop.

Title of Activity: Dramatic Play and Large Blocks—Peanut Butter Factory

- Content Objectives:

The children will label items associated with making peanut butter

The children will discuss what happens in a peanut butter factory

The children will role-play being an assembly line worker in a peanut butter factory (how things change)

- Developmental Objectives:

language
cognitive
social
fine motor
creative

- Materials:

unshelled peanuts
clean pail
pulley
spoons
spatulas
aprons
hats
scale
container to put shells in
cups or cans to put shelled peanuts in

Dramatic Play and Large Blocks—Peanut Butter Factory **continued**

blender or food processor

containers to put processed peanuts in

- Procedure:

The children will discuss the process of taking peanuts in the shell, shelling them, and then processing them into peanut butter. Then, the children, with the help of a teacher, will organize the materials and equipment around the concept of an assembly line. The children will all take turns working at each job in the peanut butter factory. The peanut butter will be used for snack with crackers, celery, carrots, or bread.

- Modifications:

Physical impairments: assist child in working with the shelling of the peanuts. A child with physical impairments that interferes with standing should be given a "job" that allows for sitting down. Adult facilitation will allow the child to be part of the socialization within the assembly line, language, and flow of activity.

Visual impairments: assist child in locating and identifying each of the items designated to be in the factory. Adult facilitation will allow the child to work with these items and in the dramatic play situation.

Social and emotional impairments: assist child in getting into the role of playing factory worker. Adult facilitation will help the child be part of a functioning group and cope with any frustration the child encounters within the activity. The adult may also rearrange responsibilities of the children if the child needs a different job.

Language impairments: assist child with vocabulary and facilitate communication between children in the activity. In addition to helping a child to learn labels of items, the adult can help the child learn verbs (i.e., crush, shell, separate, process).

Learning impairments: assist child to learn the processes involved in preparing peanut butter. Adult facilitation will help the child to be integrated into the activity and to be knowledgeable about what happens in a factory.

Title of Activity: Dramatic Play and Large Blocks—House Building

- Content Objectives:

The children will label items associated with building a house

The children will discuss what happens in the process of building a house

The children will role-play being a construction worker building a house (how things change)

- Developmental Objectives:

language

cognitive

Dramatic Play and Large Blocks—House Building **continued**

social
fine motor
gross motor
creative

- Materials:

large blocks
construction "plans"
plastic tools
hard hats
tool belts
wheelbarrow
magazine pictures of different kinds of houses

- Procedure:

The children will discuss the process of building a house. The children will work together using the materials available to build a house. They may prefer to build their own houses if the number of blocks available allows. While this possibility affords each child the opportunity to plan and execute a building, it eliminates the possibility of the social interaction that comes from working on one common structure.

- Modifications:

Physical impairments: assist child with developing a role to play in the area. A child with physical impairments that interferes with standing or carrying should be given a "job" that allows the child to pass out the tools, belts, and hats, consult on the plans, or be the building inspector. If the child is in a power wheelchair with a carrier on the back, the child may be able to transport the building materials or be the inspector making a site visit. Adult facilitation will allow the child to be part of the socialization and language of the play even if the child is not able do the same thing the other children are doing.

Visual impairments: assist child in locating and identifying each of the items designated to be used in the process of building the house. Adult facilitation will also help the child look critically at the house models placed in the area.

Social and emotional impairments: assist child in getting into the role of playing in a situation where there is one common purpose. Adult facilitation will help the child be part of a functioning group and cope with any frustration the child encounters within the activity. The adult may need to mediate for the child or help the child to observe the situation for some time before entering into the play.

Language impairments: assist child with vocabulary and facilitate communication between children in the activity. In addition to helping a child to learn labels of

Dramatic Play and Large Blocks—House Building **continued**

items, the adult can help the child learn verbs (i.e., plan, construct, inspect, cooperate).

Learning impairments: assist child to learn the processes involved in building a house. Adult facilitation will help the child to be integrated into the activity and to be knowledgeable about different types of houses.

Title of Activity: Dramatic Play and Large Blocks—Highway Construction Worker

- Content Objectives:

  The children will label items associated with road construction and maintenance

  The children will discuss what happens and what equipment is used in the process of fixing a road (how things work)

  The children will discuss safety issues involved in doing this type of job

  The children will role-play being a construction worker doing road maintenance

- Developmental Objectives:

  language
  cognitive
  social
  fine motor
  gross motor
  creative

- Materials:

  large blocks
  construction "plans"
  plastic tools
  hard hats
  tool belts
  vehicles
  magazine pictures of different roads
  highway signs
  traffic signs
  lunch boxes and thermoses for break time

- Procedure:

  The children will discuss the process of fixing a road. The children will work together using the materials available to fix the road. They will first build the road

Dramatic Play and Large Blocks—Highway Construction Worker **continued**

according to the "plan" they have. Once the road is completed, they will make necessary repairs on the road.

- Modifications:

  Physical impairments: assist child with developing a role to play in the area. A child whose physical impairments interfere with standing or carrying should be given a "job" that allows the child to pass out the tools, belts, and hats, consult on the plans, or be the road inspector or crew supervisor. If the child is in a power wheelchair with a carrier on the back, the child may be able to transport the "construction" materials, be the inspector making a site visit, or the supervisor of the job. The child may also be able to hold up the traffic signs and signal to the cars when it is safe to pass. Adult facilitation based on observation of the play will allow the child to be part of the socialization and language of the play even if the child is not able do the same thing the other children are doing.

  Visual impairments: assist child in locating and identifying each of the items designated to be used in the process of building and reconstructing the road. Adult facilitation will help the child look at the signs used in the area as well as the pattern of the road as it is built.

  Social and emotional impairments: assist child in functioning as part of working group. There may be a need for any rules of the area to be reinforced while the child is engaged in the play. The adult may need to mediate for the child or help the child to observe the situation for some time before entering into the play.

  Language impairments: assist child with vocabulary and facilitate communication between children in the activity. Adult facilitation will allow the child to be included in the play regardless of the language level. In addition to helping a child to learn labels of items, the adult can help the child learn verbs (i.e., plan, construct, inspect, cooperate, direct, supervise).

  Learning impairments: assist child to learn the processes involved in building a house. Adult facilitation will help the child to be integrated into the activity and to be knowledgeable about different types of houses.

Title of Activity: Dramatic Play and Large Blocks—Carpentry Workshop

- Content Objectives:

  The children will label items associated with a workshop

  The children will discuss what happens in the process of making something in a workshop

  The children will discuss safety issues involved in doing carpentry

  The children will use the materials and equipment associated with carpentry (how things work)

Dramatic Play and Large Blocks—Carpentry Workshop **continued**

- Developmental Objectives:

  language

  cognitive

  social

  fine motor

  gross motor

  creative

- Materials:

  woodworking table

  wood

  nails and screws

  ruler

  pencils

  tape measure

  sand paper

  furniture "plans"

  tools

  tool belts

  goggles

  shop apron

  magazine pictures of different workshops and furniture pieces

  safety posters

  broom

  dustpan

- Procedure:

  The children will discuss the rules of working with the woodworking materials and equipment. The children will work individually using the materials available to construct something out of wood. The purpose of each tool will be explained. The process of following a plan will be emphasized.

- Modifications:

  Physical impairments: assist child with the use of the tools if possible. If it is not safe for the child to attempt to use the tools, the child may still remain in the area offering advice as a "consultant" to the furniture builder. If the child is in a wheelchair or a power wheelchair with a carrier on the back, the child may be given a "job" that allows for the delivery of materials from the "lumberyard."

Dramatic Play and Large Blocks—Carpentry Workshop **continued**

Visual impairments: assist child in locating and identifying each of the items designated to be used in the carpentry shop. Adult facilitation will help the child look at the tools and recognize which parts of the tools are not as safe as others.

Social and emotional impairments: assist child in the use of the tools to avoid frustration building something. There may be a need for any rules of the area to be reinforced prior to and while the child is engaged in the woodworking. The adult may need to make sure that the wood is soft enough to ensure success for the child.

Language impairments: assist child with vocabulary particular to the woodworking activity. In addition to helping a child to learn the labels of items, the adult can help the child learn verbs (i.e., saw, hammer, measure, sand).

Learning impairments: assist child to learn the processes involved in using tools. The child might need to have only one tool available at a time.

Title of Activity: Dramatic Play and Cooking—Sandwich Shop

- Content Objectives:

  The children will label items associated with making sandwiches

  The children will discuss what happens in the process of making a sandwich

  The children will discuss safety issues involved in using knives

  The children will discuss who makes sandwiches in their homes

  The children will make sandwiches (how things change)

- Developmental Objectives:

  language

  cognitive

  social

  fine motor

- Materials:

  table and chairs

  trays

  bread

  peanut butter

  jelly

  tuna fish

  mayonnaise

Dramatic Play and Cooking—Sandwich Shop **continued**

bowl
can opener
fork
spatula
large spoon
wax paper
small plates
plastic knives
aprons
magazine pictures of different sandwiches
sponge
broom
dustpan

- Procedure:

The children will discuss health and safety as it relates to food preparation. They will work individually and cooperatively using the food available to make sandwiches to eat at snack. The original source of each food item will be explained. The process of following an appropriate sequence when preparing food will be emphasized. Once all the sandwiches are made, the children will participate in clean-up of the area.

- Modifications:

Physical impairments: assist child with the use of the kitchen utensils if possible. If it is not safe for the child to attempt to use these items, the child may still remain in the area offering advice as a "consultant" to those doing the food preparation. If the child is in a wheelchair or a power wheelchair with a carrier on the back, the child may be given the "job" of bringing things to and from the kitchen on the wheelchair tray or on the rear carrier.

Visual impairments: assist child in locating and identifying each of the items designated to be used in the process of making sandwiches. Adult facilitation will help the child look at the utensils and recognize which part of the utensils are not safe to touch with his or her fingers.

Social and emotional impairments: assist child in the use of the utensils to avoid frustration while making sandwiches. There may be a need for any rules of the area to be reinforced prior to and while the child is engaged in the food preparation process. If restraint around food is an issue, the child should be invited to this activity towards the end of the activity period.

Dramatic Play and Cooking—Sandwich Shop **continued**

Language impairments: assist child with vocabulary particular to preparation of food. In addition to helping a child to learn labels of items, the adult can help the child learn verbs (i.e., open, mix, flake, stir, spoon, spread, cover, slice, cut).

Learning impairments: assist child to learn the processes involved in preparing sandwiches. The child might need to have only one part of a task presented at a time (task analysis).

Title of Activity: Dramatic Play and Cooking—Shake Shoppe

- Content Objectives:

The children will label items associated with making healthy shakes

The children will discuss what happens in the process of making a shake using a blender

The children will discuss safety issues involved in using a blender

The children will discuss who uses a blender in their homes and what is made in the blender (recipes may be dictated by the children to be shared with the family)

The children will make healthy shakes (how things change)

- Developmental Objectives:

language

cognitive

social

fine motor

- Materials:

table and chairs

trays

ingredients for Blender Orange Cooler

(Note: Check with parents to determine if children have dairy allergies. Alternate recipes provided.)

—frozen orange juice

—milk

—plain yogurt

—ice cubes

ingredients for Strawberry-Orange Drink

—orange juice

Dramatic Play and Cooking—Shake Shoppe **continued**

—ice cubes

—strawberries

blender

cups

measuring cup

measuring spoons

aprons

magazine pictures of different shakes

sponge

- Procedure:

The children will discuss the safety issues involved in using a blender (cover on, no fingers inside the blender, remove blender jar and cover only after turning blender off). They will work cooperatively mixing the ingredients and some ice cubes. A shake should be made with each group of about four to six children so that each group is able to see the process of the frozen juice turning to liquid, the change in colors when all liquids are combined and how the ice cubes change as they are blended. The original source of each food item will be explained. The process of following the appropriate sequence when preparing this shake will be emphasized. Once all the ingredients are used up and all the children have had a serving of the shake, the children will participate in clean-up of the area.

- Modifications:

Physical impairments: assist child with correct positioning so that the child can see what is going on. If the child is in a wheelchair or a power wheelchair with a carrier on the back, the child may be given the "job" of bringing things to and from the kitchen on the wheelchair tray or on the rear carrier.

Visual impairments: assist child in locating and identifying each of the items designated to be used in the process of making a shake. Adult facilitation will help the child look at the ingredients and recognize which part of the blender is not safe to touch.

Social and emotional impairments: assist child in taking turns. There may be a need for any rules of the area to be reinforced prior to and while the child is engaged in the process of making the shake. If restraint around food is an issue, the child should be invited to this activity towards the end of the activity period.

Language impairments: assist child with vocabulary particular to preparation of a shake. In addition to helping a child to learn labels of items, the adult can help the child learn verbs (i.e., cover, mix, blend, measure, pour).

Dramatic Play and Cooking—Shake Shoppe **continued**

Learning impairments: assist child to learn the processes involved in preparing shakes. The child might need to have only one part of a task presented at a time (task analysis).

- Recipe: *Orange Cooler*

  ½ cup orange juice concentrate

  1 cup plain yogurt

  1 cup milk

  Directions:

  1. Put all ingredients in blender.
  2. Blend well.

- Recipe: *Strawberry-Orange Drink*

  1 cup orange juice

  2 crushed ice cubes

  2 strawberries

  Directions:

  1. Wash and hull strawberries.
  2. Put all ingredients in blender.
  3. Blend well.

Title of Activity: Dramatic Play and Cooking—Biscuit Bakery

- Content Objectives:

  The children will label items associated with making biscuits

  The children will discuss what happens in the process of making biscuits

  The children will discuss safety issues involved in baking activities

  The children will role-play being bakers as they prepare biscuits for snack time (how things change)

- Developmental Objectives:

  language

  cognitive

  social

  fine motor

Dramatic Play and Cooking—Biscuit Bakery **continued**

- Materials:

  table and chairs

  trays

  biscuit ingredients for Mayonnaise Biscuits

    flour

    mayonnaise

    milk

  biscuit ingredients for Pumpkin Biscuits

    canned pumpkin

    Bisquick baking mix

  muffin tins

  cookie sheet

  rolling pin

  cookie cutters

  measuring cup

  measuring spoons

  aprons

  bakers hats

  magazine pictures of biscuits

  large copy of recipe on wall or easel

  sponge

  broom

  dustpan

- Procedure:

  The children will discuss the safety issues involved in baking. They will work co-operatively following the recipe. A batch of biscuits should be made with each group of about four to six children so that each group is able to see the process of the ingredients being combined to make a batter. The original source of each food item will be emphasized. Once all the ingredients are used up and there are enough biscuits made for all the children to have two for snack, the children will participate in clean-up of the area.

- Modifications:

  Physical impairments: assist child with participating in measuring and mixing ingredients. Child can keep count of the number of biscuits prepared.

Dramatic Play and Cooking—Biscuit Bakery **continued**

Visual impairments: assist child in locating and identifying each of the items designated to be used in the process of making biscuits.

Social and emotional impairments: assist child in taking turns and sharing in the discussion. There may be a need for any rules of the area to be reinforced prior to and while the child is engaged in the baking process. If restraint around food is an issue, the child should be invited to this activity towards the end of the activity period.

Language impairments: assist child with vocabulary particular to baking biscuits. In addition to helping a child to learn labels of items, the adult can help the child learn verbs (i.e., mix, blend, measure, pour, grease, bake).

Learning impairments: assist child to learn the processes involved in preparing biscuits. The child might need to have only one part of a task presented at a time (task analysis).

- Recipe: *Mayonnaise Biscuits*

  2 cups self-rising flour

  4 rounded teaspoons mayonnaise

  1 cup milk

  Directions:

  1. Preheat oven to 425°.
  2. Mix ingredients together with a spoon or fork.

  Drop by tablespoon into 8 greased muffin tins.

  Bake for 12 to 14 minutes.

- Recipe: *Pumpkin Biscuits*

  1 cup canned pumpkin

  2 1/2 cups Bisquick baking mix

  Directions:

  1. Mix pumpkin and Bisquick together.
  2. Knead and roll out.
  3. Cut with cookie cutters and bake at 400° for 15 minutes.
  4. Serve with honey and butter if desired.

Title of Activity: Dramatic Play and Cooking—Making Pudding

- Content Objectives:

The children will label items associated with making instant pudding

Dramatic Play and Cooking—Making Pudding **continued**

The children will discuss what happens in the process of making the pudding (how things change)

The children will explore the movements of specific body parts as they prepare the pudding

- Developmental Objectives:

language

cognitive

social

fine motor

Materials:

table and chairs

trays

containers with tight lids for shaking pudding in

bowls or cups

spoons

spatula

instant pudding mixes

milk

measuring cup

aprons

magazine pictures of pudding ads

large copy of recipe on wall or easel

sponge

broom

dustpan

- Procedure:

The children will discuss the process involved in making the pudding. They will work cooperatively following the recipe. A package of pudding should be made with each group of about four to six children so that each group is able to see the process of the ingredients being combined. The original source of each food item will be emphasized. Once all the ingredients are used up and there is enough pudding made for all the children to have for snack, the children will participate in clean-up of the area.

- Modifications:

Physical impairments: assist child with participating in measuring and shaking ingredients. Child can keep count of the number of cups of pudding prepared.

Dramatic Play and Large Motor—Making Pudding **continued**

Visual impairments: assist child in locating and identifying each of the items designated to be used in the process of making pudding.

Social and emotional impairments: assist child in taking turns and sharing in the discussion. There may be a need for any rules of the area to be reinforced prior to and while the child is engaged in the process. If restraint around food is an issue, the child should be invited to this activity towards the end of the activity period.

Language impairments: assist child with vocabulary particular to making pudding. In addition to helping a child to learn labels of items, the adult can help the child learn verbs (i.e., mix, blend, measure, pour, shake, chill).

Learning impairments: assist child to learn the processes involved in preparing pudding. The child might need to have only one part of a task presented at a time (task analysis).

Title of Activity: Dramatic Play and Large Motor—Aerobic Exercise Center

- Content Objectives:

The children will label items of clothing used in exercise

The children will discuss what happens in an exercise center

The children will exercise as leaders and followers as they participate in an aerobics session (how things move)

- Developmental Objectives:

language
cognitive
social
fine motor
gross motor
creative

- Materials:

exercise clothes
towels
tape player
exercise music tapes
action photographs of exercise environments
paper and markers to make posters of body movements

Dramatic Play and Large Motor—Aerobic Exercise Center **continued**

- Procedure:

  The children will take on the roles of exercise leader and customer (follower) in an exercise center. They will see how body parts move. They will make posters of bodies in exercise positions.

- Modifications:

  Physical impairments: assist child in moving whatever part of the body the child is able to move. Adult facilitation will allow the child to be part of the socialization and language of the activity even if the child cannot do the actual exercises. The child may be able to clap the rhythm for the other children to follow. The child may be able to hand out the towels after the children finish exercising.

  Visual impairments: assist child in becoming oriented to the visual point of reference for following the exercises. Adult facilitation will allow the child to identify movements and body parts.

  Social and emotional impairments: assist child in getting into the role play in the area. Adult facilitation will help the child with learning what behaviors are appropriate for the role of leader as well as for the role of follower.

  Language impairments: assist child with vocabulary and facilitate communication between children in the activity. Adult facilitation will allow the child to be included in the play regardless of the language level. Since this activity involves considerable imitation of movement, a child without productive language should have no trouble participating. If a child has little receptive language, the instructions for movement should always be modeled.

  Learning impairments: assist child to learn the function of body parts and the purpose of doing exercises. Adult facilitation will help the child to be integrated into the activity.

Title of Activity: Dramatic Play and Large Blocks—"Mary, Mary Quite Contrary How Does Your Garden Grow?"

- Content Objectives:

  The children will learn the nursery rhyme

  The children will create their own "garden" (how things change)

  The children will role-play as gardeners

- Developmental Objectives:

  language

  cognitive

  social

Dramatic Play and Large Blocks—"Mary, Mary Quite Contrary How Does Your Garden Grow?" **continued**

fine motor
creative

- Materials:

large blocks
silk or plastic flowers
rulers and yardsticks
trowels
hand shovels
watering cans
gardening gloves
apron
gardening basket
containers for floral arrangements
florist foam to make arrangements
photographs of gardens
paper and markers to make signs indicating plantings

- Procedure:

The children will take on the role of gardener. They will plan out the garden learning about different flowers, and the requirements of each type of flower. They will pretend to water, weed, and cut the flowers to arrange in floral arrangements that can be used in the housekeeping area.

- Modifications:

Physical impairments: assist child in moving through the activity. Adult facilitation will allow the child to be part of the socialization and language of the activity. The child may be able to hand out the flowers or the gardening tools. The child may be able to help decide where certain flowers should be placed.

Visual impairments: assist child in discriminating between different tools and flowers. Show the child where the flowers are to be "planted."

Social and emotional impairments: assist child in getting into the role play in the area. Facilitation will help the child to learn how to plan cooperatively as the children plan their garden.

Language impairments: assist child with vocabulary such as flower, plant, soil, sun, water, etc. A child without productive language should be able to "plant" and engage in the other role-play behaviors. Peers will serve as role models for the child.

Dramatic Play and Large Blocks—"Mary, Mary Quite Contrary How Does Your Garden Grow?" **continued**

Learning impairments: assist child to learn the items being used in the area and the role of the gardener.

Title of Activity: Sensory—Moving Water

- Content Objectives:

  The children will move water by blowing air into it

  The children will discuss what happens when they blow through a straw (how things move)

- Developmental Objectives:

  language

  cognitive

  social

  fine motor

- Materials:

  water table or dish pan

  water

  shampoo or dish detergent

  straws

- Procedure:

  The children will each take a straw and place the end of the straw in the soapy water. They will discuss their observations of the process of moving water with straws.

- Modifications:

  Physical impairments: assist child in blowing through a straw. If the child is not able to blow through the straw, the teacher should demonstrate the process for the child so the child is able to observe and then comment on the process.

  Visual impairments: assist child in seeing where the straw should be placed and where the opening is in the straw.

  Social and emotional impairments: assist child in accepting other children in the same smaller area. Adult facilitation will help the child to interact appropriately with peers both on a verbal and nonverbal level.

  Language impairments: assist child with vocabulary such as straw, blow, move, current, force, etc. appropriate to the activity. The adult in the situation can model language based on observations made during the activity.

  Learning impairments: assist child to make observations during the activity using prompts and open-ended questions.

Title of Activity: Sensory—Moving Marbles

- Content Objectives:

  The children will observe marbles moving down a path

  The children will discuss what happens in the process of the marble moving from one place to another (how things move)

- Developmental Objectives:

  language

  cognitive

  social

  fine motor

- Materials:

  marbles

  marble rollway

  surface to work on (preferably one that can contain marbles as they move off the path)

- Procedure:

  The children will cooperatively put together a marble path. This may be done with a commercial material designed for this purpose or with small blocks. The children will place marbles, one at a time, at the start of the marble path. The children will take turns making observations and placing the marbles. The children will discuss their observations.

- Modifications:

  Physical impairments: assist child in building the marble path or placing the marbles on the path. Adult facilitation will allow the child to be part of the socialization and language of the activity even if the child cannot assist with the building of the path or the placing of the marbles. This will allow the child to make the observations of the activity so the child may be join the discussion.

  Visual impairments: assist child in seeing where the marble goes in and where it comes out. Adult facilitation will allow the child to see the direction of the marble as it moves through the path.

  Social and emotional impairments: assist child in taking turns in the process of rolling the marble through the path. Adult facilitation will help the child work with the small group of children taking turns building the path and rolling the marbles.

  Language impairments: assist child with learning the vocabulary (i.e., marble, path, slant, angle) appropriate to this activity. Present appropriate language models to facilitate language interaction between the child and the peer group.

Sensory—Moving Marbles **continued**

Learning impairments: assist child to learn how the marble rollway works. Adult facilitation will help the child learn about direction, force, and movement of sphere shaped objects.

Title of Activity: Sensory—Making Popcorn

- Content Objectives:

  The children will observe popcorn in the process of popping in a see-through popcorn popper

  The children will discuss what happens in the process of popping the corn (how things change)

- Developmental Objectives:

  language

  cognitive

  social

  fine motor

- Materials:

  popcorn

  popcorn popper

  scoops

  cups to put popcorn in

  butter and salt, if desired

- Procedure:

  The children will help pop the corn and put it into cups to be served at snack time. The children will observe the process of the corn popping and discuss their observations.

- Modifications:

  Physical impairments: assist child in participating in popping the popcorn. Adult facilitation will allow the child to help scoop the popped corn into cups for all the children. This will then allow the child to make the observations of the process so the child may be part of the discussion that follows popping the corn.

  Visual impairments: assist child in seeing where in the popcorn popper the popcorn goes and where it comes out. Adult facilitation will allow the child to see the direction of the popcorn as it moves around the popper before being completely cooked.

Sensory—Making Popcorn **continued**

Social and emotional impairments: assist child in taking turns in the process of popping the corn. Adult facilitation will help the child work within the peer group functioning together to complete a process.

Language impairments: assist child with learning the vocabulary appropriate to this activity. The adult in the area will model appropriate sentence structure for the child. Whether the child imitates immediately or not, the model will enrich the language environment for this child and all the other children.

Learning impairments: assist child to learn the function of the popcorn popper and how it works. Adult facilitation will help the child to be integrated into the activity and into the discussion that follows the observations made by all the children.

Title of Activity: Sensory—Wheels Make Tracks

- Content Objectives:

  The children will observe the movement of wheels and the tracks they make

  The children will discuss what happens in the process of a wheel rotating (how things move)

- Developmental Objectives:

  language

  cognitive

  social

  fine motor

- Materials:

  small cars with wheels with tracks

  water table or trays

  goop made from cornstarch and water

- Procedure:

  The children will help mix the goop. The children will move the cars through the goop leaving tracks. They will observe the process of the wheels leaving tracks in the goop. They will discuss their observations.

- Modifications:

  Physical impairments: assist child in participating in moving the cars through the goop. Adult facilitation will allow the child to see the process of moving wheels. This will then allow the child to be part of the discussion that follows after all the children have had a chance to move a car through the goop.

Sensory—Wheels Make Tracks **continued**

Visual impairments: assist child in seeing how wheels move. Adult facilitation will allow the child to see the direction of the wheel as it moves through the goop and how it leaves a track.

Social and emotional impairments: assist child in taking turns in the process of using the cars. Adult facilitation will help the child work within the peer group, taking turns with the different cars.

Language impairments: assist child with learning the vocabulary appropriate to this activity (i.e., wheel, track, impression). The adult in the area will model appropriate sentence structure for the child. The teacher will facilitate discussion among the children involved in the area.

Learning impairments: assist child to learn the function of wheel and the ways in which wheels rotate. Adult facilitation will help the child to be integrated into the activity and into the discussion that follows the observations of the tracks made by all the different cars the children used during the activity.

Title of Activity: Sensory—How Sound Is Made

- Content Objectives:

  The children will listen to the sounds different objects make (how things work)

  The children will guess at what makes the sound when the objects are hidden from view (in closed containers)

- Developmental Objectives:

  language

  cognitive

  social

  fine motor

- Materials:

  small objects capable of making different sounds (bells, coins, paper clips, cotton balls, popping corn, rice, rocks, buttons, etc.)

  small translucent containers with lids

- Procedure:

  The children will explore the items, label them, and discuss their use. The children will experiment with the sounds these items make. They will cover their eyes and then listen to the sounds produced by each of these items as they are shaken up in a closed container. They will discuss the results of their listening.

Sensory—How Sound is Made **continued**

- Modifications:

  Physical impairments: assist child in getting into the right position for listening. Adult facilitation will allow the child to be part of the activity.

  Visual impairments: assist child in seeing and labeling each of the items.

  Social and emotional impairments: assist child in taking turns and sitting patiently to listen to the sounds. Adult facilitation will help the child work within the peer group.

  Language impairments: assist child with learning the vocabulary appropriate to this activity. Words such as loud, soft, jingle, etc. will be emphasized. The adult in the area will model appropriate sentence structure for the child. The teacher will facilitate discussion between the children involved in the area.

  Learning impairments: assist child to learn the label and use of each of the objects. Adult facilitation will allow the child to learn how it is that these objects make the sounds they do.

Title of Activity: Sensory—Things that Make a House

- Content Objectives:

  The children will explore items that are used to make houses (i.e., bricks, wood, roofing material, insulation, metal, covered wire, piping)

  The children will discuss where these items are found in houses and where the items come from (how things change)

- Developmental Objectives:

  language

  cognitive

  social

  fine motor

- Materials:

  brick, roofing shingle, roofing paper, metal, pipe, wood, etc. without rough edges on any of the materials

  pictures of different types of houses built from different materials

- Procedure:

  The children will explore these items. The children will discuss their observations and determine which of these items are in their houses. A chart or graph can be made of the results of the discussion. The children will learn about how trees and other natural materials are changed into building materials.

Sensory—Things that Make a House **continued**

- Modifications:

  Physical impairments: assist child in exploring the items. This will then allow the child to be part of the discussion that follows after all the children have had a chance to explore the materials.

  Visual impairments: assist child in exploring the items, noting and labeling the different textures. Adult facilitation will allow the child to participate in the discussion about items found in the home.

  Social and emotional impairments: assist child in exploring the items in a safe manner.

  Language impairments: assist child with learning the vocabulary appropriate to this activity. The vocabulary to be emphasized includes the labels of each of the items and the functions of these items.

  Learning impairments: assist child with learning the function of each of the items used in building houses.

Title of Activity: Art—Marble Painting

- Content Objectives:

  The children will place marbles in cups of different colored paint, and then place the marbles one at a time on a piece of paper placed in a cardboard box

  The children will observe the movement of the marble on the paper as the box is rotated from side to side

  The children will discuss what happens in the process of rotating the marbles on the paper in the box (how things move)

- Developmental Objectives:

  language

  cognitive

  social

  fine motor

  creative

- Materials:

  several cups with different colored tempera paint

  several marbles

  plastic spoons

  paper

Art—Marble Painting **continued**

a few shallow cardboard boxes or box tops

smocks

- Procedure:

The children will place one marble in each of several cups of different color paints. The children will remove the marbles with a spoon and place the marbles one at a time onto the paper in a cardboard box. They will rotate the box to make designs. The children will observe the process of the marbles making lines on the paper. They will discuss their observations.

- Modifications:

Physical impairments: assist child in participating in preparing the marbles for painting and moving the marbles in the box. Adult facilitation will allow the child to see the process of the marbles creating designs. After participating in the process either directly or indirectly, the child will be able to participate in the discussion of observations and the finished products produced by all the children.

Visual impairments: assist child in seeing how the process of rolling the marbles around creates a design. Adult facilitation will allow the child to see that the marble moving in different directions leaves a line.

Social and emotional impairments: assist child with the process of marble painting. Adult facilitation will minimize the possibility of frustration carrying out the process. It will also encourage the child who appears to be hesitant to try the activity.

Language impairments: assist child with learning the vocabulary appropriate to this activity. The adult facilitating the activity can reinforce colors, words, and prepositions.

Learning impairments: assist child to learn the process involved in marble painting. Adult facilitation will help the child to be integrated into the activity and into any discussion about the paintings that follows.

Title of Activity: Art—Building a House of Sticks

- Content Objectives:

The children will use craft sticks to build a house (how things change)

The children will discuss the process of building

The children will discuss the differences between their houses and pictures of houses displayed in the area

- Developmental Objectives:

language

Art—Building a House of Sticks **continued**

cognitive
social
fine motor
creative

- Materials:
  craft sticks
  glue
  trays or brown paper to set houses on
  pictures of different kinds of houses
- Procedure:
  The children will use craft sticks and glue to build houses. The houses will be of their own designs. There will be pictures of houses around the area for inspiration.
- Modifications:
  Physical impairments: assist child in participating in house building. Adult facilitation will allow the child to see the process of building. After participating in the process either directly or indirectly, the child will be able to participate in the discussion of observations and the finished products produced by all the children.
  Visual impairments: assist child in seeing how houses are built.
  Social and emotional impairments: assist child with the process of building a house. Adult facilitation will encourage the child who appears to be hesitant to try the activity.
  Language impairments: assist child with learning the vocabulary associated with this activity. The adult facilitating the activity can reinforce house related words such as base, foundation, corner, wall, roof, window, door.
  Learning impairments: assist child with the process involved in building a house. Adult facilitation will help the child to be integrated into the activity and into any discussion about the houses that follows.

Title of Activity: Art—Moving Bodies

- Content Objectives:
  The children will use brads to put together parts of the body at joint points
  The children will observe the movement of the parts of the body at the various connection points (how things move)
  The children will label the joints (knee, ankle, elbow, etc.)

Art—Moving Bodies **continued**

- Developmental Objectives:
  language
  cognitive
  social
  fine motor
  creative
- Materials:
  cut-outs of body parts
  templates (for those children who can trace and cut out their own pieces)
  pencils
  scissors
  brads
  markers
  crayons
- Procedure:
  The children will trace and cut out or simply place body parts together with brads. The teacher will provide assistance where needed. The children will discuss the body parts and learn labels for the joint points as they put their bodies together. The children will observe the movement of the body parts when their bodies are completed. They will discuss their observations.
- Modifications:
  Physical impairments: assist child in participating in putting bodies together. Adult facilitation will allow the child to see how the parts go together at the joints. After the body is put together, the child can manipulate the body parts seeing how the joints work.

  Visual impairments: assist child in seeing how the body parts fit together. Adult facilitation will allow the child to complete the body and then spend time observing the way body parts move at the joints.

  Social and emotional impairments: assist child with the process of creating the completed body. Adult facilitation will minimize the possibility of frustration carrying out the process. It will also encourage the child who appears to be hesitant to try the activity.

  Language impairments: assist child with learning the vocabulary appropriate to this activity. The adult facilitating the activity can reinforce body part labels, labels for the joints (knee, elbow, ankle, etc).

  Learning impairments: assist child to learn the parts of the body as depicted by the paper body parts. Adult facilitation will help the child to have the information

Art—Moving Bodies **continued**

needed to participate in discussion that takes place as the children are working to put together their paper bodies.

Title of Activity: Art—Moving Dancers

- Content Objectives:

The children will paint pictures of people dancing

The children will observe the movement of their peers as they engage in movement activities (how things move)

The children will also observe the movement of professional dancers as depicted in action photographs decorating the easel painting area

The children will discuss the movement in their paintings when they are exhibited around the classroom

- Developmental Objectives:

language

cognitive

social

fine motor

creative

- Materials:

easel

easel paper

paints

containers

brushes

smocks

dance photographs

dance music as background

- Procedure:

The children will be encouraged to paint movement-oriented paintings. The children will be invited to observe their peers engaged in movement activity. They will also be encouraged to look at the action photographs provided for them. The children will exhibit their work around the classroom when all children have had the chance to paint. They will be invited to discuss the movement in their paintings.

Art—Moving Dancers **continued**

- Modifications:

  Physical impairments: assist child in painting by providing different brushes if necessary or modifying the easel to accommodate the child. The child may need to have the paper placed on an inclined surface at the table rather than at the easel. After participating in the process either independently or with assistance, the child will be able to participate in the exhibit. If the child does not have productive language, the other children will be able to describe what they see in this child's completed work.

  Visual impairments: assist child in seeing the movements made by the peers engaging in movement activities. The adult can point out the movement aspects of the photographs displayed around the area. The adult can also help the child to observe details in the paintings when they are exhibited.

  Social and emotional impairments: assist child with any aspect of the activity as needed. Adult facilitation will encourage the child to participate and stay with the activity until the child feels the painting is completed.

  Language impairments: assist child with learning the vocabulary appropriate to this activity. The adult facilitating the activity can reinforce movement oriented vocabulary (i.e., stretching, leaping, jumping, balancing, etc.). The adult can also facilitate the child's presentation about his or her own painting during the exhibit.

  Learning impairments: assist child in focusing on the movements of the other children engaged in movement activity. Adult facilitation can also help the child focus in on the movement depicted in the photographs displayed in the area.

Title of Activity: Art—Weaving

- Content Objectives:

  The children will see that sometimes exploring a process produces a product

  The children will learn the repetitive motion of weaving a paper mat

  The children will discuss what happens in the process of creating the mat (how things change)

- Developmental Objectives:

  language

  cognitive

  social

  fine motor

  creative

Art—Weaving **continued**

- Materials:

  mat frame with horizontal cuts made in the large paper

  strips of paper longer than the width of the mat frame

  finished mat for children to see what they will be making

  tape for finishing of edges

- Procedure:

  The children will learn the motion of over, under, over, under to complete the weaving. The children will choose the mat frame and paper strips they want to use to complete the mat. They will verbally state the pattern of over and under as they work through the process.

- Modifications:

  Physical impairments: assist child in participating in making a mat. Adult facilitation will allow the child to see the process of weaving. If the child is unable to engage in the motion necessary to complete the weaving, the child may be able to state the pattern while the adult or another child engages in the weaving process. In this way, the child will see the work required to complete a mat.

  Visual impairments: assist child in seeing the process of weaving. This might necessitate having the child work with the adult to complete a mat using the hand over hand method. It might mean that one over-sized mat may need to be made so that the child may see the process through exaggerated movements.

  Social and emotional impairments: assist child with the process of weaving. Adult facilitation will encourage the child to stay with the activity to completion.

  Language impairments: assist child with learning the vocabulary appropriate to this activity. The adult facilitating the activity can reinforce the process words of over and under as well as the vocabulary concerning the materials and the completed product.

  Learning impairments: assist child with learning about mats, what they are used for and how they are made. Adult facilitation will help the child complete the process and proudly display the finished product.

Title of Activity: Small Blocks—Transportation Vehicles

- Content Objectives:

  Over several days the children will use freight trains, passenger trains, planes, cars, and trucks to see how they move and what they move (i.e., people, cargo)

  The children will observe the movement of the vehicles and explore how each of the vehicles is fueled and loaded (how things move)

Small Blocks—Transportation Vehicles **continued**

The children will discuss what happens to make these vehicles move (i.e., engines, fuel) and the person who directs the movement (i.e., engineer, pilot, driver)

- Developmental Objectives:

  language

  cognitive

  social

  fine motor

  gross motor

  creative

- Materials:

  transportation vehicles: trains, planes, cars, trucks

  appropriate roadways to support this play

  tracks

  maps

  people

  cargo materials

  transportation pictures

  paper and markers to make signs

- Procedure:

  The children will use one type of transportation vehicle a day. They will explore each type of vehicle using appropriate accessories. They will learn about how the vehicle is loaded with cargo and how people enter the vehicle. The children will make signs as needed. They will discuss the observations they make about how things work and move.

- Modifications:

  Physical impairments: assist child in participating in the play in the small blocks area. Adult facilitation will allow the child to see how the vehicles move and how they are loaded. This will allow the child to participate in discussion. If the child is nonverbal, the adult can facilitate participation through the use of a communication board which asks the child to make choices about what to play with and who or what to put on the vehicle.

  Visual impairments: assist child in exploring the different vehicles, their parts and how they move.

  Social and emotional impairments: assist child with integrating into the play in the area. Adult facilitation will enable the child to take turns, share materials and join in the conversation and role play.

Small Blocks—Transportation Vehicles **continued**

Language impairments: assist child with learning the vocabulary appropriate to this activity. The adult facilitating the activity can reinforce names of vehicles, action words and labels for vehicle parts.

Learning impairments: point out the vehicles, their names and their purposes. Role play for the child and have the child imitate actions and words where appropriate.

Title of Activity: Music and Movement—Exploring the Way the Body Moves

- Content Objectives:

  Over several days the children will use their bodies to explore different movements (how things move)

  The children will suggest movements as well as observe the movement of the teacher and other children and imitate those movements

  The children will learn the vocabulary for the different movements they do (i.e., jump, tip-toe, walk, hop, slide, turn, twist, roll, clap, tap, tumble, forward roll, balance).

- Developmental Objectives:

  language

  cognitive

  social

  gross motor

  creative

- Materials:

  a variety of music so that children hear music that reflects the type of movement being emphasized that day

  action pictures

- Procedure:

  The children will use their bodies to explore different types of movements each day. They will discuss the ways they observe their bodies moving.

- Modifications:

  Physical impairments: assist child in participating in the movement. Adult facilitation will allow the child to participate even if only the arms or fingers can move.

Music and Movement—Exploring the Way the Body Moves **continued**

Visual impairments: assist child in exploring the pictures of people moving. Assist child with determining the physical parameters for the movement activities so the child will be safe.

Social and emotional impairments: assist child with integrating into the activity. Adult facilitation will enable the child to take turns, to move with the flow of the activity, and to handle the free-flowing nature of the activity without getting too excited.

Language impairments: assist child with learning the vocabulary appropriate to this activity. The adult facilitating the activity can reinforce movement words.

Learning impairments: provide a model for the child to imitate until the child is comfortable with the activity and can be involved on his or her own.

Title of Activity: Manipulatives—Exploring How Things Fit Together

- Content Objectives:

  Over several days the children will explore the manipulatives in the classroom to see how things fit together (how things work)

  The children will learn the language related to these different manipulatives and the actions necessary to put them together

- Developmental Objectives:

  language

  cognitive

  social

  fine motor

  creative

- Materials:

  different manipulatives each day

- Procedure:

  The children will use their hands and eyes to explore the different types of manipulatives each day.

- Modifications:

  Physical impairments: assist child in using the manipulatives. If the child cannot use the materials independently, the adult can follow instructions given by the child as to where specific pieces should be placed. If the child does not have language, the child can select pieces by an eye gaze.

Manipulatives—Exploring How Things Fit Together **continued**

Visual impairments: assist child in exploring the manipulatives pointing out the key locations for where pieces fit together.

Social and emotional impairments: assist child with using the materials. Adult facilitation will enable the child to share the materials and work within the group of children working in the same space.

Language impairments: assist child with learning the vocabulary appropriate to this activity. The adult facilitating the activity can reinforce words which describe the manipulatives and the actions required to put them together.

Learning impairments: provide a process for the child to imitate until the child is comfortable with the materials and can be involved on his or her own.

Title of Activity: Large Motor— Exploring the Way the Body Moves Outdoors

- Content Objectives:

The children will over several days use their bodies to explore different movements outdoors (how things move)

The children will suggest movements as well as observe the movement of the teacher and other children and imitate those movements

The children will learn the vocabulary for the different movements they do (i.e., climb, jump, tip-toe, walk, hop, run, slide, turn, twist, dig, pour, toss, throw, balance)

- Developmental Objectives:

language

cognitive

social

gross motor

fine motor

creative

- Materials:

outdoor equipment and materials

- Procedure:

The children will use their bodies to explore different types of movements each day when they go outdoors. They will discuss the ways they observe their bodies moving.

Large Motor—Exploring the Way the Body Moves Outdoors **continued**

- Modifications:

  Physical impairments: assist child in participating in as much movement as possible. Adult facilitation will allow the child to participate even if only the arms or fingers can move.

  Visual impairments: assist child in determining the physical parameters for moving outdoors so the child will be safe.

  Social and emotional impairments: assist child with integrating into the activity outdoors. Adult facilitation will enable the child to take turns, move with the flow of the activity and to handle the free-flowing nature of the activity without getting too excited.

  Language impairments: assist child with learning the vocabulary appropriate to this activity. The adult facilitating the activity can reinforce movement words.

  Learning impairments: provide a model for the child to imitate until the child is comfortable with the activity and can be involved on his or her own.

Language and Literacy—Exploring the Language Related to How Things Work, Move, and Change

No additional activities need be created to support this theme as the activities all support language and literacy development. The children will, over the days and the many activities of the theme, explore vocabulary and concepts related to language and literacy development.

The children will listen to stories, be exposed to signs and pictures that support the theme. Children can be encouraged to bring books to school that explore the theme. This will serve as an appropriate means to bridge the theme to home and enable parents to become involved in reinforcing the content introduced in the classroom. Literature should be selected based on the interests and levels of children in the classroom. A very fine resource for identifying theme related literature is *A to Zoo Subject Access to Children's Picture Books* by Lima (1989).

RESOURCE OF IDEAS FOR THEME: HOMES

The following section contains a resource of ideas appropriate to support the theme of homes. From this resource different conceptual strands may be developed that will incorporate these activities. Of course there are many other activities which could be developed to support this theme. This listing is designed to start your thinking on the topic. The ideas are presented in random order so that your thinking will not be directed. No two teachers will implement a theme of the same title in the same manner. Teachers exercise their individual ideas and experiences in their classrooms. Teachers also take into account the needs of the different children being taught. All of these factors fold into the decisions made concerning the development of integrated themes.

RESOURCES

ACTIVITIES

Title of Activity: Art—Shape Homes

An assortment of construction paper shapes, glue, and large pieces of paper. The children create homes from the many color shapes.

Title of Activity: Art—Spider Web

Dip a string into liquid starch. Arrange the string into a spider web on a piece of wax paper. Let it dry overnight. In the morning hang it over a tree in the classroom.

Title of Activity: Art & Small Blocks—Apartment Houses

Use half-gallon cartons. Measure a piece of drawing paper to fit around the carton. Have the children color or paint in the details of their own homes. Wrap the paper around the carton and glue in place. Add a construction paper roof to the top of the carton. If photos of the children are available, add a small picture of the child's face to one of the windows.

Title of Activity: Language, Literacy, and Art—Books about Homes

Children make books about their own homes. Compare how they are the same and different.

Title of Activity: Sensory, Art, and Large Motor—Turtle Homes

Use small shoe boxes. Go for nature walk and collect a rock for a turtle, some dirt, grass, leaves, twigs, etc. Children can paint their turtle (rock) and glue wiggle eyes on it. Then they glue the grass, etc. to the shoe box as it is standing on its side. They can also add a pond with markers or decorate the inside back of box. Last they put their "Little Turtle" in the home and recite the following poem:

There was a little turtle
He lived in a box
He swam in a puddle
He climbed on the rocks.

Sensory, Art, and Large Motor—Turtle Homes **continued**

He snapped at a mosquito, he snapped at a flea
He snapped at a minnow and he snapped at me.
He caught the mosquito and he caught the flea
He caught the minnow, BUT HE DIDN'T CATCH ME.

Title of Activity: Large Blocks, Small Blocks, and Dramatic Play—Building Castles

Invite the children to sit together. Show the children several pictures of castles. Ask the children to share what they know about castles. Encourage the children to imagine what it might be like to live in a castle. Point out that European countries have many castles. Invite the children to build a castle using the large building blocks. The children can then role play different people who lived in castles. Another day encourage the children to build castles with small building blocks. Invite them to share information about their castles with one another, such as how the castles were constructed, who might live in the castles, special features of the castles, etc. Weather permitting, children can build castles in the sandbox and put flags atop which they have made out of construction paper.

Title of Activity: Art and Language—Collage of Objects Found in a House

Child may make a collage of objects found in the house on a piece of paper. Another way to do this is to divide the paper into different rooms. Children glue pictures into appropriate rooms.

Title of Activity: Language, Literacy, and Art—Read "A House Is a House for Me"

After the children hear the story they will think of different lines (i.e., The sky is a house for the stars). Teacher will write down the children's dictated ideas. Illustrations for each verse will be done via Q-Tip painting and all will be laminated and secured together in book form to be used as a class resource.

Title of Activity: Art—Paper Bag House

Need: lunch-size paper bag, markers or crayons, one piece of white paper. Draw and color the outside of a house on the front and back of the bag. The bottom of the bag should be the bottom of the house. Leave some blank space at the top of the bag. Fold the white piece of paper in half and color it as a roof. Have the teacher staple the roof to the paper bag.

Title of Activity: Art—Housing Collage

Children will find pictures of the type of housing they want to include in their collage and will glue them down as they choose.

Title of Activity: Art—Draw Rooms as a Class or Individually

After all rooms are drawn, they may be organized into a "class house."

Title of Activity: Language, Literacy, and Art—Children Create A "Very, Very, Very Fine House"

Children create using a variety of media and skills. Teacher inquires about the attributes of their creations.

Show the big book *Homes* to the children. Sing the verses as the pages are turned. Point to the words as they are sung. Allow the children to be the "teacher" and point to the words. Copy verses of the song for the children along with a picture of the appropriate home. The task for the children is to draw a picture of the animal that lives in a particular home and finish the illustration. Put the book together with title of the childs' choice. Encourage them to make it as simple as possible, using basic shapes. If available, a photograph of the child may be added to the verse about their homes.

Title of Activity: Language, Literacy, and Art—House Collages

House collages using familiar geometric math shapes and glue. Make a class big book of A House is a House and label to store in book corner.

Title of Activity: Language and Art—Homes Collage

Pictures from various journals, realtor magazines, etc. These will be used to create a collage. Children will be encouraged to bring in pictures (either drawn or photographed) of their own homes to add to the collage and to think of ways in which the houses they have found are alike or different.

Title of Activity: Sensory—A Mix for Bricks

Children will make adobe bricks according to a recipe (source for Adobe bricks—Southwest Hoi Pueblo; *Big Book Magazine*. Issue No. 4. Topic: Home. Scholastic).

Title of Activity: Sensory and Art—Rain Stick

Have children make a rain stick from South America. Materials needed: paper towel tube; sheet of white paper; crayons, markers, paint etc. for decorating; sand, rice, beans, etc. for noise; wax paper for ends of tube and tape to hold it securely.

Title of Activity: Art—Colored Macaroni House

Using pre-dyed macaroni and outline precut houses, children glue macaroni onto the house.

Title of Activity: Language and Art—Family Tree

Materials: large piece of poster board or cardboard; pencil and poster paints; photos of the family—the older the better; double-sided sticky tape. What to do: draw a large tree on the cardboard; color the trunk of the tree brown and the foliage a bright green; let it dry; collect photos; stick them to tree; display.

Title of Activity: Art—Family Members

Using a variety of materials (scraps of construction paper, fabric, circles, squares, triangles, cotton balls, tissue paper, sequins, etc.) children can make the members of their family.

Title of Activity: Sensory and Art—Homes of Many Kinds

Split children in groups, supply each with a poster of type of land area (forest; plain—grass and mud; beach with palm trees; north pole—snow and ice; river bed or desert—very rocky; desert area—nothing but sand). Children are told that they will be building homes. They are there without any other people, no stores, no cars, etc. They can only use things found on the land to build the house. The children will get the following materials: forest (pretzels); plain—grass and mud (clay and grass); beach—palm leaves (leaves from yard); North pole—ice (sugar cubes); rocky area—rocks (pebbles); sandy area (clay). Except for the clay group, the others will build their homes around a milk carton. Use parent helpers or older children if possible. Interview each group and photograph the activities to display with final projects. Record what they tell you about their houses.

Title of Activity: Language, Literacy, and Art—Crayon Resist

Read the story *The Village of Round and Square Houses.* Crayon resist painting depicting the homes in the story.

Title of Activity: Small Blocks and Manipulatives—Making Houses

Divide the children into three or more groups and have them choose a building material available in the classroom, such as blocks, Legos, etc. Have them build a community of houses and explain who lives in the house.

Title of Activity: Art and Dramatic Play—Family Puppets

Make family puppets with tongue depressors, markers, fabric scraps, glue. Make several puppet stands with cardboard boxes. Have the children use the puppets to play out stories about their families and homes.

Title of Activity: Art—The Home Where I Live

Materials: Newsprint for each child, brushes, tempera paint, markers, easel and scissors. Outline a house shape for each child on newsprint in black marker. Child paints house to match his or her own color house. When dry, return it to easel for child to draw doors and windows. Write name and address on house and have child cut it out. Ways to extend: Attach children's houses to the wall and group them by streets or areas. Make streets of black construction paper and add paper props such as cars, trees and stop signs.

Title of Activity: Sensory and Art—Model Home

Build a model of a shelter or house that they like or would like to live in. Materials needed: small box from home; construction paper; markers; glue; popsicle sticks; raffia for straw; clay for stucco; tissue paper. To aid in their creativity, the facilitator might offer drawings of different houses as well as photos and illustrations from books and magazines. To display the work, secure a table of countertop space to put their imaginary neighborhood. (This activity comes after learning about these homes: adobe; hogan; igloo; mobile home; single dwelling; multiple dwelling.)

Title of Activity: Art and Dramatic Play—Class Map of Town

Each child contributes by drawing (or cut and paste pictures) a place where a community helper can be found. When the map of the town is completed, the children can role-play the community helpers who work near their homes.

Title of Activity: Nameplates

Children make nameplate that can be put on the doors to their rooms.

Title of Activity: Art and Large Motor—Painting Cooperation

Two-headed, one-armed painters are a great exercise in cooperation. Pair off kids, and tape the right arm of one child to the left arm of the other. Make sure the tape is not too tight. Set them in front of an easel or at a table for kids with motor impairments, and let them paint.

Title of Activity: Art and Dramatic Play—Build Log Homes

Roll paper logs and have children stack and arrange them in whatever fashion they wish. Attach with glue or tape. Can be done individually or as a class activity. If done as a class activity, the children can use the house to play house.

Title of Activity: Art, Language, and Literacy—Match Animals to Their Homes

Teacher cuts out four pictures of animals and their "homes" and scatters pictures on table in front of children. The children will then select four different animals and glue

Art, Language, and Literacy—Match Animals to Their Homes **continued**

them to the construction paper. Next the children will select a matching "home" for each of the animals and glue next to appropriate animal.

Title of Activity: Art and Dramatic Play—Building a Home from a Refrigerator Carton

Spend some time talking about the house they are going to make—what colors they would like to use, how many windows and doors they would like, any special decorations they want to add, etc. Provide paint for the outside and a variety of materials for the inside (i.e., wallpaper scraps, material for curtains, rug pieces, paint or markers to draw furniture on the walls). Care should be taken not to restrict children to realistic designs—the fun is in being creative. When the house is completed and dry, the children can use it to play house.

Title of Activity: Art, Dramatic Play, and Movement—Make a Spider Web

The children will use a variety of materials to create a large spider web. When the web is completed, the children will pretend to be spiders. They will engage in spider movements as they role-play.

Title of Activity: Art, Dramatic Play, and Movement—Make a Nest

The children will use a variety of materials to create a large nest. When the nest is completed, the children will pretend to be birds. They will engage in bird movements as they role-play.

Title of Activity: Large Blocks, Dramatic Play, and Movement—Make a Bear Cave

The children will use a variety of materials to create a large cave. When the cave is completed, the children will pretend to be bears. They will engage in bear movements as they role play.

Title of Activity: Language, Literacy, and Art—Home Decorating

Discuss different rooms found in homes, and then discuss what appliances, furnishings, or other articles would be found in a particular room. Working on one room at a time, provide the children with catalogs or advertisements and have them "decorate" a room. These rooms might be included in the project: living room, bedroom, bathroom, kitchen. When all of the rooms have been "decorated," put them together as a book and have the child draw a picture of his or her home as a cover.

Title of Activity: Art—String Painting

Cut a simple house shape for each child out of construction paper, cut 12-inch lengths of string (yarn), tie button to end of each string length for easy holding, and provide

Art: String Painting **continued**

blue, yellow, and red paint. The children dip the string in the paint and wiggle the string across the outline of the house. The children should be encouraged to use different colors each time they dip so the colors will mix.

Title of Activity: Art, Language, and Literacy—Who Lives in Your Home?

Have children trace and cut out a picture of a house. With pre-made cut outs of people (men, women, boys, girls) have them glue to the house the number of people that represent their family. When done, the teacher will ask them how many or what's the number of people in their picture. The teacher will then write the number on their picture with a marker. If interest is still there, have the children, following the pattern of the number, glue sequins to it.

Title of Activity: Art—Build a House with Popsicle Sticks.

Children construct houses of their design. They will count the number of sticks used.

Title of Activity: Art—Sponge Painting

Help the children cut or tear sponges into different shapes of parts of a house. Dip the sponges into paint and print the shapes onto the paper. Encourage the children to create patterns and to notice that the sponges make the same shape on the paper as the shape of the sponge.

Title of Activity: Art, Language, and Literacy—Making a Counting Book

Make a counting book where children have to count by twos. Make book in the shape of a house. Children cut out pictures of faces from magazine and glue to each house. Students will count eyes on each face. One face equals two, two faces equal four, three faces equal six, and so on.

Title of Activity: Art, Language, and Literacy—Architect Visits Children

This activity takes place over several weeks. To begin, an architect will visit the classroom, showing the children his or her tools, blueprints, and pictures of houses being built. The children will then "design" their own home. They will work together to decide how many and what kinds of rooms will be in the house, how many stories it will be, and which rooms will be big or small. With help from the teacher, the students will draw these plans on large sheets of paper using rulers. A local carpenter or parent will be asked to make a doll-house-size model of this building. Children will then sand and paint their home and make furniture for it in the woodworking or art area. They will also wallpaper and paint the inside walls and make popsicle stick residents.

Title of Activity: Large Blocks and Dramatic Play—Different Types of Homes

After hearing about different types of houses people in different climates live in, the children will construct these homes and engage in activities particular to this type of living.

Title of Activity: Large Blocks and Dramatic Play—Creating Rooms and Decorating Them

Children will use the large blocks to create rooms in a house. They will use materials in the classroom to fill the rooms and decorate them. They will role-play "family" after the rooms are completed.

Title of Activity: Dramatic Play and Large Blocks—Moving Day

The children will pretend they are packing and moving to a new house. They can construct their new house in the block area and set up housekeeping there once the "movers" deliver their belongings.

Title of Activity: Dramatic Play—Spring Cleaning

Children will use water, sponges, mops, etc. to clean the housekeeping area as well as other shelves in the classroom. The concept of keeping where you live and work clean will be emphasized.

Title of Activity: Art, Dramatic Play, and Cooking—Family Feast

Children will each bring in a food to contribute to a family feast prepared by all the children. Keep the recipes simple so that children can participate in most of the food preparation. Have the children decorate table coverings for the feast. Invite special guests if feasible.

Title of Activity: Art and Manipulatives—Tangram Houses

Using tangrams, have children trace and cut shapes. Then they can arrange pieces so they fit in the pictures provided. Some house or house things can be provided as shapes.

Title of Activity: Manipulative and Large Motor—Making a Birdhouse

Using woodworking materials, the child will construct a birdhouse with the aid of the teacher. Then using a simple ruler, the children will measure proper pieces of wood and put them together according to written plans.

Title of Activity: Art and Manipulatives—Making Patterns

Use construction paper, markers, scissors, chalk. After talking about patterns, copy patterns and then have children make patterns of things they would find in their houses.

Art and Manipulatives—Making Patterns **continued**

Hang the patterns around room in a chain form to use as a visual for patterns and math manipulatives for future activities as well.

Title of Activity: Art—Scrap Wood Structures

Children will use scrap wood and glue to create their own structures. Provide paint and brushes to complete the project.

Title of Activity: Art, Language, and Literacy—The Little Red House

Read the book, *The Little Red House* by Norma Jean Sawicki. This story is about a child who opens a box shaped like a red house, which when opened has a green house inside, then a yellow house, etc. Each house has a smaller house inside. For an art activity, have a series of boxes in graduated sizes. The children can paint them to match the colors in the book, then draw windows, doors, etc. The finished products will then be used in the book area for retelling the story.

Title of Activity: Art, Language, and Literacy—Where do Insects Live? Thumb Print Insects

Children sponge paint leaves on a piece of light blue paper. After the leaves dry, the students make thumb print insects on the leaves such as lady bugs, ants and caterpillars.

IDEAS FOR OTHER DEVELOPMENTALLY APPROPRIATE THEMES

The following is a list of possible themes appropriate for young children. The list is presented in alphabetical order. The most appropriate sequence in which themes should be introduced depends on these various factors: age of the children, developmental level of the children, program goals, interest of the children, availability of resources, number of hours children are in school, geographic location of program.

All about me

Animals—Pets; Farm; Wild; Zoo; Water

Apples

Breads

Celebrations

Circus

City and Country

Color

Communication

Community Helpers
Crafts
Family
Favorite Authors
Favorite Stories
Flowers
Food and Nutrition
Forests
Friends
Functional Signs and Sounds
Health
Hobbies
Insects
Musical Instruments
Neighborhoods
Oceans
Occupations
Patterns
Safety—Vehicle; Home; Community; Stranger
Same and Different
Seasons
Senses
Shape
Space
Sports
Stores
Transportation
Water
Weather
Wind, Water, and Mud

INTEGRATING THE IEP OR IFSP INTO CLASSROOM ACTIVITIES

Most goals and individualized objectives specified within an Individualized Educational Plan (IEP) or an Individualized Family Service Plan

(IFSP) can be implemented through natural or modified activities found within thematic integrated curriculum in inclusive settings. Children enjoy playing at activities or with materials and equipment requiring repetitive movements far more than they would enjoy repeating exercises designed to achieve the same goals and objectives. When teachers have information concerning appropriate goals and objectives and work in cooperation with the specialists working with the child as well as the parents, interesting, accessible activities appropriate for the child with disabilities as well as all the other children in the class can be developed and implemented.

BRIDGING CLASSROOM CURRICULUM TO HOME

Children often share the excitement and some of the details of school activities with those who share their homes. Even if this does happen on a regular basis, it is important to communicate with parents concerning ongoing classroom activities in a more formal manner. This may be done through conversations, a bulletin board describing all the activities planned for the week, informal conversations that take place at arrival and dismissal time, or through phone conversations. Occasional recipes, activities designed for the home, and special programs taking place on the weekends or during school vacations are examples of what may be sent home in a newsletter in addition to the regular weekly news. When parents are aware of the nature of activities as well as the content of activities taking place in the classroom, they are more apt to become partners in their child's educational process.

SUMMARY

There are many ways to approach the development of developmentally appropriate integrated themes for young children. There are also many appropriate resources teachers can refer to for ideas to stimulate thinking. Children themselves serve as very appropriate sources of stimulation of ideas for integrated themes. Appropriate themes and appropriate activities will include children at whatever level they are comfortable with. Each child will get something out of each activity whether the activity is new to them, a repeated activity, or a variation of an activity previously implemented. The most critical factors to keep in mind when planning for children is their developmental level and their interests. Reading the cues children provide concerning their interest in and enthusiasm for each activity and the entire integrated theme will provide teachers with the feedback they need to know if the planning being implemented is meeting their goals for the theme. Children are not the only ones who should enjoy each theme as it is presented. Teachers should enjoy what they do also!

REFERENCES

Abraham, M. R., Morris, L. M., & Wald, P. J. (1993). *Inclusive early childhood education—A model classroom*. Tucson, AZ: Communication Skill Builders.

Berry, C., & Mindes, G. (1993). *Planning a theme-based curriculum: Goals, themes, activities, and planning guides for 4's and 5's*. Glenview, IL: GoodYear Books.

Bredekamp, S. (1990). *Developmentally appropriate practice in early childhood programs serving children from birth through age 8*. Washington, DC: National Association for the Education of Young Children.

Day, B.D. (1994). *Early childhood education—Developmental/experiential teaching and learning* (Fourth edition). New York: Merrill.

Deiner, P. (1993). *Resources for teaching children with diverse abilities—Birth through eight*. Fort Worth: Harcourt Brace Jovanovich Publishers.

Dodge, D. T. (1989). *The creative curriculum for early childhood*. Washington, DC: Teaching Strategies, Inc.

Dolinar, K., Boser, C., & Holm, E. (1994). *Learning through play: Curriculum and activities for the inclusive classroom*. New York: Delmar Publishers Inc.

Eliason, C., & Jenkins, L. (1994). *A practical guide to early childhood curriculum*. New York: Merrill.

Hendrick, J. (1994). *Total learning—Developmental curriculum for the young child*. New York: Merrill.

Kostelnik, M. J., Soderman, A. K., & Whiren, A. P. (1993). *Developmentally appropriate programs in early childhood education*. New York: Merrill.

Kostelnik, M., Ed. (1991). *Teaching young children using themes*. Glenview, IL: GoodYear Books.

Krogh, S. (1990). *The integrated early childhood curriculum*. New York: McGraw-Hill Publishing Company.

Lima, C. W. (1989). *A to Zoo Subject Access to Children's Picture Books*. New York: R.R. Bowker.

Shipley, D. (1993). *Empowering children: Play-based curriculum for lifelong learning*. Scarborough, Ont.: Nelson Canada.

Trostle, S. L., & Yawkey, T. D. (1990). *Integrated learning activities for young children*. Boston: Allyn & Bacon.

Van Hoorn, J., Nourot, P. M., Scales, B., & Alward, K. R. (1993) *Play at the center of the curriculum*. New York: Merrill.

Wortham, S. C. (1994). *Early childhood curriculum—Developmental bases for learning and teaching*. New York: Merrill.

PART

3

CHAPTER 13

Parents and Families

KEY TERMS

parent readiness
parent-teacher relationships
partnership
consultation
transition

Parents are the first teachers children encounter. The teaching that parents provide is carried out in the most naturalistic environment children ever encounter, the home. The parent's role begins prior to the birth of a child and continues throughout the lifetime of the child. Whether the child is born with or without disabilities, no professional or combination of professionals will ever have the opportunity to have the impact that parents can have in the development of a child.

There are many appropriate additions and alternatives to parent care which have developed over the years either to enrich the experiences parents provide or to substitute for the parent during the time a parent works outside the home. For enrichment, children are able to attend programs in the arts, science and nature, and physical education. For the provision of substitute care there is in-home care by a care giver who may or may not be a member of the extended family, there is center-based care, and family home day care. Families choose the alternatives which best suit their needs and the needs of their children. These needs may change several times during the early childhood years. All of the alternatives parents select place children in the care of others for brief or longer periods of time.

Regardless of who provides for the care and education of young children, the emphasis should be on the provision of quality care. It is an assumption that a child cared for at home is a well-cared-for child. An at-home parent who does not actively engage in positive interactions with the child during the day is not providing better quality care than a family or center provider who does provide for positive interactions. Persons vested in the care and education of individual or groups of children and developmentally appropriate programs are important to the development and education of children with and without disabilities. Any person with less than a vested interest or a poorly run program, may be detrimental to the development and education of any child with or without disabilities. As professionals in early childhood education, regardless of the conditions under which teachers come to know children and their families, there remains an obligation to learn as much as one can from the parents and to work in partnership with them to create the most appropriate environments and approaches for young children as is possible.

ROLE OF THE PARENT IN THE DEVELOPMENT OF THE CHILD

The basic role of the parent does not change from society to society or over time. Children need to be nurtured, fed, clothed, touched, and communicated with in verbal and nonverbal ways. While it may be very natural to biologically parent a child, it takes skill and knowledge to psychologically parent a child. One of the most important jobs in the world is that of being a parent. There is no credential required for the position. Some parents appear to be naturally talented in the area and further enhance their native abilities through reading about child development and the techniques of good parenting. There is no magic formula for perfect parenting. The blend of the personalities of the child and the parent create unique combinations which require careful observation and considerations before advice or interventions are suggested. What works for one parent and child might not be effective for another dyad. Knowing what makes for positive relationships for some parents and children serves to inform parents that there are many positive approaches to working through everyday or difficult situations.

Some parents are actively involved in parenting but seem to be content with their own ways of handling matters without seeking out other parents, parenting programs, or parenting materials. A parent may be shy and thus uncomfortable in group situations. Other people have themselves been raised to believe one does not share family issues with "outsiders" and thus will not seek out the advice of another, even the child's teacher.

Some parents initially may not appear to take their child-rearing job so seriously and as such may engage in parenting behaviors which seem to be less effective for their particular children. It is often most difficult to build a partnership with this type of parent because they are not invested enough in the parenting role to take on the parent-teacher partnership. Teachers should not allow themselves to dismiss this parent as one who is not interested in an educator's help or in a relationship. Boutte, Keepler, Tyler, and Terry (1992) review effective techniques for involving "difficult" parents. They include practical suggestions for teachers to implement when working with parents who exhibit any of the following behaviors: antagonism; "know-it-all" manner; frequent complaints, negative behavior; shy or unresponsive behavior; and illiterate behavior. The authors suggest these ideas for home visits as well as for parent-teacher conferences. They point out that developing an authentic relationship with each parent goes a long way to ease difficulties.

Parent "readiness" is not something that is measured. Readiness for parenting a child with special needs is more difficult to assess. It is difficult to know what it is like to walk in the shoes of another. It is even more difficult to understand the factors that vie for attention in the family of a child with special needs. There is much to learn about being a parent. There is even more to learn about parenting a child with a disability. Readiness for parenting often begins with preparing a room, furniture, and clothing for the baby. Some parents-to-be spend time reading about the first year of life. Usually this preparation does not include preparation for parenting the child with physical disabilities, feeding problems, visual or auditory impairments, or other health impairments. Understanding the impact of the birth of a child with disabilities on the family helps the teacher to understand some of what the family has gone through prior to the time the child arrives at school. It is not possible to fully understand, but the key to paving the way for positive home and school relationships is to actively work to develop sensitivity to the issues.

When teachers first meet parents, it is conceivable that although they are ready and eager to provide support and assistance to the parent in order to establish a partnership, the parent is not ready to have teachers serve in that capacity. Parents develop their skills at different paces and in different ways, as do their children. While teachers recognize and allow for that in their relationships with children in classes, at times they are guilty of not affording the same considerations to parents. This may be due to the fact that parents are adults and as such are perceived to be fully developed persons. In fact, being a parent has a lot to do with evolving as a parent. It is a role that is learned as children grow, develop, and move from one stage of their lives to another. When a child is first born, chances are that the parent of that child could not immediately parent an adolescent. This is something one grows into as a parent, based on life experience and the enduring relationship one develops with the child. Teachers and other professionals come and go in the life of a child but in the best of all possible situations, parents provide continuity and stability.

The parent of a child with special needs has usually had many professionals to contend with prior to the time of school entrance. The early childhood educator may know some of these professionals but probably will not know all of them. Entrance into an inclusion model, early childhood program may be a shift in focus for the family. While all involved in the program will make the transition as smooth as possible, the delivery of service will be different from what the family is used to. This is a topic that will be discussed later on but is one that is very important to remember. Teachers tend to think of children making transitions but forget that entrance into a new program is a transition for the family as well. Children need support and orientation. While the approach to accomplishing this task may appear different, parents need the same considerations.

INFLUENCE OF HOME ON THE DEVELOPMENT OF A CHILD

The home has a tremendous impact on a developing child. Home is where a child hears and develops language, moves from total physical dependence to evolving independence, has developing social relationships, explores and discovers within a safe environment, is stimulated cognitively, and much, much more. Home and school partnerships provide support for the developing child. Children whose parents help them at home do better in school. Parents who participate in school have children who are more diligent in their efforts to learn and are better behaved. It is important to keep this in mind when nurturing parent-teacher relationships and parent-school relationships. Families where parents maintain partnerships with the school, the child, and the teacher are usually more comfortable with their roles and the roles being played by others.

Research supports the importance of parent-program partnerships. Family involvement in programs has been seen to improve the attitudes and performance of children in programs, raise the academic achievement of school-age children, improve parent understanding of programs and activities (Morrison, 1990), and build program-community relationships in an ongoing, problem-preventing way (Rich, 1987).

FACTORS THAT MIGHT INTERFERE WITH HOME AND SCHOOL INVOLVEMENT

Not all parents are able to participate in school activities as readily as we wish they would or as much as they would themselves like to participate. Work and family obligations may preclude their attendance at either day-time or evening events. Sometimes it is not the time or responsibility element that prevents a parent from being involved in parent-teacher relationships. The memory of what school was like for that person serves as the controlling factor. Those memories may cause the parent to stay away from school events even though the individual is a concerned parent who is actively involved with the child at home. Physical proximity to the school may bring to the surface a flood of emotions with which the parent is not able to cope. Rather than seeking help with the situation, the individual stays away from what is problematic. As a teacher, one needs to show sensitivity to such issues so that the child does not suffer because of something the parent is not able to do. Encouraging parents to attend class or school functions is commendable. Urging children to reinforce the invitation may work for some families but not for others. Chastising children when their parents do not attend the function does little if anything to enhance the parent-teacher relationship or build the child's self-esteem.

Often parents do not attend school functions because the entire presentation is conducted in a language the parent does not speak. The parent may be the only member of a certain ethnic group and feel uncomfortable being surrounded by persons from another culture. Some parents do not participate because they may not know what would be expected of them if they did attend. They stay away because they are uninformed. If another parent were to reach out on a personal level to the parent who was reluctant to attend, there is a greater likelihood that the parent will take the risk and attend. If the experience proves to be gratifying, there is a greater chance that the parent who was reluctant will return to engage in other activities. This will improve the self esteem of the parent as well as the child.

When parents of children with special needs settle their children into the school routine and help with the transition from home to school, they may be tempted to breathe a sigh of relief and attempt to take what they perceive to be a well-deserved vacation from maximum involvement. The school needs the family to be involved. The child still needs the involvement and the family still needs the involvement. It may take a few weeks for the parent to be ready to participate again or it may take a special invitation for the parent to enter into the relationship. It is understandable that the parent may view the child entering a school program as a mission accomplished. After all, this was the family goal from the beginning of early intervention. Parents need to feel as though they are still important members of the education team for the child. In fact, they are the key players because they know more about the child than any of the professionals on the team.

WHAT TEACHERS GAIN FROM PARENT-TEACHER RELATIONSHIPS

Teachers have the potential to gain much from **parent-teacher relationships.** The following are some of the ways in which parents add to teachers through developed relationships:

■ *Increased knowledge enabling teachers to be more effective with each child*

Teachers have much to learn from parents concerning the habits, interests and means through which the children communicate their needs. Parents often use special techniques for motivating their children to engage in activity, self-help tasks, or to communicate with others. These techniques may have been learned through parent education classes, from members of the extended family or may have been developed through trial and error. The information teachers glean about children can come from speaking with parents, observing parents interact with their children, and reading the information parents provide on an application or a child history form. Often, this is critical information that would not be obvious to the teacher through classroom observations or interactions. It might be information that would help explain some behavior for the teacher. A parent can relate information about difficult health situations, major or minor changes in living situations or very positive events that took place prior to the start of the school year. Whatever information parents choose to share can serve to strengthen the experience a child has in school by speeding up the "getting to know you" period.

Information gathered from parents about a child with special needs is invaluable. Techniques for calming the child, supporting feeding or eating, toileting, and favorite activities prepare teachers for including the child in the classroom. If a teacher had to discover all of this information without help, most of the initial time a child was in the classroom would be spent unearthing information that could have been obtained from the parent. A parent may tell you that the information to be shared is valid for the home environment. The information can be generalized to the classroom under most circumstances. Teachers know that children often behave quite differently in the school environment than in the home. A child with eating difficulties at home may evidence fewer problems at school. The reverse of this may be true as well. A child might be more motivated to move in the classroom than at home because of the novelty of items in the classroom. Other children might be more comfortable with the home environment and thus move about with a greater degree of confidence at home.

Something as simple as knowing what terminology children use for toileting allows the teacher to ask an intelligent question of the child. To use an incorrect term might mean that the child winds up having a toileting accident. The child will be embarrassed and the teacher will feel as though the situation was provoked by a lack of information. A child on the verge of using language may use different sounds for different responses. Without a parent providing the information, the child may experience unnecessary frustration before teachers and children begin to understand the communication attempts the child makes.

■ *Positive feedback which increases teacher feelings of competence in their profession*

When a teacher hears positive things from a parent, the teacher is gratified and fortified. Although teachers can engage in self-reflection to support their own feelings and sense of efficacy, it is even more meaningful to receive positive feedback from satisfied customers. Positive comments from a parent who appeared insecure about sending a child off to school is enough to restore faith in that teacher's abilities.

Parent participation is another form of positive feedback. Parents usually do not volunteer in the classroom if the classroom is an unpleasant place to spend time. Having parent volunteers participating in classroom activities improves the way a teacher feels about the work being accomplished in the classroom.

A relationship with a parent validates professional behavior. When a teacher receives positive feedback from a parent, the teacher is more apt to increase energy directed to the children in the class. The teacher will probably be motivated to engage in professional development if the reception received from children and parents validates the energy and effort the teacher puts into teaching.

When a parent of a child with specials needs shares the positive feelings the family has about the child being included in the classroom, the anxiety the teacher might have been feeling about the ability to be effective with a new situation tends to disappear. Gaining confidence and acceptance validates the experience and primes the teacher to be ready for other such experiences and challenges.

■ *Parental resources to supplement and reinforce teacher efforts in providing an enlarged world of learning*

Parents may have access to information and community resources not readily available to teachers or that particular teacher. Some parents have lived in the community for many more years than the teacher and know the history of the community. This parent may be able to provide an important resource when the class undertakes study of change in the local community. Parents know people in businesses or professions who might serve as vital resources to units of study. Parents may also know how to obtain recycled materials appropriate for use by the children in the class.

Parents may have hobbies that can be shared with the class. A parent who is a stamp or coin collector will add to the dimension of what is covered by the teacher. A parent who does a craft as a hobby or business can inspire children or actually teach them how to do their craft. Some parents play musical instruments and willingly come to school to play for the children.

Parents can also come to read favorite stories to children. This activity will help promote interest in reading and afford most parents equal opportunity to participate in class activities and support the learning taking place. If all parents are invited to read to the children, you may find one or more parents who are not able to read. English may not be their native language or they may have never learned to read. It is important to be sensitive to this possibility and to be ready with alternative activities for that parent to be able to do with the class.

Some parents have special things to share about their cultural heritage. Either through ethnic food preparation and sharing, music, toys, stories, or native costume, these parents can bring a dimension to the class that the teacher may not be able to bring. Many children are not aware that some of the foods they eat have origins in different countries. A parent who is able to reinforce positive concepts relating to appreciation of diversity will certainly enhance the curriculum developing in the classroom.

Grandparents who have lived in the community for their lifetimes can be very special visitors. Children may want to videotape or audiotape the stories these people are able to tell for a special project about community then and now. Grandparents in the classroom promote positive feelings towards and acceptance of the elderly. The presence of senior citizens in the classroom does much to reinforce anti-bias beliefs (Derman-Sparks, 1989). These welcome additions to the classroom can reinforce the curriculum and extend the learning that takes place.

While parents of children with special needs are people first and then parents of children with special needs, they may have many other things that they can do to add to the resources a teacher has available. In addition, these parents certainly can add to the school resources concerning disabilities. Some parents provide old braces, helmets, adaptive devices, and reading materials to add to the knowledge teachers and children can gather about disabilities.

A source of advocacy

When parents are familiar with the work teachers do, they are in a position to be advocates for these teachers. When a teacher attempts something new in the way of innovative practice, a parent spending time in the classroom can serve to report first hand knowledge of the results of this innovation. When a board member or administrator questions the innovation, the parent who has spent time in the classroom will be able to describe the climate of the room pre- and post-new practice implementation.

When parents see teachers trying really hard to enrich the classroom, they will often be more willing to fund raise or lobby the administrative source of funds to encourage the allocation of more money for certain programs. This serves to encourage the teacher to accomplish even greater things. Parents of children with special needs who are pleased with a school program will tend to be vocal advocates of the teacher and the program. They will assist the teacher in any way possible in order to maintain inclusion and the quality of the program.

WHAT PARENTS GAIN FROM PARENT-TEACHER RELATIONSHIPS

Teachers are not the only ones to gain from parent-teacher relationships. Some of the ways in which parents gain from the experience are:

Feelings of support in the difficult task of parenting

Parenting is not an easy job. Developing a relationship with a child's teacher provides a feeling of support in carrying out the responsibilities of parenthood. Many parents raise children by themselves. Regardless of whether the single parent is the father or the mother, having another adult to provide input about a child's development can be very gratifying. When a parent has a concern and does not have a spouse or someone in the extended family with whom to confer, knowing that a concerned teacher will listen and provide support is quite reassuring. Some people feel that they should be able to handle all aspects of parenting alone. In fact, people have always been dependent on others to help them with the difficult task of parenting. Extended family, neighbors, and friends have traditionally been called upon to provide coverage or support for parents in times of stress or relative to activities of daily life. It has been noted by Kunreuther (1970) that after mothers have a chance to express their feelings and concerns to others who are willing to listen, they are more relaxed, listen to their children more carefully, are more responsive to their needs, and demonstrate more patience with their children.

■ *Knowledge and skills gained to help in child rearing*

Teachers are able to provide parents with knowledge and skills to help them with child rearing through informal as well as more formal approaches. Teachers model positive child guidance techniques in their interactions with children that parents are able to observe when they bring children to school and again when they arrive at dismissal. Clearly, parents know far more about their own children than teachers are able to know about them. Teachers might know information about the child relative to school activities and routines which parents cannot possibly be aware of. This information can help the parent in fostering smoother transitions between home and school. Living with children provides information pertinent to the home and family situation. Working with a child in school often means that the teacher is privy to another entire set of behaviors which necessitate another set of procedures.

Teachers can help parents to enrich the development of their children without hurrying them through childhood. They can point out many variations on activities children enjoy which will increase the depth of their knowledge without taking them beyond their developmental ability. Teachers can be very helpful in providing parents with information about early reading and other academic thrusts. They can be reassuring in the message to parents that the children will not be behind other children if they are not already reading by their preschool years. They can reinforce the notion that children develop at differing rates and should not be compared with each other.

Teachers can share their knowledge of child development through a variety of means. Interactions with children and interactions with parents at school or through phone conversations can provide much information. Sharing of published child development material through a parent library or a child development column in a monthly newsletter is another way to share information. Parent meetings geared to the discussion of critical aspects of child development can be scheduled according to need and interest. Sometimes it is difficult for parents to attend these meetings due to work schedules or family commitments. If such a meeting is held, recording the presentation and making it available to parents on a rotating basis would allow the parent who cannot attend to receive the information anyway. The only thing the parent would miss out on would be participation in any discussion.

A classroom teacher cannot provide all the education and training some parents need but the teacher is certainly the first point of communication and stimulation of interest in further education for parents. It is important to be aware of community resources available to support continuing parent education. Developing a resource file on what is available in the surrounding community will provide parents and other teachers with the immediate information they need.

■ *Enhanced parental self-esteem from receiving positive feedback on their parenting actions*

Parents who believe in themselves in their parenting role are better able to grow and develop as parents. They are better able to ask for and accept assistance from others they respect. A parent who is secure and self-confident provides a much more secure home environment for a child than a parent who questions each and every action taken during the course of time spent with a child. The parent who constantly needs to ask "How am I doing?" is the parent who needs to be nurtured to see that the role he or she is playing is a role vital to the child's development. This type of parent also needs to know that the role he or she plays makes a vital contribution to the school life of the child.

When a parent handles a situation in a very appropriate manner it is important for the teacher to provide the parent with descriptive positive feedback. To tell a parent that a situation was handled well does not serve to educate the parent as much as describing for the parent what aspect of the interaction was really positive. Informing a parent that the situation was handled fairly, with great sensitivity to saving face for the child, or with great sensitivity to the child's feelings will encourage the parent to think further about those areas in future interactions with the child. A parent who demonstrates skill in setting age appropriate limits and following through on them should receive considerable descriptive praise from teachers.

■ *Feeling included in their child's life away from home*

Parents should be made to feel as though they have something to offer the entire class and the teacher. Whether they make a special snack for the children, assist with an activity, or accompany the class on a field trip, it is important to let parents know how much their efforts, time, and presence are appreciated. While parents are in the classroom they feel very much part of the child's life away from home. Some of the difficulty parents have with "letting go" of their children when they attend school lies in the fact that they feel they are no longer going to know what their children are doing during the school day. After spending considerable time with the child during the earliest years, sending a child off to school serves as a kind of culture shock for parents. Their identity shifts focus somewhat and they need to still feel connected to the child and everyday activities. Spending time with a child at school is one of the nicest ways parents can feel connected. It is also a nice way for a teacher to see how a child interacts with the parent rather than just hearing about or reading a report of such interactions.

Occasionally parents find that spending time in a child's classroom is not necessarily an appropriate way to foster a sense of connection. Sometimes children do not pay any attention to their parents when they are in the classroom. They not only ignore their parents, they may also try to throw the parents out of the classroom. Instead of the classroom visit helping the parent to feel connected, this rejecting behavior serves to embarrass the parent and cause some parents to think that the child is embarrassed by them. What is probably functioning is the fact that the child perceives the classroom as his or her private, personal space. When a parent shows up, the child feels as though the parent has violated that personal space by being there. The child may not be able to voice these feelings, thus the behavior display.

During the time parents are involved in classroom activities, they increase their chances of meeting with other parents and widening their social circles. Often, parents do not have friends or relatives with children the same age as their own. All parents benefit from interactions with parents who share the same concerns. Collective brainstorming and sharing responsibilities helps build parent self-esteem. Being a leader in parent circles helps to foster self-confidence for the leader. Just being part of the parent circle may serve to boost self-esteem of the other parents. As the group begins to recognize the strengths of all those involved in the group, the parent who thought he or she had nothing to offer the group may come to be pleasantly surprised.

FORGING THE RELATIONSHIP

Who first initiates the relationship is not as critical as when the relationship is established. From the first contact parents have with a teacher or school administrator, the relationship begins to form. Parents do not wait until a child begins a school program to begin to form their opinions of personnel and program. If the first contact is pleasant, the parent will feel more positive about the ensuing important transition. The first contact may be in the form of a phone call, a request for written information, a school visit with or without the child or an invitation to participate in a planning team meeting concerning the child. Some programs have an established home visit process that is part of the orientation program. The manner in which the first contact is made is not as important as the impression the family comes away with. First impressions are important and long lasting.

The first request made of parents is important to consider as well. It should be something one can safely assume can be done by all families so that undue stress is not placed on the family or the developing relationship. Parents need to be welcomed into a classroom just as children need to be welcomed. The nature of the welcome depends on the age at which the child enters a program. If a child has never before been part of an organized classroom program, this may the first such experience for the parent as well. If the teacher is overwhelming, the parent might feel the need to retreat. If the teacher is warm, welcoming, attentive, and exudes a sense of professionalism and a respect for others, parents will become comfortable very quickly. Even if all of the above is in place, an occasional parent will not perceive the school to be a warm environment. This may be due to interpersonal difficulties that parent has with any program, group, or agency.

Establishing routines for communication helps maintain a relationship. A parent handbook complete with policies, procedures, information on routines, curriculum, and special activities serves well as the first written communication of the year. Newsletters, phone calls, and informal contacts at the beginning and end of the day when appropriate, as well as scheduled conferences are some ways to establish regular contact. Some families do not transport children to school and as such rarely get to see the teacher outside of more formal conferences. When this happens, a notebook can be sent back and forth between school and home to establish regular communication. If the start of the day is very hectic and it is not an appropriate time for parents to make contact, a place for them to leave notes which will be looked at within the first hour of school can be a very reassuring alternative.

Gelfer (1991) offers many practical suggestions for enhancing communications in developing teacher-parent partnerships. He suggests documenting all parent-teacher communications in a parent-teacher portfolio so that information maintained in an organized fashion is accessible at all times. Gelfer suggests the contents of such a portfolio may include: newsletters sent to parents; notes and requests made in writing by parents; telephone conversation notes; developmental checklists and observations completed by parents; home visits; parent-teacher conferences; memos sent to parents highlighting class and individual achievements; assessment reports; parent visits and participation; and letters of appreciation to parents who have helped the school program and workshops.

Stipek, Rosenblatt, and DiRocco (1994) further suggest that by sending home appropriate materials and suggestions, parents will be educated in the developmentally appropriate approaches being implemented in the classroom. In addition, inviting parents to school for programs planned to show them school activities and explain the purposes facilitates the developing partnership.

BARRIERS TO EFFECTIVE PARENT-TEACHER RELATIONSHIPS

The best plan for establishing parent-teacher relationships will not be effective if some barriers are not attended to. Some barriers develop over time while others are put into place as soon as the teacher and the parent meet.

■ *Security in carrying out established role*

When either the teacher or the parent are insecure in their own roles and responsibilities, misunderstandings may develop. It is important to work through these as quickly as possible so that the problems that may exist do not become magnified over time. Some parents are intimidated by what they hear from individuals outside the circle of the school their child attends. Instead of checking with the primary source of information, the teacher or school administrator, the parent becomes more concerned and agitated over time. Parents can be encouraged to learn the role of the school parent, advocating for their children while providing support for the people who teach their children. Parents who are secure in their parenting skills will most usually feel secure in contacting a teacher when there is a question. Teachers who are secure in their teaching roles will feel comfortable with the questions parents ask and understand that questioning is a healthy practice for parents who are learning a role, that of being a school parent.

■ *Communication problems*

Communication is key to establishing positive relationships between parents and teachers. Communication problems may develop when systems for establishing communication are not put into place at the start of the school year. Some parents are able to and feel comfortable with coming to school on a regular basis. They may volunteer in the classroom or participate in field trips. This regular contact allows parents to maintain ongoing contact with the teacher. This is the ideal form of communication. While it may seem to be ideal in theory, there may be problems with this form of communication. A parent may overstep the welcome extended by the teacher. Parents who spend considerable time in a classroom may feel it necessary to report to other parents. What they report and the manner in which they report may cause difficulties for other parents and for the teacher. The parent needs to be helped to understand how best to visit and carry the message of the nature of the classroom activity to other parents of children in the class. Some parents wait for the teacher to call or request a meeting and are offended when the meeting does not take place in the time frame the parent would like it to happen. A teacher cannot meet all parents within the first few days or weeks of school. The teacher can avoid this communication pitfall if information about parent contact is made available to all parents at the start of the year.

When contact is established, the parent and the teacher may not be communicating with each other in such a way as to make clear what the child is accomplishing in the classroom. If a teacher uses professional jargon, the parent may not understand. The parent does not want the teacher to think that what is being said seems to be in another language, so the effort at communication is wasted. The parent leaves with little or no usable information as well as a lowered self-esteem and possibly the attitude of never wanting to return for another meeting. The teacher who finds a way to inform a parent about a child without using jargon is a teacher who will probably experience a greater degree of success with parent communication. When a teacher is unable to meet with a parent due to transportation difficulties or work schedules, a home-to-school notebook will allow a regular communication opportunity for the teacher and the parent. A phone call home to share with parents a wonderful incident that happened at school will set the tone for positive communication in the future.

One of the greatest barriers to communication is a very rigid schedule of when a parent may call. It is certainly acceptable for a teacher to designate more appropriate times for parents to call with questions, comments, or concerns. It is important for the teacher to determine whether there are any parents in the class who would be unable to call during those designated times. If that is so, then those people can be informed that a phone call may certainly come at other times. It is vital for parents to know that teachers want to hear from them and are interested in being partners in the process of educating their children.

■ *Lack of understanding of cultural differences in practice*

One of the main barriers to establishing positive parent-teacher relationships is the lack of understanding of cultural differences. Culture is something that all people have but that influences them in different ways. Cultural, ethnic, and linguistic heritage has impact on beliefs, values, and behaviors (Lynch & Hanson, 1992). There is no right and no wrong, there is difference. Perceptions voiced by parents and teachers are well worth listening to because they inform both parties about what is important to them concerning children, school, and education. When parents and teachers respect the cultural diversity of the other, the relationship will be enhanced. Cultural norms concerning dress, toileting, foods, discipline, autonomy, and independence are often nonnegotiable. Parents carry out procedures with their children in the manner in which their parents implemented practices and procedures with them when they were children. The style of communication between parent and teacher may be greatly influenced by cultural patterns. These must be honored while other patterns may be introduced which have the potential for enhancing parent-teacher relationships.

Fears of criticism

When a teacher or a parent fears criticism from the other, this becomes a certain barrier to the development of an effective relationship. Fearing criticism stems from a feeling of insecurity in the skills one has or the perception that others will be in doubt about the skills one has. When a parent or teacher attempts to do something different, moving away from the norm, it might raise a fear of criticism. Daring to be different is commendable. If one dares to be different, one should be prepared to receive some amount of criticism until the innovative idea or practice becomes more comfortable for people to handle.

Criticism may be handled in two ways. When trying something new in the classroom, a written introduction to the new idea should help to support the innovation. If this introduction is followed by periodic updates as to the progress of the innovation, parents should feel informed and remain pleased. This will serve to deter any barriers from developing in the parent-teacher relationship.

Teachers who hide behind "professional" masks

A teacher may hide behind a professional mask when being questioned by a parent about practices in the classroom. Rather than answer from a personal perspective based on a strong knowledge base, the teacher might respond by informing the parent that the school, district, or state requires the practice. This might cause the parent to refrain from asking any further questions. This in turn may create a barrier between the teacher and the parent. The parent may perceive the teacher to be unapproachable and a person who merely adheres to regulations. When a parent questions a practice in terms of his or her own child, the teacher should remain open to discussion about the relevance of the procedure even though it may be state mandated.

Fear of failure

Regardless of whether a teacher is a veteran or a novice, each new class of children and their families have the potential for creating challenges. The start of a school year with new children, parents, and possibly new support persons can create the fear of not being able to meet the needs of all involved. If a teacher dwells on this at the start of the school, this manner of thinking may develop into a real fear of failure. Recalling past success plus renewed energy and spirit will prevent fear from developing into a real barrier.

Reactions to role

Often in the transition from one program or grade to another, there are major differences between how people perceive their roles. Some teachers feel very comfortable teaching but not very comfortable with the fact that some parents feel the role of teacher also is that of parent educator and counselor. If the teacher is comfortable with the role and has expertise in assisting parents to work through some problematic situations relating to children or other home conflicts, this will probably enhance the parent-teacher relationship. If the teacher is not comfortable, it needs to be made clear to the parent that while the teacher would like to help, she or he does not feel competent to give advice. The parent may think that the teacher just does not want to help. This can develop into a real relationship barrier. The teacher may make suggestions or referrals to the parent about professionals who do have the expertise to really provide help to the parent. While this means that the parents will need to get to know yet one more person, it will be well worth it in the long run. The concern demonstrated by the teacher in an attempt to help the parent obtain the right kind of help will most probably reinforce the parent-teacher relationship.

Time

Is there anyone who has enough time to really accomplish all that he or she would like to accomplish? Setting parent-teacher relationships as a priority still may mean that there will not be as much time spent building relationships with each parent as a teacher would wish. The concept of quality time may be an important one to consider. Finding the right time to work on relationship building means more than finding a great quantity of time. A smile, a nod, or a quick phone call may not take a lot of time but they are all meaningful efforts in building relationships. Merely thinking that it takes too much time to establish meaningful relationships with parents sets up immediate barriers. Even if this thought is not voiced, it has the potential to influence the interactions that take place between parents and the teacher. A little time goes a long way in breaking down barriers.

Busyness

The responsibilities teachers have certainly do not allow for much free time. When a teacher appears to be extremely busy all the time that parents are in the classroom, the level of activity can serve as a barrier to establishing parent-teacher relationships. A parent who may be shy or just inexperienced in forging relationships with teachers may be overwhelmed by the level of activity. The result of this may be a parent who drops a child off at the door and leaves very quickly. A barrier that does not need to be there is established inadvertently.

- ***School a place for children not parents***

The notion that school is a place for children and not for parents is a certain barrier to building relationships. The time has come for the implementation of schools for the 21st century concept first introduced by Zigler in 1987. This concept supports the idea that the neighborhood school is for everyone and that parents very much belong in the school and should work in close relationship with teachers to create better programs and more options for the children and families who attend the school.

- ***Administrative policies***

Even though the classroom teacher may be a strong advocate of building parent-teacher relationships, the administration of the school may not send out the same message. Parents can sense when parent involvement is given token value in a school. Creating token slots on specific committees so that the annual report is able to list parent participation does little to help teachers develop effective parent relationships.

- ***Personal problems***

Teachers as well as parents may find themselves being involved in personal problems from time to time. When these personal problems are brought to the classroom situation, they serve as real barriers to the development of effective parent-teacher relationships. Personal problems not addressed in a timely fashion often fester and increase the distance between parents and teachers.

PARTNERSHIPS WITH CONSULTANTS AND SPECIALISTS

Most parents do not have the need to encounter consultants or specialists during the early childhood years. These parents have children who are developing along a normal sequence of behavior and skill acquisition. An occasional question or concern about development is usually able to be answered by a teacher, a relative, or the regular pediatrician who provides care for the child.

Those parents who regularly encounter consultants or specialists are those with children with disabilities. From the time a child is born with easily identifiable disabilities, or at a later point when the child is identified as having a disability, the parent is placed in regular contact with an individual or several individuals who are specialists in intervention. The success of this relationship depends on many factors but the primary factor influencing the outcome of the work with consultants or specialists is the degree to which all parties involved subscribe to the notion that they are in partnership with each other. Regardless of the level of expertise of the specialists, the family is the first source of information concerning the child and they are the individuals who provide for the greatest degree of continuity for the child throughout his or her life. Specialists are expert in identifying deficit areas and developing programs for the remediation of these deficits. They see children in clinical or classroom settings. In early intervention they see children in their home settings. The parent is the one who sees the child in the home and the community and is responsible for the implementation of intervention for the longest, most sustained periods of time, and across the greatest variety of settings. The family is the center of the child's life. Without a true sense of partnership, considerable time is wasted and the business of helping a child to improve in the areas of deficit will not be as effective.

True partnership develops from an atmosphere of being family-centered. The philosophy of family-centered care and education describes a collaborative partnership between parents and professionals in the ongoing pursuit of being responsive to strengths, needs, hopes, dreams, and aspirations of families with children with disabilities. A partnership means that all those involved in working with the child share the vision the family has for that child (Holden, Kaiser, Sykes & Tyreee, 1993). The manner in which this vision is shared and implemented is through joint meetings in which the parents are considered key team members. They have the freedom of choice as to how they will be involved and communication is multidirectional. When this happens, all parties gain from the experience. The one who stands to gain the most is the child.

The needs of the family should be considered. While a specialist may feel it is critical to work on a particular skill at the time, the family may be more interested in working on a different skill which would make life easier for the family and would help to further integrate the child into the fabric of the family. Is one skill a higher priority than another? Which skill should take precedence for the attention of all involved? In a true partnership there is give and take but what makes sense is to work on what helps the family and community to be more accepting of the child. That acceptance will make things easier for the family. In turn, the family members should wind up feeling better about the child and themselves. From these feelings, there should be renewed energy to work on other goals.

An example of a family concern might center on transportation safety. Some parents are extremely concerned about transportation safety issues. Some children seem to be able to get out of every car seat manufactured and thus pose a threat to safety. A child who is difficult to transport may not seem to be the type of issue that should be addressed at school but if the child cannot be safely transported, the child will not be able to attend school. This becomes a serious burden for the family and in turn will deprive the child of valuable educational time. Working on this issue in partnership with the family will make it safer for the child and family and allow the child to attend school. Once the child is able to travel safely, all involved will benefit.

When a **partnership** is developed, children make gains at home and they make gains at school. Sometimes a child will engage in a positive behavior at school that he or she will not do at home. A child who feeds himself at school but will only eat at home if mother feeds him is a good example of what a partnership can help with. Having an open environment in which the parent feels free to visit and observe the child feeding unassisted will help the child and the parent as well as all others involved. The behavior of self-feeding which is natural to the environment in which all the children are encouraged to help themselves may not be natural to the home environment. When the child learns that the parent now knows that he is able to feed himself and is proud of him for accomplishing this feat, the child may slowly change the behavior at home. This is an important behavior to change at home because as the child gets older, it becomes more and more inappropriate for the mother to continue feeding him. The mother can be encouraged to find new behaviors to help the child with, thus shifting her time and attention to the encouragement of new behaviors. Sitting down and talking about how shifting attention may help the child is something that can come as an outgrowth of the atmosphere of partnership with parents.

Partnership blossoms under communication. All the forms of communication previously identified are appropriate here as well. A note, a call, newsletters, communication books are all tools that allow for the maintenance of communication. Nothing is as good as being there yourself but it is often inappropriate or impossible for some families to remain at school during the day. Some children do not participate in activities or respond to anyone in the environment when a family member is in the environment. Family responsibilities may preclude the family from spending time at the school. Capturing a picture of the child for the family informs family members of the kinds of activities the child is involved in during the day. Often, they are pleasantly surprised at the information they receive.

CONSULTATION

Recognition of the parent as a viable consultant to the teachers who work with the child saves considerable time and effort. The parent and child come to a program with a history. There are techniques and procedures in place which have been developed over time which do not need to be reinvented by teachers and specialists at school. When a parent asks the teacher what information is needed when the child enters school, the teacher should tell the parent that everything that can be shared will be willingly accepted. A teacher might not know all the right questions to ask because the teacher is just beginning to get to know the child. The parent may have a lot of information that he or she thinks the teacher might think irrelevant and so does not offer it. This may mean that valuable time is lost in attempting to learn as much about the child as possible.

The family also is needed to serve as consultants to the specialists who work with the child during the school day. When the specialist undertakes an evaluation of the child, a very special piece of the evaluation should be consultation from the parents and extended family members who may have primary caregiving responsibilities. The information gathered from the family can save valuable time for direct service or support in the classroom. The specialist who spends less time with the child than either the teachers or parents is often looked to for the most information. While the information these people have is technical and specific to an area of disability, the information may not be relevant to the full-day picture of the child as a member of the family. The family can provide information about sibling interaction, neighborhood response to the child, the daily and weekly routines of the family that will round out the picture of the child as a member of the family which cannot possibly be obtained from an in-school evaluation. This information may provide alternative ideas for therapeutic intervention which will have immediate impact on the child and the family. This may also be able to be translated into appropriate school goals for the child and for other children as well.

Teachers and specialists know what is appropriate for most children to work on at a particular age. They do not know nor can they anticipate the family circumstances of all children. Knowing more about a family will help them to plan and implement programs much more effectively. When a teacher or specialist makes suggestions to a family, it is done with the best school interests of the child in mind. Unless there is real communication going on, the teacher and specialists cannot know that the mother has a serious time commitment devoted to the care of an elderly parent or that the father is on an extended business trip which has impact on the family schedule and places considerable burden on the mother. When an innocent request sent home asking the parent to work on colors or shapes comes out of the lunch box, it may not receive any attention at all. The teacher or specialist may interpret this to mean that the parent does not care and is not an active participant in the development of the child. What they do not know is that time is the critical variable and when something has to give, the child and skill acquisition may have to wait. Again, the more teachers know without prying, the better equipped they will be to plan and implement intervention.

When developing individualized education plans (IEP) or individual family service plan (IFSP) goals and objectives, parents are a very important piece of the process. Parents already know which activities are of interest to the child. Offering this information can assist the teachers and specialists in developing goals and objectives that can be immediately translated into appropriate classroom activities.

The role of the specialist is child-oriented but in that role, the specialist serves as a consultant to the family. This is done to extend the benefit of the therapeutic intervention at school and to bridge school to home. The specialist has the expertise and potential to effect major change in areas that are very meaningful to families. This meaningful intervention needs to take place within an atmosphere of respect for individuals, their values, their perspectives, and their needs. Someone who wants to consult in a manner that tells the family how to do something and how often to do it regardless of family circumstances is not going to make inroads with the family.

Sometimes the most meaningful assistance a specialist can provide for the family is a picture of how well the child is doing. Some families dwell on the deficits and the discrepancy between their children and other children. A specialist is able to consult with the family and support them in their endeavors to keep working with the child.

Consultation from parents, from specialists, and from teachers is a slowly developing process. Most usually, all of the parties who find themselves working together did not choose to be working together. They were placed together by virtue of geographic location, area of expertise, or availability. It takes time to build the trust that enables people to reach their highest potential. Learning more about parents and how to effectively work with parents will smooth the process along. Most teachers and specialists do not have specialized courses in working with parents as part of their education and training. This means that there may be some errors made in an attempt to maximize the therapeutic intervention process. Recognizing that trust is built slowly, specialists cannot come into a family picture and have the family immediately work at 100 percent effectiveness with them. A specialist professionally prepared and educated in the area of disability that a child has may not know what it is like to raise a child with that kind of disability. By sharing skills with the family, the specialist allows the family to know that he or she is ready for information from them about their child and will be sensitive to their concerns and issues.

Collaboration

Collaboration is different from partnerships. Collaboration is a process through which parties who see different aspects of a problem can constructively explore the differences and search for solutions that go beyond their own limited vision of what is possible. Collaboration is based on the notion that the more heads put together the more effective the solution (Gray, 1989).

The benefits of collaboration have been recognized in the legislation that identifies family members as key decision makers for their children during transition planning. The PL 99-457 mandates that the Individualized Family Service Plan (IFSP) must include steps that lend support to the family during the age three transition from birth to three services into a preschool, placement. School-age regulations, including those for preschool allow "parent counseling and training" to be listed as a related service in the Individualized Educational Plan (IEP) (Strickland & Turnbull, 1990).

Collaboration promotes a relationship in which family members and professionals work together to ensure the best services for the child and family. The basis of a collaborative relationship is the recognition and respect for the knowledge, skills, and experiences that families and professionals bring to the relationship. Trust is a critical part of a collaborative relationship. The trust must be of professionals by families and of families by professionals. Collaborative relationships facilitate open communication so that both parents and professionals may express themselves freely. The cultural traditions, values, and diversity of families are acknowledged and honored in collaborative relationships where negotiation among all parties is an essential parameter for success. The mutual commitment of families, professionals, and communities to meeting the needs of children and their families is the foundation upon which family/professional collaboration is built. Collaboration paves the way for all those involved with a child and the child's family to come together to begin sharing ideas and developing an action plan that is mutually agreeable and mutually beneficial.

Collaboration is essential to building and implementing developmentally appropriate integrated programs for young children. Collaboration builds relationships and allows the objectives developed by each member of the team designated to address all the concerns of a particular family to meld together instead of remaining as isolated specific objectives. Collaboration allows each member of the team to support the work of the other and integrate the purposes of all types of intervention in as many activities as possible.

Collaboration teams vary according to the needs of the child and the family. Some teams have three or four members while others have more than eight members. The size of the team sometimes has impact on the degree of collaboration. The logistics of getting that many people together in one place at one time sometimes interferes with the frequency of the meetings. The time spent trying to establish an agreeable meeting schedule is worth the effort regardless of how frustrating the process may be.

When people collaborate they share responsibility for and ownership of decisions (Holden, Kaiser, Sykes & Tyreee, 1993). Instead of decisions being handed down to a specialist from a an administrator, decisions are made collaboratively. Collaboration requires several factors to be in place in order for it to be effective. Collaboration requires communication, time and planning, coordination by all team members, establishment of common goals, networking, and most importantly it requires change. Collaboration may result in changing the focus of services from pull-out to the provision of services within the classroom. It may mean a shift in orientation from looking at the disabilities of a child to the abilities of a child and then building program interventions around those positive attributes. The degree to which teachers engage in collaboration is guided by an individual level of commitment. Shifting the focus to how "we" can provide access to the services needed for children will come to mean that everyone will be operating by the same rules so that there will be no sides and no arguments (Gallagher, LaMontagne & Johnson, 1994).

WORKING WITH TEACHERS AND SPECIALISTS TO PLAN FOR TRANSITIONS

There are several times when transition points occur for young children. Careful consideration and planning prior to the **transition** will assist all involved in making as easy a transition as possible.

Transitions from Home to School

One of the most difficult things parents ever have to do is move their children from the focus and security of their home to the world outside the home, the world of school. For some parents this is a very traumatic decision and process. The process can be eased considerably if the transition is planned for. For a child without disabilities, the family usually follows the procedure of talking to friends, neighbors, or relatives whose children are in preschools or have already entered public schools. Upon the recommendation of these persons, the family visits a variety of preschool settings, narrows down their choices, and makes the final selection. For some families, this decision is more difficult than choosing the right college. It is the first in a series of decisions that the family will make relative to a child's education and it carries with it the first real commitment to separation. When a family has a child with disabilities, there are more factors to consider when "shopping" for a preschool program. Important factors to consider are whether the school has a prior of history of accepting children with disabilities and the degree of satisfaction felt by the school, the parents, and the specialists working with the child. For a parent of a child with disabilities the appropriateness of the school program is certainly critical but the degree of acceptance of the child is also critical. Diamond and LeFurgy (1994) surveyed 141 parents of preschool children with and without disabilities enrolled in integrated and self-contained classrooms. The surveys were conducted at the beginning and at the conclusion of the school year. By the end of the school year, parents whose children had been in the integrated program held more positive attitudes toward integration than parents whose children did not attend integrated programs.

Making the transition to preschool for families with children with disabilities means getting to know a whole new set of professionals ranging from the classroom teacher to the administrator, from the specialists to the new families involved with the school. It means developing trust with another group of people and for many families it means that the child will be spending less time at home than before. It also means that the location of the child's education and therapeutic intervention will be at school rather than at home. This is a major difference from what existed prior to preschool. Helping the parent to remain connected to the entire educational process is key to the success of the program and the development of a healthy school-oriented attitude on the part of the parent.

Transitions from Preschool to Grade School

Successful experiences in the transition into the preschool environment will pave the way for the transition from preschool to grade school. There are many factors which come into the planning for this transition. Transportation may be an added feature although many children with disabilities are transported during their preschool years. Differences in the focus of services may become more pronounced with the family feeling less involved in the decision-making process as the child gets older and moves from one grade to another. Relationships with service personnel who served as the mainstay of emotional support for the family are formally ended during these transitions. This can cause feelings of abandonment for many families. Making new connections is not always easy because the family may not be in close contact with all the players. If the parent does not transport the child to school, it becomes more difficult to connect with the service providers on a regular basis. Some families may be quite comfortable with less contact as time passes. Transition planning does not have a recipe and will vary from family to family. They may feel as though the more difficult aspects of program development for their youngsters has been taken care of and now they can enjoy a kind of maintenance level of contact.

Family members who themselves grow and develop over time as the child grows and develops will find themselves moving from a high level of dependence on the various support personnel who were so critical to the welfare of the child with disabilities at the start of the process to a greater level of independence as a family and as procurers of services for their child. They may find themselves moving from very close ties with a case manager and therapists to less close and less formal contact systems. The family will have developed a resilience and a system for operating on a daily basis. From time to time, the family may need more support or a different type of support as their needs change due to relocation, change in job situations, change in caregivers, or the loss of regular respite care providers. They will usually utilize those services only until their lives return to what is normal for them. Some families with children with disabilities undergo several transitions in service provision during the course of the day. When everyone and everything is in place, life is pleasant. When one person or one aspect of a program is not in place, it may throw everything else off. That is the point at which a family may seek additional support.

Planning Transitions for Families

Families of children with disabilities often feel isolated from activities of the early childhood community, such as parenting classes and play groups (Hanline & Hanson, 1989; Stagg & Catron, 1986). Therefore it is very important to plan for the involvement of parents with children with disabilities as an essential step toward achieving full participation. Effective inclusion depends on how comfortable a family feels and the kind of welcome extended to the family by all concerned (Galant & Hanline, 1993). In planning for transition from one level program or one type of service to another, the assessment of readiness for transition may demonstrate that the child with or without disabilities is ready for transition. If the entire family is assessed, it might be found that the parents and extended family members are the ones who are not ready for transition. This needs to be considered as part of the transition planning process. After any transition the child will continue to receive attention and services. The parents may not know how to be involved in any formal or informal way and have a real need for someone to provide them with support. This may be true of any family. Children are often eager to move on while parents want to hold on to the "baby" in the young child for a bit longer. It is difficult for some parents to see that their children still need them when the children seem to be developing a greater sense of independence. Some child development education for the parents so that they are aware of the important role they still play throughout the development of the child will reinforce their self-esteem. Through continued exploration of their role as parents, their role definition will change developmentally as their child changes developmentally.

SUMMARY

The roles played by parents and families are key to the success of a child's education. Parents benefit from education and attention during the developmental years just as children do. Regardless of whether the child has disabilities or not, parents should be an important consideration in planning for and implementing early childhood programs. When parents feel welcome and comfortable, they will participate in school programs. Teachers, children, specialists, other parents, and administrators all benefit from parent participation. It is important to analyze the school environment to discern any barriers to family participation. Sometimes it is as or more difficult for parents to make transitions as it is for children to transition. Often, the identity parents develop as parents hinges on the abilities or disabilities of their children. The world comes to know parents through their children. Sometimes the fact that people who happen to be parents cease to be identified as their own persons once they have children is what hampers them from making easy transitions from one type of program to another. When teachers forge a relationship with parents, getting to know who they are as individuals is a very important part of the process.

DISCUSSION QUESTIONS

1) Describe one or more situations when you observed a teacher facilitating parent involvement when it appeared that the parent was not going to easily become part of the group or program.
2) You sent home two newsletters containing important information about upcoming events, permission slips required, etc. One particular child assures you that the newsletters have been handed over to the parents. You have received nothing back from them. You are concerned about the level of involvement of this family and want to contact them. Try to think of all the means possible to establish communication with these parents taking into account reasons why the parents have not responded to date.
3) Design a plan for establishing communication with parents of children in your classroom. In your plan, include the rationale for each form of and occasion for communication over the school year. Will the approach change over time? Why?

4) The parent of a child in your class is challenging you about what the parent perceives to be "a lack of academics" in the program. You have presented all the parents with written information about the developmentally appropriate approach to planning and implementing curriculum. You have invited the parent to visit the classroom. The parent visited once when the children acted out a story they had been reading. The parent seems to spend considerable time talking to other parents at arrival and dismissal times. What can you do to help this parent understand the process that is taking place in the classroom and the importance of the process?
5) Your goal for the year is to have 100 percent parent participation. You are not concerned about the nature of the participation but you want each parent (or family representative) to be involved in something. Create a "menu" of opportunities for parents that reflects a variety of opportunities building on a variety of interests and skills.
6) You plan to accompany a family to a PPT meeting for their child. The focus of the meeting is planning for transition to first grade. The family is uneasy about the move to what they perceive to be a more academically demanding environment. What can you help them do ahead of time to prepare for the meeting so that they will feel more comfortable in their role? What can you do at the meeting to make sure the parents hear what they need to hear?

REFERENCES

Berger, E. (1991). *Parents as partners in education: The school and home working together.* 3rd ed. New York: Macmillan Publishing Company.

Boutte, G., Keepler, D. Tyler, V., & Terry, B. (1992). Effective techniques for involving "difficult" parents. *Young Children, 47*(3), 19–22.

Boyce, G., White, K., & Kerr, B. (1993). The effectiveness of adding a parent involvement component to an existing center-based program for children with disabilities and their families. *Early Education and Development,* 4(4), 327–345.

Derman-Sparks, L., & the A.B.C. Task Force. (1989). *Anti-bias curriculum: Tools for empowering young children.* Washington, DC: National Association for the Education of Young Children.

Diamond, K., & LeFurgy, W. (1994). Attitudes of parents of preschool children toward integration. *Early Education and Development, 5*(1), 69–77.

Dinnebeil, L., & Rule, S. (1994). Congruence between parents' and professionals' judgments about the development of young children with disabilities: A review of the literature. *Topics in Early Childhood Special Education, 14*(1), 1–25.

Ehly, S., Conoley, J., & Rosenthal, D. (1985). *Working with parents of exceptional children.* St. Louis: Mosby College Publishing.

Fine, M., (Ed.) (1989). The second handbook on parent education—Contemporary perspectives. San Diego: Academic Press, Inc.

Galant, K., & Hanline, M. (1993). Parental attitudes toward mainstreaming young children with disabilities. *Childhood Education, 69*(5), 293–297.

Gallagher, R., LaMontagne, M., & Johnson, L. (1994). Early intervention—The collaborative challenge. In L. Johnson, R. Gallagher, M. LaMontagne, and J. Jordan, J. Gallagher, P. Hutinger, M. Karnes (Eds.), *Meeting early intervention challenges—Issues from birth to three.* (pp. 279–287). Baltimore: Paul H. Brookes Publishing Co.

Gelfer, J. (1991). Teacher-parent partnerships: Enhancing communications. *Childhood Education, 67*(3), 164–167.

Gestwicki, C. (1987). *Home, school and community relations: A guide to working with parents.* New York: Delmar Publishers Inc.

Gray, B. (1989). *Collaborating: Finding common ground for multiparty problems.* San Francisco: Jossey-Bass Publishers.

Hanline, M. & Hanson, M. (1989). Integration considerations for infants and toddlers with multiple disabilities. *Journal of the Association for Persons with Severe Handicaps. 14*(3), 178–183.

Holden, L., Kaiser, M., Sykes, D., & Tyreee, R. (1993). *Quilting integration: A technical assistance guide on integrated early childhood programs.* Columbus, OH: The Early Integration Training Project Center for Special Needs Populations.

Innocenti, M., Hollinger, P., Escobar, C., & White, K. (1993). The cost-effectiveness of adding one type of parent involvement to an early intervention program. *Early Education and Development, 4*(4), 306–326.

Kunreuther, S. (1970). A preschool exchange: Black mothers speak and a white teacher listens. *Children, 17,* 91–96.

Lynch, E., & Hanson, M. (1992). *Developing cross-cultural competence.* Baltimore: Paul H. Brookes Publishing.

McNaughton, D. (1994). Measuring parent satisfaction with early childhood intervention programs: Current practice, problems, and future perspectives. *Topics in Early Childhood Special Education, 14*(1), 26–48.

McWilliam, P., & Bailey, D. (1993). *Working together with children & families—Case studies in early intervention.* Baltimore: Paul H. Brookes Publishing Co.

Morrison, G. (1995). *Early childhood education today.* Columbus, OH: Merrill.

Powell, D. (1989). *Families and early childhood programs.* Washington, DC: National Association for the Education of Young Children.

Rich, D. (1987). *Teachers and parents: An adult-to-adult approach.* Washington, DC: A National Education Association Publication.

Rosenkoetter, S., Hains, A., & Fowler, S. (1994). *Bridging early services for children with special needs and their families—A practical guide for transition planning.* Baltimore: Paul H. Brookes Publishing Co.

Schulz, J. (1987). *Parents and professionals in special education.* Boston: Allyn and Bacon, Inc.

Stagg, V., & Catron, T. (1986). Networks of social supports across the life span. In R. Fewell & P. Vadasy (Eds.), *Families of handicapped children: Needs and supports across the life span* (pp. 279–295). Austin, TX: Pro Ed.

Stipek, D., Rosenblatt, L., & DiRocco, L. (1994). Making parents your allies. *Young Children, 49*(3), 4–9.

Strickland, B., & Turnbull, A. (1990). *Developing and implementing individualized educational programs.* Columbus, OH: Merrill/Macmillan.

Turnbull, H., & Turnbull, A. (1985). *Parents speak out—Then and now.* Columbus: Merrill Publishing Company.

Zigler, E. (1987). *School of the twenty-first century.* New Haven: Yale University Press.

ADDITIONAL READINGS

Galinsky, E. (1988). Parents and teacher-caregivers: Sources of tension, sources of support. *Young Children, 43*(3), 4–15.

Laosa, L., & Sigel, I. (Eds.). (1982) *Families as learning environments for children.* New York: Plenum.

Stone, J. (1987). *Teacher-parent relationships.* Washington, DC: National Association for the Education of Young Children.

CHAPTER 14

Specialists as Members of the Team

KEY TERMS

team approaches
multidisciplinary team model
interdisciplinary model
transdisciplinary model
paraprofessional
service coordination
interagency coordination and collaboration

Specialists are professionals who work with children with disabilities to attempt to strengthen weak areas or remediate deficits. Specialists are not educated as classroom teachers but are educated to have specialized expertise in a given domain. **Therapists** are involved in evaluation, therapy service planning, parent and staff training, and monitoring children's programs. The types of specialists who work with children and teachers in early childhood settings include but are not limited to speech and language therapists, occupational therapists, physical therapists, vision consultants, assistive technology consultants, and special educators. These specialists are made available to early childhood programs to enhance the level of service provided to children and provide direct therapy but mostly to work through the environment to provide the intervention necessary for the child to achieve maximum potential. These specialists work in partnership with others in the environment and consult with parents to encourage generalization to the home setting and to gather information about the child in the home environment.

ROLES OF VARIOUS SUPPORT SPECIALISTS

In order to have a better understanding of the nature of direct therapeutic services, it is important to understand the differences and similarities of the roles of therapists most usually found working with children with disabilities in inclusive environments. The following role definitions and descriptions should prove helpful to those individuals who have not yet begun to work in integrated settings as well as to clarify questions for those individuals who need it.

Occupational therapists work from a developmental rather than a medical base. Therapy is based on the age of the child and is directed to enhance the learning potential of the child. It emphasizes gross and fine motor coordination, self-help skills, vestibular (balance as determined by the inner ear), tactile, kinesthetic (sensory knowledge of one's body movements), and perceptual motor development (mental interpretation of sensation and movement based on these sensations). It directs the emphasis of all these areas to adaptive behavior and play, sensory, motor, and posture development in order to help the child develop functional skills and to minimize the impact of the disability in the school and home environment. Development of the functional skills of eating, dressing, and playing often require adapting the environment in which these skills are demonstrated (Deiner, 1993). This may mean providing adaptive equipment to enable the child to engage in a specific behavior more effectively. In the case of eating, a special spoon or bowl may make the process much easier for the child. The therapist may discover that the child needs to learn a special technique or that the child may need fewer distractions when engaging in the behavior being encouraged. In addition, an occupational therapist may observe that teachers or parents might enjoy more success with a particular child if shown another way to encourage certain self-help skills.

Physical therapists work towards preventing further disability by developing, improving, or restoring more efficient muscle function and maintaining maximum motor function. Children who wear prosthetic devices or who use wheelchairs or other adaptive equipment benefit from working with a physical therapist. The therapist works on range of motion, posture, muscle tone, strength, balance, and gross motor skills (Deiner, 1993). Working within the inclusive setting allows the therapist to see the range of positions appropriate for the placement of the child during the normal activities of the school day. The therapist is instrumental in identifying appropriate furniture and equipment for correct positioning in order to maximize the learning situations for the children in therapy. Children who are involved in classroom activities are often more motivated to participate in therapeutic activities with the therapist when the activities can include or be carried out near the peer group.

Speech and language therapists work on the development and production of speech and the use of that speech to develop communication. The classroom setting is the ideal situation for working on speech and language because there are so many adult and peer models to use in order to motivate the child with speech or communication delay. The speech and language therapist endeavors not only to encourage the production and reception of sounds and words but to enable children to use those words to communicate needs and thoughts. Many children with disabilities are very effective and efficient at getting what they need or want by shaping anticipation on the part of the adults and peers in their environments. It is sometimes very difficult to alter this pattern of nonverbal communication. The speech and language therapist will be able to assist teachers and parents to develop systems for modifying the environment which will in turn motivate the child to begin the process of verbal communication. If the development of verbal communication is not a possibility, a variety of assisted or alternative communication approaches will be tried until one is found that is effective and as portable as possible so it will be available to the child regardless of the setting. The speech and language therapist works in conjunction with teachers, parents, and other support specialists to maximize the child's experience in the classroom.

There are other support specialists who may provide indirect service to a child. This means that they will probably not be in the classroom on a regular weekly basis. Their service may be provided more through consultation to the classroom teachers, parents, and other support specialists. Their consultation services may only be required on an annual basis as the child's progress is evaluated and determinations are made concerning appropriate programming for the following school year.

In the past, therapeutic intervention during the early childhood years was provided in a "pull-out" manner which meant that a child was removed from the activity in the classroom and received therapy on a one-to-one basis in another room. Current practice is to provide as much therapy as possible through the natural environment and the natural activities that occur in the environment (Leister, Koonce & Nisbet, 1993). In this way, teachers are able to receive assistance in appropriate procedures for individual children while integrating the child with disabilities into the regular classroom activities.

UNDERSTANDING THE CLASSROOM CULTURE—HOW DOES THERAPY FIT?

In order to maximize the experience children have in the classroom, specialists who are new to the provision of direct service within the classroom environment may need the input of the classroom teacher to understand what is happening in the classroom and why. It should never be assumed that each person coming into an early childhood environment is a knowledgeable early childhood practitioner. Taking the time to explain the developmentally appropriate, integrated theme and activities being implemented will provide a framework for intervention. When a specialist understands the goals of planned activities, the specialist can integrate the therapy into the existing activity more effectively and feel more comfortable about the therapy. Serving the needs of a child with disabilities in the regular classroom translates into less direct control over therapeutic activity for specialists who were used to providing direct clinical therapy. Provision of service in the classroom does allow the therapist more control over and far more opportunity to work on the generalization and application of acquired skills. This is certainly an important feature of classroom-based therapy.

The role of support specialist in an inclusive early childhood setting is more complex than that of a traditional ancillary staff member. To enable a child with disabilities to function more effectively in an inclusive setting and to maximize the educational experience provided in that setting, the roles of the specialist must include those of team member, consultant, trainer, direct service provider, and evaluator. (Peters, Bunse, Carlson, Doede, Glasenapp, Haydon, Lehman, Templeman & Udell, 1992). The roles these specialists play are not carried out in isolation but through interactions with regular and special educators, directors or principals, coordinators, other therapists, and, very importantly, the parents.

TEAM APPROACHES TO SERVICE DELIVERY

Team approaches were developed to preclude collections of specialists from pursuing their own interests. Prior to this approach to service delivery, specialists would observe and assess a child, plan an intervention, and implement an intervention. The time, funds, and emotions spent in the process of assessment and service delivery often resulted in parents and children who were fatigued and confused as to the messages they received from the specialists. Some of the messages delivered were in direct conflict with each other. As the field develops, different models of service delivery evolve which better meet the needs of children, parents, and teachers.

The ***multidisciplinary team model*** was the initial attempt to organize related service professionals to work together as a team. Although team model members appear to work together, they actually function fairly separately. They may share common goals for a child but they basically view and treat the child in terms of their own individual areas of expertise. Each member of a multidisciplinary team typically conducts an assessment and develops and implements a discipline specific program. This program implementation is done with little communication with the other team members. While this was a positive, early attempt to build a team, the weakness in this approach necessitated the development of other models which fostered greater collaboration and communication between team members as well as a greater level of family involvement.

The ***interdisciplinary model,*** evolved during an attempt to respond to many of the problems identified in the multidisciplinary model. In this service delivery model, there is a formal structure for interaction and communication among team members. This model also includes families as members of the team. Team members conduct independent assessments and then come together to discuss their results and develop intervention plans in a cooperative fashion. Each team member implements the part of the plan that relates to his or her discipline. One of the main problems with this approach is the existence of professional turf. When team members do not understand the training expertise of other members, power struggles, and role confusion may take place. The parent may feel caught between professionals when this happens and thus find this situation quite uncomfortable. Teachers may also find the situation uncomfortable.

The ***transdisciplinary model,*** supported as the best practice in the field, attempts to rectify the problems that exist in the other models. The model is based on the belief that the child's development must be integrated and interactive and that the child must be served within the context of the family. The family is viewed as full, active, and participating members of the team. The team members accept each other's knowledge and strengths. Assessments are often conducted with the family. The team develops an integrated service plan based on the priorities stated by the family. The needs of the family and resources available within the family are considered. The intervention plan is usually implemented by one or two team members who are identified as primary care providers, in conjunction with the child's family. Members of the team provide cross-training to other members of the team in order to facilitate the process. This effective approach requires extensive training and small caseloads. A variation of this model includes an indirect, integrated therapy approach. This approach delivers related services by incorporating therapy goals within the context of naturally occurring activities in the school, the home, or both. This indirect therapy implies that therapists will serve as consultants while other team members assume the role of direct service providers (Bunse, 1992).

SUPPORT SPECIALISTS IN THE ASSESSMENT ROLE

The ideal manner for support specialists to provide service involves the coordination of assessments with other support specialists as well as with classroom personnel. The regular classroom routine provides a multitude of opportunities for assessment. It also provides specialists with situations not normally available to them in more clinical assessment situations. If the specialists and classroom teachers are to function as true team members, one person from the team can function as the facilitator so that during the regular activities the child being assessed has the opportunity to engage in the behaviors being observed and evaluated. When assessment is conducted in this manner, the child's strengths and areas of need can be identified. The need for specific items of specialized equipment, materials, or assistive technology can be identified. The type of service necessary can be identified at that point. The service need identified may range from several visits per week, to staff and family consultation, to a determination of no additional service necessary. When service is recommended, the specialist will develop goals and objectives for the child and identify a list of adaptive equipment. During the course of the school year additional adaptive equipment needs may be identified as the child masters certain skills and develops new behaviors. Additional or alternative adaptive equipment needs are also identified during the year as the child changes physically. The physical changes a child experiences may be due to growth, correction, or deterioration of the physical condition.

It is not always possible for all support specialists to be in the same place at the same time. If this is what happens, assessments may be conducted by all the support specialists at different times within a close time frame. At the conclusion of the assessment period, the specialists, classroom teacher(s), parents, and any other persons involved come together to plan for the development of common goals for the child. At this time the group will also determine whether service will be provided in terms of direct individual therapy to be conducted within the classroom environment or whether consultation will be provided. In certain cases, direct individual therapy may need to be conducted in an isolated setting due to a medical procedure or the necessity for removal of an article of clothing during therapy.

Measuring the progress of individual children with disabilities is certainly within the domain of each person working with the child both inside and outside the classroom. The support specialists are particularly responsible for monitoring the progress of the child within the areas of disability they address. That is not to say that each of the persons involved with the child does not contribute to the intervention and assessment of the child. Each person contributes a different perspective that when all added together constitute a total picture of the whole child.

SUPPORT SPECIALISTS IN THE CONSULTANT ROLE

Consultation may be provided in a variety of ways and to a variety of persons. Consultation may take the form of demonstration of skills and techniques so that the classroom teacher and parents may learn the technique and implement it consistent with the manner in which the specialist implements the technique. Another form of consultation is in the identification of specific activities for enhancing the use of certain body parts that are underutilized. Consultation may also identify resources for the classroom teacher to use with the child (Abraham, Morris & Wald, 1993). Consultation may even be provided to age-appropriate peers who wish to facilitate the inclusion of a child with disabilities. Support specialists who observe a special bond between able and disabled peers may find that a small amount of time spent supporting the helping behavior of the child without disabilities will result in a larger payoff. Children often respond more readily to their peers than they do to adults, regardless of whether the adult is a parent or a professional. It is important to inform the child of ways in which to motivate or assist a child with disabilities but it is also important to ensure that the child without disabilities is not "assigned" to the friend with disabilities. Children gravitate toward each other because they genuinely want to. Teachers want to be careful not to ruin a child's natural desire to include their friend with disabilities by forcing a relationship based more in responsibility than in fun.

A support specialist may provide in-service training to teachers and classroom volunteers to inform them of appropriate lifting, transferring or positioning techniques for individual children. If new teachers join the team, the specialist may design a specific time to provide in-service for them so that the information comes directly from the specialist rather than from the other teachers.

FIG 14.1 Specialists work closely with children with disabilities.

THE PARAPROFESSIONAL IN THE INCLUSIVE CLASSROOM

Although not considered "specialists," paraprofessionals make a valuable contribution to the inclusion of children with disabilities. Paraprofessionals deliver early intervention services within the context of home-based service delivery. They also serve as facilitators of inclusion in center-based programs (Brown & Rule, 1993). Very often it is the **paraprofessional** who becomes responsible for the implementation of the majority of the goals and objectives of the child's individualized education program (IEP). The paraprofessional as the person physically closest to the child for the majority of the school day, is usually able to provide the most information about the child and the success of activities and therapeutic interventions designed by the specialists in conjunction with the entire team. While there is a high level of responsibility that goes along with the job as well as a dependence on the paraprofessional for information and the implementation of a sophisticated program for a child, the paraprofessional is often the least trained or educated individual on the team. Some states have or are in the process of developing training programs for paraprofessionals that allow them to participate in a career ladder.

The paraprofessional should be included in as many meetings about the child as possible. The paraprofessional often winds up having the closest contact with the parent of any of the individuals who serve on the team and a great sense of trust develops as a result.

FIG 14.2 Paraprofessionals implement procedures suggested by specialists.

FIG 14.3 Paraprofessionals work as part of the teaching team.

MANAGING AND COORDINATING SERVICE DELIVERY

Moving within and among the many services available for families and children is not an easy task. The most informed family will find it an overwhelming and time-consuming responsibility. One approach that has developed in an attempt to assist with the process is **service coordination.** Families with children with disabilities find themselves in need of more than one type of service. Often each service needed may be accessed through a different agency or service delivery entity. Service coordination is a practice that assists families and children in gaining access to and integrating the necessary social, medical, educational, and other services the family needs.

Another approach to simplify systems for parents and eliminate unnecessary duplication of services for children and families involves **interagency coordination and collaboration.** A federally mandated, state-level committee appointed by the governor and comprising families, service providers, legislators, persons in personnel preparation, and agency representatives is responsible for the identification of financial services and other support services. This committee is called an Interagency Coordinating Council (ICC).

PARTNERSHIPS WITH SUPPORT SPECIALISTS AND CONSULTANTS

The first step in understanding the nature of the partnership necessary to effect maximum growth for the identified children is for the classroom teacher to understand the role of each of the support specialists who come to an early childhood program to work with children with disabilities. Familiarity with developmentally appropriate programs for young children in turn informs the support specialists concerning the mission and parameters of a developmentally appropriate, early childhood program. Armed with all this information and the knowledge of the importance of maintaining a family focus and the input of the parents, a true partnership can be established between all parties working with children with disabilities. True partnership in classroom-based intervention necessitates the involvement of all persons who come into contact with the child. It will not be an effective placement for the child if the only time the speech and language goals are implemented is when the speech and language therapist is actually in the classroom working with the child. All support specialists, teachers, and the parents need to invest in all the developed goals for the child to effect an ongoing, consistent program.

McWilliam (1993) presents an early intervention case study of a team of support specialists who do not all agree on the importance of additional services for a child who receives home-based intervention services. The tension between team members builds without a positive outcome in sight. This type of situation does nothing to help the child, the family, or the support specialists. Children are quite clever in determining when a particular person is not invested in carrying out a consistent program. If the child does not perceive a uniform "front," the child will rise or sink to the level of expectation of the person there at the time. Consistency is an important component of strong partnerships.

Consistency can be achieved when jargon is limited and professional turf issues do not exist. Every profession speaks a different language which can be intimidating to the person who is not schooled in that discipline. When all professionals speak the same language, the parents and classroom teachers, as well as the professionals benefit and learn from each other. The partnership not only enhances the growth of the child, it enhances the quality of service delivery of each professional as well. When a professional works in isolation, there is a limit to the ideas that the one individual is able to develop and consider. When professionals and parents sit around a table and share ideas, the possibilities are able to increase exponentially. The child benefits and the partnership expands the horizons of the adults involved as well as provide the necessary service to the child. Professionals observing each other at work with children in an inclusive setting can develop an avenue for professional growth for these specialists. On-site learning provides each person with the opportunity to combine procedures to effect maximum change in a child. When a physical therapist works with a child and is concentrating on limbs and muscles, the therapist speaks to the child during the therapy. When that therapist knows about the goals the speech and language specialist has identified and is aware of the techniques designated as appropriate for working with that child, the physical therapist can use the techniques and reinforce the language intervention by integrating it into the physical therapy.

Partnership promotes the integration of therapeutic goals, the delivery of service and the integration of all persons involved with the child. In turn, this partnership and integration results in the integration of the child in the inclusive classroom and the integration of the parts of the child. The child will not be separated out into component parts to be worked on at different times of the day or days of the week, but the child will be treated as a whole child. This supports the ultimate goal providing for the inclusion of a child with disabilities in a regular classroom because the child is a child first and a child with disabilities second.

COLLABORATION

Collaboration can be a confusing factor in the development and implementation of early childhood services in inclusive environments (Kagan, 1991). While there is little research to date on the process and outcomes of collaboration, the necessity of collaboration seems quite obvious and is a practice that is advocated as an important component of planning for inclusive environments (Bruder, 1994). Collaboration with specialists entails cooperation and communication. Collaboration is the result of programs and staff joining forces to come up with a solution to a service problem.

SUPPORT SPECIALISTS WITHIN COMMUNITY EARLY CHILDHOOD PROGRAMS

When a child is of preschool age and the local school system in which the child lives does not have a preschool program within the district or the number of children it is able to accommodate is small, the child whose family desires an inclusive experience for the child usually attends a community early childhood program. In order to provide classroom-based support services to this child, the sending school system needs to send the appropriate support specialists to work within that setting. Collaboration in this type of situation then involves the support specialists, the parents, and the teaching staff of the early childhood program the child attends. Professionals who have been trained to work mostly with individual children are now being asked to work as members of a team in a parent-teacher-professional relationship. They are also being asked to collaborate with the staff of the early childhood program in which the child with disabilities is enrolled. It is likely that the teachers in the program have also not received training in collaboration since the focus of most traditional teacher training programs has been on the teacher working as the sole individual in the classroom. Occasionally, teachers discuss the importance of working with parents as well as school personnel. Rarely is one prepared for the quantity of professionals who will spend time in the classroom.

These professionals should be welcomed with open arms for they are the people who will help the classroom teacher to better understand the needs of the child with disabilities. Support specialists, while being welcomed into programs, also need to understand the capability of both the program and the teachers to carry out the suggestions they wish to have implemented when the specialists are not working with the child. What might appear to be a very logical intervention procedure to a therapist who is able to devote one-to-one time with a child may not be a feasible procedure for teachers to implement. Support specialists need to consider the logic of the procedures they recommend and the appropriateness of someone with less expertise being responsible for their implementation.

Collaboration is certainly to be valued and the manner in which communication is established is key to the success of collaborative efforts

(Gallagher, LaMontagne & Johnson, 1994). For communication to be effective, it needs to be carried out on a regular basis, in an honest manner, and delivered in language all are able to understand. Collaboration is designed to share the responsibility of intervention while sharing the strengths and weaknesses of specific approaches and techniques. Communication should speak to these issues. Collaboration is to be developed in the spirit of cooperation and not competition. Walker and Singer (1993) speak to the issue of developing an atmosphere where collaboration is valued and is based on a family-focus. When the atmosphere is one of collaboration, the outcome may yield increased exchanges of information that take place between parents and teachers as well as positive expectations for productive interactions (Brinkerhoff & Vincent, 1986). Sometimes the desired behaviors do not occur naturally. Brief communications and relationship training directed to family members and professionals can improve the interactions between these people (Lewis, Pantell & Sharp, 1991).

Teachers have a long history of establishing communication with parents. There are many things that teachers do to establish this communication relationship with parents. They seem to focus on the daily contacts with parents and judge the success of their relationships on the parent's responsiveness to initiations, the degree of cooperation with requests, the amount of agreement or conflict regarding day-to-day program activities and long-term intervention programming, apparent support or challenge of their efforts to work on the child's behalf, and the perceived success or failure of their efforts to influence parents or be helpful (Walker & Singer, 1993). With this model in mind, other professionals who work with parents on a regular basis should be able to establish communication in a more comfortable fashion. Taking the time to get to know each other as individuals rather than always getting to know each other only as professionals would greatly enhance communication and set the tone for more cooperative and collaborative working relationships. Working this way in the beginning of a relationship should help to smooth out differences that might occur during the time that the team needs to meet together. If any individual on the team is not honest with all the others, each time the team comes to the table, tensions will develop and the stress level in the room will become measurable. When people are feeling stressed, they are usually not the best listeners. When they are not able to listen carefully, they may miss something being reported or overlook something they wanted to discuss. They leave the meeting frustrated and full of doubt concerning the level of service the child is receiving. This feeling leads to tension at home and the child eventually winds up feeling the tension as well. Much of this negative activity can be avoided by valuing the relationship, valuing the "culture" of each member of the team, making an effort to maintain jargon-free discussions, and attempting to maintain flexible partnerships with parents. Flexible partnerships invite the sharing of responsibilities concerning the child to allow the parents as much of a role in the child's program as he or she wants and is able to undertake (Walker & Singer, 1993).

Professionals working in early childhood settings are used to delivering feedback to children, teachers, other support specialists, and to parents. They may not be as used to receiving feedback from teachers and parents. The nature of feedback received may be very hard to swallow when the specialist thinks he or she is doing an excellent job. It may be difficult to receive this information without becoming defensive. It is usually not healthy to be defensive in interactions with parents concerning feedback. If a parent becomes brave enough to provide feedback, it should be listened to without ascribing what they say to the fact that the parent just does not understand (Zeitlin & Williamson, 1994). Specialists need to be understanding of parents while maintaining their professional demeanor. They need to know that sometimes they ask too many questions of the child with disabilities. When the child is unable to answer or does not care to answer, this may give a parent a false impression which then gets turned into negative feedback to the specialist. Specialists need to educate parents in an understanding way. This will help foster positive communication between all parties.

Formal individualized educational plan (IEP) meetings are required by mandate to occur once a year. The development of the IEP requires a collaborative team process. The parents in attendance at these meetings are greatly outnumbered by the number of professionals in attendance. This fact alone can be extremely intimidating to the parent. In an attempt to be efficient and effective, the meetings sometimes move along very quickly with little or no time for "chatting" about the child. It is important to make time to hear about the child and the child's activities in addition to hearing the reports from each professional sitting around the table. Much energy is directed toward the child during the IEP process. It is important to keep the momentum of the IEP process in place through regularly scheduled team or collaboration meetings in which all parties, in a less formal situation, are able to sit around the table to discuss the progress observed and the concerns still unaddressed. As the year progresses, additional issues may develop that could not have been anticipated when the IEP meeting was held. Some children make amazing progress in a short time and need to have additional or higher level objectives specified. All of these things can be addressed through informal monthly or bi-monthly meetings. Ideas for program modifications can be tossed around without all of the ideas having to be recorded. People sometimes feel freer to share ideas under these conditions than they do at more formal IEP meetings.

COMMUNICATION WITH PARENTS

In addition to regular meetings with parents, support specialists need to develop systems for regular communication with parents. Some parents appreciate weekly phone calls so they are able to ask questions of and share information about progress in the home with the support specialist. This may be difficult to arrange due to work or family commitments on the part of the parents and the therapist. Some parents and support specialists work out a communication notebook arrangement. After each visit, the therapist writes a note to the family about the time spent with the child. The family responds with a note to the therapist. Though this process is not as immediate as phone calls, one benefit is that there is a written record of communication which allows for clarification of issues or concerns if need be.

THE EARLY CHILDHOOD TEACHER AS COLLABORATOR AND COMMUNICATOR

Children with disabilities are enrolled in inclusive early childhood programs in order to benefit from the program and the expertise of the individuals who implement the program. The expertise of the teachers and director or principal extend beyond program implementation to coordination of service and communication between those involved with the child (Chesler, 1994). Early childhood staff become the core of the service delivery and coordination by virtue of the fact that the program the child attends is in their classroom or school and by virtue of the fact that they are the professionals who are on site all the time. The support specialists and parents spend time in the classroom but the classroom and school personnel are the ones who see the child the most and have the most contact with all the parties involved.

How welcome and comfortable support specialists feel in an early childhood environment greatly influences the effectiveness of their work with the children with disabilities. Teachers must be sensitive to the fact that these professionals coming into established early childhood programs have much to learn about the children with disabilities they are to serve, the other children, the early childhood staff, the parents with whom they need to consult and collaborate, and the nature of the program and activities. Each early childhood program has a unique flavor and emotional climate. While there may be many common denominators to developmentally appropriate programs, the children and teachers in each program coupled with the geography and physical facility create the difference in how the program develops. It is not easy for a support specialist to move from one program to another, keeping track of children, objectives, parents, staff, and program. While a program may honestly and earnestly welcome these professionals, the professionals may still may feel as though they are guests in that house. Learning the culture of each program and the personalities of the early childhood teachers who work in them takes time.

In planning and implementing an inclusive environment, there are many things that early childhood teachers and directors can do to facilitate the inclusion of support specialists as well as children and their families. When the specialists arrive for the first time, greet them and give them a tour of the facility while taking the time to explain the dimensions of the program. Introduce them to everyone in the classroom and anyone else in the building they will be in contact with each time they come to the program. Be sure to inform them of the daily and weekly schedule. If you have a printed calendar, share it with them. They may be spending time in a variety of schools that each have different schedules and vacations. Tell them about field trips which are scheduled on their regular therapy days at least a week in advance. They may wish to join you to facilitate the experience for the children with whom they work or they may wish to reschedule for another day. Be hospitable and share your food with them. Spending time in a program where delicious things to eat are being made and not offering some to the adults working with the children does not make anyone feel welcome. Treat the professionals who come to work with you the same way you would wish to be treated if you made regular visits to another program.

Communication takes time. Consistent, meaningful communication builds relationships that are mutually beneficial. There are many signals people give during communication that negate the verbal message being delivered. The words may indicate a willingness to cooperate and collaborate but the physical posture and lack of eye contact may indicate just the opposite. A positive message delivered in an overly assertive, controlling tone of voice tends to upset those listening to the message. Demonstrating real concern for the daily family routine and responsibilities may help all at the table to see that it would be unreasonable to request that the parents spend one hour per day on intervention activities.

Nothing can be more upsetting than coming to a meeting with parents, thinking everything is going well and facing upset, angry parents. Sometimes this happens no matter how well you thought you were communicating. A friend, neighbor, or relative may have said something to the parent that led the parent to become immediately disenchanted with the child's program. When this happens, it is best for all the support specialists and teachers to listen carefully before saying anything. Parents have a right to be heard before any attempt is made to set the record straight.

Some parents are so vulnerable that whatever anyone else says to them—even if they were satisfied with everything up to that point—causes them to doubt the program. The professionals, in their most professional but caring manner, need to respond without defensiveness. Validation of the parent's feelings while the team continues to work together on important tasks can be the outcome of such a discussion. Each child is precious to each parent. It takes a bit of "walking in their shoes" to imagine what it is like to care for and raise a child with disabilities. This feeling needs to be conveyed to the parent during the times the team meets. Sometimes parental self-esteem needs some attention in order for the parent to be able to continue the important work outlined by the team.

WORKING WITH FAMILIES IN PLANNING FOR TRANSITIONS

To a family with a child with disabilities or to any family with a child in the early childhood years, it may seem that just about the time a child and family are settled into a routine and are comfortable with every facet of the school program, it is time to move on to a different program or different classroom with different people. The trust that has been developed through time and effort needs to be transferred to others. Planning for transitions can make the journey to the next teacher, classroom or school a much easier one. It is important for all involved in planning for the transition to know about the program the child will be moving to. This means that anyone unfamiliar with the setting should make at least one classroom visit to the new setting. If there is a decision to be made between several possible sites, it would be important to gather information about all the settings, make visitations, and then come to the table with a much better idea of the range of options. When possible, it makes sense to include the child in the visits to other classrooms because observing the child in the setting will help to inform the parents, teachers, and support specialists concerning the viability of the setting for that particular child. For this reason, it is important to start planning for transition early in the school year so that the end of the year does not arrive without all persons involved in the transition planning having had a chance to gather the necessary information.

It appears that transition is not a single event but an ongoing process that begins early in the school year and continues throughout the period of adjustment to a new program (Hains, Rosenkoetter & Fowler, 1991). The role of support specialists is an important one as plans are outlined for the transition to the next environment. Rather than a simple transfer from one set of support specialists to another set in the new classroom, there should be some carryover so that the children, parents, receiving teachers, and therapists have time to become acquainted with the whole situation. The information a team of support specialists can convey to the receiving team in a short amount of time is more meaningful than having the receiving team learn about the child from written reports only.

There is a big question about the actual preparation of a child for the next level classroom. Whether the child making the transition to a new classroom or school is a child with disabilities or not, some specialists, parents, and teachers place an emphasis on the identification of the skills anticipated as necessary for survival in the new environment. The notion of identifying skills important for the next level classroom and teaching to those skills is in contradiction with the notion of developmentally appropriate and individually appropriate curriculum and practice. Identifying functional skills that a child needs regardless of what kind of classroom the child is to be in is much more in keeping with a developmental approach. Studies looking at the issue of preparation of specific skills for the transitions children undergo found that teachers preparing children for inclusion in kindergarten classrooms preferred to nurture the development of global abilities such as the ability to complete a task with minimal teacher supervision, attending and following instructions during group activities, and positive play-based social interaction (Beckoff & Bender, 1989; Hains, Fowler, Schwartz, Kottwitz & Rosenkoetter, 1989).

Support specialists can be instrumental in planning for transition by identifying materials and equipment appropriate for the nature of the classroom experience to which the child will be moving. One of the things that interferes with more immediate inclusion into the classroom routine and a success orientation for the child is a lack of or delay in acquiring equipment that allows the child to be "where the action is" at the same physical level as the other children. If the team following the child always has to wait until the start of the school year to identify the equipment and materials needs of the child with disabilities, precious time may be lost. During the time spent waiting for the new equipment, accommodations can be made for the child but the best possible situation will not be in place.

Support specialists usually focus on transition planning for the child with disabilities. Parents are in need of transition plans as well and often look to the therapists who have been working with the child to provide or at least think about the issue of transition. Parents need help in understanding what will be expected of them in this new setting. They need assurance from the therapists that they will not be dropped by the therapists when their child enters the new setting. By the time a child enters kindergarten or first grade, the parents have worked with a minimum of two teams of professionals between early intervention services at home and in the preschool environment. The professionals who have provided therapy for the children have become part of the extended family. They have often provided emotional support and strength for the family during previous transitions and difficult adjustment periods. These professionals have been a source of information and referral as well. Adjusting to an entire new team is another emotional adjustment parents are required to make. A transitional period during which the current and receiving support specialists are able to be in contact with the parents paves the way to a smoother transition for the child, the family, and the support specialists as well.

Sometimes children are not authorized for therapeutic services during the summer months. Toward the end of the school year, the support specialists on the team should make available some goals and objectives for the summer in order to promote maintenance of gains accomplished during the school year. Parents often want to know what they can do at home over the summer to provide for generalization of acquired skills and behaviors. They may also feel ready to tackle some new skills and behaviors and would welcome suggestions from the support specialists.

As the child matures and moves from one level of education and service delivery to another, parents need to know that they are still very important to the advancement of their children. They need to know that what they reinforce in the home environment can make the role of the support specialists and classroom teachers easier and frees them up to work on other behaviors and skills in the classroom. Parents also need support from the support specialists to know that their role as parents comes first and their role as interventionist comes second. Sometimes parents who have experienced a great deal of stress related to the very early years of a child's life, find that as the child's development becomes more stable, they are unsure of their continuing role. They know that there is still much to do to encourage maximum growth in their children but their own identity has changed and they are in need of a redefined role. Some parents do not take the positive change in their children for granted. Some parents report that they are "always waiting for the other shoe to fall" because they cannot believe their good fortune and the progress the child has made after the very difficult start in life the child experienced. Helping parents to make the transition to a new purposeful identity will serve the entire family and the team of professionals too. Each transitional step toward family independence and a more gratifying parenting identity will help to foster a higher degree of child independence. Transitions happen in the lives of all families regardless of whether they have children with disabilities or not. Families have different resources at their disposal. Some families have an extended family network that is available to them to help them through transitions. Even if a family does have a wonderful support network, professionals assisting parents with planning for transitions will make the transition take place as smoothly as possible.

SUMMARY

Specialists working with children with disabilities in inclusive settings are members of a large team of people. These specialists play a very important role in the development and implementation of developmentally and age-appropriate programs for these young children in inclusive early childhood settings. Support specialists are expected to work with a variety of professionals, parents, and classroom teachers. Since current preferred practice is to provide classroom-based therapy, specialists who were not trained to provide this type of service are finding themselves working in environments that might be completely new to them. Working in a new environment with new people always takes time. Learning the culture of the integrated classroom and the other specialists working as part of the team is critical to the success of the intervention. Collaboration is the key to providing the most integrated, appropriate service delivery possible. Collaboration is not something that happens automatically but is the outcome of teachers, parents, and professionals working together. Working in a collaborative fashion improves service delivery, integrates the therapeutic intervention and opens up the channels for communication between all persons involved with the child. Establishing honest, meaningful communication assists with planning for the transitions that occur during the early childhood years. Successful transitions play an important role in the successful integration of children with disabilities in inclusive early childhood environments.

DISCUSSION QUESTIONS

1) Develop an approach to integrating specialists into an inclusive classroom. Indicate the steps you would take to explain your program and make the specialists feel as comfortable as possible.
2) Think about how frequently you would want to have team meetings with all individuals involved with a child with disabilities. What will influence your decision as to frequency? Who do you think will be in charge of organizing and calling the meetings? Discuss your plan with another member of the class, comparing decisions and discussing rationales.
3) You have never included a child with disabilities before this year. Now that you have a child with disabilities, you also find yourself with a complement of specialists as well. You are aware of the role of each type of specialist but do not understand all the language and details of therapy goals. With another class member, brainstorm several ways in which you may gain the necessary expertise you need in order to gain the maximum possible from the situation.

4) A specialist is assigned to deliver service to a child in your classroom. The therapist is new to working in applied settings, having spent many years working in clinical settings. You attempt to explain the nature of your program to this person but the specialist appears to want to proceed with business as usual. Develop a way to bring the therapist to understand the importance of what happens in your classroom.
5) Parents of children without disabilities need to be kept up to date concerning all the personnel they may see working within the classroom setting. Think of several ways in which you may keep parents informed while preserving the privacy of each family with a child in your room.
6) Some of the children in your room are curious about the children with special needs and seem to want to help them. How can you as the classroom teacher, with the support of the specialists, maximize this potential without giving the children too much responsibility?

REFERENCES

Abraham, M., Morris, L., & Wald, P. (1993). *Inclusive early childhood education—A model classroom*. Tucson, AZ: Communication Skill Builders.

Beckoff, A., & Bender, W. (1989). Programming for mainstream kindergarten success in preschool: Teachers' perceptions of necessary prerequisite skills. *Journal of Early Intervention, 13*, 269–280.

Brinkerhoff, J., and Vincent, L. (1986). Increasing parental decision-making at their child's individualized educational program meeting. *Journal of the Division of Early Childhood, 11*, 46–58.

Brown, W., & Rule, S. (1993). Personnel and disciplines in early intervention. In W. Brown, S. Thurman, and L. Pearl (Eds.), *Family-centered early intervention with infants & toddlers—Innovative cross-disciplinary approaches*. (pp. 245–268). Baltimore: Paul H. Brookes Publishing Co.

Bruder, M. (1994). Working with members of other disciplines: Collaboration for success. In M. Wolery and J. Wilbers (Eds.), *Including children with special needs in early childhood programs*. (pp. 45–70). Washington, DC: National Association for the Education of Young Children.

Bunse, C. (1992). The role of related service providers. In J. Peters, C. Bunse, L. Carlson, L. Doede, G. Glasenapp, K. Haydon, C. Lehman, T. Templeman, & T. Udell, *Supporting children with disabilities in community programs—The teaching research integrated preschool*. (pp. 105–113). Monmouth, OR: Teaching Research Division.

Chesler, P. (1994). *A place for me—Including children with special needs in early care and education settings*. Washington, DC: National Association for the Education of Young Children.

Deiner, P. (1993). *Resources for teaching children with diverse abilities*. Fort Worth, TX: Harcourt Brace Jovanovich College Publishers.

Gallagher, R., LaMontagne, M., & Johnson, L. (1994). Early intervention—The collaborative challenge. In L.Johnson, R. Gallagher, M. LaMontagne and J. Jordan, J. Gallagher, P. Hutinger, M. Karnes (Eds.), *Meeting early intervention challenges—Issues from birth to three*. (pp. 279–287). Baltimore: Paul H. Brookes Publishing Co.

Hains, A., Fowler, S., Schwartz, I., Kottwitz, E., & Rosenkoetter, S. (1989). A comparison of preschool and kindergarten teacher expectations for school readiness. *Early Childhood Research Quarterly, 4*, 75–88.

Hains, A., Rosenkoetter, S., & Fowler, S. (1991). Transition planning with families in early intervention programs. *Infants and Young Children, 3*(4), 38–47.

Kagan, S. (1991). *United we stand: Collaboration for child care and early intervention and education services*. New York: Teachers College Press.

Leister, C., Koonce, D., & Nisbet, S. (1993). Best practices for preschool programs: An update on inclusive settings. *Day Care and Early Education, 21*(2), 9–12.

Lewis, C., Pantell, R., & Sharp, L. (1991). Increasing patient knowledge, satisfaction, and involvement: Randomized trial of a communication intervention. *Pediatrics, 88*(2), 351–358.

McWilliam, P. (1993). In P. McWilliam & D. Bailey, Jr. (Eds.). *Working together with children & families—Case studies in early intervention*. (pp. 219–225). Baltimore: Paul H. Brookes Publishing Co.

Peters, J., Bunse, C., Carlson, L., Doede, L., Glasenapp, G., Haydon, K., Lehman, C., Templeman, T., & Udell, T. (1992). *Supporting children with disabilities in community programs—The teaching research integrated preschool*. Monmouth, OR: Teaching Research Division.

Rosenkoetter, S., Hains, A., & Fowler, S. (1994). *Bridging early services for children with special needs and their families—A practical guide for transition planning*. Baltimore: Paul H. Brookes Publishing Co.

Walker, B., & Singer, G. (1993). Improving communication between professionals and parents. In G. Singer & L. Powers (Eds.), *Families, disability and empowerment—Active coping skills and strategies for family interventions*. (pp. 285–315). Baltimore: Paul H. Brookes Publishing Co.

Zeitlin, S., & Williamson, G. (1994). *Coping in young children—Early intervention practices to enhance adaptive behavior and resilience*. Baltimore: Paul H. Brookes Publishing Co.

CHAPTER 15

Observation and Assessment

KEY TERMS

observation
assessment
observation as assessment
anecdotal record
running record
event recording
duration recording
interval recording
latency recording
rating scale
checklist
portfolios
diagnostic assessment
performance assessment
continuous assessment
arena assessment
curriculum-based assessment
play-based assessment

Observation and assessment are terms used widely and easily by early childhood teachers and specialists. What procedures and processes are actually meant by these terms has varied considerably over the years. Observation is currently widely accepted as an appropriate means of measuring the behavior of young children by early childhood educators and early childhood special educators (Bredekamp, 1987).

Observation as a systematic process of gathering information about children and their environments (Cohen & Spenciner, 1994), consists of watching children where they are, in settings that are natural to them, and in ways that yield descriptions and quantitative measures (Goodwin & Driscoll, 1980). Observation involves watching and listening to a child or a classroom of children. The observation results in a written record of what occurred during the period of time the person was making the recording. The purpose of the observation may be to measure a specific aspect of behavior or program or to log a more free-flowing record of what transpired in the environment. The free-flowing record may serve to focus future observation direction or the single record may become part of a profile of activity that takes place during the course of the school year.

Assessment is defined as procedure to determine the degree to which an individual child possesses a certain characteristic or attribute (Gullo, 1994). Assessment is the process of observing, recording, and otherwise documenting work that children do and how they do it, as a basis for a variety of educational decisions that affect the child (NAEYC & NAECS\SDE, 1991, p. 21). It also refers to testing and alternate forms of measurement that might include observations, interviews, and reports gathered from specialists, all of which are recorded and integrated into a working plan for instruction and intervention. Assessment is the term sometimes used to mean one appraisal or one measure of a child's performance to avoid the negative connotations of the words test or evaluation. Assessment can be conducted in the classroom as well as in a more test-oriented environment. Assessment should be part of each child's early childhood program regardless of whether the child does or does not have disabilities.

Prior to or concurrent with using observation as a means of assessment, or developing other means of assessment in the classroom, the early childhood classroom teacher would benefit from acquiring an understanding of the types of children's testing which have been a part of traditional assessment (Aylward, 1991; Nuttal, Romero & Kalesnik, 1992; Wodrich & Kush, 1990). It is from the frustration of working within the confines of these types of traditional tests with the population of young children, that the current movement to develop more age-appropriate and curriculum-appropriate assessments developed.

OBSERVATION AS ASSESSMENT IN INCLUSIVE DEVELOPMENTALLY APPROPRIATE SETTINGS

The process of **observation as assessment** is not intrusive and allows for the informal gathering of information about children in natural environments. Seeing a child in an environment native to the child reveals a picture different from observing a child in a more clinical environment. Observations made on children in school may reveal a picture unlike one gathered from observing a child in the home environment. Classroom observations provide for assessment in context (Hills, 1993). Hills advocates that children are most themselves when they are in familiar environments with adults and children they know and trust. What adds to their comfort level is the fact that they are engaged in tasks which allow them to use the skills with which they are most comfortable. Under these conditions, they should demonstrate their best abilities. Weber, Behl, and Summers (1994) discuss the benefits of using play as an assessment tool. They describe play as being "user friendly" as well as naturalistic, nontraumatic, and enjoyable for both the child and teacher or parent. Play scales that are currently available have practical applications for both intervention and assessment.

Observation also provides a means of monitoring a child's progress without "testing" the child. Monitoring progress in the natural environment provides for a success orientation rather than a deficit orientation. Sometimes the notion of testing a child is directed towards gathering evidence of what a child cannot do and what a child does not know. By observing the child in a developmentally appropriate environment, the observer will learn how the child functions in the environment, what interests the child and will hopefully be able to observe ways the environment can be modified to ensure a greater level of success for the child. In the natural environment, early childhood teachers are usually the assessors as well as the users of the information gathered (Hills, 1993). Benjamin (1994) points out that observation should be something that is planned for and based on clear goals as to why and what you want to observe. In order to maximize the potential of observations, she advocates narrating observations directly into a small tape recorder for transcription at a later time.

Parents want to know how a child is performing in a given area and how the performance will impact future learning. In addition to sharing information with parents, parents should be able to contribute to the observation picture. Diamond & Squires (1993) review the role of parental report in screening and assessment of young children. They specifically recommend the wider use of parent report as the basis for initial developmental screening. Parental report may be able to give a more accurate picture of the child's current behavioral repertoire than could be captured by the use of an initial screening tool. The authors also speak to the cost effectiveness and time effectiveness of parental reporting. Dinnebeil and Rule (1994) conducted a literature review of congruence between parental estimates and professionals' assessments of children's abilities. The results of their review suggest that there are strong, positive correlations between parental and professional judgments. Henderson and Meisels (1994) combined the results of an early screening inventory (ESI) with information from a parent questionnaire. They found that the use of a parent questionnaire enhanced the effectiveness of the developmental screening process. The study supports the recognition that parents can supply unique information about the child's growth and development.

Since the process of observation does not involve anything technical, parents come supplied with ready information that merely needs to be accessed with the right questions. Parents can contribute information about the child in the home and neighborhood environment. Through the provision of observations, parents are able to feel more closely connected to the school environment and the program planning directed towards their child. Parents can share information about behaviors that occur spontaneously in the home which may never have been seen at school because of the nature of difference between home and school.

Observation may be used as a tool by itself or it may be used as part of a comprehensive assessment strategy. There are many strategies to organize observations which can range from the formal to the informal, from the structured to the flexible. Guidelines for conducting observations may be tailored to individual early childhood programs or may be adopted or adapted from established, published curriculum and assessment packages. The benefits of observation as assessment include the fact that observations produce the most naturalistic information about children, usually gathered by persons who know the child quite well and who spend more time with the child than most other people. Other benefits include the inexpensive nature of observation, the portability of procedures and the potential for collecting information about children across settings. The variety of settings and situations in which children may be observed is great. The following list of situations which may be observed may prove useful to stimulate thinking about observation as assessment. With each situation is included some behaviors that might be observed:

current events group discussion: questions asked or answered; information voluntarily shared; participation; prepared with article to discuss

filmstrip presentation or video presentation with follow-up activity: questions asked or answered; information voluntarily shared; participation

work on a class play: lines said correctly; offers to help peers; offers to help adults

oral presentation to class: vocabulary used; organization; eye contact; level of comfort with material recess: spontaneous peer interaction; gross motor skills; ideas for activity

free time: choice of activity; time spent with activity of choice; time spent with which peers

independent reading time: time spent reading; time spent out of seat; questions asked of teacher or peers; physical position used for reading

OBSERVATION TECHNIQUES

The following observation techniques are appropriate for use with any young children in any early childhood environment. Children with or without disabilities emit multiple behaviors that provide teachers with considerable information. Some of the behaviors emitted are situation specific and some occur in all situations.

One type of observation technique is the ***anecdotal record.*** Anecdotal records are specific and brief narrative descriptions of children's behavior (Abraham, Morris & Wald, 1993). Anecdotal records are usually written but they may also be taped. Details to be included in the anecdotal record are the date, time, and location of the observation. As accurate a description as possible of what transpired during the observation should be recorded. Since the observation is a description and not an interpretation of what was observed, the observer needs to be as objective as possible (Sattler, 1988). Anecdotal records can be conducted in an impromptu manner so that if something is going on that the teacher wished to make a record of, a written record can be undertaken. Anecdotal records taken in this manner often have to be transferred to a more permanent location or file. The sticky backed notepads that are currently available are very convenient for making brief recordings about individual children. At the end of the day, these convenient records can be transferred to a child's file for future reference. The mechanics of maintaining anecdotal records need not be difficult. In addition to the sticky backed notepads method of recording information, records can be kept either on index cards which are transferred to files, notebooks for each child, or file folders or file pockets for each child. Whatever works best for each classroom is what should be implemented as a procedure.

During the child-directed activities of the day such as free choice of planned activities, snack and lunch times, and outdoor play, teachers may find themselves more likely and available to make such recordings than during the more teacher-directed times of the day such as circle time or transitions. It is important to keep track of the number of anecdotal records made on individual children. If a particular child is the subject of multiple recordings, a flexible schedule of recordings can be developed to ensure that equal records will be made on all the children in the class.

There are benefits to the use of anecdotal records as an observation technique. It does not take much special training to learn how to conduct an anecdotal observation. If a child begins to exhibit a new behavior or skill in a spontaneous manner, the process can record it. During the anecdotal observation process, authentic behaviors are recorded. In addition, if observation is used as a portion of a comprehensive assessment, it can provide a "reality check" for the remainder of the assessment.

Although there are several benefits to the use of anecdotal records, there are some deficits as well. In order to record everything seen during the allotted time, the observer needs to be able to write quickly and have a good memory. The more time that elapses between the observation and the writing of the record, the greater the likelihood of forgetting something that was observed. Observer bias, which is a factor in many types of observations, may play a role in the creation of anecdotal records. As the recording of the observation may take considerable time, it is possible that the observer will only record some of the events seen during the observation period (Cohen & Spenciner, 1994). Selective recording of only positive or negative behaviors would present a slanted profile of a child. When an observer is asked to observe specific behaviors, the observer may want so much to accomplish that task that behavior that actually did not happen might be assumed to have happened.

Running records are observations that keep a record of events as they occur. In a **running record,** the time and flow of activity is critical to the observation. Running records are sometimes called continuous records. The concept behind this type of observation is to record everything that takes place. If recording everything were possible, the information gathered would be able to help teachers and parents see how a child spends every moment of the school day. To do this type of observation is extremely time consuming and may lead to some details being overlooked. If the person serving as observer takes shorthand, it may be possible to record everything if one child is the subject of the observation. If the target is a small group of children, it may prove impossible. Running records are factual and thus are not subject to judgment.

When what you desire to collect is a record of a behavior each time it occurs, you will want to use ***event recording.*** During a specified period of time, a defined behavior is recorded each time the behavior is observed. A clear definition of behavior is critical to the success of any observation process. If a behavior cannot be easily defined, it will be impossible to collect data. This technique requires paying very close attention to the particular child who is the subject of the observation. Regardless of whether the behavior occurs frequently or infrequently, event recording is an appropriate method. Event recording allows the teacher to see changes over a period of time. It provides an opportunity to see differences in behavior during different activity periods. The method of recording can be as simple as making tally marks on a piece of paper and then transferring the data to a more permanent record. Some teachers find it helpful to place a strip of masking tape on a sleeve and make tally marks in that way. In order to have a clear idea of the quantity of behavior that occurs each day, the observation periods need to remain constant and they should occur during the same time period each day. Some behaviors only occur during specific times of the day due to the environmental variables operating at those times. Once this has been determined, it would not make sense to record behavior all day every day. One of the drawbacks to event recording is the fact that if you are recording an isolated behavior, you may not have an idea of what sets off that behavior. The changes in the targeted behavior after modifications were introduced to the environment would be assumed to occur due to the procedures implemented. With event records of only the targeted behavior, you might not be able to determine the accuracy of your assumptions. If event records were kept of targeted procedures as well, the teacher would have a much better idea of the relationship between behavior and environment. An example of this might be recording a child's responses to questions. If you only record responses and not the number of questions asked, and type of questions asked, you may not know that the child responds to only one type of questioning. This information would be quite valuable when attempting to determine how to elicit more answers to questions. Occasionally it might be useful to probe during the remainder of the day to make sure that the targeted behavior is not happening. One advantage to event recording is that it is portable, flexible, and extremely inexpensive. It is also something that classroom teachers are able to implement while they carry out their responsibilities. If a behavior is extremely low rate, missing the behavior in the flurry of other activity that transpires during the day might occur. Regular observations over a longer period of time will confirm the actual pattern of behavior.

When the concern over a behavior is more how long it lasts than how often it occurs, ***duration recording*** is a logical observation technique. Duration recording collects information concerning the persistence of the behavior. If a child has tantrums, while it is important to know how many times the behavior occurs it may be more important to know how long the tantrums last. If a child participates in an activity it may be important to know how long the child participates as well as how many times a day it occurs. Measuring duration necessitates beginning the recording at the onset of the behavior episode and concluding the recording when the behavior stops. This means that the definition of the behavior needs to be very clear about when to start and stop recording.

Duration can be recorded with the start and stop of a stopwatch or by the marking of time intervals on a recording sheet. When a daily record is complete, it is possible to figure the average length of behavior episodes for the day. The range of duration can also be analyzed from the data collected. As a child is assisted to either increase a low-rate behavior or decrease a high-rate behavior, looking at the frequency and duration of the behavior will provide information as to the effectiveness of the intervention.

When you are looking to collect the most precise, detailed information possible on one or more behaviors, the use of ***interval recording*** will provide the most quantifiable data. Interval recording allows for the recording of several behaviors simultaneously so the relationship of one behavior to the other may be analyzed. In this fashion, both child and teacher behavior may be recorded to see what, if anything, can be modified in the behavior of the teacher to support change on the part of the child. Figure 15.1 shows an example of what a simple interval recording sheet might look like. The sheet illustrates how in a 10-second interval, information may be gathered concerning whether one or more of the defined behaviors occurred during that interval.

The manner in which the behavior is defined will influence the quantity of behavior recorded. Within the definition of the behavior it must be specified whether the behaviors must be observed for an entire interval for a recording to be made or whether the behavior may be observed only within a portion of the interval for it to be counted. If the partial interval option is in place, there may be a tendency to have more occurrences of the behavior than if the total interval must contain the behavior. It is also possible to designate the end of the interval as the time to observe the child. This momentary time sampling technique allows for the observation of an entire group of children once every time interval. The observer would look up at the end of the interval and record the occurrence or non-occurrence of each child at that time. This type of observation is helpful when the behavior observed is participation, on-task, or something else of that nature. When developing the observation strategy, it is important to be aware of the level of behavior considered within the norm for children of the age you will be observing. It is also important to be aware of whether the behavior to be observed occurs within entire intervals for children one would consider the norm for this behavior. With this information in mind, a reasonable, measurable definition of behavior may be developed that will be able to show behavior changes that occur over time.

The length of interval used and the decision to observe continuously, time sample, or use longer recording intervals will influence the kind of information that results. Observers can record only so much information within brief recording intervals. If the observation process is designed to document multiple behaviors, behaviors across several children, or to ob-

Time	10 sec.	10 sec.	10 sec.	10 sec.	10 sec.	10 sec.
Subject Initiations	X	O	O	O	O	X
Peer Responses	O	X	O	O	O	X
Peer Initiations	O	X	O	O	O	O
Subject Responses	O	O	X	O	O	O
Teacher Initiations	O	O	O	O	X	O
Subject Responses	O	O	O	O	X	O

FIG 15.1 An interval recording form using 10-second intervals. An X indicates at least one occurrence of the behavior during the interval; an O indicates no occurrence of the behavior during the interval.

serve a very high-rate behavior, it may be difficult to record all the information with great accuracy and reliability. In this instance, it may be helpful to design a process of observation followed by a recording time. For example, in a 10-second interval observation may occur during the first seven seconds with three seconds remaining for recording the behavior. This would establish a pattern of observe, record, observe, record. While there is a chance that this process may cause some behavior to be missed, it would allow for greater accuracy of measurement of what was observed. It is also possible to specify longer intervals for recording. With a longer interval, there is a greater amount of time in which the behavior may be observed and the pace of observation and recording may be more conducive to accuracy.

Some behaviors are very intense. The intensity of behavior in the classroom may be more of the issue than the frequency of the behavior. While duration recording may be one way to obtain a measure of intensity, defining different levels of behavior may be another. When a child engages in negative interaction it might range from the child saying something negative to another child or adult or it might involve kicking, hitting, spitting, or swearing. It is not enough to call it all of it negative interaction. It is important to know the *intensity of the behavior*. The negative comment is a less intense behavior than the kicking or hitting. Defining levels of behavior allows the classroom teacher to see the change in intensity of behavior as well as the change in frequency of behavior. Encouraging a behavior to occur less frequently is advisable but with a very intense behavior it may be advisable to work on intensity at first and frequency second. Less intense behavior may seem like less frequent behavior in the classroom situation.

In situations in which it is important to know how long it takes a child to begin to carry out a task, answer a question, or to follow a request after it has been issued, ***latency recording*** is the appropriate means of observation. In latency recording, the person recording the information starts to record time when a request is issued, a question is asked, or a task is given. Although latency may be difficult to measure because it is difficult to carefully define the behavior that initiates the behavior episode, latency information may be very helpful in designing appropriate interventions.

When a classroom teacher is interested in what children produce during the school day, ***evaluation of permanent products*** they produce can yield considerable information. Teachers can collect work samples supplying the information generated by:

cooperative learning groups working on a social studies or science project

any task that results in a paper being generated

creative writing activity

math worksheets completed individually or in a small-group situation

math activities conducted with manipulatives that generate a permanent product completed either individually or in a small group

art activities such as drawing, painting, collage, sculpture

drafts of a story that is being developed

recordings of a dictated story

block play

computer activity involving problem solving

daily entry in a personal journal in the form of drawings or writing

manipulative play that leaves a completed design (i.e., pegs, cubes, beads, parquetry blocks.)

The evaluation of these products can include measures of completion, accuracy, the number of items attempted compared to the number of items completed, and the number of items completed correctly. The product can also be evaluated for creativity, new words used, new pieces used, or the number of forms used. This form of evaluation can be maintained throughout the school year. While block structures and constructions made with other manipulatives may not be permanent for the entire school year because the materials need to be used by other children, a photograph taken of the product can be added to the permanent product file for the child. It can be used for ongoing evaluation, to share at parent meetings or for a child to see his or her own growth in a given area.

A ***rating scale*** records inferences or judgments about the quality of a behavior (McAfee & Leong, 1994). Rating scales can be given to all those involved with a child to document general impressions of a situation as well as to make an evaluation of the climate in a classroom environment. Rating scales are best used in conjunction with other measures. It is too easy to read into the results of a rating scale. Some published rating scales focus predominantly on negative behaviors. If one or more persons are assigned to look for negative behaviors, chances are that they will find them. In the process, they may overlook the positive behaviors the child does exhibit because the positives were not emphasized in the rating scale. Repeated use of the same rating scale sometimes produces mixed results. If teachers or parents are asked to rate a child's behavior on a daily basis, the more times the scale is used, the less seriously the scale is taken. It becomes another daily task using the same instrument. The potential for people eventually not paying close attention to the items on the scale develops. The accuracy of the ratings diminishes over time. In addition, without a clear definition for the terms "sometimes, usually, always" observer bias and judgment will play a large role in how the situation is rated. The same observer using the same scale may differ in the use of the scale from one time to the next. If qualifiers such as the range of times something happens can be added to the terms of the rating scale, the person conducting the ratings will have a better guideline for use of the rating scale.

Checklists can be very helpful for teachers to use while teaching. Children generate a considerable amount of data each day. Some of the data they generate revolves around the skills they demonstrate in both social and academic areas. A **checklist** can help focus attention on specific skills. Checklists may be kept in each area of the room so that all the adults who work in a classroom may record information on a checklist that identifies specific skills appropriate for that area.

Most checklists require only a simple yes or no response (Cohen & Spenciner, 1994). An example of such a checklist may be seen in Figure 15.2 In this checklist, a teacher is able to obtain a record of whether a child participated, completed a task, the length of time spent in activity, and the degree of self-sufficiency appropriate to the activity area.

In this very efficient method of collecting information, patterns of flow of activity, activity preferences, and amount of time spent in activity

Behavior	Child 1	Child 2	Child 3	Child 4	Child 5	Child 6
Participated in Activity	yes	no	yes	yes	yes	yes
Completed Activity	no	no	yes	no	no	yes
Time in Activity	9:10–9:30	no	9:15–9:35	9:25–9:30	9:30–9:40	9:10–9:40
Needed Help	no	no	no	yes	no	no
Interacted with Peers	yes	no	yes	yes	no	yes

FIG 15.2 Checklist for classroom observation. A yes or no recording can be made in each box as appropriate.

areas will be evident. Large amounts of information may be collected through the use of checklists that are used in an ongoing fashion. According to Wortham (1995), checklists are best used when a great number of behaviors are to be observed. This will allow teachers and parents to see progress over time. At the start of a school year a child may not participate in all activities. During the course of the first few weeks at school, children begin to explore other areas. A checklist system will document these changes very easily. McAfee and Leong (1994) make important recommendations for using checklists which include the following:

Group similar items and put them in sequence with space between groups of items

break subskills into subgroups, levels, or steps listing each separately

state items in the positive to avoid confusion

choose representative items that are important indicators and decide on and use a consistent marking system

As children are able to recognize and then write their own names, they might be able to record their own participation in an area by putting a check mark next to their names or eventually sign themselves into an area. In this way, a method of observation also provides more opportunities to make other observations.

Checklists are very helpful in preparing progress reports as well as in preparing for parent conferences. They also inform teachers about skills that should be emphasized within future curriculum themes. The important thing to remember about checklists is that they are valuable as part of an assessment and that when kept for an entire year, they will provide considerable developmental information for teachers and parents.

Some general issues involved in the use of observation as a means of assessment revolve around establishing the reliability of the observations made. The best way to measure reliability is for two people to sit together in the classroom and begin and end their observations at the same time. It is essential the each observer use the same definition(s) and the same type of recording form to collect the data. This means that an observation code should be developed that contains all of the procedures necessary for conducting the observation. The observation code should include the following information: name of subject to be observed, age of child, conditions under which the observation should take place (during which periods of the day), definition of all behaviors to be observed, and rules for recording the behavior. It takes some training to become an accurate observer who is able to observe only the targeted child or adult in the classroom environment. Early childhood classrooms abound with distractions because young children are engaging. Therefore it takes great concentration to focus specifically on the subject of the observation. It may take several observation sessions until all in the environment, including the observers, children, and teachers are comfortable enough with the situation to obtain a reliable observation. Observation should not interfere with the environment. The results of observation well done should enhance what happens in an early childhood environment because the information gained should serve to inform teachers of what needs to change or be added to the environment to make it a better one for children and adults.

OBSERVATION AS ASSESSMENT IN DIFFERENT ACTIVITY AREAS

Early childhood classrooms contain multiple activities and multiple opportunities for observation as a means of assessment. Considerable behavior can be observed whether the child is involved in activity by him- or herself, with peers, peers and adults, or an adult. The following is a description of the types of observation information that can be gathered from each of the activity areas. It is not difficult to see that some of the same behaviors may be observed across activity areas while several are unique to each specific activity.

In the *art* area, the following behaviors can be observed from the papers that are generated from children's drawings, paintings or collages, from prints taken from finger paintings done on a table top, from photos taken of paintings in progress, or from sculptures. These products may be observed for colors used, lines and forms made (Goetz, 1973), amount of space used on the paper, location of drawing on the paper (does the child use only the center of the page or the entire paper?), stage of development of the art (scribble, representational, etc), and intensity of what is drawn (how dark is the line). While the child is in the process of creating the art, observations may include how the child uses the materials, whether the child is more concerned about remaining clean than getting involved with the materials and how long the child stays with the art activity. Observations may also be made on how much language the child generates during the activity, whether the child uses appropriate vocabulary for each art tool used and whether the child seeks peer or adult approval for the work produced.

In the *music* area observations can be made during the activity but tapes can also be made of a child singing. The value of the tape is that it can be analyzed later for tone, vocabulary of the songs sung, how in tune the child sang, and other musical variables. While the music activity is taking place, participation can be measured, in addition to recording whether the child volunteers to sing or to name a song to sing.

Movement activities can be captured on videos and through photographs. From the videos, the behaviors of different movements can be recorded. Leaping, sliding, bending, stretching, twisting, on toes, on flat feet, or any other different movements can be noted. The sequence of moving from one movement to another would be interesting to record. During the activity, recordings can be made indicating whether the child imitates the movements of others or initiates movements that others follow.

The *block area* provides opportunities for interesting observations. Finished products can be captured through sketches, photographs, and videos of the child in the process of creating a structure. Information collected on the number of blocks used, the variety of forms used (Goetz, 1971) and the actual type of structure built can provide a rich source of development during the year. Observing children during the process of building allows for the collection of information on problem solving, planning, and cooperation with peers.

A favorite activity area is that of *manipulative play*. Children have many different styles of approaching manipulatives. Some children just start to put pieces together and see where that takes them. Other children have an idea in mind when they start out. They search for specific pieces and settle for nothing less. This process information can only be observed while the child is busy "constructing" whatever it is they are making. Finished products can be "preserved" through a sketch, or photographs. Sometimes constructions may be saved for a period of time in a "museum" that is located somewhere in the classroom or in the hallway. In this way, structures can be compared over time with regard to number of pieces used, color of pieces, and the representation of the structure.

Many children who are described as quiet are sometimes very talkative in *sensory activities*. Since there is no finished product from sensory activities, on-site observation is the way in which information needs to be gathered. Verbal and non-verbal social interaction, looking at both initiations and responses, participation, concern for cleanliness, and amount of time spent in the activity are all measures that can be taken during sensory play.

An interesting area of the classroom in which to collect information about young children is in the *book corner*. Direct observation can be made of the child's choice of book, time spent "reading" to self, correspondence of "reading" to the actual text, responses to questions posed about the story by an adult reading to the child, and the sharing of books with peers. If tapes of "reading" to self can be made, repeated "readings" may be compared over time with vocabulary, sentence structure, and story line being measured.

Play is one of the most fascinating behaviors to observe. Children engage in solitary, parallel, and cooperative play in a developmental sequence. Recordings made of these levels of play is just one aspect of observation of play. Measuring the amount of time a child spends in play, who the child plays with, what the child plays with, themes the child plays, and comparisons of the child's play indoors and outdoors are other aspects of play behavior providing important information about play as a skill as well as play as a developmental progression. Cohen and Spenciner (1994) present a summary of the developmental aspects of play as a progression of skill, object use, and as an activity with specific characteristics. Play may be viewed as the natural behavior of the child and through play, teachers, parents, and specialists are able to learn much about the language, cognitive level, social development, and physical development of a child. All of these domains present themselves in play situations. Information gained about children during play can support the information gained about the child through other more structured means of assessment. When a child does not respond well to an assessor or therapist in a more traditional assessment format, most of the same information may be obtained from observations of a child's play in the natural setting.

Observation of *routine times* of the day provides information on a child's ability to follow instructions and routines, to make transitions, and to use context clues in order to know what to do next. Information can also be gathered on the child's independence, self-help skills, and language.

Although not a specific activity area, *social interaction* is an activity in which teachers encourage young children to engage. Social interaction encompasses many behaviors including physical, language, cognitive and emotional. Social interaction can be nonverbal as well as verbal and when observing children in any activity area in an early childhood classroom, social interaction should be one of the targeted behaviors to observe. When a child without disabilities interacts with peers in the classroom environment, interval recording, or a checklist may be used to capture the skills the child demonstrates. When a child with disabilities is in the proximity of interaction with peers, interval recording and checklists may be appropriate but a more sensitive method of assessment might be to use the Social Strategy Rating Scale (Beckman & Lieber, 1994). This scale measures social competence in children with disabilities across multiple contexts. Bronson (1994) also speaks to the importance of observation as a measure of a child's social and mastery behaviors in early childhood classrooms. The author discusses the Bronson Social and Task Skill Profile as a tool for assessment. Regardless of the approach or tool used to assess social interaction, collecting information on this behavior has impact on the total assessment picture of a young child.

PRESERVING AND COMPILING INFORMATION ON CHILDREN

Collecting data on children is one part of the process of observation and assessment. Finding a workable, appropriate means of preserving and compiling the information in a manner which renders it accessible and meaningful to those who need to use the information to plan and implement programs for children validates the process of observation and assessment. If considerable time is spent collecting information and nothing is ever done with the information to influence program or behavior management decisions, collecting the information becomes nothing but an exercise of going through the motions. A program based on another program that was based on data was visited to look at the model as a potential for implementation in another community. When the persons in the preschool program were interviewed to find out the details of program implementation, they related that parents with children in the program were trained to collect data and did so on a daily basis. When asked what happened after the data was collected, the visitors were informed that the data were filed. The data were never used to determine whole program or individual child program modifications. While the original model utilized the data to inform change, in this program, several generations from the original one there was no one who knew what to do with the data; they just knew data had to be collected.

Several methods to compile information exist that are appropriate to use in early childhood classrooms. The ideal situation would be the initiation of one approach when the child first enters the school system that could be used cumulatively during all the years the child is in school. Starting a videotape and an audiotape record to be added to each year would be a very informative way to compile information on language, social interaction, physical development, and cognitive development.

In addition to the cumulative tapes, **portfolios** can be initiated as another cumulative assessment project. Portfolios are informative for teachers, administrators, specialists, children, and parents. Portfolios are both a process and a product (Gelfer & Perkins, 1992). These authors point out that while portfolios have been used by artists, actors, and writers, they are appropriate for use in the classroom as well. One of the benefits of portfolios is that they reveal a lot about their creators. School portfolios should include a series of examples of actual school performances that demonstrate how skills have improved. Gelfer and Perkins (1992) indicate that the portfolio product represents the processes and outcomes in the child's educational program.

Davidson (1993) points out that portfolio is not a single assessment practice but a group of strategies for documentation and assessment. There are three basic approaches to developing portfolios. Portfolios may contain a child's best works, collections of work, or serve as process portfolios. Portfolios are purposeful collections of a child's work that exhibit efforts, progress, and achievements. Portfolios are part of authentic or alternative assessment formats (Martin-Kniep, 1993). In addition to determining the type or types of portfolios to be maintained, it is important to think of the physical structure of the portfolio and the location of the portfolio in the classroom. Gelfer and Perkins (1992) suggest that the portfolio may be housed in an expandable file folder but it is more than a container, file, or collection of a child's work. The portfolio should contain samples of a child's work that document performance, growth, and development over time. A portfolio is an evolving concept rather than a strict standardized format. Portfolios are well suited to storing, organizing, and preserving informal, authentic primary, and summary data about all aspects of a child's development (McAfee & Leong, 1994). The portfolio should not be a depository of checklists, notes, test results, and other information and records. This type of information has been maintained in cumulative files in the main offices of schools for many years.

The portfolio can be arranged by subject area, developmental knowledge, skills, or daily progress. From program to program, portfolios will appear in different formats and contain different materials. Since portfolios should reflect what happens in the classroom and the content of classroom curriculum differs from program to program, it is only natural that portfolios will reflect these differences. Portfolios should contain checklists for minimal information to be contained within them. After the minimal information is obtained, each portfolio can contain unlimited information specific to the individual child. The Work Sampling System (Meisels, 1993) is a performance assessment system that offers an alternative to product-oriented, group-administered achievement tests in preschool through Grade three. Meisels lists the domains of the system: personal and social development; language and literacy; mathematical thinking; scientific thinking; social studies; art and music; and physical development. While school systems are in the process of evolving from being test-oriented to developing their own unique systems for collecting functional information about children, the system may have strong value.

Those wishing to establish potential content lists for portfolios may think about including some or all of the following as suggested by Gelfer and Perkins (1992):

1. samples of child's work selected by the child or selected by the child with the support of the teacher: samples from writing; storytelling tapes; photos of experiments or projects; drawings of stories; drawings and collages; creative self-expression projects; lists of written words; videotaped of projects
2. teacher observations: anecdotal observations; checklists
3. child's own periodic self-evaluations reported by the teacher: interest inventories; attitude inventories
4. progress notes contributed by both the student and teacher
5. logbooks
6. parent observations
7. summaries of parent-teacher conferences
8. parent-teacher communications: lists and descriptions of phone conversations; brief discussions; notes; reports

Best Works Portfolios

Best works portfolios are devoted to only those items that reflect the highest quality work a child has produced. This may be a difficult type of portfolio for young children to contribute to because at the beginning of the process of self-assessment, a child may not be able to judge what constitutes "best work" and thus include everything or nothing. Children contributing to this type of portfolio should be helped to understand that they can add things to the portfolio just as they may delete items from the portfolio.

Collections of Work or "Works-in-Progress" Portfolios

These portfolios contain stories, artwork, or anything else the child is working on. To save all of a child's works-in-progress may soon turn into an unwieldy process since in short time, all of a child's work may soon be in the portfolio (Gullo, 1994). It is important to date all entries so the teacher is able to evaluate progress over time and the child is also able to see how projects, stories, etc. evolve over time. If the works-in-progress portfolio serves only as a depository of work, there is no way of having an understanding of the quality of the work collected. The collection of work documents what happens in a classroom; it may not serve as a reliable or comprehensive tool for learning and teaching (Davidson, 1993). An analytic component may be added to the collection of work which requires children and teachers to reflect on the work in the portfolio.

Process portfolios forge a connection between collecting work and linking it to the process of learning (Davidson, 1993). The process portfolio is used by the teacher to help children focus on learning and understanding, to develop and expand the vision of what work is, to see what path growth takes, and to observe how standards develop. A process portfolio can encourage the child to be self-reflective by asking for descriptions of the process involved while producing the work, and asking the child to relate what was accomplished in this work to what was accomplished in previous work, and asking the child to relate what new learning resulted from the work accomplished. Essentially, a process portfolio is a means for a teacher to determine what and how a child learns by using the child's reflections of his or her own work as the measure. A child will become more accountable for learning if what the child learns is assessed by the child and is connected to previous and future learning. Teachers have long known that children learn well what they want to learn. When children have a hand in assessing their own learning, they are more accountable for the learning and retain much more because they have applied the information and not just memorized it for a test.

There are several cautions to the use of portfolios (Cohen & Spenciner, 1994). When designing a portfolio process one should ask whether the contents of the portfolio are representative of the child's work, whether the criteria for the selection and evaluation of contents are clear, who evaluates the contents, and who owns the portfolio. Children who are encouraged to feel a great sense of ownership in their portfolios and the process through which they were developed may have a difficult time understanding why they cannot take the portfolio home at the end of the year. Much thought should be given to who receives the contents of the portfolio and how much information should be maintained in the portfolio to give the receiving teacher, recognizing that the next teacher will begin adding to the portfolio as soon as the school year begins.

Preparing to Begin the Portfolio Process

Until a system or individual school is ready to begin the portfolio process, individual teachers may prepare themselves for the process by developing their own procedures for collecting information such as finished products, journals, audiotapes, videotapes, and parental reflections. Once a teacher is in the habit of collecting these items, the shift to actually establishing portfolios for each child in the class will not be as cumbersome a process as if the teacher must start from scratch.

ETHICS OF "ASSESSMENT"

Sometimes assessments are conducted to determine the appropriateness of a child for a specific early childhood program. These assessments are conducted under conditions unfamiliar to the child. The parents sometimes experience a great deal of stress related to the testing situation and this anxiety filters down to the child. When poor performance on a test results in exclusion from a program the parent really wants the child to attend, there is a great chance that the child will not perform at optimum level.

WHAT IS ASSESSMENT?

Observation and recording by themselves do not constitute assessment. These two processes become assessment when teachers and parents reflect on what has been observed in relation to the goals of the program and the individual child objectives. As a reminder, assessment is the process of observing, recording, and otherwise documenting work that children do and how they do it, as a basis for a variety of educational decisions that affect the child (NAEYC & NAECS\SDE, 1991, p. 21). Interviews may be an important part of the assessment process (Wolery, 1994). Interviews may be conducted with parents, specialists, and former teachers.

Traditionally assessment for the purpose of identifying children with disabilities in order to provide the best program possible for the child begins with screening and diagnosis. Screening and diagnosis is not a process that is necessary for every child during the early childhood years but is appropriate for children who exhibit behaviors or lags in development that are of concern to parents, health providers, or teachers.

Screening

Screening is a brief, inexpensive standardized procedure designed to serve as a quick way to determine which children in a group are in need of further assessment. Diagnoses cannot be made from screenings nor can screenings inform instructional program decisions (Wolery, 1994). While widely accepted as tools of early identification, screening tools are usually not studied for their accuracy. Glascoe and Byrne (1993) studied three screening tools, the Developmental Profile II, the Denver II, and the Battelle Developmental Inventory Screening Test. The screening tools were administered to 89, 7- to 70-month-old children in five day care centers. The Battelle was seen to be more accurate than the other tests and identified correctly 72% of the children with difficulties and 76% of the children without diagnoses. This raises an important question about the use of screening tools. Often, if a project of screening all children in a program is undertaken, the top criterion for selection of a screening tool might not be reported accuracy but cost and time to administer. Another feature people often investigate is the ease of administering the tool. If these are the criteria by which administrators select screening tools, the use of screening tools may not be as meaningful as if accuracy is the main characteristic for use of a particular tool.

Diagnosis

Diagnostic assessment or evaluation is an in-depth look at an individual child by a specialist usually done after a child has been identified through screening to be in need of further assessment. Diagnosis determines the nature of treatment or intervention. The specialists who are part of a team (speech and language therapist, occupational therapist, physical therapist, physician, psychologist, audiologist) are the persons who usually make diagnostic evaluations. Once an initial diagnosis is made, specialists in the areas of deficit will conduct specialized assessments to further pinpoint the range of deficit and to identify more specific techniques and materials appropriate for intervention implementation. Cohen and Spenciner (1994) present an overview of the specialized tests and types of deficits found in young children in the areas of vision, hearing, motor, and communication. A classroom teacher would not ever be the person to administer those assessments but should be aware of what they are and what they assess.

WHY MUST TEACHERS ASSESS?

Assessment is a process that informs those involved with the program, the parents, teachers, administrators, children, and funding sources, concerning the appropriateness of program, and the accomplishments of the children and teachers within the program. All involved want to know that the children in the program are learning and growing. When a program does not engage in any form of assessment, formal or informal, the effectiveness of the program cannot be measured, only speculated about.

Early childhood programs should engage in assessment to be able to prepare progress reports based on solid information. Progress reports prepared for parents are appreciated. When parents receive progress reports that contain specific information based on classroom observations, they not only learn about their children but they learn more about the nature of early childhood education. This may serve to positively influence them in the home environment, encouraging them to provide more developmentally appropriate activities for the children at home. Ongoing assessment techniques make the process of preparing progress reports much easier because "testing" does not need to be done in order to communicate with parents.

Assessment is the basis for placement determination for young children with disabilities. Often, prior to an inclusive placement, a child is assessed in a more clinical fashion sitting with a therapist in a location apart from children and other adults. It is important to make placement decisions based on information gathered in an inclusive setting as well as in clinical situations.

CASE STUDY

A family requesting an inclusive classroom for their child with multiple disabilities was informed by their school system that the child would need to spend many weeks in a special education preschool classroom in order for them to assess the child and make the determination concerning the appropriateness of an inclusive classroom. The child came to the school system with multiple evaluations conducted at regular intervals by multiple specialists. The parents requested a hearing and at the hearing, after many days and considerable testimony by school system personnel and outside witnesses, the hearing officer determined that in order to assess the child for appropriateness for an inclusive setting, evaluation should be conducted in an inclusive setting as well as in a segregated classroom. The child attended both types of programs for a few weeks each. The final determination in the case was that the child would certainly benefit from an inclusive classroom experience. This case further supports the value of classroom observation as the basis for meaningful assessment. Assessment of children in settings in which they will not be asked to operate, is assessment that supplies information about what a child is able to do, or chooses to do in a setting in which the child will not be placed.

Assessment is used to determine what should be undertaken as the next step in appropriate classroom curriculum. Traditional testing does not inform the teacher about appropriate curriculum decisions. It simply informs a teacher the results of a situation in which a child was asked to respond to questions and scenarios to which the child might not have been inclined to respond (Schweinhart, 1993). In a standard testing situation a child may become distressed when unable to deliver what is considered the one right answer. Children in testing situations are often asked to relate to the tester when having no previous relationship with the person. There is no trust, no rapport, and no common experience. Children are often cautious when meeting new adults. Why should they respond to questions and commands from these new people? The conditions of traditional testing do little to bring out the best performance in many children. A child who is unsure of a response often looks to the adult for feedback. In a traditional testing situation, the adult is not supposed to provide any feedback. The child may become very anxious and the anxiety may cause the child to perform poorly on the test. The child may also cease to respond under these conditions. All in all, the testing situation may produce a profile of a child that is not like the one the child would produce in the natural environment.

Assessment is also undertaken to determine the eligibility of a child for special services not available to the general public (Wolery, 1994). These services may consist of speech and language therapy, occupational therapy, physical therapy or any other therapy deemed appropriate to assist the child with developing learning strengths.

WHEN DO TEACHERS ASSESS?

Assessment may be done at regular intervals during the school year or it can be an ongoing process. Assessment linked with teaching and curriculum is assessment that documents that teachers teach children how to learn rather than teaching them isolated facts and behaviors (Bergan & Feld, 1993). In addition, this type of assessment philosophy is one that will be taken seriously and be undertaken on a regular basis. If assessment is done in the fall, winter and spring, who is to say that the child being assessed will be performing at an optimum level? Even if the nature of the assessment undertaken at these times is child-friendly, the child may be at a learning plateau or recovering from an illness. The child may be tired or just not having a good day. Assessment that is conducted as an ongoing process linked to curriculum and teaching is assessment that is fair for all children. It looks at the performance of children on a daily basis as well as over time to measure the level of performance as well as the effectiveness of the learning situation for the individual child and for the group.

HOW DO TEACHERS ASSESS?

Assessment can be done through the processes already described: many types of observation, interviews, portfolios, checklists, rating scales, evaluation, or finished products. The process of assessment may also include dynamic assessment, authentic, direct or performance assessment, classroom assessment, arena assessment, criterion-based assessment, and play-based assessment. There are three approaches to working with others to complete assessments of young children. In multidisciplinary assessment, each member identified to carry out a piece of an assessment does so with minimal amount of interaction with the others during the assessment process. The results of all these assessments are reported in a team meeting. At this team meeting, all members would develop their piece of the intervention plan and provide direct service to the child to implement the intervention. In interdisciplinary assessment, team members conduct their own assessments and develop an intervention plan together. This approach leans more toward cooperation and collaboration but each discipline is still largely responsible for its own interventions. During direct service, there may be some attention paid to the intervention goals of other disciplines. This helps the child because all skills are not taught in isolation. In transdisciplinary assessment, team members assess and plan the program together. Implementation of the plan is carried out by one team member in consultation with the others. The family only has to deal with one person but that person has the support of the rest of the professionals in carrying out the plan.

Dynamic Assessment

Dynamic assessment occurs when the assessor gives clues, leads and hints, asks questions, or poses problems to see what the child being assessed can do with as well as without assistance. This form of assessment works well within the classroom environment. If a teacher can simultaneously assess knowledge and instructional approaches for the best match for the child, considerable time may be saved. Instruction becomes assessment-oriented and assessment becomes instruction-oriented. Dynamic assessment serves to integrate curriculum, teaching, and assessment.

Authentic, Direct, or Performance Assessment

Authentic, direct, or **performance assessment** evaluates the child while engaged in tasks that are as close to the real situation as possible. Instead of asking a child to circle an answer, draw a line to an object, or color in a "bubble sheet" the child is asked to perform real tasks in the classroom environment. The assessment is made on the child's performance on the real task accomplished with real materials (McAfee & Leong, 1994). There are some distinctions between the terms performance assessment and authentic assessment. Performance assessment refers to the child performing the action that corresponds to the behavior being assessed. Gardner (1991) describes performance-based assessments according to developmental levels. A child may perform at one end of the continuum at a novice level when beginning to acquire a behavior or skill or at the other end of the spectrum, at the expert level of performance when the child achieves mastery. In performance assessment the child may engage in a task that is somewhat contrived while authentic assessment necessitates that the task in which the child is asked to engage is true to life. In performance assessment, a teacher may ask a child to tie shoes or demonstrate the number of jumps that he or she can accomplish. Authentic assessment measures are embedded in the curriculum (Martin-Kniep, 1993). In authentic assessment, the teacher would observe the child putting shoes on after changing from snowboots and watch the child in gross motor activity when the classroom trampoline is available for use.

Continuous Assessment

Continuous assessment occurs within the daily framework of the classroom. Evaluation of children's responses, actions and questions are conducted as part of the daily routine and as such becomes the basis for curriculum and teaching decisions and modifications. This type of assessment is ongoing and serves to inform teachers, administrators, and parents.

Arena Assessment

Arena assessment is a model of assessment in which a facilitator works with the child in assessment activities across disciplines. Other team members including the parents sit away from the child and assessor and observe and record information during these activities. Arena assessment may take place through the observation of a video tape if several people in the proximity of the child may inhibit the performance of the child.

Curriculum-Based Assessment

This approach links assessment to instruction, another test, or another outcome measure. The three purposes of this approach to assessment are to determine eligibility, to develop goals for intervention, and to evaluate the child's progress in the curriculum.

Play-Based Assessment

There are several models of **play-based assessment.** Play assessment is designed to allow the observation of all developmental domains as well as the observation of a child's strategies for initiating and responding to verbal and nonverbal initiations of others in a play situation. Play is a familiar behavior for most young children. Play assessment in conjunction with other assessments presents a complete picture of a child's development.

Play can be assessed during the regular classroom play activities or a situation may be created for the express reason of assessment. The specially designed play situation is appropriate to assess behavior that might not occur in the regular planned activity for that particular day.

Play assessment is very appropriate for all children but it is very important as an assessment tool for children who do not respond to other forms of assessment. In the naturalistic environment of play, the environment in which the child is comfortable, the child is free to engage in his or her best behaviors. The child does not feel a sense of being judged so the child does not feel threatened (Linder, 1990).

The person conducting the play assessment is familiar to the child and thus can elicit the richest responses possible from the child. Parents can participate in the assessment. If the parent participation works well, the parent may be able to provide interpretation of behavior that is new to the person conducting the assessment. Sometimes children do not perform in their most natural fashion when a parent is in a school-based situation. A judgment needs to made as to the appropriateness of the presence of the parent in the assessment situation. While the child may be comfortable with the play situation, the parent may want so much for the child to perform well, that an air of anxiety creeps into the environment.

In a play assessment the child is in control of the materials and equipment. In traditional testing situations, the assessor is in control. Play assessment is open-ended while other forms of assessment have more finite possibilities. There are no specific questions to ask in play assessment. Any means of communication a child uses are acceptable.

While a more traditional form of assessment has a beginning and an ending, play sessions can last as long as appropriate. There is no limit to the number of play assessments that can be conducted. Sessions can be compared over time to assess the differences in content of the play observed. Since play content depends on the materials the child uses, it is difficult to compare sessions directly. The comparison of sessions would have to look toward appropriateness of play with materials, appropriateness of role development, and appropriateness of language used during play.

When a child with disabilities does not play at the same level of peers the same age, it is still appropriate to use play-based assessment. The nature of the play situation offered to the child may be the same as would be offered to a younger child. If the child demonstrated skill in those play activities, more sophisticated play situations can be offered. A child with special needs, in a structured assessment situation, may not even reach out to touch any materials. In a play situation, with familiar toys, the child may be comfortable enough to engage in play for sustained periods of time.

There are some limitations of play assessment. If the children in the classroom where the play assessment is to be conducted are not used to having observers, the process may prove intrusive. The results from the observation may not be as representative as they would have been if the children were accustomed to additional people being in the environment. If there were fewer than usual children in school the day of the observation due to illness or inclement weather, the observation may not yield the typical picture. If there was a substitute teacher in the class that day, that might influence the resulting observation. These factors need to be taken into account when analyzing the results of the observation.

Persons carrying out play assessments need to be comfortable with play, recognize the value of play, and understand how play can serve as an indicator of a child's development. They also need to be able to convey what they observe to those who may not share the same enthusiasm for the value of play as a tool of assessment.

WHAT HAPPENS TO ASSESSMENTS?

Assessments that remain in a file are assessments that were not worth conducting. Assessment should inform curriculum and instruction. Assessment carried out by teachers is assessment that links curriculum and instruction. Each assessment undertaken should become part of an overall, comprehensive assessment package.

Assessment is an ongoing process that adds value to a child's program as well as adding value to the feedback a teacher needs in order to plan and implement developmentally and individually appropriate early childhood programs. When a teacher is comfortable with the notion of ongoing assessment, it becomes part of the daily routine and provides a teacher with feedback about individual children, program effectiveness, and teacher effectiveness. Some teachers are accustomed to waiting for feedback from administrators in order to know how they are doing in the classroom. An effective ongoing assessment process should be able to provide this type of feedback on a regular basis.

Many schools are grappling with the dilemma of what information to send on with a child to the next teacher, what information to place in a child's permanent file, and what information to send home. Information gathered through the means described in this chapter can be shared by all persons interested in the child's development. It is information gathered from the classroom environment and if it is well documented before it is placed in a portfolio or some other file, it should be of continuing value throughout a child's schooling.

SUMMARY

Observation and assessment are currently in the forefront of evolving practices in early childhood education. While the entire area of early childhood assessment is being developed and refined, it is obvious that there will never be one single assessment that will meet the needs of all situations and all young children. It has been demonstrated that it is critical to include as much information as possible from as great a variety of resources as possible in order to understand the full picture the child presents. Early childhood educators have long known that one very vital way to know about a child is to watch the child in as many different activities and settings as possible. Children demonstrate their abilities in different ways. Different teachers, and the child's parents as part of the partnership interested in the child, should pool their resources to plan for the child. When working with children with disabilities, cooperation and collaboration between teachers, parents, and specialists are part of a meaningful assessment approach.

DISCUSSION QUESTIONS

1) Develop a rationale for observation as assessment for an early childhood program. The rationale will be used in a parent handbook to explain the process of observation versus other more traditional means of assessment that parents may be more familiar with.
2) A parent asks for an appointment with you to find out how his child is doing. You begin the meeting by asking the parent how he thinks the child is doing. The parent seems to be bothered by this line of questioning. What can you do to remedy the situation with the parent and how can you get the parent to understand that he has considerable information about the child which can add to the information you are gathering?
3) Think about the various forms of assessment available. Discuss the pros and cons of each of these approaches with a member of your class.
4) The community you are in has conducted traditional standardized assessments over the years. Recently, a committee of concerned teachers came together, determined to change the way assessments are conducted on children from preschool to third grade. You have joined the committee as a student member. What issues would you want the committee to look at in considering undertaking this major change?

5) The principal of your school has asked you to serve on a committee to develop a design for portfolio assessment for the early childhood grades. If the use of portfolios is deemed appropriate and beneficial after a period of two years, other grades will join the effort. With a classmate, brainstorm a list of ideas for the types of things that may be included in the portfolio.
6) A parent comes to you and asks you how her child is doing compared to other children in the class. How will you respond to this parent?

REFERENCES

Abraham, M., Morris, L., & Wald, P. (1993). *Inclusive early childhood education—A model classroom*. Tucson, AZ: Communication Skill Builders.

Aylward, E. (1991). *Understanding children's testing: Psychological testing*. Austin, TX: Pro-Ed.

Beckman, P., & Lieber, J. (1994). The social strategy rating scale: An approach to evaluating social competence. *Journal of Early Intervention, 18*(1), 1–11.

Benjamin, A. (1994). Observations in early childhood classrooms: Advice from the field. *Young Children, 49*(6), 14–20.

Bergan, J., & Feld, J. (1994). Developmental assessment: New directions. *Young Children, 48*(5), 41–47.

Bredekamp, S. (Ed.). (1987). *Developmentally appropriate practice in early childhood programs serving children from birth through age 8*. Washington, DC: National Association for the Education of Young Children.

Bronson, M. (1994). The usefulness of an observational measure of young children's social and mastery behaviors in early childhood classrooms. *Early Childhood Research Quarterly, 9*(1), 19–44.

Chesler, P. (1994). *A place for me—Including children with special needs in early care and education settings*. Washington, DC: National Association for the Education of Young Children.

Cohen, L., & Spenciner, L. (1994). *Assessment of young children*. New York: Longman.

Deiner, P. (1993). *Resources for teaching children with diverse abilities*. Fort Worth, TX: Harcourt Brace Jovanovich College Publishers.

Davidson, L. (1993). Portfolio assessment and exhibits: Moving from recall to reflective understanding. *Holistic Education Review*, 45–51.

Diamond, K., & Squires, J. (1993). The role of parental report in the screening and assessment of young children. *Journal of Early Intervention, 17*(2), 107–115.

Dinnebeil, L., & Rule, S. (1994). Congruence between parents' and professionals' judgments about the development of young children with disabilities: A review of the literature. *Topics in Early Childhood Special Education, 14*(1), 1–25.

Gardner, H. (1991). *The unschooled mind*. New York: Basic Books.

Gelfer, J., & Perkins, P. (1992). Constructing student portfolios: A process and product that fosters communication with families. *Day Care and Early Education, 20*(2), 9–13.

Genishi, C. (Ed.). (1992). *Ways of assessing children and curriculum—Stories of early childhood practice*. New York: Teachers College Press.

Glascoe, F., & Byrne, K. (1993). The accuracy of three developmental screening tests. *Journal of Early Intervention, 17*(4), 368–379.

Goetz, E., & Baer, D. (1971). Descriptive reinforcement of "creative" blockbuilding by young children. In E. Ramp & B. Hopkins (Eds.), *A new direction for education: Behavior analysis*. Lawrence, KS: University of Kansas Press.

Goetz, E., & Baer, D. (1973). Social control of form diversity and the emergence of new forms. *Journal of Applied Behavior Analysis, 6*, 209–217.

Goodwin, W., & Driscoll, L. (1980). *Handbook of measurement and evaluation in early childhood education*. San Francisco: Jossey-Bass.

Gullo, D. (1994). *Understanding assessment and evaluation in early childhood education*. New York: Teachers College Press.

Hains, A., Fowler, S., Schwartz, I., Kottwitz, E., & Rosenkoetter, S. (1989). A comparison of preschool and kindergarten teacher expectations for school readiness. *Early Childhood Research Quarterly, 4*, 75–88.

Henderson, L., & Meisels, S. (1994). Parental involvement in the developmental screening of their young children: A multiple-source perspective. *Journal of Early Intervention, 18*(2), 141–154.

Hills, T. (1993). Assessment in context—Teachers and children at work. *Young Children, 48*(5), 29–34.

Kagan, S. (1992). Readiness past, present, and future: Shaping the agenda. *Young Children, 48*(1), 48–53.

Kamii, C., (Ed.). (1990). *Achievement testing in the early grades—The games grown-ups play*. Washington, DC: National Association for the Education of Young Children.

Linder, T. (1990). *Transdisciplinary play-based assessment*. Baltimore: Paul H. Brookes Publishing Co.

Martin-Kniep, G. (1993). Authentic assessment in practice. *Holistic Education Review*, 52–58.

McAffee, O., & Leong, D. (1994). *Assessing and guiding young children's development and learning*. Boston: Allyn and Bacon.

Meisels, S. (1987). Uses and abuses of developmental screening and school readiness testing. *Young Children, 42*(2), 4–6, 68–73.

Meisels, S. (1993). Remaking classroom assessment with the work sampling system. *Young Children, 48*(5), 34–40.

Morison, P. (1992). Testing in American schools: Issues for research and policy. *Social Policy Report, Society for Research in Child Development, 6*(2), 1–24.

Morrow, L., & Smith, J. (Eds.). (1990). *Assessment for instruction in early literacy.* Englewood Cliffs, NJ: Prentice Hall.

National Association for the Education of Young Children & the National Association of Early Childhood Specialists in State Departments of Education (NAEYC & NAECS\SDE). (1991). Guidelines for appropriate curriculum content and assessment in programs serving young children ages 3 through 8. *Young Children, 46*(3), 21–38.

Nuttall, E., Romero, I., & Kalesnik, J. (1992). *Assessing and screening preschoolers—Psychological and educational dimensions.* Boston: Allyn and Bacon.

Perrone, V. (1991). On standardized testing. *Childhood Education, 68*, 132–142.

Sattler, J. (1988). *Assessment of children.* San Diego, CA: Jerome M. Sattler, Publisher.

Schweinhart, L. (1993). Observing children in action: The key to early childhood assessment. *Young Children, 48*(5), 29–33.

Weber, C., Behl, D., & Summers, M. (1994). Watch them play, watch them learn. *Teaching Exceptional Children, 27*(1), 30–35.

Wodrich, D., & Kush, S. (1990). *Children's psychological testing—A guide for nonpsychologists.* Baltimore: Paul H. Brookes Publishing Co.

Wolery, M. (1994). Assessing children with special needs. In M. Wolery and J. Wilbers (Eds.), *Including children with special needs in early childhood programs.* (pp. 71–96). Washington, DC: National Association for the Education of Young Children.

Wortham, S. (1995). *Measurement and evaluation in early childhood education.* Columbus, OH: Merrill Publishing Company.

ADDITIONAL READING

Martin, S. (1994). *Take a look: Observation and portfolio assessment in early childhood.* Toronto: Addison-Wesley Publishers Limited.

Appendix

EARLY CHILDHOOD VIDEO RESOURCES

A Classroom with Blocks
In video format, *The Block Book* brought to life. 13 minutes. NAEYC.

Anti-Bias Curriculum Video
Child care staff show why the Anti-Bias Curriculum is important to them and how they implement it with children. 30 minutes. Redleaf Press.

Appropriate Curriculum for Young Children: The Role of the Teacher
This program depicts developmentally appropriate practices in programs for young children, illustrating the important role of the adult in helping children learn in a play-oriented environment and showing the adult's role in child-initiated activity. 28 minutes. NAEYC.

Block Play: Constructing Realities
The program presents various skills children practice in block play and the stages of building. Block play is illustrated as a natural method of constructing knowledge and developing the skills children need to grow and negotiate in their world. NAEYC.

Building Quality Child Care: Health and Safety
This video focuses on health-and-safety practices in a group child care setting. 28 minutes. NAEYC.

Building Quality Child Care: Relationships
Focuses on the developmental stage of independence and the importance of adults recognizing and working through this stage with young children. Explores the aspects of independence in children's behaviors, the design and setup of the classroom, curriculum building, and the role of the teacher. 20 minutes. NAEYC.

Caring for Children: An Introduction to the Child Care Profession.
This series of twelve videos stresses the interrelationship between all areas of development through developmentally appropriate activities and experiences that promote social interaction, self-expression and communication, and positive growth development. Emphasis is on the importance of the parent-provider partnership and respecting the primary role of parents as children's first teachers and caregivers. Delmar Publishers Inc.

Caring for Infants and Toddlers
A discussion with Bettye Caldwell. How can the unique needs of infants and toddlers be met in group care? 17 minutes. NAEYC.

Communicating Effectively with Young Children—Yvonne Gillette
Effective communication strategies for families of infants to 3-year-old children who have communicative, physical, social, or cognitive impairments. 38 minutes. Communication Skill Builders.

Count to Five and Say I'm Alive!—Two Poetry workshops with Michael Rosen and Judith Nicholls
The joy as well as the instructional value in writing poetry. Many ideas and ways of composing poetry are introduced. 30 minutes. Stenhouse Publishers.

Culture and Education of Young Children
A discussion with Carol Phillips. How can programs show respect for our cultural diversity and use this richness to enhance children's learning? 16 minutes. NAEYC.

Curriculum for Preschool and Kindergarten
A discussion with Lillian Katz. What is appropriate for four and five-year-olds? 16 minutes. NAEYC.

Developmentally Appropriate First Grade: A Community Of Learners
Spend a typical day in David Burchfield's first grade classroom in rural Virginia. See how David translates the concept of developmentally appropriate practice into a thematic, interactive learning experience for 23 children, ages five through seven. 30 minutes. NAEYC.

Developmentally Appropriate Practice: Birth Through Age 5
Depicts teachers and children in action in developmentally appropriate programs. Also points out inappropriate practices. 27 minutes. NAEYC.

Discipline: Appropriate Guidelines for Young Children
Positive guidance of young children toward healthy social and emotional development is the foundation of a good early childhood program. This video shows ways to handle the difficult situations—hitting, not taking turns, temper tantrums—that inevitably arise among preschool children in early childhood centers and family day care homes. 28 minutes. NAEYC.

Early Intervention with Special Needs Children—The Research Foundation of State University of New York
An introduction to the services and agencies available for children birth to five years with special needs. Demonstrates special characteristics and development to parents and staff. Three videos and a manual with complete scripts. 60-, 45- and 30 minutes. Communication Skill Builders.

Environments for Young Children
A discussion with Elizabeth Prescott and Elizabeth Jones. How the materials and arrangement of your environment help meet your goals for children. 18 minutes. NAEYC.

Family-Centered Care
This video presents ways in which family-centered care is implemented in a variety of settings. 28 minutes. Association for the Care of Children's Health.

How Young Children Learn to Think
A discussion with Constance Kamii which explains Piaget's theory of how children can acquire knowledge. 19 minutes. NAEYC.

Infant Curriculum: Great Explorations
This program focuses on stages of development from birth through 15 months, individual temperament and style, shaping the environment, and using routines to support an infant's explorations. 20 minutes. NAEYC.

Learning Can Be Fun
Ella Jenkins demonstrates how she sings and uses music to promote learning. 57 minutes. NAEYC.

Let's move, let's play—Developmentally appropriate movement activities for preschool children.
KinderCare Learning Center, Inc. (Distributed by AAHPERD Publications)

Men Caring for Young Children
This video celebrates a diverse group of men who have chosen careers working with infants, toddlers, preschoolers and young school-age children in a variety of educational environments. 30 minutes. NAEYC.

Music Across the Curriculum
An interview with Thomas Moore and examples of music in an early childhood classroom showing the integration of music in the classroom and the structured use of music to build processing skills. 20 minutes. NAEYC.

New Room Arrangement as a Teaching Strategy—Diane Trister Dodge
This video teaches the basic principles of room arrangements and illustrates the impact room arrangement has on children's behavior. Looks at the basic organization, pathways, compatibility of different equipment and activities. 20 minutes. Redleaf Press.

Partnerships with Parents
This video dramatizes the importance of the parent-teacher relationship for children, how to establish and maintain positive communication, and how to handle the most common problems teachers face in working with parents. 28 minutes. NAEYC.

Play and Learning
A discussion with Barbara Biber. Why is play important? What do children learn when they play? 18 minutes. NAEYC.

Preparing Paraprofessional Early Interventionists—Samera Baird
Curriculum to train paraprofessionals serving infants and toddlers birth through two years. 37 minutes. Communication Skill Builders.

Promoting Family Collaboration
This video provides information on coping strategies used by families during children's long-term hospitalizations. 23 minutes. Learner Managed Designs, Inc.

Raising America's Children—A Video Series
A series of ten 30-minute video programs that examines child rearing between infancy and kindergarten. Each video focuses on one aspect of development, showing adults and children in a variety of real-life settings. Children with special needs are also included in each video, and there is one program dedicated to focusing on the educational options for children with special needs. Delmar Publishers Inc.

Reading and Young Children
A discussion with Jan McCarthy. What can teachers say to parents who want their children to learn to read in preschool? 15 minutes. NAEYC.

Sensory Play: Constructing Realities
This program examines how a child's first-hand experience with sensory exploration contributes to overall development. Children's sensory play is illustrated as a natural means of supporting each child's individual learning style whether auditory, visual, or kinesthetic. 18 minutes. NAEYC.

Sharing Nature with Young Children
This video demonstrates ways of making ordinary and commonplace natural phenomena into exciting learning experiences. 18 Minutes. NAEYC.

Spoonful of Lovin' Video Programs
This series of five, 30-minute video programs is designed to help day care providers improve their skills. The programs cover a wide range of topics. Delmar Publishers Inc.

Teaching the Whole Child in the Kindergarten
This program depicts elements of developmentally appropriate teaching, curriculum, and assessment in two kindergarten classrooms, public and private, in Hawaii. 27 minutes. NAEYC.

The Adventure Begins: Preschool and Technology
This video shows how children and teachers in early childhood programs across America are using computers to enhance learning in developmentally appropriate ways. 10 minutes. NAEYC.

The Creative Curriculum for Early Childhood—Diane Trister Dodge
Demonstrates the power of a well planned environment. The scenes of children working and playing in seven learning centers capture the essence of the Creative Curriculum. Teaches new and experienced staff to use their environments to support their curriculum. 37 minutes. Redleaf Press.

The Family Experience
This video provides information about families and allows professionals to respond more sensitively to families of infants born with prematurity and other conditions. 45 minutes. Learner Managed Designs, Inc.

The New Room Arrangement as a Teaching Strategy
A 15-minute slide or videotape which presents concrete ideas for arranging early childhood classrooms to support positive behavior and learning. Teaching Strategies, Inc.

Toddler Curriculum: Making Connections
This program explores how toddlers, 12 to 36 months of age, develop and learn. It depicts developmentally appropriate curriculum in the toddler classroom. 20 minutes. NAEYC.

Video Observations for the Early Childhood Rating Scale—Thelma Harms, Jana Fleming, and Debby Cryer
Multimedia package demonstrates how to use the Early Childhood Environment Rating Scale (ECERS). 21 minutes. Teachers College Press.

We All Belong: Multicultural Child Care That Works—Australian Early Childhood Association

Introduces the principles that transformed this Australian center into an exciting place where everyone feels at home. 20 minutes. Redleaf Press.

Whole Language Learning
This video explores the role of the teacher and parent in language development and the use of whole language philosophy in an early childhood classroom. 20 minutes. NAEYC.

RESOURCES

American Alliance for Health, Physical Education, Recreation and Dance (AAHPERD)
1900 Association Dr.
Reston, VA 22091
703-476-3400

Association for the Care of Children's Health
7920 Woodmont Avenue #300
Bethesda, MD 20814
301-654-6540

Communication Skill Builders
3830 E. Bellevue
P.O. Box 42050-CS4
Tucson, AZ 85733
602-323-7500

Delmar Publishers Inc.
3 Columbia Circle
P.O. Box 15015
Albany, NY 12212-5015
800-347-7707 or 518-464-3500

Learner Managed Designs, Inc.
2201-K West 25th Street
Lawrence, KS 66047
913-842-9088

National Association for the Education of Young Children (NAEYC)
1509 16th Street, N.W.
Washington, DC 20036-1426
800-424-2460 or 202-232-8777

Redleaf Press
a division of Resources for Child Caring
450 N. Syndicate Suite 5
St. Paul, MN 55104-4125
800-423-8309

Stenhouse Publishers
P.O. Box 1929
Columbus, OH 43216-1929
800-988-9812

Teachers College Press
P.O. Box 20
Williston, VT 05449-0020
800-575-6566

Teaching Strategies Inc.
P.O. Box 42243
Washington, DC 20015
800-637-3652

Index

Q

R

S